PROUD AGES

A story of England from earliest
times to 1900

Come the three corners of the world in arms,
And we shall shock them.
Nought shall make us rue,
If England to itself do rest but true.

SHAKESPEARE

PROUD AGES

A story of England from earliest times to 1900

GEORGE E. TAIT

Professor of Education, University of Toronto

Illustrated by
VERNON MOULD
Art Master, Preparatory School, Upper Canada College

THE RYERSON PRESS TORONTO

Published, 1958

ACKNOWLEDGMENT

The author wishes to express his sincere thanks
to Mr. W. D. Gilmore of Malvern Collegiate
Institute, Toronto, and Mr. H. J. P. Schaffter
of Upper Canada College for their sympathetic
reading of the manuscript and for suggestions
which have been incorporated in the text of
Proud Ages.

Maps by
M. RICHARD HARGRAVE

The cover illustration is reproduced through the courtesy
of the British Travel Association.

PRINTED AND BOUND IN CANADA
BY THE RYERSON PRESS, TORONTO

FOREWORD

TO TEACHERS AND STUDENTS

Proud Ages is a chronological history of England from the invasion by Julius Caesar to the close of the Victorian era.

Careful attention has been given to the organization and development of all materials included in this book. To assist pupils in locating information, such devices as unit headings with date lines, unit summaries, time-charts, marginal headings, appendices and index have been included.

Illustrations have been designed to trace the historical development of certain typical features such as weapons, armour, architecture, ships, costumes and household articles. The comprehensive captions appearing below the illustrations have been prepared with the purpose of supplementing the facts supplied by drawings and text.

Because various tales have added colour and richness to England's story, a short collection of these has been placed in the appendix. Also in the appendix is a complete list of British monarchs and a classified list of British possessions in 1900.

We hope you will enjoy reading *Proud Ages*.

G.E.T.

FOREWORD

TO TEACHERS AND STUDENTS

CONTENTS

III

END OF THE FEUDAL SYSTEM (1377—1485)

IV

THE RISING POWER OF MONARCHY (1485 = 1603)

V

THE TRIUMPH OF PARLIAMENT (1603-1702)

VI

GROWTH OF BRITISH POWER (1702 - 1763

VII

REVOLUTIONS AND WARS (1763 - 1815)

VIII
THE REFORM PERIOD (1815 — ~~1900~~ 1850)

IX
GROWTH OF DEMOCRACY (1850 - 1901)

APPENDIX

INTRODUCTION

Although they are but bits of land "set in a silver sea," the British Isles hold a peculiar charm, a rare beauty, which is known the world over. They have had an effect on world affairs out of all proportion to their size. From these islands have come the people who have made English the most common language spoken in two continents and the language of scholars and travellers all over the world. From Great Britain has come our modern concept of democracy. The British Commonwealth of Nations, which grew out of the British Empire, was founded by sailors who set out from British ports.

The British Isles lie a few miles out from the mainland of Europe. They consist of two main islands, Great Britain and Ireland, together with a host of tiny islands sprinkled about their coasts. The largest of these contains three countries: England, Scotland and Wales; the second largest is divided into the Republic of Ireland and Northern Ireland.

In the south, Great Britain is separated from France by the **Coast** funnel-shaped English Channel. The narrow north-eastern end of **waters** this funnel is the Strait of Dover. The town of Dover, in southeast England, is just twenty-two miles from Calais in northern France, and on clear days the shores of France may be seen from the cliffs of the English coast. Beyond the Strait of Dover the North Sea separates Britain from Belgium, Holland, Germany, Denmark and Norway. Much broader than the English Channel, the North Sea is 450 miles across at its widest point.

At one time in the distant past the British Isles were not islands, **Ancient** but formed part of the mainland of Europe, being joined to the con- **land** tinent by a broad plain which stretched north of Scotland and west **formation** of Ireland. Gradually this plain sank into the sea, forming what is now a continental shelf covered by shallow waters no more than 600 feet deep. The floor of the sea about the British Isles is not flat, but has valleys dipping downward and plateaus rising upward, almost to the surface of the sea. On the Dogger Bank, a fishing ground in the North Sea, the depth of the water is little more than 100 feet.

Thousands of years ago people may have crossed the plain, or **Ancient** land bridge, from Europe and Asia to what is now Britain and Ireland. **peoples**

1

This map shows ancient northwest Europe. The shaded section has gradually disappeared below the sea, leaving shallow banks in many places. Note how the present rivers tend to follow old river valleys.

They probably found a rough region of forests and swamps, a region where lived giant elephants known as mammoths, cave lions, rhinoceroses and sabre-toothed tigers. Settling along the rivers, these early people made their tools and weapons from flint and stone, and so are called *Palaeolithic* Men, or Stone-Age Men.

Ages passed. The climate slowly changed as glaciers like great bulldozers pushed down from the polar regions, grinding and gouging their way over much of Ireland and Great Britain. In order to escape the ice and snow, the Stone-Age Men moved to the extreme southerly parts of England, where they lived in the shelter of caves. There they maintained a crude, primitive kind of life, shivering in their rocky homes, hunting with stone weapons, fighting savage animals.

Then, as more ages passed, the climate warmed, the glaciers slowly retreated, leaving lake-spotted regions which may have looked like the barren lands of northern Canada. Warmer and warmer became the climate until the forest grew, and the isles were green again. The land bridge to the continent sank slowly into the sea, so that the British Isles stood by themselves in the open waters.

From the mainland of the continent newcomers invaded Britain, newcomers we call the *Neolithic* people, or New Stone-Age people, whose stone weapons were polished, hard and well-made. More than mere hunters, the New Stone-Age people cleared the land, planted crops, and raised farm animals. Avoiding the dense forests of the British valleys, the settlers made their clearings on the upland regions where, with crude hoes, they stirred the fertile soil.

From the Mediterranean regions in southern Europe more settlers moved into western Britain and Wales. These people, the *Megoliths,* or Great Stone Builders, constructed gigantic circles with massive

2

Stonehenge is a great double circle of stones probably erected later than 2,000 B.C. by the Megolithic people of Britain. It was used as a temple of worship. Some of the huge stones are twenty-one feet in height and may have been transported by water as far as 200 miles.

blocks of stone. One of these mysterious structures, now partly in ruins, may still be seen at Stonehenge in England.

Still later came fair-haired Germanic tribesmen, the Celts, of northern Europe and Asia, who spread over many parts of the British Isles. It was the Celts who were the most important people in Britain when English history was first recorded in written form.

It has already been stated that Britain and Ireland are the two **Size of** largest islands of the British Isles, but they are not large in comparison **British Isles** with some other land masses. From north to south Great Britain is about 565 miles in length, a distance about the same as that between Toronto and Quebec City, or between Lake Ontario and James Bay, or between Winnipeg and Regina. At its greatest width the island is 280 miles across, and at its narrowest point no more than sixty miles. Of the countries within the Isles, England is the largest, having an area of 50,000 square miles, or slightly larger than Newfoundland. Ireland with 33,000 square miles and Scotland with 30,000 square miles are each somewhat larger than New Brunswick. Wales, the smallest, is 7,000 square miles in area.

A look at the map of the British Isles reveals a very irregular **Coastline** coastline with numerous gulfs and inlets pushing their fingers into the land. The western coast is rougher than the eastern one. Here in the west are hundreds of small islands, while very few stand in the North Sea or the English Channel. The indented coast of the British Isles offers many useful harbours, free from ice, so that trade may be carried out at all times of the year. British ports on the western shore face America, those on the east face Germany and the Scandinavian countries, while those in the south face France. Some of the ports in England are Liverpool, Bristol, Cardiff, London, Hull, Newcastle, Southampton, Plymouth and Portsmouth; in Scotland there are Leith and Aberdeen; in Ireland Belfast, Dublin and Cobh.

Trade Because the country is small in relation to its population, Britain must trade with countries around the world . . . to get food and raw materials for manufacturing. Lumber, minerals, oil, wheat, eggs, butter, cheese, cotton, wool, meat, sugar, coffee, paper, furs, tobacco, rubber and hundreds of other things must be brought in ships to the Islands. In order to pay for these products, great quantities of manufactured goods must be made and sold. Trade is the life blood of the country, and if it were to be cut off or reduced, results would be most serious.

Inland regions Inland regions of the British Isles are just as interesting as the coast for there lie mountains, highlands, plateaus and flat plains. In general, the northern and western parts of Great Britain are marked with highlands, while the southeastern portion is a low plain. The northern half of Scotland is crossed by the Highlands, the southern section is traversed by the Southern Uplands, and in between are the Lowlands. The once high mountains of Scotland have been worn away, so that Ben Nevis, the highest peak is but 4,406 feet above sea level. This compares in size with the Appalachian mountains of North America, but is much lower than the lofty peaks of the Rockies.

Running from the Southern Upland of Scotland, a great plateau called The Pennines thrusts its way southward, forming what is known as the "backbone of northern England." To the west of this lies the beautiful Lake District, and to the southeast the English Lowlands. Wales is a rugged, mountainous country with a narrow fringe of flat land along its twisting coast. In Ireland, the low mountains rise in scattered patches along the shores, leaving a wide plain running through the centre of the island.

Climate Westerly winds, moving across the Atlantic, carry moist air to the British Isles, and since these damp air currents strike the western portion of the islands first, it is there that the rainfall is heaviest. Regular showers at all seasons maintain a heavy vegetation, and provide water for many medium-sized rivers. As in our Maritime Provinces, the British Isles are subject to heavy, deep fogs which darken the cities and lie like a grey blanket over the waters. Although the islands are in the same latitude as Hudson Bay, the British winters are much milder than those we have in Canada; warm winds blowing off the Gulf Stream current of the north Atlantic are the kindly agents which modify the weather of the wintry months. Summers, on the other hand, are cooler than those in Canada, because winds and ocean waters tend to cool the air. It is an odd fact that hardy

Introduction

Canadians, accustomed to cold winters, still shiver in the chill, damp climate of England.

London

Almost one quarter of the people of Britain live in Greater London which, with the towns about it, has a population of ten million . . . more than half the population of Canada. Greater London, like Metropolitan Toronto, is composed of a number of municipalities lying close together.

London is located on the Thames River which flows eastward across southern England, breaks through a gap in the chalk hills, and empties into the North Sea. This river provides London with its water supply, and provides the city with the greatest port in the Isles. Passing up a dredged channel in the river, ships from a hundred shores land their cargoes at endless docks that line the banks. Of all the goods coming into Great Britain, almost half make their way up the Thames to the Port of London.

London is more than a port, more than a seat of government, more than a populous centre: London is a city with noble character stamped on its ancient face. Here are some of the greatest tourist attractions on the globe. Westminster Abbey, Buckingham Palace, The Tower of London, Nelson's monument, St. Paul's Cathedral, the National Gallery, the Houses of Parliament and Number 10 Downing Street are familiar places even to those who have not yet visited them.

The British people

The people of the British Isles are a remarkable folk with a mixture of blood in their veins: the blood of Celts and Romans, the blood of Iberians and Gaels, the blood of Angles and Saxons, the blood of Danes and Normans. For two thousand years the Isles have seen wars and invasions, each bringing its own tragedies and blessings, each adding something to British character. From these trials a nation arose destined to form a mighty empire drawing broad patterns on the map of the world. These were the people who were aggressive, merciless and ruthless, but at the same time progressive, forgiving and generous. These were the people who fought great battles, wrote great books, painted great pictures, made great explorations, created great industrial empires, and developed one of the greatest of modern democracies.

Traditions which developed slowly during 2,000 years of British history form an important part of our Canadian heritage. Events which took place centuries ago still influence our speech, our literature, our laws, our customs and our government.

5

I. A NATION IS BORN

B.C.	55
	0
	100
	200
	300
	400
	500
	600
	700
	800
	900
	1000
	1100
	1200
	1300
	1400
	1500
	1600
	1700
	1800
	1900
A.D.	2000

Julius Caesar in Britain • Life of the Britons • Return of the Romans • Roman civilization comes to Britain • The fall of Rome • Conquest by the Jutes, Angles and Saxons • English ways replace Romans ways • Coming of the Danes • William of Normandy defeats Harold Godwin at Hastings • Norman life in Britain • The Feudal System • Strong government • Foundations of a united nation

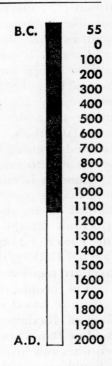

1

ROMAN RAIDERS FROM THE SEA

During the centuries directly before the birth of Christ the Romans of Italy conquered all the lands about the Mediterranean Sea, and built up the great Roman Empire. Having completed the conquest of Gaul, which we now call France, the Roman general, Julius Caesar, turned his attention to the islands which lay just across the English Channel.

It was an August morning of the year 55 B.C. Above the water on the brink of the tall white cliffs stood an army of Britons, dark against the morning sky. There were young lads, sturdy tall fellows with broad shoulders, and older men with crooked hands and grey

The Roman trireme was a long slender vessel built for speed. It was propelled by a square sail and long oars which were worked by slaves. The word trireme indicates that there are three banks of oars on each side of the ship. A drum on deck beat the stroke for the rowers.

beards. Horsemen dashed about, chariots rattled by, their riders swaying with the jolt of heavy wheels. A feeling of tenseness and expectation lay over the army, as if the men were expecting some strange thing to rise from the sea.

A shout that startled the sea birds rose from one end of the long line, and hands pointed out to sea. Away over the flat surface of the Channel through the thinning mist, appeared white shapes, scarcely visible in the distance. With the passing of minutes the watchers could make out eighty vessels, Roman sailing ships from across the Channel, from the shores of Gaul. A roar went up from the waiting Britons, an odd roar, half in anger, half in joy at the coming battle.

As the ships sailed nearer, they shifted course, moving along the shore, seeking a flat, level place for landing. Foot soldiers, horsemen and charioteers on the chalk cliffs seized their arms, and hurried off in the same direction. The sound of running hoofs and the ring of chariot wheels carried over the waters.

7

Hours later, the Roman transports and warships swung toward a
flat beach which was already swarming with great masses of Britons
a few miles from Dover. On came the ships, their banks of oars flashing
in the light, their decks alive with soldiers. As keels scraped on the
pebbly bottom of the Channel, the forward motion of the vessels was
checked.

Even for Roman troops, a terrifying sight lay ahead, for horsemen
were dashing through the spray and war chariots plunging into the
shallows. Britons in horned helmets, their long blond hair flying in
the wind, drove onward toward the ships, while a shower of stones
and javelins poured from the beach. In the face of the fierce attack
the Romans hesitated momentarily, but a standard-bearer of the Tenth
Legion slipped over the side of a transport, into the water, and with
the precious standard held high, he advanced toward shore.

The Roman general, Julius Caesar, ordered the warships to
open fire on the beach. Catapults flung missiles from their long
arms, and flights of arrows from Roman bows hissed overhead. Soldiers
leaping from the transports formed into ranks as best they could and
waded toward the beaches. All was confusion . . . a wavering mass
of charging horsemen, wheeling chariots and wading foot soldiers.
There was the clash of iron swords on bronze shields, and the cry
of men slipping below the waters. Slowly the Britons were pushed
back to dry land, and the Romans, swarming ashore, formed themselves
into tight ranks. Faced with the iron wall of the Roman legions, the
Britons fled from the beaches.

Julius Caesar set up camp on the shore, and waited for the arrival
of a second fleet bearing cavalry troops that were to support the inland
march across the island. A fierce gale, however, drove the fleet down
Channel, forcing it back to the mainland of the continent. A second
stroke of ill fortune for the general came with the high tide of
the full moon; many of the Roman transports and warships were
driven ashore, wrecking some and damaging others. Caesar, who had
planned a swift conquest of Britain, was now left in a dangerous
position, for he had lost much of his transport, and he had no food
stores for a winter on the island. Parties of soldiers were ordered
inland to raid farms and villages, and so successful were these forays
that the Romans lived for two weeks on grain stolen from the nearby
fields.

When the Britons realized the precarious position of the invaders,
they harried the wandering bands of soldiers, and made hit-and-run

On a beach in southeastern England the Britons rush to meet Roman invaders under Julius Caesar. The sturdy chariots employed by the Britons had iron tires on the wheels, and sometimes were fitted with sharp knives attached to the axles. Describing the charioteers, Julius Caesar wrote, "They begin by driving all over the field, hurling javelins, and the terror inspired by the horses and the noise of the wheels is usually enough to throw the enemy ranks into disorder."

attacks on the Roman camps. While these tactics did not seriously threaten the invaders, they did make conditions very uncomfortable for the legions. Anxious to get away from the island, Caesar repaired a number of ships, crowded his troops aboard, and sailed for Gaul, taking with him hostages and prisoners.

The following year, 54 B.C., Caesar was back in Britain with a **Julius** larger army of foot soldiers and cavalrymen, all transported in a fleet **Caesar,** of 800 ships. This huge armada threw terror into the Britons, for **54 B.C.** they had seen nothing like it. After landing, Caesar marched north, destroying forts and scattering settlements, but the victorious campaign was cut short when the Roman general received news that another vicious storm had battered his invasion fleet. Returning to the coast, Caesar spent some time repairing ships before he was able to continue the conquest of the island. Then once again he advanced

9

Because the Roman siege weapon, the onager, kicked and jumped when fired it was named after the wild donkey. Heavy stones were shot when a thick skein of twisted cords was released. Weapons of this type were still in use in the fifteenth century.

inland and reached the Thames River in the vicinity of what is now the city of London.

Casivellaunus

In the meantime large numbers of Britons rallied under the leadership of a shrewd chieftain, Casivellaunus, who utilized a most effective plan of fighting the invaders. He sent all foot soldiers home, keeping only a powerful striking force of swift-moving horsemen and charioteers. With this hard core of an army, Casivellaunus harried the Romans, attacking their flanks and cutting off small raiding parties. But even such daring manoeuvres as these could not keep Julius Caesar from capturing more strongholds and gaining more ground. In the end, Casivellaunus wisely made peace with Caesar, submitting himself and his army to the power of Rome. With prisoners and hostages, the Roman general left Britain and returned to the shores of Gaul. Although the Romans went home boasting of a new conquest, it was really a victory for the Britons, because the legions did not come back to the island for another hundred years.

2

THE BRITONS

The Britons who had humiliated the famous legions of Rome were a mixture of European, Asiatic and perhaps African peoples who, through the ages, had moved westward into the British Isles. Considerable mystery still surrounds the origin of these peoples, but we do know something of their later history through Roman records and through relics found by archaeologists.

During the first stages of recorded history, the islands we call Great Britain and Ireland were settled by tribes of people closely related to the races of the European mainland. There were the dark Iberians who originally came from the Mediterranean lands, and there were the fair-haired Celts who came from northern Europe and northern Asia. It is thought that the Iberians tended to gather to- **People of** gether in villages, while the Celts preferred the greater freedom of **Britain** the open country. The tall, blond Celts were a proud, generous people who revelled in hunting and fighting, while the short, dark Iberians stayed close to their villages, taking an interest in farming, handicrafts and business. Both peoples lived side by side, but since the Celts were more powerful and more numerous, as time went by Celtic became the common language.

At the time of the first Roman invasion the islanders seem to have been divided roughly into three large groups: the Britons or Brythons of southern England, the Scots or Gaels of Ireland and western Scotland, and the Picts or Caledonians who lived in the far northern regions.

It was the fair-haired Britons of Celtic origin who came into contact with Caesar's legions. These people were similar in speech and appearance to the Gauls who lived across the English Channel in the land we call France. A friendly relationship existed between the two, for the Britons provided some assistance to the Gauls in their fight against the legions; this was one reason why Caesar had decided to invade the island across the Channel.

The Romans felt much superior to the Britons. Roman records **Life of the** deal rather sketchily with the civilization of the islanders, but archae- **Britons** ology has shown that the Britons were no primitive savages. They

11

The Britons shown here have gathered to worship in a sacred grove beside a sacred pool. With arms upraised the chief Druid stands before the wooden

knew something of farming, for they kept herds of cattle, pigs, sheep, goats, and they grew crops of wheat, oats, barley and flax. Their round, wooden homes had conical, thatched roofs made from grasses, branches, ferns and straw. They wove woollen and linen cloth, worked in metals and constructed small ships. Skilled artisans were able to make pottery, jewellery, tools, knives, chariots, harness and weapons of iron and bronze. A difficult process of applying coloured enamels to metal was known to the Britons, so that some of the best enamel work of the time was produced in England, Ireland and perhaps in Scotland.

Coracles A small circular boat, the coracle, shaped like a round basket, was used by the Britons for fishing and for travelling along the rivers and seashores. It was constructed by fastening hides over a light wooden framework, and was moved in the water by the use of a paddle. It is curious to note that the bull boat made by Indians of western Canada was very much like the coracle. Oddly enough, too, the coracle is still used in some parts of Wales which long ago was populated by the Britons.

12

image of a three-faced god, while other Druids play music on curved bronze
trumpets. Offerings to the gods have been cast upon the surface of the pool.

It seems strange that a people who were very skilled in certain
crafts did not make better homes for themselves. The Briton's house
was built by setting a circle of poles into the ground, weaving strips
of thin wood in and out all around this framework, and then topping
the whole with a thatched roof. An open fire on the earthen floor
served as stove and furnace, filling the hut with a heavy eye-smarting
smoke. Single houses, or groups of houses, were protected from raiders
by earthen walls, or thick thorny hedges, which in turn were surrounded by ditches as an added protection. Here and there on hilltops
circular forts with earthen walls were maintained as strongholds during
warfare. These safety measures were necessary, for the tribes were
frequently fighting each other for reason of land or power.

Much of what is now called England was covered with forests
and swamps, so that the trails, or tracks, used by the people ran along
the higher parts of the country. Here the rich green grass served to
feed herds of sheep driven from one place to another, and here the
firm sod made solid paths for horsemen and chariots. Winding trails
led from ford to ford, from village to village and to places where the
craftsmen found flints and minerals.

The small boat in the foreground is a coracle made from hides stretched over a circular framework of wood. Julius Caesar was so impressed by coracles that he ordered some made for a military campaign in Spain. The dugout in the background was a primitive boat formed by hollowing out a log.

Druids Britons, like other early peoples, were superstitious, holding many strange religious ideas which had arisen ages before in Europe, Asia and Egypt. One of the odd facts of history is that religious beliefs spread from land to land, from tribe to tribe, across continents and over wide seas. Priests of Britain, the Druids, were powerful men who held great influence among the tribesmen. More than simple priests, the Druids acted as judges, lawyers, teachers and witch doctors. No written records were kept by the Druids because they wished the secrets of their profession to remain a mystery among the ordinary Britons. Young men training for priesthood spent years of schooling under the Druids, learning by memory the rules, regulations and religious customs of the priests. Britons believed that spirits lived in trees, rivers, springs, birds, animals and insects, and, for this reason, religious ceremonies were held in the open beneath the trees of the forest. Oak trees and the mistletoe which grew upon them seem to have been particularly sacred in the religious rites. To seek the pleasure of the gods, the Druids offered sacrifices of grains, birds, animals and sometimes human beings. Victims, placed in huge wicker baskets were hurled into blazing fires, or others, tied hand and foot, were slowly stabbed to death with long bronze swords. The Druids chanted and the Britons watched.

14

3

RETURN OF THE ROMANS

Because he was busy with successful conquests in France, Italy and Egypt which finally led to his becoming dictator of the Roman Empire, Julius Caesar never returned to Britain. At the height of his power he was murdered by a group of rivals who were jealous of his success. Caesar's attacks upon Britain had little effect upon the history of England, but the same cannot be said of later invasions launched by his countrymen. Rome was to have an important influence upon the development of the little isles across the Channel.

In A.D. 43, ninety-eight years after the attempted invasion by Julius Caesar, Emperor Claudius decided that the land of the Britons should be added to the Roman Empire. He ordered four legions from Gaul to cross the Channel, and as soon as possible Claudius joined the troops, an act which showed the importance of the campaign. Marching inland, the legions fought Britons in battles along the Thames River, and finally captured an important stronghold commanded by a powerful chieftain of the Britons. This victory broke the resistance of the tribes in the southeastern part of the island, making it possible for the invaders to occupy much of the country.

Southern England was made at once into a Roman province, Britain, a which, like other provinces of the empire, was garrisoned by imperial Roman troops and ruled by a governor. By means of warfare and peace Province treaties, during the following years governors spread Roman rule westward to the coast of Wales and northward to the Highlands of Scotland. The Scots of Ireland and the Picts of the far north remained free. Conquest and control of the Britons were aided to a great extent by the magnificent system of roads which the Romans established. Quick movement of troops from one place to another made it possible to crush uprisings and to invade new districts.

The Britons were not easily conquered by the invaders because Caractacus a number of vigorous leaders led resistance movements among the tribes. A daring chieftain, Caractacus, who fought the Romans from the very beginning, slipped like a phantom from one unconquered tribe to another, and during nine years he caused continuous trouble for the Roman legions. Eventually Caractacus was betrayed, captured and taken to Rome where he with other prisoners was paraded through the streets of the city. His proud appearance and his fame as a fighter

15

This Roman chariot is being driven along a road, or *Pavimentum*, and is about to pass one of the mile-posts, called milliaria. The inscription carved on the

won the admiration of the Emperor Claudius who pardoned Caractacus and permitted him to live in Rome as a free man.

The Island of Mona (Anglesey) off the west coast of Britain became the refuge of a number of unconquered Britons and escaped Druids, thus forming a troublesome spot for the Roman rulers of the country. In the year A.D. 61 a massive force of troops was thrown at the island; the Britons were overwhelmed, and a Roman garrison was stationed at Mona to keep control.

Queen Boadicea There were rebellions among some of the tribes who had been conquered during the early stages of the invasion. While Roman troops were attacking the Island of Mona, the Iceni people of the east arose in a wild revolt, A.D. 61, under the command of their courageous widow-queen, Boadicea. Fighting savagely, large numbers of Iceni warriors wiped out Roman garrisons, cut the Ninth Legion to pieces, and destroyed the city of Londinium, (London). Modern archaeologists have lately uncovered burned brick walls which are relics of this destructive attack. When powerful Roman reinforcements were hurried to the rebellious area, the Iceni were defeated and punished in a merciless manner. Queen Boadicea committed suicide.

Roman roads The Roman military roads spread in a network across the country. These were no mere trails, but straight solid roads built in a direct line between important fortifications. When building highways, the Romans ploughed two parallel furrows across the land, and then

16

post says: *Emperor Caesar Trajan Hadrian Augustus, the High Priest, with the power of a Tribune, father of his country, 3rd Consul, 8 miles from Kanovium.* Such inscriptions were among the earliest highway signs.

proceeded to flatten the earth between them. This flat, level strip of hardened earth was called *Pavimentum,* a Roman term from which we have derived our word "pavement." Over this was poured a kind of concrete made of mortar and gravel. Even then the roadway was not complete, for the next came a layer of small stones and lime, then a layer of lime, chalk and earth, and finally a coating of heavy carefully-fitted flagstones or gravel.

Along the military roads were towns, villages, camps and resting places for travellers. All important roads were marked at regular intervals with posts called *Milliaria* which were spaced one thousand paces apart. This distance, equal to 4,834.38 feet, was the measurement which eventually developed into the "mile" we use today.

Military camps scattered throughout Britain were of different **Military** types. The first was a small camp which was used only when needed **camps** for a definite purpose; the second was larger in size and more strongly protected; the third type was large, permanent and heavily fortified. Roman camps, large and small, were square or rectangular in shape rather than round as were the old Briton strongholds. A Roman legion of 5,000 or 6,000 men required a walled camp which was about 2,300 feet in length and about 1,600 feet in width. Surrounding ramparts were six feet high and eight feet thick, while the outer ditch, or moat, was three feet deep and five feet across.

17

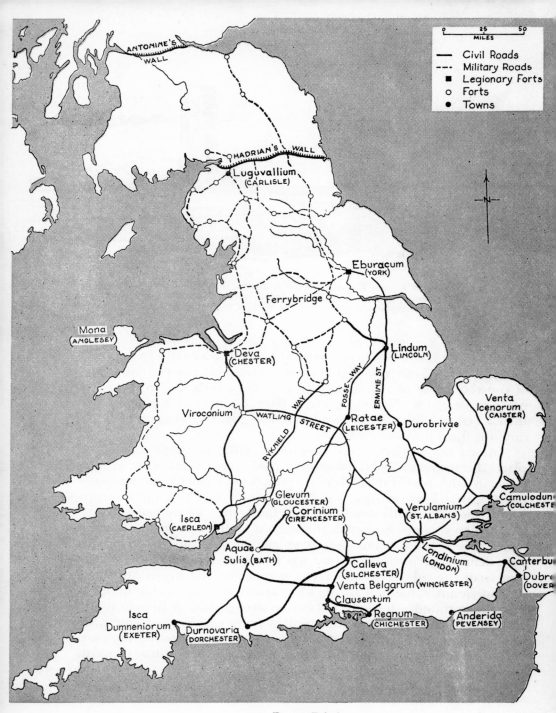

Roman Britain

Britons wore helmets and carried elongated shields made of bronze or wood. Shields and helmets were sometimes decorated with brightly-coloured enamel work.

The Roman name for camp was *castra,* a word which in various forms still finds use in our language. For example, the names of English cities such as Lancaster, Gloucester and Manchester have endings resembling the word *castra.* All of these places, and others, were once fortified Roman towns serving in the control and defence of Britain.

To keep the unruly Picts **Hadrian's** from invading the southern **Wall** regions, the Romans built in the reign of Emperor Hadrian a defensive system called Hadrian's Wall, seventy miles in length, stretching from Solway Firth to the mouth of the Tyne. It was composed of two parallel walls; one of heavy stone facing north, and a smaller one of earth facing south. Between the two was a complex series of forts, guard houses, watch towers and military camps. Although considered a powerful means of defence at the time, Hadrian's Wall, if used in modern warfare, would be no more effective than a cardboard wall. However, even today in Canada we have a northern wall of defence, not made of stone or of earth, but consisting of lines of radar stations projecting invisible barriers of radio waves. Like Hadrian's Wall, the radar lines are designed to form a protection against raiders from the north.

By modern standards the Roman army of occupation in Britain **Roman** was not large, containing as it did about 20,000 foot soldiers **occupation**

This Roman legionary, or infantry man, wears the famous short sword which was double edged and perfectly straight. The best of these swords were made in Spain. He holds in his right hand the *pilium*, a long wooden spear with an iron head. For body protection he has a helmet, chest armour and a rectangular shield. The height of the shield was supposed to be the length of the soldier's arm.

and nearly 2,000 horsemen. All troops in the infantry were armed with a shield, a sword and a lance approximately six feet in length. When in battle, the first rank of soldiers hurled their lances, and then charged the enemy with sword in hand. The second rank launched lances over the heads of their advancing comrades and held themselves ready to attack when needed. The ranks behind acted as reinforcements and formed a solid wall behind which tired and wounded soldiers took refuge.

Cavalry troops took up protective positions on each side of the legion, ready to check the charge of enemy horsemen, or to launch an attack upon retreating forces.

The excellent training and discipline of the Roman soldiers was revealed clearly in some of the more important engagements which took place between the Britons and the legions. During one battle with the Iceni warriors, the outnumbered Romans killed thousands, while losing only 400 of their own soldiers. It is little wonder that the tribesmen, bold fighters though they were, bowed before the might of the imperial legions.

4

LIFE IN ROMAN BRITAIN

Life in Britain was changed after the Roman conquest, for the Romans brought with them ideas, luxuries and customs which were unknown to the Britons. Roman law and Roman rule brought a period of comparative peace during which towns were born, industry developed and trade expanded. These improvements were not planned merely for the good of the people, but were carried out for the glorification of the Roman Empire.

Just as North American Indians gradually learned the ways of the conquering Europeans, so did the Britons acquire the habits and customs of the invaders. They learned to dress in Roman clothing, to use Roman tools, to enjoy Roman goods, and, in some cases, to read and write as the Romans did.

Roman law, while severe, was just, and protected the weak and **Roman law** innocent from the strong and ruthless. No person accused of crime was punished without a fair trial; no person was killed on the word of an official; no person was sacrificed to please Druid priests; and the ancient wars among the tribes were no longer permitted. In many ways the Britons benefitted by these conditions, and yet they longed for the days of liberty when they were free from heavy taxes and exempt from military service in the Empire.

Young Britons found their way into the Roman army, some by force and some voluntarily. They were not allowed to remain in their homeland, but were sent abroad to garrisons in various parts of Europe and Africa where many of them served with courage and distinction. Occasionally as a reward for long and devoted service, Britons with their wives and children were given full citizenship, an honour which carried with it a number of privileges not granted to the ordinary conquered peoples. By the year 212, however, citizenship in the Roman Empire was granted to all who were not considered slaves.

Roman officials and wealthy Britons built large rambling homes **Roman** resembling those found in Italy at the time. The first villas, or country **homes** homes, may have caused as much wonder among the Britons as did Champlain's habitation among the Indians of New France. The Roman villas were a collection of rooms and galleries built about

21

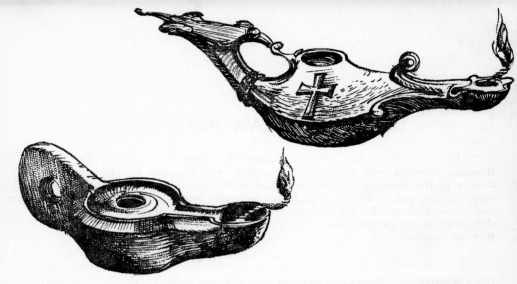

Vegetable and animal oils were used as fuel in Roman lamps. The lower lamp is a simple pottery object, while the upper one is an elaborate bronze lamp. The cross appearing in the decoration of the upper lamp is probably a Christian symbol. Wicks used in lamps were of flax tow, an improvement over the rushes of earlier times.

large courtyards which were paved with flat stones. Because the climate of England was cool, the Romans heated their homes by narrow passages beneath the floors which carried warm air to the rooms used most frequently by members of the household. Large furnaces were tended constantly by slaves. In addition to the living quarters of the villas, there were storehouses, workshops, bathing houses, kitchens and great banquet halls.

Because the upper parts of the houses were made from wood, plaster and stucco, they have long ago disappeared, leaving only the ruins of floors, foundations and paved courts. Of special beauty were the mosaic floors of the villas made from countless tiny blocks of coloured stone, all laid in a bed of cement. Under the training of the Romans, British craftsmen became remarkably skilful in the design and construction of these amazing floors. Complete pictures with fine details all done in stone have been found in the ruins of the old villas in Britain.

Entertainment

Romans, longing for their native land, made some attempt to enjoy the pleasures, the comforts and the entertainments which had pleased them in their homeland. One of their greatest pleasures was public bathing, a pastime which led them to build large and ornate bath houses in the larger centres of population. Most of these have

22

not survived the passage of years, but ruins may still be seen at Bath. Bathing among the Romans was a social event where men gathered not only to bathe, but to talk, to gossip and to discuss important matters. Romans enjoyed, too, entertainment at the theatres where plays were performed, and at great amphitheatres where military contests were held. Little today remains of these, but it is believed that the structures were small compared with the magnificent ones which existed in some other parts of the Roman Empire.

Britons had coins before the coming of the Romans, but after the conquest, the amount of coinage increased. Trade with the continent which had been carried on in a small way, became more extensive after the conquest. From Britain went cargoes of grain, lead, tin, iron, cattle, sheep, furs and oysters. British dogs, noted for their hunting skill, were prized in many parts of the Roman Empire. **Trade and industry**

For use at home in Britain, many goods were manufactured in the growing towns. Among these products were woven fabrics, slates for roofs, tools, weapons, pottery, glass, brick and tiles. There were, of course, goods brought into Britain which could not be grown or manufactured on the island. Most of these were luxuries for the wealthy which came from faraway points in the Orient. There were wines, spices, cottons, silks, rare woods, jewels and golden ornaments. It seems likely that only the highest Roman officials and the wealthiest of Britons could afford these expensive imports.

Of all the towns built by the Romans, the largest and most important rose on the site of a British village on the Thames and was called Londinium. Londinium became a vital name in English history, for eventually the little village was to become London, the largest city in the world. **Londinium**

Under the Romans, London was an important centre of business and government, and the city grew so fast that the brick and tile makers could scarcely keep pace with the builders. Among the important features of the city were a covered market place, a bridge across the Thames, a track for chariot races, an amphitheatre and a number of temples and public baths. Beautiful homes with brightly painted walls lined the important streets. London, an unfortified city, fell in A.D. 61 an easy prey to Boadicea's warriors as the city was burned and the citizens massacred. London was not to remain a heap of ruins, for the Romans rebuilt rapidly, making the city larger than ever before. At the peak of its glory Roman London contained about 350 acres and had a circumference of five miles.

Inside a walled Roman town of Britain, citizens move about the streets. The man in the foreground is wearing a cloak, the famous Roman toga. A woman at the right is making a purchase at an open stall. In the background may be seen the wall and gate of the town.

Language and religion

As time went by, the population of Britain became more and more mixed owing to the fact that soldiers who made up the garrisons came from widely scattered parts of the Empire. Latin, the language of Rome, probably became the common speech of the island, although groups of Britons in isolated areas kept their own Celtic language and customs.

The ancient religion of the Druids slowly disappeared. For nearly two centuries of Roman rule, the Roman gods remained the centre of attention and then Christianity, reaching the island about A.D. 200, gradually spread to many parts of the Roman province. Among the greatest workers in the early Christian church was St. Patrick who is thought to have been born in what is now western Britain. After being trained as a monk in France, he was sent to Ireland in the year 439 to spread the Christian gospel. It is estimated that during the course of his missionary career he founded 365 churches, baptized with his own hands 12,000 persons, and ordained a large number of priests. It is not surprising that he became Ireland's patron saint.

24

The glory of Rome was not to last, because it suffered decay from within and attacks from without. Part of the waning prosperity arose from unbearable taxes forced upon the provinces to pay for the expenses of military forces and costs of government. Jealousy spread among the highest officials, and quarrels arose among the provinces. Wild tribes of barbarians along the fringe of the Empire kept a constant pressure on the defences, launching annoying raids and small invasions. They looted lands along the boundaries. In some cases they stayed as unwelcome citizens. Some bands of the barbarians, taken into the Roman legions, became good soldiers, but were dangerous risks to security.

Britain itself felt the heavy weight of barbarian attacks as Picts from the north, Scots from Ireland and Saxons from across the North Sea pressed in on the Roman province.

In northern Europe the savage Goths were an ever-present menace to the very heart of the Empire, and so great was the danger that troops from Britain and other imperial outposts were hurried home to protect the city of Rome. Then came the final blow, when the Goths swept through Italy, smashed the central defences and, in 410, marched into Rome. The whole civilized world could scarcely believe that Roman power was lost, shattered beneath the feet of barbarian hordes.

And what of Britain? Without the strength of the imperial legions, she stood weak and unprotected, an easy victim for the hungry raiders that eyed her shores.

5

THE ANGLO-SAXON CONQUEST

Half-naked Picts from Scotland and wild Scots from Ireland raided England, but made no lasting settlements in the Roman province. It was a different story, however, with the Germanic pirates who sailed their little ships from the shores of northern Europe.

Even before the shocking collapse of the Roman Empire, bands of Jutes, Angles and Saxons harassed the coastal area of England. From Holland, northwestern Germany and southern Denmark these marauders flung their high-prowed vessels southward across the North

This Anglo-Saxon warrior wears mail armour, a helmet and carries a heavy shield. Saxon shields were oval or circular in shape and often were made of linden wood. Notice the long woollen stockings held in place by leather cross garters. The shoes, too, are made of leather.

Sea to the outpost of the Roman Empire. Then, landing at a river's mouth or some quiet beach, they ravaged the nearby villages and villas, killing people and taking whatever they wanted.

Conquest by Jutes, Angles and Saxons

After the Roman legions had left the island in 410, the attacks became more frequent, more violent, until they formed minor invasions. No longer brief raids of short duration, these new ventures were attempts to make lasting settlements in Britain, so with warriors came women and children. In some cases the invaders quietly occupied thinly settled districts, and in other cases fought bloody battles with the islanders. Their earliest permanent settlement was established about 499, some forty years after the imperial troops rushed home to protect Rome. During the next 150 years more than half the island was overrun by the Jutes, Angles and Saxons who formed themselves into a number of separate kingdoms. The Angles occupied northern, central and eastern England, while the Saxons and a smaller number of Jutes took over the southern regions. Saxons were separated into groups according to location—East Saxons, Middle Saxons, South Saxons and West Saxons. The locations of the settlements later came to be known as Essex, Middlesex, Sussex and Wessex.

Whether the German tribes destroyed great masses of the island people, or merely became their masters is not known, for this question

26

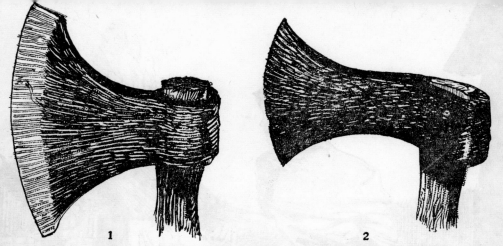

Illustrated here are Anglo-Saxon axes. (1) A broadaxe with a long handle which was swung as a battle axe. (2) The taper axe with a short handle which was thrown during conflict very much in the same way as the North American Indian threw his tomahawk.

has long been argued by historians. It may be that some of the Roman-Britons were killed in battles, others were murdered for their wealth, and still others thrown into slavery. Bands of stubborn fighters, too, fled to the mountains of the west after defeat in hard-fought battles.

In contrast with the civilization of the Roman Empire, the cus- **The English** toms and habits of the newcomers were rough and crude. Latin **people** languages disappeared, and the Celtic tongue survives now only in the region we call Wales. Law and justice, which had been see p.395 fair and constant under the Romans, fell upon sorry days. Strong and wealthy men were punished lightly for their crimes, while the poor and defenceless suffered severe penalties. Rank and wealth played such an important part in Saxon ways that each man's life was given a special value in terms of money. A slave was worth nothing; a serf or farm servant was worth fifty shillings; a churl or farmer 100 shillings; an eorl or nobleman 300 shillings; and an atheling or prince 1,500 shillings. If by chance a prince killed a churl, he would be forgiven his crime on the payment of only 100 shillings, but if a churl were to murder a prince, he paid 1,500 shillings. Persons who could not afford to pay their fines were killed, tortured, imprisoned or became slaves. Under this unequal system of justice wealthy and powerful men could commit crimes as long as they had the wealth to pay their fines.

Coming as they did from northern Europe, the invaders had been accustomed to a rough forested homeland with little farming or in-

The Anglo-Saxon settlement was surrounded by a wooden stockade for protection. Farm animals were often driven inside the walls at night. In the centre stands the great hall, surrounded by smaller buildings which could

dustry. To them Britain was a golden land, a highly developed country with well-tilled farms, herds of cattle and sheep, gardens, orchards, vineyards and fields of rippling grain. Along with the fertile farmlands were mines, iron-works, potteries, brick-kilns, quarries, fisheries and glass factories. Linked together by good straight roads were thirty fortified towns. Sturdy bridges arched over waterways, and the crossings at the river fords were paved with stones. Harbours along coasts were snug, well-protected havens for ships which came from and went to foreign countries.

When the invaders, who came to be known as the English, took over the land of Britain, they let the beautiful Roman villas go to ruin, and set up for themselves establishments resembling those in their homeland. Noblemen with large land holdings built big timber houses surrounded by a clutter of barns, workshops, storehouses, stables, wagon sheds and thatched huts for the workers. Each season of the year brought its own special tasks: in the spring there was ploughing, seeding and the care of new-born lambs; in summer came haying, harvesting and the shearing of sheep; in the autumn, there

include stables, serfs' huts, cattle sheds, beehives and gardens. The vegetables grown were cabbage, lettuce, onions, peas, turnips, parsley, mint, beets and leeks.

was hunting, hawking, butchering, salting of meat, the brewing of ale; and in winter came the chores of threshing, winnowing, carpentry and blacksmithing.

The working day of the farm labourer is described in an Old English Dialogue which has the ploughman say:

I work hard; I go out at daybreak, driving the oxen to the field, and I yoke them to the plough. Be it never so stark winter I dare not linger at home for awe of my lord; but having yoked my oxen, and fastened share and coulter, every day I must plough a full acre or more. I have a boy driving the oxen with a goad-iron, who is hoarse with cold and shouting. And I do more also. I have to fill the oxen's bins with hay, and water them, and take out their litter . . . Mighty hard work it is, for I am not free.

In the days of the Roman Empire, European civilization had **Decline of** glowed like a lamp in the night, but with the victory of barbarian **Roman** hordes, the lamp went out, leaving the continent in the chill twilight **civilization** of the Dark Ages. In England, culture and learning disappeared as people forgot their Latin and were forced to write simple messages in a crude runic form. Where order had existed before, there was now confusion; where laws had been fair, there was now injustice; where imperial unity had held the people together, there was now disunity and distrust. Even the good influence of the Christian religion was swept away from all the island except the mountains of Wales and in Ireland where it found a sheltered haven.

Christianity But Christianity was not to remain in hiding; it was destined to return through the good services of a kindly man in Rome. An ancient story tells of a priest called Gregory who, when visiting the Roman market place, saw handsome fair-haired boys being sold as slaves. When the priest asked from what race the boys came, he was told they were Angles from the heathen island of Britain. Sadly, Gregory remarked that it was a fitting name for the young slaves for they indeed had the faces of angels, but what a pity they had been brought up in a land of barbarians. Years later, when Gregory became Pope, he recalled the fair faces of the English boys—a memory which forced him to take an important action. Collecting a group of monks under a priest named Augustine, Pope Gregory sent them across France, over the Channel to the English kingdom of Kent where they arrived in the year 597.

King Ethelbert King Ethelbert of Kent, although a barbarian himself, had married a princess from France who was a Christian and so devoted to her faith that she worshipped by herself in a ruined Roman church. Ethelbert, not altogether pleased with the coming of the missionaries, nevertheless met the newcomers in an outdoor ceremony. There under the open sky Augustine preached to a quiet king and wondering attendants of the royal court. In time Ethelbert's distrust of Christianity disappeared, leading the way to his final baptism and acceptance of the faith. Many subjects followed their king to Christianity.

In a few brief years all Kent was Christian and neighbouring Wessex was following quickly. Not all missionary work was directed from Rome, for monks from France, Wales and Ireland joined in a drive to make all England a Christian land. The missionaries met with success, because they had energy, enthusiasm and a burning love for their chosen faith.

Venerable Bede With the return of Christianity, England took a renewed interest in learning and education, a movement which was helped by scholars within the church. Monks and priests who lived in monasteries had the time and the opportunity to study and to write. Among the religious scholars none was more important than a monk named Bede

Britain in the Eighth Century

The Saxon baker seen here is mixing dough in a large wooden vessel. *Bread* and *yeast* are Saxon words which have become part of our language. Strict laws were enforced against dishonest bakers. The offenders were whipped, pilloried or displayed publicly with their bad loaves hung about their necks.

who was born in northern England about the year 673. Gifted with a bright and enquiring mind, Bede took his greatest pleasures in reading, studying, teaching and writing. So active was he in his studies and his authorship that he produced textbooks in such varying subjects as history, astronomy, science, grammar, music and medicine. In addition to his writing, the "Venerable Bede" directed a school where he taught 600 monks who travelled long distances to study at the monastery. Bede may have been the first to realize that the English people made up a nation, even though at the time they were divided into a number of quarrelling kingdoms. To Bede's writings we owe much of our present knowledge of life in early England, and from him we have gained our practice of numbering calendar years from the birth of Christ.

So it was through the teachings and studies of Christian churchmen that a spark of culture and learning began to glow through the dimness of the Dark Ages.

6

COMING OF THE DANES

At the end of the eighth century a new menace arose in northern Europe which once again threatened the shores of England. Here was another group of sea-rovers who eyed the English kingdoms. These were the dreaded warriors of Denmark, Norway and Sweden who fought with equal ferocity on land and sea. Among themselves, these fighters were known as Vikings, but in Europe they were called Northmen; in Ireland they were called Ostmen; and in England they were called Danes.

Not content with pirate raids on the continental coasts, the Danes made three powerful thrusts through and around the land mass of Europe. Hordes of them marched overland from Sweden, across Russia, and on to the city of Constantinople. Others, in square-rigged, dragon-prowed ships sailed around Spain through the Strait of Gibraltar, and into the Mediterranean where they scourged the shores of southern Europe and northern Africa. A third group ranged the seas to Iceland, Greenland and the British Isles and even came, in the year 1,000, to our own continent of America.

It was the seaworthy and graceful long-ships which made possible **Danish** the amazing voyages of the Danes. One of these vessels in remarkably **long-ships** fine condition was found eighty years ago in Norway. Seventy-six feet from bow to stern and seventeen feet across the beam, the ship drew less than three feet of water. She was able to navigate shallow rivers and approach close to sandy beaches. Fitted with a single mast, a square sail, and thirty-two oars, the long-ship was ready for movement in windy weather and calm.

In sail on the ocean, the Danish vessel was a breath-taking sight. Below the wind-tightened sail, warriors pulled on the long oars. Along the bulwarks, round wooden shields were locked in a row like a giant chain of beads. At the back of the ship the high stern rose in a graceful curve, and at the bow the prow thrust upward to a grotesque, carved head.

The first recorded attack of Danes on the coast of England was in **Danish** the year 789. Defence against the Danes was difficult because they **invasions** came so suddenly, and appeared in the most unexpected places. By the time the local English chieftain had rallied his fighting men, the Danes had completed the attack, and were off to sea again. Even

33

The Danes often wore a thick leather jacket called a *corselet* which was covered with iron scales or rings. They also had chain mail armour, but probably this was worn only by the wealthy. Helmets were close-fitting metal caps, sometimes decorated with horns or wings. Principal weapons were the sword, spear and axe.

when an army of English troops met a strong group of Danes in battle, the invaders were apt to get the better of it. With their helmets, chain mail and great battle-axes, the reckless Danes were more than a match for the English with their swords and spears.

After years of raiding, the Danes began more serious invasions which carried fear and terror to many parts of England. Rowing their long-ships into rivers, small armies of Danes went ashore on headlands where they threw up earthen walls, from beach to beach. Behind these protective walls they set up camps which served as invasion headquarters. When possible, they stole horses from the nearby farms and with these made quick raids throughout the surrounding districts. Living in the camps, many bands of Danes were able to hold their positions permanently on the island. It was a fearful period for the English, because the Danes were cruel and merciless. Sometimes after battles the invaders ate victory feasts among the fallen men of the English.

With the passing years, the districts held by the Danes grew larger and larger until much of eastern England lay in the hands of the heathen invaders. Monasteries were looted and destroyed, villages were burned, and thousands of people were killed. Saxon kings ruling their little kingdoms lost their thrones to Danish rulers. Then began a period of settlement in which families from northern Europe arrived in England to make their homes in regions controlled by Danish kings

Danish settlements

34

A well preserved Danish long-ship was found at Gokstad in Norway. Made of oak, it was seventy-six feet in length. Long-ships were clinker-built, meaning that they were made from over-lapping planks fastened together with iron rivets. Power was supplied through a large square sail and a row of oars on each side. Steering was accomplished by an oar placed on the right side of the ship at the stern.

or chieftains. Some indication of Danish settlement is still found on the English maps of today through place names ending in *by* and *thorpe* such as Rugby and Burnam Thorpe. The Saxons, on the other hand, had used some place names ending in *ton* and *ham* such as Northampton and Buckingham.

In time all eastern England and much of northern England was under the power of the Danes, although a continuous struggle flared along the borders of this region. The whole of England might have fallen to the Danes had it not been for a Saxon prince, Alfred, who was brother of King Ethelred of Wessex. Having captured the city of London, the Danes prepared to move into the district of south-western England. About fifty miles west of London, the Saxon army waited the coming of the Danes. While King Ethelred was praying to God for help, the Danes attacked, so it was Alfred who led the Saxon charge. After a bloody, bitter struggle, the Danes gave in and fled from the field leaving their dead scattered across the Berkshire hills.

This Battle of Ashdown, fought in 871, had not smashed the strength of the Danes, but it had taught the invaders a stern lesson; it taught them to respect the power and the courage of the West Saxons. Here was a vital English victory, for had the Danes been successful, all Christian England would have sunk under heathen rule.

7
ALFRED THE GREAT (871—   )

The war between the Danes and the West Saxons dragged on. King Ethelred died, and was succeeded in 871 by his brother, Alfred, who was only twenty-two years of age.

Continuing the fight against the Danes, King Alfred* won some battles, and lost others. At one time after a serious defeat, he was forced to run for his life, hiding like an outlaw in swamps and forests. Eventually, however, he came out of hiding, rallied an army, and once again took up the struggle.

Alfred and the Danes A clever military leader, Alfred set up a defence system which later proved valuable. He built permanent forts, armed the towns and constructed war vessels to fight the long-ships of the Danes. For this reason, King Alfred is sometimes called the founder of the British navy. In addition, he arranged matters so that half the men in each community were occupied in military service, the other half remaining home on farms or in villages. By this system, agriculture and business could be carried on even when fighting was in progress.

Seven or eight determined battles were fought with the Danes, and then King Alfred made peace. The Danes might have conquered the West Saxons had they been willing to make great sacrifices of soldiers on the field of battle but they too were satisfied to have peace because their losses had been extremely heavy. By the peace treaty King Alfred made, in 886, England was divided into two parts, one

*For legends concerning King Alfred see page 395.

36

King Alfred the Great is seen here studying and arranging old Saxon laws, or dooms. Early Saxon books were sometimes covered with slabs of oak, beech or fir. Alfred's costume consists of a loose tunic with long sleeves and belt. Anglo-Saxons liked gaily-coloured clothing.

in the east under the Danes, and the other in the south and west under the West Saxons. Since Danish law was to govern eastern England, this section came to be known as the Danelaw.

Following this time, the Danes, tired of fighting, gave greater attention to settlement, to farming and to trade. Their old love of the sea, and their joy in fighting slowly waned. Within the Danelaw, Danes and Saxons settled down in peace. They mixed together, traded among themselves, intermarried, and in time the two races grew together. To this day there are noticeably more fair-haired, blue-eyed people in the east of England than in the west. This mixture of the races was a good thing, for it brought fresh vigour and vitality to the people who were to make a new and powerful nation.

King Alfred was more than a good soldier; he was an intelligent, Christian man, interested in law, in order, in prosperity and in education. His love of learning had begun years before in the days of his

Danelaw, 886

Alfred the Great

EPICTLAND AND DALRIADA
(United 844)

The five Danish boroughs
are underlined

STRATHCLYDE

NORTHUMBRIA

BERNICIA

· Lindisfarne

· Jarrow
Wearmouth

CUMBRIA

ISLE OF MAN

✗ *Brunanburgh*

DEIRA

· York

THE DANELAW

· Manchester

· Chester

R. Trent

Lincoln

Derby ·

Nottingham

WALES

Offa's Dyke

WATLING

R. Severn

Leicester ·

Stamford ·

EAST

✗ *Thetford*

ENGLISH
MERCIA

Warwick ·

ANGLIA

R. Wye

STREET

· Bedford

R. Thames

· Oxford

Malden ✗

I. OF MERS

Aston ✗

London ·

Chippenham ·

Merton ✗

I. OF SHEPPE
I. O

Wedmore ✗ *Ethandun*

Farnham ✗

Rochester ·

THA

Glastonbury ·

Canterbur

Athelney ·

Wilton ✗

· Winchester

✗

W E S S E X

Exeter ·

· Wareham

100

FRAN

0   40   80

MILES

England after the Treaty of Wedmore, 886

A lamp of the time of King Alfred the Great. It is of very simple construction, in sharp contrast with the beauty of the Roman lamps shown on page 22.

boyhood, at a time when his mother promised a manuscript of Saxon poems to the first of her five sons who memorized all the verses. Even though Alfred was the youngest member of the family, he had studied hard, learned the verses, and won the prize.

The King's early education proved most valuable to him in the years of uneasy peace that followed the wars. Anxious to improve the state of his kingdom, Alfred introduced a number of reforms which affected the life of his people. To establish justice and order, Alfred organized a set of laws or dooms connected with English life. He did not create new laws for his subjects, but collected and rearranged old Saxon dooms which he thought were suitable for the people. One such Saxon law read in this manner, "If anyone dig a waterpit, or open one that is shut and close it not again; let him pay for whatever cattle may fall therein."

During the long struggle with the Danes, literature and education had suffered greatly, almost disappearing in some parts of England. Determined to improve this state of affairs, Alfred founded new abbeys and monasteries, and encouraged the writing of books. In order to set a good example for scholars, Alfred himself wrote long passages in English prose.

Learned men from Wales, France and Germany were brought to Alfred's kingdom where they were given important positions as teachers and professors. At his court the King set up a school for the sons of nobles and wealthy Saxons, and here the boys learned to read in Saxon and in English. The King himself continued to study with such good effect that after middle age he was able to translate Latin books into English—a remarkable feat for a busy ruler. Today Alfred's translations are considered good though he himself apologized for the quality of his work.

King Alfred seems to have been altogether a wonderful person wholly devoted to the welfare of his people. It is not surprising, then, that he won from his subjects the title of "Alfred the Great," a name which holds a high place in the history of England. His work in defence, in law, and in education brought western and southern

A spoon and fork of the time of King Alfred the Great. This is either a cooking fork or a dessert fork, both of which were used at this time. The dinner fork as we know it today was not introduced into common use in England until early in the seventeenth century, after travellers had seen Italian forks.

England into closer union than ever before; a nation was beginning to form. It was fortunate for the Saxons that this unity existed, for war broke out once again. At the time of his death, in 901, Alfred was fighting the Danelaw and fresh invaders from the mainland of Europe.

Alfred's son, Edward, became king, and soon showed that he, too, was a skilful soldier and an able ruler. The fight against the Danes went on and on, with battles won and battles lost. A vital victory for the Saxons, in 910, however, turned the tide of warfare. Shifting from defence to attack, Edward invaded the land of the Danes. Joined by his widowed sister, Ethelfleda, who led a second Saxon army, Edward marched into the Danelaw with the purpose of conquering the whole of it. For eleven years brother and sister hounded the weakening Danes, occupying towns and smashing armies, until, in 917, most of the Danes gave in. Danish leaders submitted to Edward's authority, and, in return, were allowed to keep their lands, their estates and their customs.

Edward the Elder, 901

In the years that followed, Edward pushed his conquests northward, and all Wales bowed to his control. Edward's son, Athelstan, who succeeded as Saxon king, added still more successes. King Alfred had called himself "King of the West Saxons;" his son, Edward, had called himself, "King of the Anglo-Saxons;" but his grandson, Athelstan, gloried in the title of "King of All Britain."

Athelstan, 924

8

DANES AND NORMANS

After the defeat of the Danes, conditions improved in England. Law and order were restored, the country was divided into shires for local government, Christianity flourished, and learning made progress. The future appeared bright, but dark clouds loomed ahead.

The great-grandson of King Alfred, Edgar, carried on for seventeen years the good work of his noble ancestors, but he was the last strong man in the line of Wessex kings. His successor, Ethelred the Unready, was weak and foolish with no strength and no will to improve his kingdom.

With a weakling on the throne, England was once more an easy target for Danish marauders from Europe, and in 980 the attacks began. Instead of rallying a powerful army and fighting the Danes, Ethelred tried bribing the Danes with large sums of money. The raiders came back again and again and the climax came in 1013 when the King of Denmark and his son Canute* defeated the English. Ethelred the Unready lost his throne, dying soon afterward. In a valiant effort to regain lost ground, King Alfred's great-great-grandson, Edmund Ironside, fought the Danes, winning back half of England, but he, too, died when only twenty-two years of age. Tired of the struggles, all England joined in proclaiming Canute as the new king.

Canute* was a powerful ruler, for besides his English throne he controlled the kingdoms of Norway, Denmark, Scotland, Wales and other parts of Europe. But of all the lands he ruled, Canute liked England best, so it was there that he set up his court. A surprisingly kind and gracious ruler, the new king disbanded his invading army, and set about the work of uniting his newly-won domain. He married the widow of Ethelred the Unready, established strict courts of justice, built Christian churches, and encouraged the growth of education.

While these events were taking place in England, across the Channel in what is now France a powerful military group was rising. Danish settlers, a hundred years before, had settled in the region of Normandy named after the Northmen, and there they developed an unusual state. The remarkable feature of the state was the system by which Norman knights and nobles were given large land grants in

More Danish invasions, 980

King Canute, 1016

The Normans

For a legend concerning King Canute see page 396.

41

The morning star was a Saxon weapon which was a variation of the mace. Its heavily-spiked head was attached to a sturdy handle by means of a length of chain. Mail armour was only slight protection against this effective weapon.

exchange for military service. Nobles and knights in turn granted small plots of land to tenants who were required to follow their lords in times of war. Through this state organization called the feudal system the Normans became a strong, well-disciplined people.

Edward the Confessor

King Canute died in 1035, leaving three sons —rough, ignorant men who had little of the wisdom of their father. For a time they managed to control the kingdom, but after seven years the English throne was empty. The crown was placed on the head of a descendant of Alfred the Great, who had spent his life in Normandy. More Norman than Saxon in his ways, the new king, Edward, brought many of his friends from the continent, placing them in important positions. Edward was a disappointment to the English people, for he had little interest in ruling and absolutely none in warfare. A fat, friendly man, Edward's whole life was concerned with religion, so that in time he lived very much as a monk. As the years went by, the English gained an admiration for the king's saintliness, even though they regretted his lack of kingly qualities. Because of his monk-like habits, the king came to be known as "Edward the Confessor."

Earl Godwin

During this period England was really ruled by an ambitious nobleman, Earl Godwin, and his family, who managed to lay their hands on a great deal of land, wealth and power. In the year 1051, however, Godwin suffered a serious defeat when he was exiled from the country by a strong group of Normans in the court of Edward the Confessor.

William of Normandy

It is believed that while Godwin was out of the way, William, Duke of Normandy, paid a visit to the English King. It may be, too, that on the suggestion of the Norman Duke, Edward the Confessor agreed that the Norman ruler should be the next king of England. Such an agreement was a natural one, for Edward had always been favourably inclined toward the Normans. If such a plan was arranged between the King and the Duke, it received a rude set-

42

back by the sudden return of Earl Godwin, supported by his son Harold and a stout body of fighting men. Through this show of power, the Godwins regained their former importance, and took prompt revenge by expelling a number of Normans from England.

Less than a year after his return, Earl Godwin died, leaving lands **Harold** and power to his oldest son, Harold, who was a vigorous and clever **Godwin** young man. Like his father, Harold Godwin became the strong man of the land, ruling England for thirteen years, even though Edward the Confessor sat on the throne. Unfortunately there was discontent within the Godwin family, because Harold's brother, Tostig, had become jealous and troublesome. Instead of supporting Harold, the unreliable Tostig took up Norman ways, became a favourite in Edward's court and was made Earl of Northumbria. As a result the two brothers became bitter enemies, a condition which led to sad results for the House of Godwin.

Then by a strange trick of fate, in 1064, Harold Godwin fell into **Harold's** the hands of Duke William of Normandy. While making a trip along **oath** the eastern coast of England, Harold's ship was blown by strong winds across the Channel to the coast of France, where Harold was captured and held prisoner. Some time later he was taken to the Norman court and handed over to William. Instead of treating him as a prisoner, the Duke greeted Harold as a guest, granting him a knighthood and other favours. The two men became good friends, hunting and feasting together as the days passed by. Realizing what power his guest held in England, the Duke made a private treaty with Harold. By this agreement William was to become the next king of England and Harold was to rule in the province of Wessex. Together they swore an oath to keep the treaty, but Harold did not realize until later that trickery had been used in the ceremony. Below the table at which they sat the Duke had hidden certain sacred relics—perhaps the bones of a saint—which made the oath both sacred and binding.

In January, 1066, Edward the Confessor died, prophesying on his deathbed that dark days lay ahead for England. Although he had been a weak king, Edward's saintliness lingered long in the minds of the people.

It is possible that before his death Edward the Confessor forgot **Harold** his promise made to William of Normandy, and declared that Harold **crowned,** Godwin should be named the new king. However that may be, Harold **1066** did become king in 1066 after a coronation ceremony in Westminster Abbey.

Norman cavalry troops charge English infantry at the Battle of Hastings. The celebrated Bayeux Tapestry, made shortly after the Battle of Hastings, provides us with most of this information. A new kind of warfare was introduced to Britain by the Normans through the use of well-disciplined, armoured cavalry.

Harold's breaking of the sacred oath with Duke William, of course, caused shock and anger in Europe. Through an odd coincidence Halley's Comet appeared in the night sky at this time, causing the Normans to say that even Heaven was displeased at Harold's actions.

The Normans were not the only people annoyed by the English coronation. King Harold Hardrada of Norway, a descendant of Canute, decided that his family, too, had been insulted by the events which had taken place in the island kingdom.

Harold Godwin's* treacherous brother, Tostig, who had been exiled from England, joined King Harold Hardrada in Norway, and the two prepared troops and ships for an invasion of the island. In the meantime, the angry Duke of Normandy was collecting his powerful forces for a second invasion of the English shores.

In London, Harold Godwin waited anxiously, wondering where the two invading fleets would strike.

*For a legend concerning Godwin and Harold see page 397.

Norman horsemen used long, kite-shaped shields because they were more easily managed in the saddle. Straps attached to the shield enabled the warriors to wear them when necessary. Simple patterns were painted on shields to identify the owners. The Norman lance was generally wielded in a free manner, rather than being held in a firm position beneath the arm.

9

THE BATTLE OF HASTINGS

Of the two invading forces the Norwegian army reached England first, landing in Yorkshire to the north of London. Harold Godwin with his Danish household troops marched up the old Roman road to York, and then met the enemy at Stamford Bridge. In the battle which followed, the Norwegians were defeated; the King of Norway and Tostig were killed. But even in the hour of victory there came alarming news for Harold Godwin. Duke William of Normandy had landed strong forces in southern England.

In about five days Harold retraced the two hundred miles which lay between Stamford Bridge and London—an amazing journey for tired men wearing chain mail and bearing heavy weapons. After arriving at the city, Harold sent out a call for more troops to face the invading Normans. Reinforcements poured toward the city under the command of knights and nobles. Impatient to be off, and contemptuous of the enemy, Harold did not wait for all his troops to gather, but set out to meet Duke William. Moving southward, he reached a point about seven miles north of Hastings and there on a hill he took up a position blocking the road to London. It was not a steep hill, but a hill with a slope which would be difficult enough for an attacking force.

Harold reaches Hastings On the morning of October 14, 1066, Harold lined up his men in a tight formation, and waited the coming of the Normans. Solid masses of English axemen behind heavy shields stood as firm as the oaks on Senlac Hill.

The Norman army approaching in the distance was different from the English both in weapons and fighting methods, for here came cavalry troops and companies of archers carrying short tough bows. It was to be a battle between standing soldiers and swift-moving horsemen supported by bowmen.

As the invaders drew close to the foot of the hill, a Norman knight came forward alone, tossed his lance high, caught it in mid-air, and charged straight at the English army. Plunging into the ranks, he disappeared, dying among the swinging battle-axes.

Battle of Hastings, 1066 Norman cavalrymen followed him up the hill, throwing themselves against the rock-like wall of English troops. Norman arrows, flying overhead, struck English shields, but the foot-soldiers on the hilltop stood steady. English battle-axes swung in vicious circles, and English javelins arched over the wall of shields, falling among the horsemen. Wounded horses stumbled, throwing Norman knights to the ground where, burdened with armour, they lay in peril. Unnerved by the stubborn defence of the English, the left wing of Norman cavalry folded, gave way and fled down hill.

Eager for a quick victory, the half-trained troops on the right wing of Harold Godwin's army broke ranks, running down hill in hot pursuit of the Norman horsemen. This was a serious blunder, for, separated from the solid mass of their fellow soldiers, the English were an easy mark for the enemy. Seeing his chance, Duke William threw a fresh group of horsemen at the advancing foot-soldiers, and cut them to pieces.

Hour after hour the battle dragged on with more charges by Norman cavalry and more flights of arrow fire from the archers. The

(a) This is a small section of mail armour known as the *hauberk*. Notice its link construction. (b) This simple spur was used until the fourteenth century when it was beginning to be replaced by the rowel spur.

work of the bowmen began to tell, as many an Englishman died by an arrow that plunged through his chain mail. So close were the English standing, that the wounded and dying had scarcely space to drop to the earth. Both armies were beginning to tire, but there was no sign of victory or of defeat on either side.

Then, late in the afternoon, following a strong cavalry charge, **Defeat of** the right wing of Norman horsemen broke in confusion and retreated **the English** down hill. Then again came the fatal English error; a group of half-trained soldiers took up the pursuit, rushing down the slope only to meet the savage charge of cavalry surging up from the foot of the hill. There at the mercy of the horsemen they died in a wild effort to beat back the Norman lances. This was the turning point in the battle, for the English had made a tragic mistake in leaving their hill position.

As twilight fell on Senlac Hill, Harold Godwin fought on with **Death of** little more than his own well-disciplined bodyguard to keep off the **Harold** **Godwin** Norman riders. Taking advantage of the dim light, the enemy archers shot their arrows in high curves over the wall of shields, among the exhausted English. One such arrow caught Harold directly in the right eye, and a moment later he was cut down.

In the gathering darkness the valiant English retreated from the hilltop, and took refuge in the woods beyond. Numbers of Norman horsemen galloping in swift pursuit rolled and tumbled into a deep ditch; there in the night they were slaughtered by English axes and javelins.

The invaders had won the day. William the Conqueror camped as victor on the battlefield.*

*For a legend about this battle see page 397.

10

NORMAN RULE IN ENGLAND

On Christmas Day, 1066, the Archbishop of York crowned William the Conqueror as King of England, although even then the conquest was not yet complete. It was not until five years later that the last Saxon chieftain gave in to Norman rule.

By the year 1071 King William I could say in truth that he was king of all England, but control of the country had been won at the cost of sieges, battles and massacres. Towns were captured, villages burned, captives put in prison and rebellions smashed. An old record describes the ruthless crushing of an uprising in northern England:

When King William heard the news, he at once gathered an army and hastened to Northumberland with exasperation at heart, and all winter without ceasing laid waste the country . . . so great a famine prevailed that compelled by hunger men ate horses, dogs and cats, and anything whatsoever is loathesome; some sold themselves into perpetual slavery, so long as somehow they could support a miserable existence; others leaving the country as exiles gave up the ghost in the middle of their journey.

These were days of sorrow, days of bitterness for the English, and yet out of this dark period there grew a strong and united nation, largely because the Normans had a special talent which the nation needed.

Strong government At this time the countries of Europe were breaking up into small states or provinces, each ruled by a nobleman. Such had been the trend in England before the Norman conquest, but under the rule of William there was only one king, and he ruled with a firm hand. The Normans were an able people possessing a remarkable talent in politics and government. So effective was their work that for centuries England was to have the strongest government in all Europe.

William was a hard and merciless king in many respects, and yet he was a Christian man who held a sense of rough justice. Few other kings of England have introduced such sweeping changes into the life of the nation. Soon after his coronation he set about the work of making Britain a Norman state, a process which in time was to give the nation a greatness she had never known before.

48

The mail shirt, or *hauberk*, worn by this Norman knight offered protection to the head as well as to the body. The split in his *hauberk* permitted the knight to sit more comfortably in the saddle. A cone-shaped helmet worn over the head mail, had an iron bar, the nasal, which protected the nose. It was said to have been a good handle by which knights were dragged from the saddle during close combat.

After the first days of conquest, King William extended friendship and protection to those who accepted his rule. The city of London was given a royal charter promising fairness and justice to all its citizens. This famous document still may be seen in the Guildhall of the city. In other parts of the land, however, where English chieftains rose in rebellion, estates were taken away and granted to Norman noblemen.

One of King William's greatest accomplishments was the keeping of peace and order throughout England. Because there was no written code of Norman laws, the King was content to rule his subjects under the old Anglo-Saxon laws. Thieves, murderers and other criminals received swift punishment, so that citizens could travel anywhere in England without fear of attack or robbery.

Defence and control of the country were maintained through a system of forts and castles scattered throughout the land. Each of these was held by a knight or nobleman who commanded a body of armed men. In the beginning the forts were little more than fortified

49

The early Norman castle bears little resemblance to the elaborate castle of later times. Earth dug from ditches helped form the large mound on which the wooden castle was built. On top the mound stood the central citadel, or *motte*, which commanded the entire area of the castle. The wooden walls were not unlike the stockades of early forts in America. Below the *motte*, and also surrounded by a stockade, was the *bailey* or forecourt, where cattle were sometimes kept. A drawbridge connected the *bailey* with the central portion of the castle. The *bailey* was the first line of defence and the *motte* the second.

camps, and the castles were timbered buildings, but eventually these gave way to large stone castles capable of withstanding long sieges.

Tower of London

Among the most important of these structures was the Tower of London, built on the spot once occupied by a stronghold of Alfred the Great. The famous Tower of London was a palace, a fort and a prison all contained in one building. Additions were made to the Tower in later reigns, but William's portion of the famous place still stands firm—one of the great landmarks of British history.

Doomsday Book

The careful attention given by William to the small details of government is shown clearly in his establishment of the Doomsday Book which was the written record of a survey made in England during the years 1085 to 1087. These amazing records indicated the lands held in England, the names of landholders, the kinds of crops grown, the farm animals, and the valuation of all property. Information included in the records was useful in numerous ways, but particularly in the matter of raising taxes. The name Doomsday Book was given to the records by the English people because they compared the listing of property and the raising of taxes to "the day of doom."

Death of William I, 1087

William the Conqueror ruled both Normandy and England for twenty-one years after the battle of Hastings, and during that time he was never free from troubles and worries. French troops raided Norman lands . . . Robert, William's son, plotted against his father

50

. . . Queen Matilda died. Then in 1087, William attacked a French town, pillaged it, and set the place afire. As the King rode through the flaming streets, his horse stumbled, throwing him violently against the pommel of the saddle. For months through the hot summer William suffered from his wound, and then he died. Even in death the Conqueror was not to have peace, for, as he was about to be buried in a Norman churchyard, a citizen protested that the land belonged to him. Only after sixty shillings were paid by the embarrassed priests, was the body of the King lowered into the grave.

Before his death, William had declared that his eldest son, Robert, should be King of Normandy; the second son, William, was to be King of England; and the youngest boy, Henry, was to receive 5,000 pounds in silver. Strangely enough, a prophecy of the time stated that it was young Henry who finally would become the king.

William the Conqueror's second son became King William II of England in 1087, and ruled for thirteen restless years. It was a troublesome reign, as the King quarrelled with nobles and churchmen, and imposed heavy taxes upon his people. The unpopular monarch came to be known as "William Rufus," probably because his face was red in colour. Very few of his subjects shed tears when in the year 1100 the King was found lying in the New Forest, a hunting arrow driven through his heart. Whether he was murdered by a bitter countryman or killed in a hunting accident is not known. The body of William Rufus was carried on a cart to Winchester, and there he was buried without so much as a prayer said over his grave.

Then the prophecy came true, for William the Conqueror's youngest son, Henry, was crowned in 1100, King Henry I of England. The new King by custom had less right to the throne than did his brother, Robert, so he took quick action to tighten his hold on the kingdom. He promised to rule justly, and in return the powerful men of the realm agreed to support him. Wisely, too, Henry married an English woman, Matilda, who was descended from Alfred the Great and related to William the Conqueror. This marriage, of course, won the approval of most Saxons and Normans.

Henry was a well-educated man for his time, a fact which won him the name *Beauclerc* which means "fine scholar." In time he took control of Normandy, captured his brother, Robert, and held him in prison for life. For thirty-five years Henry ruled England, and through this period he gained among his people the reputation of being a good king, if not a great one.

51

Here we see agents of the king collecting information for the Doomsday Book. This ancient document indicated that 5,000,000 acres of land were under cultivation at the time. Information was so detailed that an Anglo-Saxon writer declared that "not even an ox, nor a cow, nor a swine was there left that was not set down in his writ." The Doomsday Book was originally recorded on rolls, and later in book form. The original document still exists in the Public Record Office, London.

11

LIFE IN NORMAN ENGLAND

As we have seen, there were four conquests of England — Roman, Saxon, Danish and Norman. The last of these conquests, like the others, brought important changes into the lives of the English people.

(a) After the Battle of Hastings, about 5,000 Normans settled in England, and these became the governing class of the country. It is true that a few Saxon nobles were allowed to keep their land, but most lost their estates, their wealth and their power.

In Saxon England there had been a tendency for the lower classes

This serf working in the field wears the standard garment of medieval times—a loose fitting woollen tunic girded at the waist. Such a costume with some alterations was worn by men over several centuries during the middle ages. The iron cultivator used by the serf would be considered very heavy and ineffective today.

Feudal system of people to hold land granted by the powerful lords in return for military service. King William I (The Conqueror) strengthened and organized this custom into a pattern which is called the *feudal system*. It cannot be said that the Normans invented feudalism, for it was found in different forms extending far back to earliest times. It became more common in Europe after the fall of Rome. It was the Normans, however, who brought the feudal system to its highest level of perfection.

The holding of land became the very foundation of social, political and economic life in Norman England. As head of the nation, the king was recognized as being owner of all the land within the nation. He granted vast sections of it to powerful nobles and churchmen called tenants-in-chief who swore allegiance to the King and promised military support when needed. Tenants-in-chief then granted sections of their holdings to lesser nobles called middle-tenants who in turn gave promises of loyalty and military assistance to the tenants-in-chief. Middle-tenants could, if they wished, grant portions of their holdings to other lesser nobles.

English land, then, was divided so that nearly every acre of it was placed directly under the control of a nobleman. Huge areas were granted to the Church, and the King himself had an estate in nearly every county.

Manors The local rural community in Norman England was the estate or manor which contained a small village where stood the lord's manor house, the priest's home, and the huts of the workers. All about the village lay fields, pastures and forests. Every villager on the manor

53

held a few strips of land in the cultivated portion of the area where he grew his crops and planted his garden. On the common pasture lands he had the right to graze so many geese or cattle, and in the forests he could feed his pigs and cut his firewood.

Strange as it may seem, most of the people of England at this time were not free. The Doomsday Book reveals that of the 232,021 workers only 36,513 were freemen. The others, called serfs, did not have the liberty allowed the freemen who could move about as they wished. Without the permission of his lord, the serf could not leave his village, and, if the manor were granted to another owner, the serf was passed over to the new lord. Both freemen and serfs paid rent for their strips of land by working on the fields of the nobleman. Sometimes part of the rent was paid in the form of produce such as eggs, butter, meat or grain.

The long narrow fields or strips were not marked off by means of fence or hedge as they are now, but the divisions were shown by piles of sod or stones. Crops produced on the land were poor, so that an acre of ground probably did not grow a quarter as much grain as it would today. No better than the crops, the farm animals, pigs, horses, sheep, cows, were scrawny beasts, much smaller and thinner than those now found on farms.

The work and duties of the serf differed in the various parts of England. In some places the serf could not send his children from the village, or sell his animals, or allow his daughter to marry without the consent of the lord of the manor. On many estates, too, the serf had no choice but to have his grain ground in the mill of the nobleman.

In addition to his land duties, the villager was required to make payments called tithes to the church. Every tenth animal and every tenth bushel of grain were considered tithes which rightly belonged to the church. Villagers who grew careless in the payment of these church taxes were fined or punished in some way or other. Military service, too, was another duty which fell upon many of the freemen and serfs. At the call of the lord, they were required to drop their work, pick up their weapons and march off to a battle or siege.

Local Officials Under feudalism there arose a number of officials whose names are very familiar to Canadians. In each manor there was a bailiff who acted as manager of the estate, and a reeve elected by the tenants to keep a record of duties performed by serfs and freemen.

It will be remembered that Saxon England had been divided into a number of kingdoms such as Essex, Sussex, Wessex and Kent. In

This drawing of a feudal village includes the following items: (1) manor house and manor park, (2) pigeon cot, (3) the mill, (4) the church, (5) the priest's home, (6) tithe barn, (7) common pastures, (8) ploughing with oxen, (9) fields of growing wheat, (10) serfs' huts dotted throughout the village, (11) woodland where trees are being felled.

later years these districts were called shires by the Saxons and counties by the Normans. The chief official, or the King's officer, in each country was called a "shire-reeve" or sheriff.

Even the nobles, wealthy though they were, led lives which we would consider difficult and uncomfortable. Simple conveniences taken for granted in later years were unknown to the people of those days. There was little glass for windows, no comfortable beds, few baths, and no effective way of heating the homes. It is not surprising that the nobles living in cold draughty houses went to bed with their clothing on.

Barons The most important nobles, the barons, became rich and powerful as rents from their estates poured in year after year, and hundreds of men stood ready to fight at their leader's call. Quarrels broke out between rival barons, resulting in battles and sieges. Even disagreements among groups of barons and the King occurred, so that a constant struggle for power was in progress. It took a strong and powerful monarch to rule the turbulent barons.

Norman castles Every important baron built a stone castle, usually on a hill, constructed so that it was easy to defend and difficult to attack. The central part of the castle, the keep, was a large rectangular tower marked by smaller towers and slit-like windows. At the base of the keep the stone walls were sometimes thirty feet in thickness, but even these massive barriers were not considered protection enough, for they were surrounded by more walls, and beyond them a deep moat filled with water. Across the moat stretched a drawbridge which was raised at night or in any time of danger. The main entrance in the outer walls of the castle was protected by a heavy grating, the port-cullis, which was raised upward to open the gateway, and could be dropped in an instant to bar the way.

A visitor arriving at the castle rode over the drawbridge, through the gateway, under the port-cullis, and into a courtyard on the sides of which stood the chapel, offices, tool shed, blacksmith shop, woodyard and the great hall which was the most important room of the castle. Inside, the great hall was decorated with tapestries, weapons and antlers of deer and stag. Flames leaped in the enormous fireplaces and minstrels sang from a gallery. It was here in the hall that guests were entertained, and all the people of the castle ate their meals. A large salt-cellar stood at a certain point on the long tables, and this dish formed a dividing line, because the baron, his family and guests sat at the end of the table "above the salt." Others of lesser rank

The sport of hunting with hawks was sometimes called the "mystery of the rivers" because it was conducted on the banks of streams. Young gentlemen were taught hawking as an important branch of their education. They were required to know how to train hawks, feed them, hold them and call them. Frequently a goshawk, a bird then plentiful in Britain, was used in hunting.

were required to seat themselves "below the salt." Dogs wandered about the hall, crawling under the tables, begging the diners for scraps of meat.

When bedtime came, the lord and his family left the hall, and walked up an outside staircase to apartments high in the castle. Servants, soldiers and workers dragged straw mattresses into the great hall, and settled themselves to sleep on the floor. The dogs found places near the fire or among the sleepers.

The city of London was a busy and prosperous centre fringed **London** with fields, pastures and forests. Houses, stores, shops and churches lined the narrow streets, so that when fires broke out, flames raced through the wooden buildings. The number of people in the city was considerable, for in time of war London could muster a substantial army.

It would appear that the citizens of London led a more pleasant and exciting life than those who lived in the country. A story of the time states: "The citizens of London everywhere, and throughout

A medieval hawk vendor with hunting birds for sale. The selling of hawks in streets, in markets and at fairs was common. Such birds remained on a frame which could be placed on the ground when necessary. Leather hoods covered the birds' eyes and head to prevent escape by flight. A feather placed on top of the hood permitted the hood to be removed without injury to the bird's head.

the whole of the kingdom, are esteemed as the politest of all others in their manner, their dress and the elegance and splendour of their tables."

People of London were fond of sports, and among these the most popular were hawking and hunting. In the sport of hawking, trained hawks, or falcons, were used to kill game birds. Men of the time

Sports enjoyed watching a number of cruel amusements such as bear-baiting and bull-baiting. In these savage spectacles fierce dogs were set loose in an enclosure to fight with a bear or a bull. The wide-jawed, sturdy English bull-dog was frequently used in the sport of bull-baiting. Because of its courage and determination the bull-dog is sometimes used as a symbol of England.

On Shrove Tuesday, the last day before the beginning of Lent, London boys took their fighting roosters to school, and spent the morning fighting them in the classrooms. This holiday was often marked, too, by rough, wild games of *foot-the-ball* in which hundreds of men and boys took part. Players were injured, clothes were torn and quarrels broke out in these contests which were governed by few rules. It was from this ancient English game that modern games such as soccer, rugger and football developed.

Boys belonging to the noble families practised fighting with shields and swords. Mounted on horses, they played at jousting, battling with wooden lances, imitating the actions of the knights who fought in tournaments.

58

In summer, men and boys were active in contests of archery, swimming, boating, running, jumping, wrestling and throwing heavy stones. In winter, boys tied bones to the soles of their shoes, pushing themselves with poles as we use skis. Sometimes the boys fought duels. Starting at some distance apart, they pushed themselves swiftly over the ice, and, just at the moment of meeting, they raised their poles striking fiercely at one another. One or both would crash to the slippery surface, occasionally suffering a broken arm or leg.

We may think of this as a rough period of history but perhaps a thousand years from now our sports, or the accident toll of our highways, or our wars will shock people who read about them.

SUMMARY—SECTION I

The attempted invasion by Julius Caesar in 55 and 54 B.C. had no permanent effect upon England. However, one hundred years later in A.D. 43 the Romans returned and conquered most of the land. Roads were constructed, towns built and trade established. London became an important city. Many of the conquered Britons learned the Latin language and accepted Christianity which arrived in England during the time of the Romans.

After the Roman troops were withdrawn in 407 to protect the imperial city of Rome, England was left open to the attacks of the Jutes, Angles and Saxons of northern Europe. The Britons were driven westward into what is now Wales and Cornwall, while the invaders set up a number of Anglo-Saxon kingdoms in eastern and southern England. By 830 King Egbert of Wessex had emerged as the most powerful among the Saxon kings.

Then began the Danish, or Viking, invasions which troubled England for two centuries. During the reign of King Alfred the Great of Wessex, 871 to 901, the West Saxons regained some of their lost territory and came to terms with the Danes. England was divided roughly into two parts: the Danelaw in the eastern and northern parts under the Danes and large sections in the south-west under the West Saxons.

In the later Danish invasion of 1016, Canute of Denmark defeated the West Saxons and gained control of England. He was accepted as King by both the Saxons and the Danes. This invasion made little difference, for Canute interfered very little with the customs and laws of the people.

A major change, however, came with the Norman conquest of 1066 when William the Conqueror of Normandy defeated Harold Godwin at the Battle of Hastings. Under Norman rule England was placed under a highly-organized feudal system with the King as supreme head. This had the effect of giving England a strong government at a time when many European lands were divided into quarrelling states. England, though not yet united in all respects, had become a nation.

TIME-CHART

55 B.C.-A.D. 1135

	B.C.	
	55	COMING OF THE ROMANS
	A.D.	
Birth of Christ	**1**	
	43	RETURN OF THE ROMANS TO BRITAIN
	200	BEGINNING OF CHRISTIANITY IN BRITAIN
	410	ROMANS LEAVE BRITAIN
	449	COMING OF THE JUTES, ANGLES AND SAXONS
	597	ST. AUGUSTINE IN BRITAIN
	787	DANISH ATTACKS BEGIN
	871-901	ALFRED THE GREAT
	886	THE DANELAW
	959-975	EDGAR
Eric the Red in Greenland	**980**	
Bjarni reaches America	**985**	

TIME·CHART — *(continued)*

Leif the Lucky in America	**1000**	
	1016-1035	CANUTE
	1042-1066	EDWARD THE CONFESSOR
	1066	BATTLE OF STAMFORD BRIDGE BATTLE OF HASTINGS DEATH OF HAROLD GODWIN WILLIAM THE CONQUEROR CROWNED KING
	1071	WILLIAM I, RULER OF ALL ENGLAND
	1087-1100	WILLIAM II
Beginning of the Crusades	**1096**	
	1100-1135	HENRY I

II. BEGINNINGS OF NATIONAL UNITY

The weak rule of King Stephen • Henry Plantagenet becomes Henry II of England • The new King establishes a system of law and justice • Beginning of trial by jury • Quarrel between Henry II and the Church • Murder of Thomas Becket • Henry II becomes one of most powerful rulers in Europe • People begin to think of themselves as being Englishmen and not Saxons, Danes or Normans • King Richard I goes on the Third Crusade • John succeeds his brother Richard I • Signing of Magna Carta, the Great Charter • Westminster Abbey rebuilt by Henry III • Edward I conquers Wales and Scotland and fights France in the Hundred Years' War • Increasing importance of Parliament • Feeling of national unity

B.C.	55
	0
	100
	200
	300
	400
	500
	600
	700
	800
	900
	1000
	1100
	1200
	1300
	1400
	1500
	1600
	1700
	1800
	1900
A.D.	2000

12

HENRY PLANTAGENET

The first hundred years after the Battle of Hastings was a period of transformation in England. Anglo-Saxon customs became Norman customs, the feudal system became general, trade grew, literature showed new life and architecture improved. The coming of the Normans had brought a higher level of civilization to the country.

King Henry I died in 1135 after expressing the wish that his daughter, Matilda, might be crowned; but the barons of England had no desire to have a woman on the throne. So it was that for a time no ruler was proclaimed. Then, from Normandy came a handsome, good-natured nobleman, Stephen, who was a nephew of the dead **King Stephen, 1136** King. After securing encouragement from some important nobles, Stephen laid claim to the throne and was crowned. Although he was pleasant, Stephen never made a satisfactory military commander or a ruler. He lacked the strength of will and the intelligence to control the barons of his realm, so England drifted into a period of turmoil.

To make matters worse, civil war developed when Princess Matilda pressed her own claims to the throne. For fifteen years the senseless war dragged on, causing misery, suffering and death. Captives were thrown into prison, tortured and fined, and on several occasions men, women and children were herded into churches and the buildings set afire.

Stephen's disastrous reign came to an end in 1154 when the King **Henry II, 1154** died; he was succeeded by Henry of Anjou, son of Matilda. King Henry II was a bull-dog of a man with short red hair and a freckled face, a man whose legs were bowed from endless hours in the saddle. One of the most active kings that ever wore the English crown, he spent a bustling life, travelling, fighting, making new laws, talking with his ministers and enjoying his favourite sport of hunting.

King Henry II and the seven English monarchs who follow him are called the Angevin line of kings, the word Angevin referring to Anjou, the King's birthplace. These rulers are also called the Plantagenet family because Henry's father had the nickname Geoffrey *plant de genêt* meaning "broom flower." It is not known with certainty how this name first arose, but it may be that Geoffrey loved to hunt

63

Early English furniture was crude and unattractive but at the same time rugged and strong. Meals were eaten at trestle tables like the one shown here. Such tables could be taken apart and stored away when necessary. In the castles and manors most people sat on benches and stools, chairs being provided only for the lord, his family and honoured guests.

in the hills bright with broom flowers, or perhaps he wore a sprig of broom in his jacket.

In addition to being ruler of England, Henry II controlled a little empire consisting of Anjou, Normandy, Maine, Brittany, Touraine, Aquitaine and Gascony all of which were in the region we call France. He married Eleanor of Aquitaine, divorced wife of Louis VII of France, the most powerful woman of her time and one of the most interesting in history. It was through her that Henry laid claim to much French territory. Besides these, Henry claimed rule over Wales, Scotland and Ireland. While attempting to control all these lands, he was a very busy man settling the problems which arose. He travelled hurriedly from state to state accompanied by wagons carrying his business papers. It pleased him very much if he could arrive unexpectedly, surprising the officials of the region.

It was not a united England over which Henry II ruled, for there were many things to keep the people apart. There was, for example, the fact that no less than three languages were used throughout the kingdom—men of the church spoke Latin, noblemen spoke French and the lower classes spoke Anglo-Saxon. Another factor which hindered complete unity was the constant struggle for power which existed among the barons, the Church and the King. It was not a

64

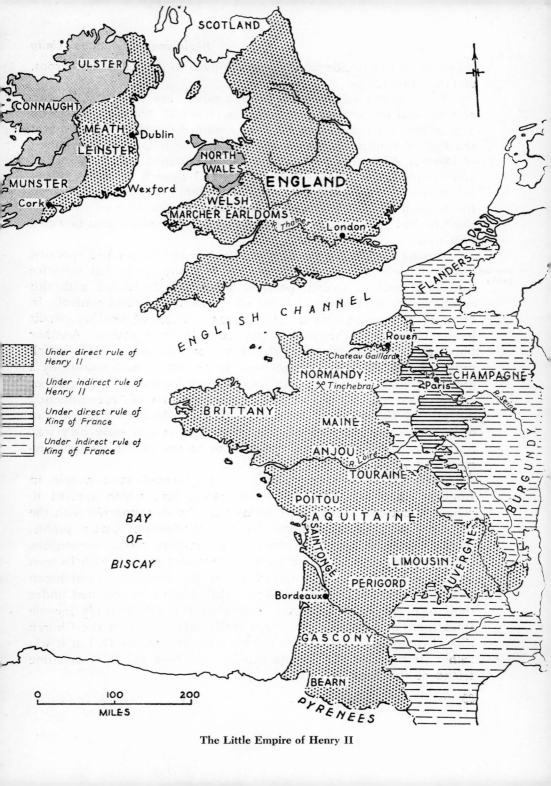

SCOTLAND

ULSTER

CONNAUGHT

MEATH

Dublin

LEINSTER

MUNSTER

Cork

Wexford

NORTH
WALES

ENGLAND

WELSH
MARCHER EARLDOMS

R. Thames

London

ENGLISH CHANNEL

FLANDERS

Rouen

Chateau Gaillard

CHAMPAGNE

NORMANDY

Tinchebrai

Paris

R. Seine

BRITTANY

MAINE

ANJOU

R. Loire

TOURAINE

POITOU

BURGUNDY

Under direct rule of
Henry II

Under indirect rule of
Henry II

Under direct rule of
King of France

Under indirect rule of
King of France

AQUITAINE

BAY

OF

BISCAY

SAINTONGE

LIMOUSIN

AUVERGNE

PERIGORD

Bordeaux

GASCONY

BEARN

PYRENEES

0   100   200

MILES

The Little Empire of Henry II

simple matter to decide what rights belonged to the King, the barons, and the Church.

England was still far from being a solid, closely-knit nation with one law and one central government. Henry II, however, was to do a great deal toward making England a unified country. He also sent the Earl of Pembroke, known as Strongbow to Ireland at the request of Dermot, King of Leinster. Strongbow regained Leinster's estates, and Henry called himself King of Ireland though it was centuries before the whole of Ireland was subdued. Henry's armies also captured the Scottish King, William the Lion. He was not allowed to return until he had paid homage to Henry who could then say that he ruled Scotland. *(- 1154)*

During the weak reign of King Stephen the barons had operated the local law courts to suit themselves with the result that injustice was often done to accused persons. Henry II, dissatisfied with this arrangement, determined to bring all courts under royal control. In order to accomplish this he revived the practice of sending circuit judges throughout the land to try cases in local courts. Another important step was taken by the *Assize of Clarendon,* 1166, which provided that the King's judges were to be met in each county by a group of local men who were to "present" citizens suspected of crime. Such a group of local men, forming a jury of "presentment", did not try the accused, but merely decided whether or not a man ought to be tried for any offence. Imperfect as this early jury was, it grew during the following centuries to be one of the greatest safe-guards of English liberty.

In addition to common-law which governed most people in England, there was Church law, or canon law, which applied to religious matters. There were numerous officials connected with the Church — archbishops, bishops, canons, archdeacons, parish priests, monks, nuns and other workers such as teachers, clerks, messengers, stewards and servants. More than 200 monasteries, each with its own buildings and staff, were spread across the country. Churchmen were an important, wealthy and powerful group who operated under their own laws, and supported themselves through a steady income from tithes and estates. It was not really surprising that the Church should come into conflict with the hot-tempered Henry II, but it was rather strange that the dispute should have been led by a one-time friend of the King.

(marginal note: Law and justice)

Judges, or justices, of Henry II travelled about the country on horseback trying special cases in court. This was necessary because King Henry could not trust serious cases to corrupt courts controlled by the barons. Even today justices go on circuit.

The person who held the vital post of chancellor in England was Thomas Becket Henry's friend, Thomas Becket*, a brilliant, handsome nobleman who was full of life and energy. A wealthy man holding large estates, Becket dressed in a magnificent manner and lived a life of luxury. When the Archbishopric of Canterbury, the highest office in the Church, became vacant, the King requested Becket to take the position. With his friend as head of the Church, Henry thought, there would be no more trouble with the powerful churchmen.

Thomas Becket was not at all eager to be Archbishop of Canterbury, for he realized that it would lead to conflict with the King. Henry II, nevertheless, stuck obstinately to his plan, and Becket assumed the position as head of the Church in England.

The recognized church in England and other countries of Europe was the Catholic Church with the Bishop of Rome, called the Pope, as supreme head.

*For a legend concerning Thomas Becket see page 399.

Thomas Becket was not a man who could be untrue to the position
Henry and he held. When he became Archbishop of Canterbury, he made himself
Becket a champion of Church rights, and even defied King Henry II in a
quarrel number of important matters. The quarrel between the two became
so hot that Becket and others were forced to seek refuge on the
continent.

While Thomas Becket was in exile, Henry II arranged the succession of his own son, Henry, to the throne. In order to insure succession,
Henry ordered a coronation, and this was conducted by the Archbishop
of York and six other bishops.

After six years of exile Thomas Becket returned to England, and
made a triumphant entry into London where he was given a warm
welcome by the people. Becket was very much annoyed that Henry's
son had been crowned by men of the Church. Perhaps unwisely,
Becket took revenge on the bishops by declaring that they no longer
belonged to the Church. When this news reached Henry, he was in
Normandy with his court. In fury the King turned to his followers
and roared, "What a pack of fools and cowards I have nurtured in my
house, that not one of them will avenge me of this turbulent priest!"

Four knights who heard the bitter words of the King, travelled
Murder of swiftly to the Norman coast, crossed the Channel, reached England,
Becket, secured horses and galloped to Canterbury. On December 29, 1170,
1170 they found Thomas Becket in the cathedral. The archbishop with
cross in hand faced the armed intruders, showing no sign of fear. After
sharp words were exchanged, the knights drew their blades and flung
themselves at Becket. In a moment the swords had done their fatal
work . . . the archbishop sank to the floor . . . dying in a pool of blood.

The murder of the Archbishop of Canterbury caused alarm
throughout all England, for an Archbishop had been killed in his
own cathedral. Thomas Becket was declared a martyr, and anger
burned strongly against the King. Henry II himself was just as
alarmed as were the English people when he heard the news, because
he had not intended murder even though his angry words had suggested
it. For the rest of his life he tried to make up in every way possible
for the tragic blunder which led to Becket's death. On many occasions
he visited the archbishop's grave, and several times he allowed himself
to be beaten by monks. Two years after the murder in the cathedral
Henry II made his peace with the Pope so that relations between
Church and state were improved.

No English king dared to question the authority of the Church

Before the fatal encounter Becket had met and argued with King Henry's knights. After they left, Becket was persuaded to take refuge in Canterbury Cathedral. When the knights returned, they entered the Cathdral and murdered Becket where he was standing near the northwest transept, or wing.

for four centuries following Henry's disgrace and as a result some churchmen grew to abuse the tremendous power which was held by religious bodies in England.

Henry's power and his influence grew until he was one of the most powerful monarchs in all the Christian world. His crime was almost forgotten when the Pope invited Henry to lead a crusade against the Turks in the Holy Land. Henry might have been content with his life's work but for one thing . . . his four sons caused him ceaseless trouble. Dissatisfied with the lands they had been given to rule, the sons — Henry, Geoffrey, Richard and John — were anxious for still greater power. They plotted against their father, led rebellions and assisted the King's enemies. Because Henry loved his sons (particularly the youngest boy, John), their disloyal actions caused him to become bitter.

69

13

RICHARD I AND THE THIRD CRUSADE

In 1076 the Mohammedans, or Saracens, captured Palestine where Christ had lived and died. The Christian peoples of Europe, shocked that the Holy Land should be held by infidels, sent military expeditions, or crusades, to recapture the sacred places. In 1099 during the First Crusade French troops captured Jerusalem, and fifty years later on the Second Crusade French and German soldiers fought more battles in Palestine. At the close of Henry II's reign Jerusalem was again taken by the Saracens under their famous leader Saladin.

Henry II died while he was preparing to take part in the Third Crusade. Just before his death he realized that he himself could never see the Holy Land, so he expressed the wish that his son and heir, Richard, should lead English troops in the holy war.

Richard I, crowned King in 1189, was a tall, athletic man with a hot temper like that of his father. Not at all interested in ruling his dominions, Richard spent only seven months in England during a reign of ten years. A proud man, Richard could be cruel and treacherous, but was also warm-hearted and exceedingly courageous, earning the name "Richard the Lion Heart."

Richard I, 1189

In order to set out on the Third Crusade, King Richard had to raise large sums of money to supply men, arms and ships. In securing these funds, he followed some practices which his father never would have permitted during his lifetime. Richard collected heavy feudal taxes, offered royal charters to towns in exchange for money, sold royal lands and offered titles for sale. He even said that he would have sold London itself, if there had been anyone wealthy enough to take it.

Richard and his followers became crusaders along with men from France, Germany and Italy. It was the custom of the time in these armies for knights to wear large red crosses on their breastplates as they travelled toward the Holy Land, but wore the crosses on their backs as they journeyed homeward. The word crusade comes from a Spanish word *cruz* meaning "cross." The use of the cross as a symbol during the crusades probably was suggested by Christ's words, "If any man will come after me, let him deny himself, and take up his cross and follow me."

70

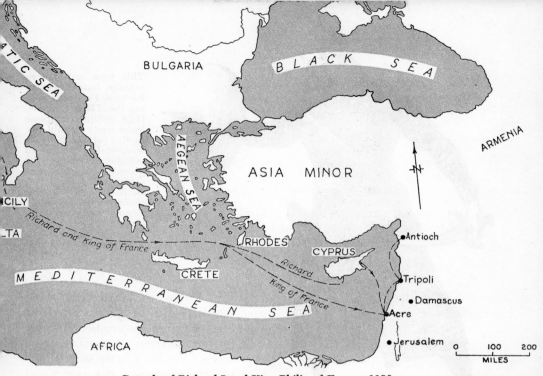

Crusade of Richard I and King Philip of France, 1190

In 1190 Richard I sailed the long voyage from England by way Third Crusade, 1190 of Gibraltar and the Mediterranean Sea to Sicily. There English troops along with their French allies spent the winter. Richard and the French King, who had been friendly, began to quarrel so that conditions in the camp were not pleasant. In the spring the French sailed directly to Palestine, while Richard remained to capture the island of Cyprus. Having completed this task, the English reached the Holy Land and took part in a siege of the city of Acre. King Richard fought so effectively in this engagement that his leadership played an important part in the capture of the city. After the fall of Acre, the invaders ransacked the city and killed 3,000 Saracens.

Moving southward from Acre the Crusaders marched toward Jerusalem, hoping to seize the Holy Place in an overpowering attack, but the Saracen leader, Saladin, stood firmly in their path. With extreme courage and brilliant generalship, he fought the invaders, blocking the road to Jerusalem. In the battles which followed, both Richard the Lion Heart and the Saracen leader became famous for their bravery.

71

This type of Saracen warrior fought against Richard I's troops during the Third Crusade. His military costume bears some resemblance to that of the Norman warrior, but there is an oriental touch in the pointed helmet, pointed shield and pointed toes on the shoes. Saracen chain mail was quite loose to provide greater freedom of movement and Saracen swords were curved.

Twice the crusaders came within sight of Jerusalem, but both times they were beaten back by the Saracens. Constant quarrels among the Christian military leaders weakened the command of the crusading armies, and made victory impossible. The King of France gave up, collected his troops, and sailed for home, but Richard remained to fight on. For another year the English King stayed on in the Holy Land, sometimes battling the Saracens, and sometimes talking peace with their leaders.

End of the Third Crusade, 1192 During this period there were a number of conferences held between the Saracen and Christian commanders, and these were friendly affairs marked by feasting and entertainment. Richard gained a certain admiration and liking for Saladin, and even suggested that his sister Joanna might marry the brother of Saladin. This proposed marriage never was arranged. Eventually the two warring parties agreed to a peace treaty which held advantages for both sides. By the treaty, Christian pilgrims were permitted to travel in the Holy Land and certain coastal ports were to be kept by the Christians. Control of such ports were important to some European peoples, especially the Italians, who were keenly interested in trade.

72

A group of crusaders bombard a town with a siege weapon called a *trebuchet* which was the largest of medieval artillery pieces. The *trebuchet* was usually constructed on the scene from heavy timbers. Often the whole trunk of a tree was employed to make a throwing arm. Stones were its usual projectiles, but animal carcasses, or even live prisoners were sometimes thrown over castle walls. Note that the crusaders are wearing a cloth surcoat over mail armour to serve as protection against sun and weather.

On the return voyage to England, Richard* was shipwrecked and captured while travelling across land in disguise. Strangely enough, he was held prisoner by the Emperor of Germany who had been a fellow crusader in Palestine. Even at this time, holding Richard as captive was not considered an honourable action, for crusaders by tradition were expected to help each other in times of difficulty. Nevertheless, the English King was not released until his people had raised and paid a very large ransom.

Richard's personal courage and his skill in combat seem to have been his most important kingly qualities, for during his reign he did nothing to improve conditions in England. Indeed, it may be said

*For a legend of King Richard see page 400.

73

that he neglected his royal duties to carry on the life of adventure he so enjoyed. In spite of the heavy losses in men and money caused by Richard's adventures, the English people loved and almost worshipped their wandering monarch. Richard the Lion Heart, warrior King and gallant crusader, was the type of man most admired in this robust age. His name became a legend, and his bravery a romantic subject for songs sung by minstrels in the castles of France and England.*

Death of Richard I, 1199
Richard I died of wounds while fighting in Normandy during the year 1199. During the siege of a small castle he was struck in the shoulder near the neck by a bolt from a crossbow. During the removal of the arrowhead the dangerous wound was made still deeper, and infection set in. Realizing his life was running out, Richard sent for his mother, Queen Eleanor, and cheerfully divided his possessions among his friends. He declared his brother, John, to be the next King, making those in his presence swear loyalty to Prince John. Then in a generous action he pardoned the captured bowman who had shot the crossbow, granting the surprised prisoner a sum of money. After Richard I had died, his followers tortured and killed the archer.

14

KING JOHN AND THE GREAT CHARTER

Richard's brother, John, came to the throne at a time when the Crusades were still being fought in the Holy Land; at a time when in central Asia the great Mongol Empire was rising under Genghis Khan.

If one were to ask a hundred Englishmen the name of the most hated king in England's history, the common answer would be . . . John. There are good reasons for such an answer. John was cruel, ruthless, grasping and dishonest. In one way, however, the English people are grateful to King John because his selfish actions eventually led to a greater freedom and liberty for all citizens.

King John, 1199
At least one historian has tried to prove that John was mad, but there seems to be very little to support this belief. Indeed, there is much evidence to show that the King was a clever, able person with

*For a legend of Robin Hood, who was supposed to have lived in this period, see page 399.

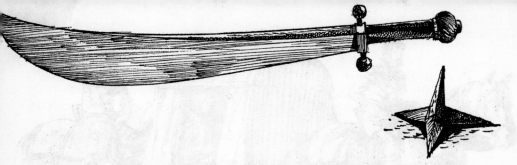

(1) The falchion was a sword widely used at this time. It was approximately three feet in length, and was made like a knife or cleaver with a heavy, thick-backed blade. (2) A knight's horse was often his weakest point of defence, and in battle (not in tournaments) was the object of attack. Shown here is a small four-pointed device, the caltrop, with points so arranged that one was always upright. The caltrops were scattered in the enemies' path to cripple horses and render riders helpless.

a searching mind and a love of books. Had he chosen to use his abilities wisely, he might have become a great ruler.

Unfortunately John's chief aim in life was to grasp as much power as possible, no matter what suffering he caused in securing his desires. He made promises and broke them; he ignored the laws of the land; he put men in prison without trial; he quarrelled continuously; and he took whatever he wanted without regard for the rights of anyone.

Before his death in 1199, Richard I had declared John to be the next king, but there were others who thought his nephew, Prince Arthur, had a better claim to the throne. The young prince was the son of Geoffrey, John's older brother who had died. In England John was accepted as the new king, but in the royal lands across the Channel it was a different story. In Normandy and other states under the English crown, there was a growing restlessness, because the people there were beginning to feel a closer connection with France than they did with England. It is not surprising that they, and the French, opposed John and supported the royal claims of Arthur, Prince of Brittany.

In the war which followed, King Philip of France gradually gained **War with France, 1202** control of Maine, Poitou, Anjou and Normandy. Conquest was not too difficult because many barons deserted to the French and the English put up rather a poor defence. King John was not able to rally and inspire his soldiers as his brother Richard I had done. In a surprise attack, however, John captured Prince Arthur along with a group of rebel knights outside a castle in Poitou. After being taken prisoner

75

Medieval transport was relatively primitive with its emphasis upon the movement of goods by means of pack animals, carts and boats. The heaviest of commodities were moved most conveniently by water transport. Travel was difficult, uncomfortable and sometimes hazardous. Shown in the illustration is a horse-litter which was employed in travel by the nobles and wealthy citizens. The horse-litter had one great advantage—it could move over roads which were impassable to wheeled vehicles.

Prince Arthur disappeared and his fate remains a mystery. It may be that he was tortured and murdered on orders from his Uncle John.

Victory after victory was won by the French, so that John had to withdraw his troops from Europe and return to England. All the English possessions, except Aquitaine, had been lost to the French. The English people, of course, considered this a heavy blow, and they were inclined to blame John for poor leadership during the war. No one seems to have realized that the loss of the lands across the Channel was a blessing in disguise. Barons who had held estates both in Normandy and England were forced to decide whether they were going to be Frenchmen or Englishmen. John's successors were to spend their energies ruling England instead of wandering about in small continental states. The result, in time, was a stronger and more united England.

When the Archbishop of Canterbury died, King John stated his **Stephen** right to appoint the next Archbishop, but Pope Innocent III of Rome **Langton** claimed the same privilege. Setting aside the churchman named by King John, the Pope declared Stephen Langton to be the new Arch-

King John signs the Magna Carta at Runnymede. On top of the chest is the press used to affix the Royal seal. Kings and knights of this time were beginning to use designs marked on various personal belongings. This system known as heraldry later developed into a complicated science. King John's personal design was the crescent and flaming star.

bishop of Canterbury. As might be expected, hot-tempered John was so furious he began to take revenge upon the Church in England. He seized religious properties, and made conditions as miserable as possible for the churchmen. In answer to this challenge, the Pope placed England under an *interdict* which had a marked effect upon the whole country. Church doors remained closed; no services were held indoors; the steeple bells were silent; and bodies of the dead were laid in ground outside the cemeteries. None of these things, however, bothered King John, for he went on stealing Church wealth, and he continued to persecute the churchmen.

In a second attempt to humble John, the Pope excommunicated the English King. By this act, the King was no longer a member of the Church, and his subjects were not required to remain loyal to him. Still unmoved by this latest punishment, John took more Church estates, abbeys and money until the royal treasury was overflowing with wealth.

77

Interdict,
1208
Neither the interdict nor excommunication had affected King John, but a European event caused him much concern. The King of France and Pope Innocent, after making an agreement between themselves, made preparations to invade England with strong military forces. As a result, John decided very quickly that it would be wise to give in to the wishes of the Church. Pretending to be ashamed of his past sins, John agreed that the Pope was to be his feudal lord, and that he himself was to be a servant of the Church. In return for this surrender, John was forgiven by the Pope, and England became a favoured nation under the protection of the Catholic Church which had its centre in Italy.

This changed situation was not at all pleasing to a great many people. The King of France was disappointed because he could not invade England. Some English barons disliked being under the direct authority of the Pope. Even the English churchmen were unhappy with changes in Church affairs. All of this brought about a strange condition in which John and the Pope were good friends, while Stephen Langton and a group of barons were in opposition.

Having made peace with the Pope, John launched war against his chief enemy, the King of France, hoping to get back his lost possessions in Europe. For two years the war dragged on, and then came final defeat for the English. On his return home, John found a determined group of barons, knights, churchmen and other citizens under the leadership of Stephen Langton, Archbishop of Canterbury.

Tired of long wars, high taxes and cruel injustice this group had decided to force the King to change his ways. Probably there would have been a bloody revolution in England had it not been for the wise leadership of Stephen Langton. Anxious to avoid civil war, the Archbishop told his followers that they could gain their wishes without actually using their weapons. They drew up a charter listing the just rights of the people, and asked the King to sign it. John refused. Then the barons and knights collected their troops, and marched on London, gathering more men as they travelled. When they arrived at the city the people opened the gates, cheering the troops as they marched in.

No one stood by King John except for a few servants and some royal officials. A selfish, grasping monarch stood helpless before the rising anger of his people . . . he had no choice but to give in.

78

King John and the Great Charter

Although Stephen Langton and his followers could have imprisoned or even killed their King, they chose a more civilized way of solving their problems. On June 15, 1215, they met John in an open meadow at Runnymede along the River Thames not far from London. A strange hush fell over the gathered men as the King dismounted from his horse, and took his place on a little throne set up in the field. A group of stern-faced nobles and churchmen stood in front, while in the background were ranks of men, their arms and armour glowing in the morning light. One of the leaders, probably the Archbishop, presented a document written on parchment and explained the demands of the English nobles. John was angry, but without argument he signed, and the royal seal was fixed to the parchment. Some days later the short agreement made at Runnymede was enlarged into a long charter called *Magna Carta,* or the Great Charter. So important was this agreement between the King and a group of his people that it had a vital effect upon all the future history of the British Isles. The Great Charter is sometimes called the keystone of English liberty. Some of the freedoms enjoyed in Canada and the United States today may be traced back to this famous document.

Magna Carta, written in Latin, was in general a collection of agreements which had been accepted by former kings such as Edward the Confessor, Henry I and Henry II. Among all the terms in the Charter, three stand out as being especially important:

The law must be obeyed by everyone, even the king.

No one may be imprisoned, fined or punished without a lawful trial.

No taxes must be collected except those authorized by law.

The signing of *Magna Carta* was important since it represented the first time that the barons and churchmen had united to force terms upon an English monarch. In effect they were saying, "His majesty has not been keeping the rules. In future he must keep them, and in case there is any doubt about it, here they are in black and white!"

It is said that King John was so enraged at having to sign the Charter that later in a rage he chewed up pieces of wood and straw. He had no intention of keeping his promises if he could find a way

News that Parliament would now include representatives from the towns created lively interest among the people. In the background of the picture is a typical street. The towns were often walled and the buildings within them constructed of various materials. Houses packed tightly together were made of stone or of

of escaping them. In a letter to the Pope he complained about the outrageous behaviour of the nobles, and asked the Pope to cancel the Charter. To this request the Pope agreed, setting aside *Magna Carta*, and excommunicating the men who had rebelled against King John.

Death of John, 1216

John was pleased, but not for long, for the barons invited Prince Louis, son of the French King, to take the English throne. Delighted with the invitation, Louis landed in England with an army at his back. Not all the English people favoured a French King, so it appeared that a civil war was about to develop. Fortunately, in 1216, John died, perhaps of overeating, and his son Henry was declared King. With this change of situation the barons deserted Prince Louis, defeated him in battle, and drove him back to France.

wood with a framework arranged in elaborate patterns. Roofs were of tile, of reeds, or of straw. Windows were small. The shops were generally narrow and high with goods displayed and business conducted on the street which was usually filthy.

15

HENRY III AND PARLIAMENT

John's son, Henry III, ruled as King of England for fifty-six years—1216 to 1272—one of the longest reigns in English history. It was during this time that Marco Polo made his famous journey from Venice to the land of Cathay.

King Henry III was by no means as cruel, cunning and selfish as his father had been, but he did possess some of John's own faults. Quarrels with the barons continued as the struggle for power went on and on. Henry soon found that he could gain increasing power over his realm without actually breaking the terms of the Great Charter. Powerful barons were removed from high offices, and replaced by friends of the King; good positions in the government were granted to noblemen from France who were related to Henry's French wife, Queen Eleanor. The Pope and King Henry were excellent friends, so Italian clergymen took high offices in the English Church.

With hordes of foreigners gaining posts of power, the English barons and churchmen became very much alarmed. It was only natural that they should unite to protect their interests in the kingdom; it was only natural that they should raise the cry of "England for the Englishmen."

(c) *(i)*
Parliament For many years English kings had, on special occasions, called together a group of nobles and churchmen to discuss affairs of importance. Under the Saxons such a meeting had been called the *Witan,* and under the Normans it had been called the *Great Council.* During the reign of Henry III, however, these meetings came to be known as *Parliament,* a word derived from the French verb *parler* meaning "to speak." In Henry III's time the meetings of Parliament

(ii) were held about once a year which was much more frequent than in former times. In Parliament the nobles, the churchmen and Henry had many hot disputes over high taxes, government policy and affairs of the Church.

(d)
Simon de Montfort A strong leader among the barons at this time was Simon de Montfort, a French nobleman who had inherited the earldom of Leicester in England. De Montfort married Henry III's sister, and became a noble of great influence. In spite of his French birth, he became an ardent Englishman, and in spite of being Henry's brother-in-law he supported the barons against the King.

Provisions of Oxford, 1258 In 1258, during two meetings of Parliament Simon de Montfort and the barons forced Henry III to sign the *Provisions of Oxford* by which the King lost much of his power. A committee of nobles and bishops was established to take control of the government and to manage the actions of the King.

Henry was not at all pleased with the restrictions which had been placed upon his rule, and in anger he threatened to set aside the Provisions of Oxford. Strangely enough, King Louis IX of France supported the English King, saying that the barons had no right to control their monarch.

De Montfort rules England Ignoring this statement, the barons, rallying their troops took up arms against the King. Henry III, his son Edward and their supporters were defeated in battle, a defeat which ended in the King's capture and imprisonment. Simon de Montfort, the victor, took over the

82

government, ruling in the King's name. When de Montfort called
Parliament in 1265, he included men from the towns as well as the
country nobles, an action which showed his sympathy for the middle
classes of England. This was one more important step in the slow
growth of Parliament.

Henry's son, Edward, escaped from Montfort's control, and soon
was very active in gathering support for his father. It was not too
difficult a task, for some of the barons were jealous of de Montfort's
success, and some were not pleased with his interest in the lower classes
of people.

On August 4, 1265, the famous battle of Evesham was fought in a **Defeat of De Montfort, 1265**
driving rain beneath dark skies. Edward's cavalry smashed the enemy
ranks, leaving Simon de Montfort fighting for life in a small circle of
his men. Falling beneath the force of overwhelming numbers, he died,
struggling gallantly to the last breath. Poor old Henry III, mistaken for
an enemy knight, was wounded and almost killed by his own troops.
His life was saved in the nick of time when he shouted frantically, "Slay
me not. I am Henry, your King!'"

Even after the battle of Evesham, there was some restlessness and
some discontent throughout the country. Barons who had fought
against the King were punished by having their estates taken away. The
people remembered de Montfort as the man who had championed their
cause against the might of monarchy. To them the dead earl was a
saint who had died a hero on the field of battle. Although Simon de
Montfort was gone, the spirit which he had aroused lived on through
the centuries of the future.

Although Henry III's reign was marked by bitter disputes and by **Architecture**
civil war, it was a period in which England made much progress. Architecture was one of the arts which made great strides, developing a new
kind of building which contained grace and beauty. The age of the
crusades was a period when many churches and cathedrals were built
throughout Europe. During the Norman times in England churches
and other religious buildings had been constructed with thick pillars
and low round arches to give the appearance of strength and solidity,
but in Henry III's reign a fresh form of architecture became important.
In this new kind of construction groups of graceful, thin pillars were
used, along with tall pointed arches and vaulted roofs. Although the
new buildings appeared fragile and elegant, they were in reality stronger than those made by the Normans. Salisbury Cathedral built between

Salisbury Cathedral of Early English architecture possesses a lofty, soaring style so different from the earlier Norman. The tall spire added in the first half of the 14th century is 404 feet in height, almost as high as Canada's tallest skyscraper. This cathedral created without the aid of machinery offers remarkable evidence of the skill of medieval builders. Within Salisbury Cathedral are magnificent carvings in stone and wood, and a great number of vivid, glowing windows in stained glass, adding great beauty and richness to the interior.

the years 1220 and 1258 is a good example of the new architecture now known as *Early English*.

Henry III was a religious man interested in books, art and learning. The erection of a great and beautiful church had been one of his greatest dreams, a dream which came true with the rebuilding of Westminster Abbey church. On his order, the old Abbey erected in the time of Edward the Confessor was torn down, and a fresh building slowly rose in its place. The new Westminster Abbey, a masterpiece of architecture, was marked by a continental style called French Gothic, but in some respects it had, too, some resemblance to the Early English form. In later centuries, changes and additions were made to the Abbey so that the building of Henry's day is but part of the present structure.

Westminster Abbey

84

It is difficult for us today to appreciate how valuable books were before the use of printing presses. Monks working in tiny rooms within the monasteries spent months, and sometimes years, in the copying of a single manuscript. The monk in the illustration is writing with a quill pen on a parchment made from sheepskin. Notice that the sheet of parchment is held flat by large straps fastened on either side. In addition to writing, the monk decorates the pages with elaborate coloured drawings and large letters, often using an ivory rod to press the parchment flat at the spot where he is working.

During this period, too, **Universities** there was much interest in education, which largely came under the authority of the church. All the larger cathedrals and monasteries had special schools for the training of boys and young men who were to become clergymen. Oxford and Cambridge Universities were founded during the century before Henry III's reign, but it was during his time that they began to grow rapidly, attracting many teachers and thousands of students. The word university comes from the Latin word *universitas,* which in the beginning was used in connection with any organized group of persons such as the merchants of a town, or the priests of a cathedral. Gradually, however, the word had narrowed in meaning until it became attached to any group of teachers and students gathered together for the purpose of advanced study.

Great teachers in surprising numbers collected in the universities, and there they did a remarkable work of inspiring and teaching the students. During Henry's reign these able men added much to knowledge, and influenced the thinking of the English people. Among the scholars were skilled writers who organized English common law, and wrote important books on history.

The universities built up libraries, while in the monasteries monks made beautiful copies of religious books on parchment. In those days before the invention of printing, books were precious things reproduced only after months and years of patient work.

It must not be imagined that all young people had the opportunity of getting an education as they do in England today. Schools and universities of the time were meant chiefly for boys and young men who were to enter the professions of the ministry, law and medicine. Boys and girls of the lower classes were put to work at an early age without the chance of securing an education. It should be remembered that it was less than one hundred years ago that free schools open to all were to be found in England and in Canada. Education for everyone is a modern idea not dreamed of in the days of the thirteenth century.

The last years of Henry III's life were his happiest and most peaceful. In 1272 he died and was buried at Westminster Abbey.

16

EDWARD I, WALES AND SCOTLAND

Henry III's son, Edward, was away on a crusade at the time of his father's death. It was 1274 before he returned and was crowned.

"Longshanks" is hardly a fitting term for one of England's most able kings, and yet that is the nickname he bore. King Edward I was a very tall man with a striking face and thick black hair. His broad shoulders and muscular arms made him a dangerous swordsman, and
Edward I, his long legs gripped his saddle like a vice. Fond of active sports, Edward
1272 delighted in tournaments and took great pleasure in hawking and hunting. Altogether he had the qualities which made him a strong king for that period in history. He had the courage and military skill of Richard the Lion Heart together with the good sense of King Henry II. He was a real Englishman who loved England and intended to see that the country grew in power and strength; Edward I had no intention of allowing foreigners to take over important positions in Church and state.

One of the great gifts given by Edward I to England was an
Improved improved Parliament, one which represented more truly the people
Parliament of the nation. In the days of the Great Council only the interests of the nobles and the churchmen had been considered, while the great masses of Englishmen were ignored. Another group of citizens, however, had made its appearance in England and was assuming an important place. These were the middle class landowners and merchants who over the

The English longbow was often as tall as the archer himself. It was made from ash, hazel or yew, of which yew was by far the best. Bow strings were of hemp whipped with a fine linen cord. Bowmen used two types of arrows—the long flight arrow for distance and the shorter sheaf arrow. In battle the archer often placed his entire sheaf of arrows on the ground, and perhaps put his foot on them as shown here. Peasants were trained in the use of the longbow when young.

years had been gathering wealth and influence. King Edward, like Simon de Montfort, realized that this group was a rising power in England, that the taxes they paid were large, and their rights, too, must be protected.

In 1295 Edward established a new plan of sending representatives to Parliament, a plan which formed a model for all later parliaments. According to custom, he invited nobles and senior officials of the Church, but in addition he asked each county and each self-governing town to send two men. When Parliament met in the winter of 1295, there were in attendance two archbishops, eighteen bishops, seventy abbots, seven earls, forty-one barons, seventy men from the counties and two hundred from the towns.

Representatives from the counties and towns had very much the same interests, for they were new to Parliament, they represented large groups of people, and none of them were nobles. As time went by, they were considered to be one group, and were given the name *commons* to indicate that they were different from the noblemen and churchmen. In the beginning all members of Parliament sat together in one body, but later they sat in two different bodies. The nobles and churchmen collected in a group called *The House of Lords,* while the men from counties and towns met in *The House of Commons*. This division of Parliament into two sections has been continued in England to the present day. In Canada, United States and many other countries the same practice is followed although the two bodies of government may not be known by the names originally used by the English.

King Edward I was keenly interested in the improvement of law as well as the reform of Parliament. During his reign many changes were made in old laws and some new laws were introduced. The name "English Justinian" has been applied to Edward because he, like the Roman Emperor Justinian, did so much to improve the laws within his country.

If Edward I was a good king, he was also a very demanding one. In an effort to maintain a strong army, he was continually demanding higher taxes from his people. Eventually this annoyed Parliament so much that the members asked the King to sign a document stating that he would keep the terms of the Great Charter. They also required Edward to make several other promises, one being that he would collect no taxes without consulting Parliament.

The King's desire to keep a strong army was a natural one for a monarch of the time; Edward I did not trust France, and he wanted to add more territory to his realm.

Wales had never formed a true part of the royal lands, because it was a rugged country where a determined people still clung to their old Celtic customs. From time to time the Welsh had been forced to swear loyalty to English kings, but having done so, they went on living their own free way. Along the borders between England and Wales there was constant trouble as the Welsh raided the English and the English raided the Welsh. From the days of William I Wales was hemmed in by a line of English castles held by warlike barons called the *lords marchers*. In a long period of struggle the barons drove the Welsh slowly back into the mountains. At each forward step made by the barons new castles appeared on the green Welsh hills.

Rebellion in Wales Eventually the fighting spirit of the Welsh burst forth under the leadership of a local prince named Llewellyn. In 1277 Edward I led an army into Wales to subdue the rebellious prince who kept his army in the mountains. Instead of chasing the Welsh through the rugged country, Edward blocked all the passes and sent a fleet to patrol the Welsh coast. In the end, Llewellyn was starved out, having no choice but to surrender. Surprisingly enough Edward I treated his prisoner kindly and let him off with an oath of loyalty. Five years later, however, Llewellyn rebelled again and this time lost his life in combat.

An old story says that Edward promised the Welsh a prince who was born in Wales, a prince who could speak not a word of English. He kept his word, for his own baby son, born in a Welsh castle, was given the name *Prince of Wales*. Since that time it has become the custom to give this title to the eldest son of the English kings.

In 1284 Wales was annexed to the English crown and divided into counties. Edward I wisely allowed the Welsh people to keep their own laws, customs and language.

Edward I had used many paid soldiers in the English army fighting in Wales. The old feudal practice of calling out men when needed was gradually disappearing. Edward wanted a standing army, ready for action at any time, ready to fight for years if necessary. Many barons, knights and freemen by this time were quite willing to pay sums of money instead of fighting in time of war.

Another change, too, was becoming apparent in the English army. The importance of cavalrymen dressed in armour was decreasing in favour of foot soldiers who came from among the common people. These men carried weapons that could shoot a great distance, and could strike with such force that armour was no protection. This new weapon was the Welsh long bow, a much better weapon than the old short bows of the Saxons. It was made from a six-foot piece of yew from which a three-foot arrow was shot. Some ideas of the longbow's power is revealed in the story of an English knight struck by a Welsh arrow which passed through three thicknesses of armour, through the man's leg, through the saddle and into the horse's side. With such a weapon as this in the hands of foot soldiers, mounted horsemen were no longer kings of the battlefield. The longbow was to bring a new and different kind of warfare.

Wales was not the only region on the island which was to see fighting during the days of Edward I. Scotland too was to feel the sting of English blows. In 1286, the King of Scotland died in an accident when his horse tumbled over a cliff at night, and his granddaughter, Margaret, fell heir to the Scottish throne. It was suggested that it would be an excellent plan if Princess Margaret were to marry the son of King Edward I. The marriage, it was thought, would be a fine thing for both Scotland and England. Edward I was pleased with the idea, but the marriage never took place for the Princess was drowned during a voyage from Europe.

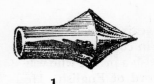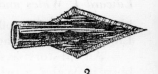

1   2   3

Illustrated here are arrowheads of the fourteenth century. Making arrows was highly specialized, for an arrowsmith made the heads and a fletcher made the shafts. Arrowheads fall into two main divisions—the broad and the pile. The arrows (1), (2) and (3) above are pile heads, (1) probably being the most

A serious problem, of course, was created by Margaret's death. Who was to sit on the throne? A dozen of Scotland's noblemen were quite willing to be the new king, but just two of them seemed to have suitable claims to the crown. They were Robert Bruce and John Balliol. Both of these men had followers in Scotland, so it appeared that a dangerous struggle might break out within the country. In order to prevent such a disaster, King Edward I was persuaded to study the claims of the two men with the purpose of naming the new King of Scotland. Edward agreed to do this providing the Scottish people accepted him as their feudal lord. The Scots finally accepted this plan, but with no great amount of joy.

Rebellion in Scotland A meeting was held on the border between Scotland and England, and there King Edward I named John Balliol as the Scottish monarch. Some suspected that Edward deliberately chose the weaker man but Balliol was crowned king. Following this event, Edward I treated Scotland very much as if it were just another big estate within his kingdom. This kind of treatment was by no means agreeable to the freedom-loving Scots, so they were soon at war with the English.

It was not a wise move on the part of the Scots, for they were no match for Edward's troops. Defeated in battle, John Balliol lost his throne and was exiled from Scotland. English officials were sent to Scotland where they took up important positions in the government, and English garrisons were stationed in castles throughout the land. The Scottish crown was taken to London, as was the stone of Scone, a square block of stone on which the Kings of Scotland sat while being crowned. In London the stone was fitted in the English coronation chair, and there it has remained to the present time, though in 1950 some Scottish nationalists stole the stone and returned it to Scotland briefly.

Although Scotland had been conquered by English troops, there

90

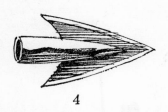
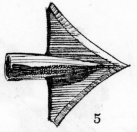

4   5

common. This head could penetrate mail armour at 200 yards. Arrow (4) with its broader head was used in hunting, and (5) with its very broad head was excellent in sea warfare where it could slice up sails and rigging.

still was strong resistance in some parts of the country. An active leader among the Scottish rebels was William Wallace, a bold and clever warrior who gave much trouble to the English. Wallace slowly gathered an army of tough, hard-fighting Scots. It was a stern, well-disciplined army in which death was the penalty for disobedience. Castle after castle was captured from English garrisons until the Scottish army presented a threat to Edward's power in Scotland.

In September, 1297, an English army faced Wallace's troops at the Battle of Stirling Bridge. Eager to attack the enemy, the English general sent his soldiers marching across the long narrow bridge. William Wallace waited until the English were spread out . . . some on one side of the river . . . some on the bridge . . . some on the other side of the river. Then with all his own troops the Scottish commander struck hard, hitting the advance troops of the English with such power that 5,000 men were slaughtered on the field. It was a great victory for the Scots, but a humiliating defeat for the English.

The following year, 1298, Edward I led a large army of cavalry troops and archers northward to Scotland, and there he met William Wallace at the Battle of Falkirk. Among the Scottish troops there were a few horsemen and archers, but the most important section of the army was made up of sturdy spearmen. Edward's archers poured a hail of arrows into the Scottish ranks, opening up great holes through which the English knights dashed on their horses, their lances doing a deadly work among the Scottish spearmen. When once Wallace's men wavered and broke, they were defeated. A savage massacre followed, so that the ground was soaked with blood and strewn with broken bodies.

Those Scots who escaped from the arrows, the lances and the swords fled from the battle, trying to find refuge in the forest and hills. William Wallace made his escape, and remained a free but hunted man until 1305 when he fell into the hands of the English.

Battle of Stirling, 1297

Scottish victory

Battle of Falkirk, 1298

Scottish defeat

Death of William Wallace

91

William Wallace waits for the English troops and prepares to strike. The Scots excelled in the use of the long lance which is seen here. Note also that many soldiers are wearing the kilt. On his horse and surcoat Wallace uses the red lion of Scotland which was adopted as part of the Royal coat of arms earlier that century.

After a trial, he was sentenced to die, sentenced to the savage execution of the times . . . hanged, drawn and quartered.

Even then the determined Scots were not beaten, for they found a new champion in Robert Bruce*, grandson of the man who once had claimed the Scottish throne. When Bruce was crowned as King of Scotland, Edward I swore that he would smash the rebel of the north. Leading an army into Scotland, the English monarch defeated the Scots in the summer of 1306. Robert Bruce was forced to flee, but by the next spring he was gathering men to continue war.

Edward I, however, was never to fight again, for he died near the Scottish border. Before his death, he ordered that his bones should ride with the English troops into Scotland, and that his heart should be sent with a hundred knights to the Holy Land. Neither of these wishes was carried out by his weak son.

*For a legend concerning Robert Bruce see page 401.

92

17

BEGINNING OF
THE HUNDRED YEARS' WAR

Edward I, one of England's greatest kings, left his son Edward, to rule the kingdom. Unfortunately, King Edward II was an insignificant man who had little effect upon English history. Following a period of restless rule, he was put off the throne and placed in prison where he died. Perhaps he was murdered. His thirteen-year-old son was crowned King Edward III of England in 1327.

The old quarrels between England and France went on and on, for even yet there were good reasons for bitterness. England still held a few small possessions in what is now southern France . . . a fact which did not please the French. During the war between Scotland and England, France had aided the Scots . . . a fact which did not please the English. The hatred existing between the two countries revealed itself in the frequent minor battles which took place between French and English seamen who sailed the coastal waters. It is small wonder that the two nations growled at each other across the English Channel.

When the French throne became vacant, King Edward III of **Edward III,** England claimed it because his mother had been the daughter of the **1327** French king, Philip IV. Although Edward's claim may have been legal and reasonable, the French wanted no foreigner on their throne, much less an Englishman. Consequently, Philip, Count of Valois, was crowned King of France, and was accepted as ruler by the French people.

As a boyish king, Edward III was not strong enough to challenge the French, but as he grew into manhood, he renewed his claim to the French throne, and made ready, in 1337, to invade France. The young monarch probably did not realize at the time what serious events he was putting into motion, for his attack on France was the beginning of a long conflict which was to be known as the Hundred Years' War.

In 1337 the war began as Edward III marched deep into France, **War with** spreading destruction throughout the countryside. Towns were burned, **France,** crops destroyed, orchards flattened, farm animals driven off, leaving a **1337** desolate scene in the wake of the English armies. In the meantime, the French were active, for their ships were darting along the English shores, their seamen raiding towns, looting shops and killing people.

A Genoese crossbowman with his weapon. There were many types of crossbows, some more elaborate than the one shown here. The handle at the end is really a stirrup in which the bowman placed his foot when drawing and setting the bow. An arrow called a quarrel was fired when the bowman pulled the trigger. Approximately fifteen inches in length, the quarrel was much shorter than the arrow of the English longbow also shown.

After two years of fighting, Edward III returned to England, gathered a fleet and started back to the continent. His fleet numbering about 147 vessels, sailed on June 22, 1340, and by the following day was off the Dutch harbour of Sluys[1]. There lay the French fleet of 190 ships manned by 35,000 soldiers and sailors. As day was breaking on Saturday morning, the French and English both prepared for battle. Instead of sailing out to meet the enemy, the French formed their ships across the entrance to Sluys harbour. They were placed in three lines with the largest ships in front, linked together with heavy chains. Standing on the high decks French soldiers stood ready with swords, stones and other weapons.

In the early afternoon the English fleet came forward in three **Battle of** divisions with the biggest ships in advance of the others. With kettle **Sluys, 1340** drums beating and instruments playing, the English smashed into the

[1]Sluys, now called *Sluis,* is today an inland town. The old harbour was filled in by silt.

front rank of French ships. Volleys of English arrows poured toward the French vessels alive with men-at-arms. As the ships came alongside each other, their decks became battlefields writhing with hand-to-hand encounters. From high in the big French vessels showers of stones rained on the English below. So fierce was this barrage that at least one English crew was wiped out entirely. Stones, however, were no match for English arrows which cleaned many a French deck. Several of the French ships were captured, manned with English archers, and turned against the enemy.

Seeing that the battle was lost, one French admiral with a group of galleys escaped to the open sea, but the remainder of the ships were caught in the awful destruction. In a frantic attempt to get ashore, some French sailors and soldiers crowded into small boats many of which turned over, spilling the occupants into the harbour. By sundown 166 French ships had been captured or destroyed. One French admiral had been killed in combat and a second one hanged from a yard-arm.

The importance of this decisive victory was that for a generation to come it gave England command of the Channel. Without this advantage it is doubtful if the English could have continued the war with any hope of success.

By 1346 Edward III was smashing his way through Normandy, **Battle of** but eventually he was brought to bay by a powerful French army. **Crecy, 1346** Edward decided to make his stand on the slope of a gentle hill located near the village of Crecy. Setting up his headquarters in a windmill, he planned the battle he knew lay just ahead. The English were seriously outnumbered. This caused some concern to King Edward, but he realized his own men were better trained and better disciplined than were the French. He had confidence, too, in the power of the English longbow.

Early on an August morning King Edward and his seventeen-year-old son, the Black Prince, lined up 10,000 English troops in three great divisions. Dressed in a red and gold coat, Edward rode about on a small horse cheering and encouraging his men. As the day advanced, great masses of French soldiers appeared in the distance . . . company after company of footsoldiers and horsemen. It was not a pleasant sight for the English.

King Philip, arriving with the vanguard of French troops, ordered his men to camp for the night and rest for the next day's battle. But as more and more French troops arrived, the scene became one of

During the middle ages ships developed very slowly. The ship shown here was actually little improved over the early Danish vessels. Because there was no regular navy, the king in time of war was empowered to take over stout merchant vessels and modify them for fighting purposes. Platforms were erected at the bow and stern of such ships and in later times platforms became a permanent feature of ships.

confusion. Not at all willing to wait for the next day, some of the eager French pushed on in spite of the king's command. Some of the troops stood still in obedience to their commander's wishes, while others began a restless advance. Even the French King himself was caught up in the fighting spirit of his men.

Within the French army was a body of 6,000 hired crossbowmen from Genoa, Italy. These were the shock troops who were to lead the main advance, troops who were expected to shoot great gaps in the

The Black Prince fights the French. By this time plate armour was worn over mail for protection. Less exposed parts of the body such as the backs of legs and the inside of arms were covered only with mail. The head was enveloped in a protective helmet known as a *bascinet*. A coat of arms is emblazoned on the shield of the Black Prince. The design is that of King Edward II together with three bars, indicating the Prince to be the eldest son.

English ranks so that French horsemen could charge through the broken wall of the enemy. But the crossbowmen had marched eighteen miles with heavy arms, and had no desire to fight so late in the day. In spite of this they were ordered into action.

As the weary crossbowmen led the way forward toward the English, a sharp shower of rain fell from dark clouds, and a flock of black crows flew over the heads of the attackers. Then to make matters worse, the sun bursting forth, shone directly into the eyes of the advancing Frenchmen. With a hoarse shout, the Genoese crossbowmen fired their bolts from wet bowstrings, but little harm was done for the thick heavy missiles fell short.

Then the English bowmen, who had been standing like statues, came quickly to life. Their bowstrings were dry, for their bows had been in cases during the shower of rain. Thousands of arrows were fitted into longbows; strong hands drew back to the bowmen's ears,

97

and, a flight of arrows, thick as a snowstorm, poured into the ranks of the enemy crossbowmen. The result was terrible to see, for in minutes thousands of them were dead, lying on the field, feathered arrows sticking from their crumpled bodies. The survivors were helpless in this hissing storm of death, for their own weapons could not reach out to the English bowmen. Those who escaped the arrows struggled frantically to get away, and to reach the main body of the French.

In a cold merciless fury, King Philip ordered his cavalry to clear the remaining crossbowmen from the battlefield. "Kill me these scoundrels," he commanded, "for they stop our road!" Thundering into action, the French horsemen charged the floundering Genoese, cutting them down with the vicious swing of swords. But in so doing, the cavalry made a fatal blunder, for now they themselves were within range of the English longbows. Flight after flight of arrows fell among the horsemen, cutting through armour, striking horses and knocking men from their saddles. One description of this action says:

> For the bowmen let fly among them at large, and did not lose a single shaft, for every arrow told on horse and man, piercing head, or arm, or leg among the riders and sending the horses mad. For some stood stock still, and others rushed sideways, and most of all began backing in spite of their masters, and some rearing and tossing their heads at the arrows . . .

More French horsemen pushed forward from the rear, but the deadly hail of English arrows beat on and on. It was a scene of horrible confusion as wounded horses, neighing in agony plunged over the dying and the dead . . . and still the arrows whispered their song of death. Welsh footsoldiers slipping through the ranks of bowmen, reached the struggling enemy and with long knives killed hundreds of the French.

The battle was not yet over, for the French still had squadrons of fresh cavalry troops. Waves of them launched themselves at the English, avoiding as far as possible the flights of arrows. Some of these determined horsemen reached the English troops commanded by the Black Prince. Seeing the Prince in a dangerous position, an officer sent a messenger to the King, asking for help. At the windmill Edward said to the messenger, "Return back to those that sent you, and tell them from me, not to send again for me this day, or expect that I shall come, let whatever happen, as long as my son has life: and say, that I command them to let the boy win his spurs." In spite of this order the King sent a body of thirty knights to assist the Prince.

In the darkness of the night the battle raged on, but the attacks of the French became weaker and weaker until they died away entirely. Then the English built fires and lighted torches to lighten up the blackness. In the glow of the flickering lights King Edward put his arms about the Black Prince, saying, "You are my son, for most loyally have you acquitted yourself this day. You are most worthy to be a sovereign."

The victory secured at the Battle of Crecy was one of the greatest military achievements of all British history. Following the battle King Edward marched to the Channel, and laid siege to Calais, a troublesome spot for the English, because here was the home of sea raiders who harried the coast of England.

The French fortress at Calais was well protected by double walls **Capture of** and moats which made a direct assault almost impossible. Edward III **Calais** drew a tight rein of troops around Calais on the land side while English ships patrolled the waters off shore. Barriers made from piles, or stakes, were driven in the shallow waters to keep small French boats from securing supplies. Bombards (early cannon) were used to hurl heavy stone balls at the fortress walls. In spite of the constant pressure, the determined French in Calais held out month after month, although they suffered from hunger.

King Edward III appeared to be master of the situation, but he, too, was having troubles. His troops were anxious to go home, his navy was tired of the siege and Parliament complained of the high taxes needed to support the war. Nevertheless, after eleven months of the siege the ragged starved people of Calais surrendered to the English, and were granted generous terms of peace.

The capture of Calais was as important to the English as Gibraltar was to be in later years. Edward III established this coastal point as a powerful military stronghold and a centre of trade. In order to maintain its commercial position, Edward ordered that all English exports to the continent should pass through the port of Calais. For over 200 years this outpost on the French coast was to remain in English hands.

Edward's successes in France established England as a military nation. The victory of the longbow at Crecy not only shocked France but surprised England. Having gained such a high reputation as warriors, the English tried hard in future struggles to keep this fame.

Here is an early bombard, or cannon. It was constructed of iron bars bound together like a barrel with hoops. The balls projected from the bombard were of stone, sometimes bound with iron. Balls varied in size, ranging up to twenty-five inches in diameter. Because the barrel tapered toward the back end, it was not necessary for balls to fit exactly. Thoroughly unreliable at first, it took a long time for the bombard to surpass the mechanical siege weapons. Gun powder of the time was weak and very dirty.

18

BLACK DEATH AND WAR

While the French and the English were at war, a new enemy arose to threaten all Europe. This was an enemy against which the most powerful weapons and the best disciplined armies were powerless.

The new enemy came silently, stealthily and with such strength **Bubonic** that it killed many more people than died on the battle fields. The **plague** disease, bubonic plague, spread from Asia into Europe; by 1348 many countries were suffering from it. It is difficult for us to realize the terror and the tragedy of those years, for it may be that as many as 25,000,000 people died in the great epidemic known as the Black Death.

Perhaps the bubonic plague was carried to England by Italian merchants who brought oriental goods from the Mediterranean to the lands of western Europe. However it came, the Black Death reaped a grim harvest in England, wiping out whole families and reducing the population of the towns and cities by as much as a third or even half.

Black Death and War

The plague attacked swiftly, causing headache, high temperature and sleeplessness. On the second day hard painful swellings appeared in the armpits or groin, while the organs of the body were usually affected. As the disease progressed, the victims became delirious. Few people once infected with the disease escaped a horrible death.

A description of conditions in England reads as follows:

The grievous plague penetrated the sea-coasts from Southampton, and came to Bristol, and there almost the whole strength of the town died, struck as it were by sudden death; for there were few who kept their beds more than three days, or two days, or half a day; and after this the fell death broke forth on every side with the course of the sun. There died at Leicester in the small parish of St. Leonard more than 380; in the parish of Holy Cross more than 400; in the parish of St. Margaret of Leicester more than 700; and so in each parish a great number.

Bodies of the dead being carted away during the terrifying days of the "Black Death." Bubonic plague was to some degree spread by rats which thrived in the dirt and filth of the medieval towns. People died so quickly and in such numbers that proper burials could not be conducted. In some places bodies were simply placed in great pits which served as common graves. The scene below takes place in a walled town of England. In the background may be seen the thirteenth century gatehouse with its clock tower. Clocks made their appearance during this century, although for a time they had only one hand which marked the hours.

The tragic loss of so many citizens had a serious effect upon English life . . . the churches lost priests . . . estates lost serfs . . . industry lost workers . . . universities lost students and teachers. It was a crippling blow to the nation, but when the Black Death had run its fearsome course, the people set themselves to carry on as best they could.

But even the bubonic plague could not wipe out the old rivalry and hatred which existed between England and France. There were several years of truce following the capture of Calais but, as these drew to a close, the fighting was renewed.

The Black Prince who had won fame at Crecy became an important military leader as the war progressed. A striking figure dressed in black armour, the Prince fought beside his father in many engagements and himself led several expeditions into France.

The Black Prince

To the people of his time the Black Prince was the ideal knight in an age of chivalry. During this century, knights were bound by a code of rules which was supposed to govern their actions in war and in peace. In addition to being courageous, they were expected to be courteous in manner, generous in combat, loyal to their lords, gracious to ladies and devoted in religion. These rules and customs of chivalry appeared in the songs and poems of the period. While such were the ideals of knighthood, they were not always carried out in actual practice, for knights could be brutal, and often they did not treat common people with the same degree of kindness as they offered to men of their own rank. The Black Prince probably held all the virtues and faults possessed by most knights of his time. He was daring in battle, loved to fight in tournaments, enjoyed hunting and could be very charming in his manners. In time he became the most famous warrior in all Europe.

Battle of Poitiers, 1356

In 1355 King Edward III took up the Hundred Years' War once again, sending the Black Prince and his younger brother, John of Gaunt, into France with two separate armies. By the following year the Black Prince found himself in a dangerous situation. In full retreat with only 4,000 men, the Prince was pursued by a French force five times as large as his own. Choosing to make his stand at Poitiers, the Black Prince stationed his men so that the flanks were protected by forest.

King John of France saw his chance to avenge the French defeat at Crecy, and to end the war with one powerful blow. It was an army of mail-clad foot soldiers that hurried forward to meet the English,

102

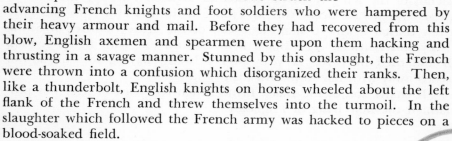

This is a fourteenth century pottery jug with a mask lip and eyes. The medieval potter set up his rude workshop wherever clay beds were available. Some potters travelled about from place to place. Monasteries are thought to have had their own potters. People generally ate off wooden plates which were cleaned by scouring with ashes.

for the French realized that horsemen were no match for the dreaded longbowmen.

The prospect appeared grim for the English, but the military genius of the Black Prince arose to meet the challenge. Instead of remaining still in one spot, the Prince chose to fight a battle of movement and surprise attack. Showers of arrows struck the advancing French knights and foot soldiers who were hampered by their heavy armour and mail. Before they had recovered from this blow, English axemen and spearmen were upon them hacking and thrusting in a savage manner. Stunned by this onslaught, the French were thrown into a confusion which disorganized their ranks. Then, like a thunderbolt, English knights on horses wheeled about the left flank of the French and threw themselves into the turmoil. In the slaughter which followed the French army was hacked to pieces on a blood-soaked field.

King John of France was taken to England and there he was **Peace of Bretigny, 1360** confined in the Tower of London. By the Peace of Bretigny, signed in 1360, England was to hold the states of Gascony, Aquitaine, Ponthieu and the city of Calais. What appeared to be a victory for England was scarcely a victory at all, for the small gains achieved had been won at dreadful cost. King Edward III had failed in his goal of conquering all France.

During the years that Edward had been waging war, important changes were taking place in Parliament. The King's constant need for money to support his armies had caused Parliament to meet at **Importance of Parliament** frequent intervals. The House of Commons, which had been comparatively unimportant before this time, gained steadily in power and influence. Before the end of his rule Edward III recognized that the Houses of Parliament held considerable authority in the raising of taxes and in the forming of national policy. This was a great advance

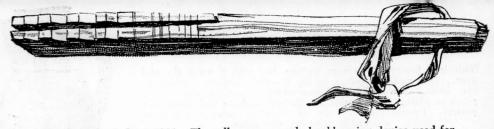

A tally stick of about 1361. The tally was an early bookkeeping device used for recording business transactions. A long stick had notches cut into it, each notch representing an amount of money. After the notches were made, the stick was cut in two, the longer piece being given to the customer and the shorter one to the seller. Later, if necessary, the pieces could be fitted together to see if they "tallied."

toward freedom for the people because Parliament was now considered to be a necessary part of English government.

The last period of Edward III's reign was a sad and disappointing time for the old warrior. There were serious quarrels among the noblemen and the churchmen, each group jealous of the other. Former friends of the King turned against him. Queen Philippa died. Conquests which had been won in France dwindled away, leaving only a few coastal towns to stand as token of the great victories of Sluys, Crecy and Poitiers. The Black Prince, worn out with fighting, took ill and died in 1376. A year later Edward, having lost his mind, passed away with few to mourn his death.

Richard, son of the Black Prince, then ten years of age, was proclaimed the new King of England.

SUMMARY—SECTION II

King Henry I died in 1135 and was succeeded by his nephew, King Stephen, who proved to be a very weak monarch. After Stephen's death in 1154 Henry II (Henry Plantagenet of Anjou) came to the throne. One of the most active kings in English history, Henry II spent a busy life controlling England and his possessions in Europe. One of his greatest contributions was the establishment of a system of law and justice. From the practices he put into force there arose the custom of trial by jury.

A clash of power arose between the Church in England and Henry II. Thomas Becket, a former friend of the King, who became Archbishop of Canterbury, led the Church opposition against Henry. As a result of the quarrels which followed Becket was murdered in 1170 by followers of Henry. All Europe was shocked by the tragedy, but in time the King made his peace with the Church and the Pope. Before his death in 1189 Henry II was one of the most powerful rulers in Europe.

104

Through his efforts the people of England were beginning to think of themselves as Englishmen and not as Danes, Normans or Saxons. A feeling of national unity was just beginning to assert itself.

Next to the throne there came the popular adventurer King Richard I (Richard the Lion Heart). Although he won fame in the Third Crusade and other military campaigns, he was not an effective King. He was never in England long enough to carry out his royal duties. After he was killed in a siege, 1199, his brother John was crowned.

The one important event in King John's selfish, troublesome reign was his enforced signing of *Magna Carta*, 1215. This famous document is considered to be the keystone of English liberty.

John's son, Henry III, came to the throne in 1216. He, like his father, was a selfish person, but during his long reign England made remarkable progress. Parliament won new power, Westminster Abbey was re-constructed and the universities showed new growth.

Henry III's son, Edward I, was a warlike King who conquered Wales and fought a war with Scotland. It was during his reign, 1272 to 1307, that Parliament was divided into the House of Commons and the House of Lords.

After the weak reign of Edward II, another warlike monarch, Edward III was crowned in 1327. Edward III found himself involved in the Hundred Years' War with France. During the struggle the English won fame as warriors through the naval victory at Sluys, the capture of Calais and the Black Prince's triumph at Poitiers. This first portion of the Hundred Years' War came to an end with the Peace of Bretigny, 1360.

The growth of prosperity, the increasing importance of Parliament and the war with France, all of which took place during this period from 1135 to 1377, tended to increase a feeling of unity within the nation.

TIME-CHART

1154-1360

	1154-1189	HENRY II
Birth of Genghis Khan— rise of the Mongols	**1162**	
	1170	MURDER OF THOMAS BECKET
	1189-1199	RICHARD I

TIME-CHART—*(continued)*

	1189-1192	THE THIRD CRUSADE
	1199-1216	JOHN
	1206	STEPHEN LANGTON BECOMES ARCHBISHOP
	1215	MAGNA CARTA
	1216-1272	HENRY III
Death of Genghis Khan	**1227**	
Jerusalem captured by the Turks	**1244**	
	1264	CIVIL WAR—THE STRUGGLE BETWEEN HENRY III AND SIMON DE MONTFORT
Kublai Khan becomes emperor of the Mongols	**1260**	
Marco Polo travels to Cathay	**1271**	
	1272-1307	EDWARD I
	1284	CONQUEST OF WALES
Marco Polo returns to Venice	**1295**	
	1298	DEFEAT OF WILLIAM WALLACE
	1307-1327	EDWARD II
	1327-1377	EDWARD III
	1337	BEGINNING OF THE HUNDRED YEARS' WAR
	1340	BATTLE OF SLUYS
	1346	BATTLE OF CRÉCY
	1347-1350	THE BLACK DEATH
	1356	THE BLACK PRINCE AT POITIERS
	1360	PEACE OF BRÉTIGNY

Discontent of the lower classes in England • Richard II faces the rioters in the Peasants' Revolt • Death of Wat Tyler • John Wycliffe and the "poor priests," or Lollards • Henry of Lancaster takes throne from Richard II • England fights France in a renewal of the Hundred Years' War • Joan of Arc becomes leader of French forces • England loses all French possessions but Calais • Wars of the Roses fought between Lancastrians and Yorkists • Civil war weakens the power of the barons • Feudalism falls into decay • Serfs gain new freedoms • Henry Tudor comes to throne as Henry VII

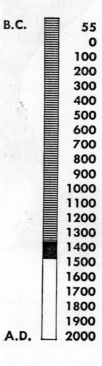

B.C.
55
0
100
200
300
400
500
600
700
800
900
1000
1100
1200
1300
1400
1500
1600
1700
1800
1900
A.D. 2000

19

RICHARD II AND THE PEASANTS' REVOLT

John of Gaunt, younger brother of the Black Prince, ruled England until young Richard II was old enough to assume his royal duties.

The old feudal pattern of life in England had begun to crumble. **Richard II, 1377** English kings themselves had played a part in this change, for they had given up the practice of calling out troops from the estates in favour of using hired soldiers in time of war. Another factor in the gradual decline of feudalism, too, was the appalling number of deaths which had been caused by the plague.

(1) A picture drawn by a medieval artist shows a swineherd knocking down acorns for his pigs. Such a drawing now appears stiff and unnatural. (2) This represents the same subject as we would draw it today. Pigs were inexpensive to keep, for they lived largely on roots, stubble and nuts. They were kept by most village citizens. Fees were paid to professional swineherds for looking after the pigs, and to landowners for the use of fields and forests. Note the rough, bristly hides and the long snouts of the animals.

Many of the great landowners found themselves short of freemen and serfs to work their estates. In some cases the nobles had been forced to reduce their rents and pay wages to have their lands cultivated. The old severe laws by which serfs were bound to remain **Greater** on the manors were being ignored by serfs and nobles. Serfs who **freedom** **for serfs** ran away from their own villages frequently found employment with other landowners who asked no embarrassing questions. Then, too, serfs often disappeared from manors only to appear as workers in the towns. By custom, any serf who lived for a year and a day within a town was considered a free man. This tendency for serfs to become either hired workmen in the country or labourers in towns, of course, speeded the breakdown of the feudal system. It also led to the growth of towns and the rising importance of the middle classes of people.

It is true that England had become a united nation with one **New Poll Tax, 1381** language and one government, but still there was ill feeling between the upper and lower classes. Burdened with taxes and hampered by old customs, the lower classes felt a great discontent with their lot in life. The feeling of discontent burst into hot anger when Parliament levied a new form of taxation known as the poll tax. Unlike older taxes levied on property or on goods, the poll tax was levied on people, so that persons over twelve years of age were subject to the tax.

When, in 1381, the poll tax was being collected for the second time, the peasants in the southeastern part of England started riots and attacked the tax collectors. Thousands of angry rioters reached London, surging through the city in violent waves. There, under the leadership of Wat Tyler they set up a reign of terror. Buildings owned by nobles were burned, the Tower of London was seized, and a number of officials beheaded. Terror ran through the streets as foreigners and others were beaten and murdered.

John of Gaunt was absent in the north, but Richard II, then sixteen years of age, took a cool and courageous stand in the face of a dangerous situation. He met a large assembly of the rioters at a meeting where Wat Tyler on behalf of the people demanded freedom from serfdom, freedom from forced labour, lower rents, division of Church lands, free use of forests and abolition of cruel game laws. Knowing that his government was helpless against the power of the masses, Richard agreed to grant the demands of the people.

The following day a second meeting was held between the King **Richard II and the rioters** and a large group of the rioters. Soon after discussion had begun, a sudden quarrel broke out between Richard's followers and the leaders of the revolt. Wat Tyler rode so close to the King that "his horse's head touched the edge of the King's saddle." The Mayor of London, thinking that he meant to attack King Richard, cut Tyler down with a sword. In a swift flurry of action Wat Tyler, stabbed twice, fell dying from his mount. There was a moment of shocked silence, and then the rioters in fury reached for their bows.

With remarkable presence of mind, young King Richard II spurred his horse forward, shouting, "I will be your leader! You shall have from me all you ask! Only follow me to the fields outside."

Bewildered and confused by the swift turn of events, the rioters followed the King beyond the city gates, where to their alarm they found themselves surrounded by an armed force. When a horseman appeared with Wat Tyler's bloody head held aloft on a lance, the rebels gave in, surrendering their arms. After disbanding quietly, they left London and returned to their homes.

With the death of Wat Tyler and the end of the London riots, the revolt had spent its force. Smaller disturbances still continued in other parts of England but were smashed by powerful nobles. Many of those who had taken important parts in the rebellion were brought to trial and executed. In spite of the promise made by Richard II, no new laws were passed to improve the lot of the lower classes. This fact was not surprising, for the King had not intended to keep his word once the revolt was over.

It is true that Parliament gave up collecting the poll tax, but the bitterness between upper and lower classes continued. Some of this feeling was a result of religious conditions of the time. Important churchmen lived like wealthy nobles on large estates while the Church as a whole controlled some of the best lands in England. Many of the priests scattered about the nation were ignorant, lazy and selfish. People of the lower classes could not help feeling that the churchmen were a privileged group more interested in wealth than they were in religion.

John Wycliffe John Wycliffe, a clergyman and a teacher at Oxford University, became leader of a group who protested against religious conditions throughout the land. Wycliffe believed that churchmen should devote themselves wholly to the work of God and take no interest in property and wealth. As a result of his teachings and writings, a number of men called "poor priests" began to move about the country preaching to the people in English rather than the Latin of the Church. These devoted men dressed themselves in simple clothes and lived on the plainest foods. In addition to preaching and teaching the "poor priests" distributed copies of the Bible translated into English. This made it possible for people to judge the teachings of Christ for themselves. Unintentionally, then, Wycliffe and his followers were undermining the whole foundation of power of the established Church.

The Lollards Those people who accepted the teachings of John Wycliffe came to be known as Lollards, a term meaning "heretics" or "unbelievers." At first the church authorities took little action against the Lollards, but as the movement grew, a more serious attitude appeared. The

110

Archbishop of Canterbury began a stern campaign against the religious rebels, and John Wycliffe was put out of Oxford University. Retiring to a parish, Wycliffe went on with his writings, and continued to direct the work of the "poor priests."

More pressure was placed on important Lollard preachers who were brought into Church courts and accused of crimes against the Church. Many of them begging forgiveness, confessed their crimes and gave up their former work among the people. Nevertheless, the Lollard movement within the mass of people remained strong, and even at Oxford University many students and teachers held firm to their beliefs.

In the year 1401 Parliament passed a severe act which aimed at stamping out the Lollards. By law, then, no person was to preach or teach religious matters without permission granted by a bishop of the Church. Penalties for disobeying such law ranged from imprisonment to burning at the stake. During the same year in which the act was passed by Parliament, a Lollard priest was actually burned alive and in the next few years others followed.

The work of the Lollards had served to further the use of English in spoken and written form. Latin was still the language of the churchmen and the learned scholars of the universities, but English was increasing in general use by all classes of people. By the year 1362 a law was passed making English the official language of the law courts. Literature, too, began to reflect an interest in the common tongue, so that poems and stories appeared in English.

The greatest poet of the time was the noted Geoffrey Chaucer, **Geoffrey Chaucer** son of a wealthy London merchant, who as a boy served as page in the royal household. His most famous poems, *Canterbury Tales,* tell of a group of pilgrims travelling to a shrine at Canterbury. As the pilgrims make their way along the English roads, they tell stories to each other to pass away the time. *Canterbury Tales,* then is largely made up of these stories told by the pilgrims. Although the English spelling of Chaucer's day was somewhat different than that used today, we have no great amount of difficulty in understanding the poet's meaning. Here is a verse from *Canterbury Tales*:

> A Knight ther was, and that a worthy man,
> That fro the tyme he first bigan
> To ryden out, he loved chivalrye,
> Trouthe and honour, fredom and curteisye.

The Pilgrims are shown approaching Canterbury Cathedral which lies in a valley among beautiful hills. Although not visible here, the city of Canterbury had a wall about it like most medieval towns. In the foreground one pilgrim is seen carrying a leather water bottle at his waist. A friar is dressed in long black robe and hood. The shaved patch on top of his head is known as the tonsure and indicates that he belongs to the Church.

Later in history when the art of printing arrived in England, *Canterbury Tales* was one of the first works to appear as a printed book. Today the writings of Chaucer are still much admired, and are studied by students in our universities.

At first Richard II was a popular king among his people, but he was not an effective or a kindly monarch because he possessed a desire to rule with absolute power. As time went by, he used a number of illegal and dishonest means to gain a tighter control over the nation. He surrounded himself with armed men, abused Parliament, executed and banished nobles, spent money foolishly, and generally acted in a manner which angered his people.

One of his greatest mistakes was to banish from the country his **Henry of** first cousin, Henry of Lancaster, who was son of John of Gaunt. The **Lancaster** banished Henry took up residence in France, and there he waited patiently for a chance to strike back at Richard. An excellent opportunity opened in 1399 when the King was out of the country on a military expedition to Ireland.

Appearing suddenly in northern England, Henry of Lancaster made his way toward London, gathering an army of supporters as he went. So great was his increasing strength that he eventually decided

112

During the fourteenth century windmills began to dot the English countryside, supplementing the old but reliable watermills. The mill shown here was called a post mill because it turned on a large central post to face the wind. Sails were laced to the blades of the mill, and as the wind blew against these, a mechanism turned the mill stones which ground grain into flour. Peasants taking grain to the mill to be made into flour paid the miller, or owner, a small portion of the grain for his services.

to claim the English throne. When Richard II returned from Ireland, he was dismayed to find that his people had turned against him in support of his cousin.

Realizing he had no chance of regaining his authority, Richard II made little effort to battle against his fate. Held in prison, he signed a document stating that he was giving up his royal rights and his power as the English monarch. Then followed an impressive meeting of Parliament at which Richard was officially deposed and Henry was named as the new King. On the day of his coronation in 1399, Henry **Henry IV,** IV rode through the streets on a beautiful roan horse which had been **1399** the favourite mount of the imprisoned king.

Richard II, secretly removed from the Tower of London, was hurried away to a castle in northern England. A few weeks later there reached London a solemn procession in the middle of which a black-draped carriage rolled along carrying the body of the former king.

His hands were folded awkwardly across his chest; his face was wan and haggard; a gold band encircled his forehead. As his body lay in state at St. Paul's Cathedral, hundreds of people came to gaze curiously on the pathetic form of Richard II.

Perhaps they wondered how and why he died.

20

RENEWAL OF THE HUNDRED YEARS' WAR

Henry IV, son of John of Gaunt, Duke of Lancaster, became King with little difficulty in 1399, but his ascent to the throne caused English quarrels which lasted for years.

The power of Parliament had been growing steadily for a hundred years, ever since the time of Edward I. Its division into two bodies, the House of Commons and the House of Lords, was well established. Meetings of Parliament were held at least once a year and sometimes more frequently. Over the years Parliament had gained certain powers which were recognized by the people and by the king. These powers included the right to approve all taxes, the right to approve new laws, the right to dismiss the advisers of the king, the right to advise the king in all important matters of government.

When Henry IV* came to the throne in 1399, he promised to respect the rights of Parliament, and not to abuse them as Richard II had done. For the most part Henry kept to his promise, ruling the nation in accordance with the wishes of Parliament. His reign of fourteen years, however, was not a happy one, for he was troubled by disturbances within and without the country. The Church's struggle against the Lollards was still in progress. There were several groups of men who, remaining loyal to the memory of Richard II, still resented the seizure of the English throne.

Revolt in Wales

Wales which had been conquered by King Edward I stirred uneasily under the harsh rule of Englishmen known as the "Lords Marchers," who lived in fortified castles. Early in the reign of Henry IV, a determined Welsh leader, Owen Glendower, rose in revolt against the English rulers of his native land. Winning the support of the Welsh people, Glendower was proclaimed as the Prince of Wales. With extreme courage and with remarkable military skill, he captured a number of English-held castles in Wales and made bold raids into the nearby counties of England. So successful was he that in time he defeated several English armies, making Wales almost an independent country.

*For a legend concerning Henry IV see page 402.

114

By the 15th century the knight's body was completely enclosed in plate armour. The surcoat had vanished, although it was to return later in the century. Steel gauntlets cover the hands, and guards called *pauldrons* protected the shoulders. Straps and buckles are not worn on the outer surface of the limbs, because in battle they could be cut away. The pointed metal shoes reflect the fashion of the day.

To make matters even more difficult for Henry IV, the Earls of Northumberland and Worcester rose in revolt, joining the Welsh rebellion. Along with these rebels was "Harry Hotspur", son of the Earl of Northumberland, a fiery young warrior who lent strong support to the cause. For a time it appeared as if the rebels might overthrow Henry, but in the Battle of Shrewsbury, 1403, their hopes were smashed: Hotspur was killed and the Earls captured. In time, Henry IV and his son, Prince Henry, recaptured the English castles in Wales, and restored order in that green and hilly land. *Battle of Shrewsbury, 1403*

After the death of Henry IV, in 1413, his son Henry V came to the throne. Young Henry, who had been trained as a soldier, was very anxious to win glory for himself and his nation. It was quite natural then that he should consider renewing the Hundred Years' War with France. It was an excellent time to attack the old enemy, for the King of France was suffering from a mental disorder and the country was on the brink of civil war. *Henry V, 1413*

During the second year of his reign, Henry V led a small but well-armed force into France. In the first important military engagement, the Battle of Agincourt, 1415, the English repeated the triumphs of Crecy and Poitiers, as the longbowmen defeated a large French army. *Battle of Agincourt, 1415*

King Henry V, instead of marching about and ravaging the land as Edward III and the Black Prince had done, spent his time in the

Minstrels were wandering musician-poets. They often composed love songs and battle songs to entertain nobles in the banquet halls and courts of the medieval world. In addition to the songs they composed, the minstrels repeated the old ballads and folk-lore of former days. In this way some ancient songs have come down to us.

siege of important cities and towns. When the insane King of France, Charles VI, died, Henry was powerful enough to take the throne of France, and by marrying the daughter of the dead King, he made his position still stronger. Then as quickly as possible he went on to conquer the remaining districts of France which held out against him.*

Henry VI, 1422
After a brief reign of nine years, Henry V died in 1422, leaving a baby son, Henry VI, as King of England and of France. The war dragged on, for the son of the former French King, the Dauphin of France, was determined to regain his father's throne. English troops for some years managed to hold most of France, but in time the tide of fortune turned in favour of the French.

Joan of Arc
The revival of the French fighting spirit was due to the actions of an amazing peasant girl, Joan of Arc, who felt that she was called by God to save her country. After a dangerous journey across France, she appeared in the court of the Dauphin and speaking directly to him she said, "I am Joan the Maid, sent on the part of God to aid you and the kingdom, and by His order, I announce that you will be crowned in the city of Rheims."

So great was her calm confidence, and so spiritual was her appearance, that the Dauphin granted permission for Joan of Arc to lead an army against the English. Then came one of the miracles of history . . . a young French girl in plain armour at the head of French troops . . . marching on the famous warriors of England. At this stage of the war, 1429, the city of Orleans was being starved out by a tight ring of English besiegers. It was here that Joan of Arc began her work of recovering France from the invaders. In the struggles which

*For a legend of this time see "Dick Whittington and his Cat" on page 402.

116

Joan of Arc appears before the Dauphin of France. Note the boy's tunic and the peasant simplicity of her dress in comparison with the elaborate costumes of the court. Women of the court are wearing dresses which reflect Gothic style. On their heads is the conical *hennin* made from the fine materials stretched over a wire frame. Women frequently revealed their brows and temples, but concealed their hair beneath the pointed *hennins*.

took place about Orleans, she was struck by an arrow and later knocked from a scaling ladder as she climbed a wall.

Awestruck by the heroism of the girl, and fearful of her spiritual powers, the English lost their fighting spirit and became cautious in their movements. In time they were beaten, and Orleans was saved. French successes

Other victories followed, and then Joan of Arc urged the Dauphin to march to Rheims for a coronation ceremony. It was a hazardous journey, for Rheims lay in territory still held by the English. Nevertheless, the Dauphin, after some persuasion went, and everywhere the French people welcomed him and shouted their loyalty. In a ceremony of pomp and splendour the Dauphin, with Joan of Arc at his side, was crowned King Charles of France.

Following the coronation, Joan of Arc, feeling that her great mission had been completed, asked permission to return to her home. Permission was refused, so the tired girl, carrying on her military duties, was badly wounded in a French attack on the city of Paris.

With the passing of time, Joan of Arc gradually lost favour with the French King, with the Church and with a number of the French nobility. Then tragically, in 1430, she fell into the hands of an unfriendly group who, in a treacherous act, handed her over to the English for a sum of money.

To many of the English, Joan of Arc was a supernatural being of unearthly power who must be destroyed before she could do more harm to England's cause in France. But she was a prisoner of war, and by the customs of chivalry could not be condemned to death merely because she had fought against her enemies. It was with the crime of heresy and sin against the Church that she was accused. For over a year her fate was argued. To the everlasting disgrace of the French king, it must be said that he made little attempt to save the gallant girl who had placed him on the throne.

Death of Joan of Arc

Finally, on May 29, 1431, Joan of Arc was taken into the marketplace of Rouen, and there she was bound to a stake standing high over a great pyramid of dry firewood. As the flames licked upward and the smoke swirled around her pathetic figure, Joan raised a little cross and cried, "Jesus."

An English soldier with a look of anguish on his face, turned away from the haunting scene, shouting, "We are lost. We have burned a saint."

English losses

The struggle for France continued for another twenty-two years after the fiery execution of Joan of Arc. Military successes begun by the maiden soldier were carried forward, so that more and more land was won back from the English. Finally, in 1453, the Hundred Years' War came to an end with England losing all her possessions except the city of Calais.

It was sad for the English to reflect that even the brilliant victories of the longbowmen could not make up for the appalling losses which had been suffered in more than a century of senseless and wasteful warfare.

118

21

THE WARS OF THE ROSES

Henry VI, who inherited the crown of England while still a baby, was a dull-witted but kindly and religious monarch, not strong enough to control the restless barons of his realm. He was a grandson of Henry IV who had pushed Richard II from the throne. This seizure of royal power was still remembered in England, a memory which rankled in the minds of certain noblemen.

The power and wealth of the important barons was very great during this period, for, left uncontrolled by a weak King, they built up private armies to protect their castles and attack their enemies. Following the closing of the Hundred Years' War, many soldiers who returned from France, joined the service of nobles. Groups of barons made treaties among themselves in opposition to other strong groups.

Eager for power, rival bands of barons in an effort to influence **Rivalry of** the King plotted against each other in a vicious manner. Eventually **the barons** these conflicts led to a series of battles lasting thirty years, 1455 to 1485, which are known in history as the Wars of the Roses. This was a struggle between groups of barons and *did not* involve the country as a whole.

When Henry VI began to suffer from fits of insanity, the Duke of York was named Protector, and ruled England in the royal name. A number of the King's friends, jealous of the Duke, resented his high position in the nation's government, and Henry himself did not appreciate the efforts of his Protector. With the passing of time, there developed a bitter struggle for the throne itself.

Two strong parties opposed one another: the *Yorkists* who fol- **York and** lowed the Duke of York and the *Lancastrians* who supported the King's **Lancaster** family of Lancaster. The emblems used to distinguish the two groups were the white rose of York and the red rose of Lancaster.

There were a number of military clashes, and then at the Battle **Battle of** of Wakefield, 1460, the Yorkists were beaten, and the Duke of York **Wakefield,** was killed. His head, hacked from his body, was decorated with a paper **1460** crown and placed on top a wall. Following this defeat, the leadership of the House of York fell to young Edward, the Duke's son.

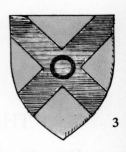

Heraldry is the name given to the system of personal designs and markings worn by knights of the middle ages with the purpose of identifying themselves. Such designs were worn on shields, surcoats, helmets, horses and elsewhere. In time a complicated system developed with regard to the use of the heraldic designs. Here are a few samples: (1) This is a family design or coat of arms. In the practice of heraldry each son was given a specific mark which was added

Events moved swiftly. A year after his father's death, Edward of York whipped the Lancastrians in battle, claimed the throne, and was crowned King Edward IV. Driven from power, Henry VI took refuge in Scotland.

Queen Margaret

It may be that the Wars of the Roses would have ended at this point had it not been for Henry's Queen, Margaret the Princess of France. A beautiful woman of great courage, she secured help from France and Scotland in an effort to win back the throne. More battles and sieges followed with victories and defeats on both sides. It was a cold-blooded conflict, as wounded were murdered on battle fields and prisoners were beheaded without mercy.

But not even the courage of Queen Margaret could stem the Yorkist tide, for the English government made peace treaties with her allies, France and Scotland. Poor demented Henry VI was captured in Lancashire and brought to the Tower of London, his feet tied to his saddle stirrups and a straw hat thrust on his head.

Edward IV, 1461

Magnificent warrior though he was, Edward IV was not an able king. Fond of hunting, feasting and drinking, he was quite content to let his ministers look after the tiresome details of ruling the kingdom. The Earl of Warwick, who had supported Edward's rise to the throne, became the most important man in the government. It is not surprising that the Earl was known as "Warwick the Kingmaker."

Warwick the King-maker

Warwick, hoping that the King would marry a French princess, was very much annoyed when he discovered Edward's secret marriage to an English widow of no high rank. Feeling between Edward IV and Warwick was not improved when the King proceeded to grant important positions to relatives and friends of the Queen. It was

120

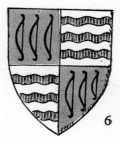

4
5
6

to the family coat of arms. (2) Shows the mark or *label* of the eldest son and (3) the mark or ring of the fifth son. Some designs were based on a notable feat performed by the owner, and some were based on the family name. Shown in (4) is the coat of arms of the Bowes family. (5) Indicates a new design resulting from a marriage. Note that the arms of both families are placed side by side. (6) The division of a design into four parts is known as quartering. This type might be used by the grandchildren of (4) if there were daughters but no sons to carry on the family coat of arms.

actions such as these that turned Warwick from a good friend to a dangerous enemy of the King.

The last period of the Wars of the Roses was noted for shifting alliances and sudden upsets of power. The Earl of Warwick (a Yorkist) with the King's brother Clarence (a Yorkist) and Queen Margaret (a Lancastrian) all joined together to push Edward IV from the throne.

Invading England with French support, Warwick the Kingmaker marched to London, took insane Henry VI from the Tower and put him on the English throne. Conditions then became so dangerous for King Edward IV that he was forced to flee to the continent, where for a while he remained in exile. Many men would have surrendered to fate after such an experience, but Edward IV was not one of them. Landing in England with only 300 men, he collected more troops and marched to meet the Earl of Warwick.

During the battle which followed, Warwick was killed, an army led by Queen Margaret was beaten, and Henry VI died or was murdered. Edward's cause was helped when his treacherous brother Clarence deserted Warwick and came to the King's assistance.

Lancastrian power was smashed; the white rose of York stood supreme. King Edward IV took up his reign with little fear of further challenge.

Suddenly at the age of forty-two, Edward IV died, leaving his throne to his son Edward V. The future of the House of York appeared bright, but unexpected events were to change all that.

Edward V, who was crowned in 1483, was soon pushed from the throne and probably murdered by his uncle, the Duke of Gloucester. **Edward V, 1483**

121

Warwick the Kingmaker was killed in battle during the Wars of the Roses. His shield is shown falling with two crossbow quarrels embedded in it. Horses are protected by armour with flaring surfaces to ward off direct blows. Although very strong, horse armour was remarkably light, some outfits weighing as little as seventy-two pounds. Warwick probably was wearing Italian armour which was far superior to any other of the time.

This ruthless nobleman became King Richard III of England, but he was not to enjoy victory for long. In another rapid switch of royal power, Henry Tudor of the Lancastrian family defeated Richard III at the Battle of Bosworth and he himself in 1485 became King Henry VII.

Henry VII, 1485 In the long strange struggle for the throne the Lancastrians had been victorious, but even then Henry VII thought it wise to marry Princess Elizabeth of the House of York. This was the beginning of a new and famous line of English monarchs, the Tudors, who were to play a vital and colourful part in the development of the nation and in the birth of an empire.

122

The Wars of the Roses is a dark period in the island's history, for there had been much bloodshed, needless cruelty, shocking treachery and no good reason for such a costly struggle. One of the chief results was the weakening of the authority of the barons of England. Noble families lost their lands, their fortunes and their sons in the dizzy play of power which swung like a pendulum between the white rose and the red.

As the power of the nobles declined, the strength of the middle classes increased, so that in time they became an important and influential group in English life.

Feudalism was drawing its last weak gasps of life. The nobles **End of the feudal period** had lost power and prestige through the suicidal Wars of the Roses. The struggle for power now lay among the Church, the King and the middle classes. The following chapters will show how the King and the middle classes joined forces to destroy the power of the Church . . . leaving Parliament and the King to fight it out in the seventeenth century.

22

CHANGING WAYS OF WAR AND LIFE

The latter part of the feudal period saw changes in English customs and traditions. Many factors varying from the introduction of gunpowder to the breakdown of serfdom caused these changes.

The Wars of the Roses which came to an end in 1485 illustrated the lawlessness then existing among the nobles of England. Of the nine kings who sat on the throne after Edward I, four were murdered and one died in battle. The old chivalry of crusading days had disappeared leaving little but cold-blooded treachery and merciless vengeance.

The fighting equipment of the nobles had altered since the days **New arms and armour** of Richard the Lion Heart. At the time of the Crusades knights wore *mail armour* consisting of tunics and leggings covered with rings or small plates of metal. Knights dressed in mail carried lances, shields and swords.

With the coming of the longbow, mail armour was no longer able to withstand the striking force of arrows. In consequence there gradually developed the use of heavy *plate armour* which provided much

123

greater protection. Plate armour enclosed most of the warrior's body in solid sections of steel. This type of armour had one disadvantage, but it was a serious one. Knights thrown from their horses during battle were almost helpless because of the weight of their metal suits. Heavy armour, too, was so expensive that only the most wealthy warriors could afford to have it made.

Just as the longbow spelled the doom of mail armour, so did gunpowder spell the eventual doom of plate armour. By the time of the Wars of the Roses hand guns were in use, but they were of very crude construction. They were cumbersome in size and awkward to handle. Powder and balls had to be poured into the muzzle, and firing was accomplished by lighting with a "match." Actually this type of firearm did not become really effective in battle until it was improved in later years.

Cannon had been used in England even before hand guns, ever since the year 1327 when Edward II used them to a limited extent against the Scots. They were difficult to move and even more difficult to aim. The early cannon were little more than heavy metal tubes mounted on thick timbers of woods. They were of little use in swift moving battles, but could be used effectively in sieges.

Edwardian castles

The early Norman castle had consisted of a keep surrounded by walls, drawbridge, portcullis and moat. A castle of this kind was a cramped, cold, dark structure which offered little in the way of com-

The cut-away drawing shown on the opposite page illustrates a castle gatehouse of the type constructed during the second half of the thirteenth century. Approaches to the gatehouse were commanded from arrow-loops placed in the walls. Notice the moat, the drawbridge and the deep pit. Working on a pivot, the drawbridge could be raised at night or in any time of danger. Above the drawbridge was an overhanging structure which had openings in its floor. Through these flaming tar, boiling water, hot oil or stones could be dropped on attackers. The pit also was overlooked by similar openings. The soldier in the illustration is pouring hot water through one of these openings. (1) This shows a section of curtain wall and a small tower. Such towers began to appear in the early part of the twelfth century. Notice the overhanging parapet from which the defenders could guard the wall and watch for signs of under-mining. In the process of undermining, the attackers dug a tunnel below the castle walls. The walls and roof of the tunnel were strengthened with heavy wooden timbers. When finished, the tunnel was partly filled with straw which was set afire. As the great timbers burned away, the tunnel caved in and a portion of the castle wall collapsed. In (2) there are openings, or crenellations in the castle parapet. These openings were sometimes covered with wooden shutters which could be removed when necessary. In (3) is seen an arrow-hoop through which arrows were shot. Behind the narrow slot the opening in the wall widened at a sharp angle so that archers could shoot in different directions. Early arrow-loops were simple vertical slots, but later ones included some form of horizontal opening to accommodate the cross-bow.

V. Muilo

fort. By the time of Edward I the English had begun to build what is now called the Edwardian castle. It was a more spacious building whose wall inclosed a separate house for the lord, and sometimes a church and other buildings. It was still a fortress, but much airier and more comfortable than formerly. Only a king or a very wealthy noble could afford to build and maintain such an establishment.

The increasing use of cannon in sieges, eventually rendered the castle useless as a means of defence. There was little use in defending a castle whose walls could be battered down by cannon balls. By the beginning of the Tudor period, then, the castle was fast losing its former place as a military stronghold. Wealthy noblemen were building palaces without thick walls and protecting moats.

At a time when nobles were behaving in such a lawless manner, others of lesser rank copied their vicious actions. Robbers and outlaws preyed on the weak and the defenceless. Farmers were forced to keep fierce dogs to protect their homes. Women and children were kidnapped, and murder by "lynching" took place.

The keeping of law and order was extremely difficult under such circumstances. By Norman law and custom, men were all expected to be members of a *tithing*—a group of ten men who were responsible

The first Norman castles were of wood, but around the year 1100 they began to be built of stone. (1) A stone keep containing the "great hall" of a castle. (2) By the end of the twelfth century round towers had replaced square towers because it was believed the former provided a stronger defence. Towers and gate-houses became so important in castle construction that they eventually replaced the central keep. (3) During the latter half of the thirteenth century new castles had no keep and were built in a rectangular fashion. This castle is completely surrounded by an artificial moat. Some changes in the structure of the English castle were influenced by what crusaders saw in the countries of the Mediterranean. Drawings shown here, of course, do not indicate all the types of castles which appeared in England, for castles displayed a variety in shape, size and design. Some were actually combinations of the types illustrated. Castle styles changed continuously to take advantage of new discoveries in defence. Assaults on castles were assisted by a number of effective devices. In addition to undermining which has been mentioned, attackers used battering rams, mantelets and siege towers. (4) A battering ram working under cover of a shelter called a "cat." This was wheeled into position beside the castle wall, and the battering began. The top of the "cat" was protected with wet hides to guard against hot materials poured from the parapets. (5) Illustrates a portable barrier from behind which archers could shoot in comparative safety. (6) The siege tower such as the one shown was moved close to the castle. Attackers climbed stairs inside and rushed across a short drawbridge to the top of the castle wall. Such siege towers were protected by wet hides. Also shown in the same illustration is a scaling ladder fitted with hooks to grip the top of castle walls.

Norman architecture, massive and solid in appearance, made use of rounded arches which were Roman in influence. Shown here is a portion of the interior of a Norman cathedral. Norman churches were often covered inside and out with a smooth coat of white plaster. Interiors were decorated with brightly-coloured mural paintings. Any carvings used in church design were created with the axe as a carving tool.

for each others' conduct. They were required to report any misdeeds done by fellow members of the tithing.

When a crime was discovered and the alarm raised, all men in the vicinity were required to join in the "hue and cry" after the criminal. But, because crimes usually took place at night, the culprits often disappeared in the darkness and were never caught.

Trial by jury which had begun in the reign of Henry II began to change its form. In the beginning the jurors were really witnesses who testified for, or against, the accused person. Later, jurors ceased to be witnesses, and became a body which heard evidence and gave a verdict. In this way our modern form of jury came into being.

Trial by jury was not possible unless the accused person gave his consent to the procedure. He was asked, "How will you be tried?" If he replied, "By God and my country," the trial began. If, however, he refused to make this answer, he was tortured until he did so. Numbers of men actually suffered death by torture rather than agree to trial by jury. Such men preferred death by this means rather than hanging through a jury's verdict. Thus they remained unconvicted in court, and their property passed on to their families instead of going to the government.

As feudalism declined, the English towns flourished, many of **Rise of the towns** them becoming centres of manufacturing. Cloth woven from English wool became one of the nation's most important products. With an ample supply of coal and iron in the country, the making of metal goods increased. Ship building rose as a vigorous industry. By Norman

128

Early English architecture is of the Gothic group. The style is much lighter and more delicate than Norman. Instead of single massive pillars, there are clusters of smaller pillars, frequently made from English black marble. High narrow pointed arches take the place of rounded Norman arches. Delicate carvings and stained glass windows add to the beauty of the design.

custom the lords had exercised the right to control towns which grew up on their estates, but in time this authority passed away. Gradually the towns gained self-government by purchasing these rights or through charters granted by the king. Citizens took turns as policemen, patrolling the streets at night. Cattle were pastured on common fields which belonged to the town.

Among the organizations within the towns were the *guilds*. These societies were formed by groups of merchants or artisans with the purpose of assisting one another and of protecting their own interests. Members of the guilds were so jealous of their rights that it was often difficult for outsiders to gain membership. Many of the guilds became wealthy, powerful organizations which built expensive guild halls in the towns. It is true that the guilds were sometimes selfish and dictatorial in their actions, but on the whole they encouraged good workmanship and fine quality in the manufacture of products. Some of the old guilds have survived to the present day.

The increasing wealth of the middle class could be seen in the new buildings which appeared in the towns. A new style of architecture known as *perpendicular Gothic* made its appearance. This style, found chiefly in churches, used straight lines in large window openings instead of the elaborate decorations used in *Early English Gothic*. The high vaulted stone roofs of the new churches were exquisite in their delicate patterns. King's College Chapel of Cambridge University is an excellent example of perpendicular Gothic.

Other indications of an improved English civilization are revealed **Music and** in the activity being displayed in music and education. Music was so **education**

129

well advanced in England during the fifteenth century that the nation led Europe in this field. Wealthy men interested in education encouraged the establishment of private schools. Among the most noted of these was Eton College founded by King Henry VI in 1440 before the Wars of the Roses.

SUMMARY—SECTION III

In 1381 during the reign of Richard II the peasants of southeastern England rose in revolt over the new poll tax which was levied on persons over twelve years of age. The revolt was crushed with little gain for the lower classes.

John Wycliffe led a protest against the worldly ways of the Church in England. His "poor priests" preached in English to the people and encouraged the reading of the Bible among the masses. Followers of Wycliffe and his teachings came to be known as Lollards, meaning "heretics." Eventually Wycliffe was expelled from Oxford University because he had aroused the resentment of the Church. Gradually the government began to take action to stamp out the Lollards of England.

Henry of Lancaster took the English throne from Richard II in 1399, thus himself becoming Henry IV. His son, Henry V, in 1415 renewed the Hundred Years' War against France. Under Henry VI the war continued. The French led by Joan of Arc gained a new fighting spirit which eventually led to important victories for France. The Dauphin was placed on the French throne. In 1453 the long war came to a close with England losing all her French possessions except Calais.

Between the years 1455 and 1485 the Wars of the Roses were fought between the Lancastrians and the Yorkists. This was a struggle for the throne between two rival groups of barons, and did not affect the English people as a whole. After thirty years of wasteful, cruel conflict the Lancastrians were victorious and Henry Tudor (Henry VII) was on the throne. Henry married Princess Elizabeth of the House of York, thus founding the famous Tudor line of English monarchs.

The Wars of the Roses so weakened the nobility of the nation that it ceased to be a powerful force within the country. From then on the struggle for power was to be among the King, the Church and the middle class of people.

The Norman feudal system which had been established in the eleventh century under William the Conqueror fell into decline and eventually broke down entirely. The Black Death, the Wars of the Roses, the breakdown of serfdom, the rise of the English towns and the introduction of gunpowder all had a part in reducing the power of the nobles and ending feudalism.

During the fourteenth century England was beginning to be an important manufacturing and trading nation. A new style of architecture called perpendicular Gothic made its appearance. Englishmen were leading Europe in music and wealthy men were promoting the establishment of private schools.

TIME-CHART

1376-1485

1376	DEATH OF THE BLACK PRINCE
1377-1399	RICHARD II
1381	PEASANTS' REVOLT—WAT TYLER
1399	HENRY OF LANCASTER DEFEATS RICHARD II
1399-1413	HENRY IV

The Mongol Empire is shrinking **1400**

1401	PARLIAMENT PASSES AN ACT TO STAMP OUT THE LOLLARDS
1403	BATTLE OF SHREWSBURY—HOTSPUR KILLED
1413-1422	HENRY V
1414	RENEWAL OF THE HUNDRED YEARS' WAR

Prince Henry of Portugal begins to send ships down west coast of Africa **1415** BATTLE OF AGINCOURT—VICTORY AGAINST FRENCH

1422-1461	HENRY VI
1429	JOAN OF ARC AT ORLEANS
1431	BURNING OF JOAN OF ARC

The Turks capture Constantinople **1453** END OF THE HUNDRED YEARS' WAR

1455-1485	WARS OF THE ROSES
1461-1483	EDWARD IV
1483	EDWARD V
1483-1485	RICHARD III
1485	BATTLE OF BOSWORTH—HENRY TUDOR DEFEATS RICHARD III—END OF THE WARS OF THE ROSES—BEGINNING OF THE TUDOR LINE OF KINGS

IV. THE RISING POWER OF MONARCHY

Restless times after the Wars of the Roses • Strong monarchy under Henry VII • The barons brought under control by the Court of the Star Chamber • A time of peace, trade and prosperity • Effects of the Renaissance • Henry VIII quarrels with the Church • Dissolution of the monasteries • Church of England as the established Church • Queen Mary restores the Catholic Church • Loss of Calais to the French • Elizabeth I comes to the throne • Church of England re-established • Mary Queen of Scots plots against Elizabeth • Execution of Mary • Exploration in America • Battle against the Invincible Armada • Supremacy of crown over barons and churchmen

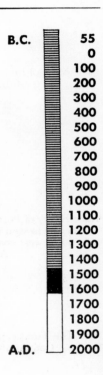

B.C.

55
0
100
200
300
400
500
600
700
800
900
1000
1100
1200
1300
1400
1500
1600
1700
1800
1900
2000

A.D.

23

HENRY VII AND STRONG MONARCHY

The five Tudor monarchs, beginning with Henry VII, reigned for more than one hundred years . . . an exciting century of progress, warfare, exploration, discovery, trade and settlement. It was during this time that European seamen sailed around Africa to India and pushed across the Atlantic to America. It was an age in which nations struggled for land and power in a new world of great opportunity.

Henry VII was a hard-working, able and self-disciplined man, devoted to the duties of his royal position. One of his most useful talents was the wise selection of good men for posts in government, and in this selection he did not always choose persons of noble birth.

An alarming amount of lawlessness had crept into English life during the turmoil caused by the Black Death and the Wars of the Roses. A Venetian envoy described conditions in these words:

There is no country in the world where there are so many thieves and robbers as in England; insomuch that few venture to go alone in the country in the middle of the day, and fewer still in the towns at night, and least of all in London.

From the beginning of his reign, 1485, Henry VII determined that peace and law should be restored throughout the country. Several armed rebellions against the King were crushed, and the leaders put to death. It is revealing to notice, however, that such men were brought to trial and condemned in accordance with law. Rebels were not executed hastily as they had been during the Wars of the Roses.

As a further step in the promotion of peaceful conditions, Henry VII took measures to control the noble families already weakened by losses during the war. In 1487 the *Court of the Star Chamber,* so named because of the decoration of the room in which it met, was established to deal with noblemen who persisted in gathering armed forces, noblemen who interfered with justice, and noblemen who took part in riots or other unlawful meetings. So powerful was this court that it had a peaceful effect upon the nation. The days were gone when restless barons could take the law into their own hands.

Court of the Star Chamber

133

The Royal treasury

Such strict control of the barons placed King Henry VII in a high position, thus developing a kind of government which may be called strong monarchy. While looking after the interests of the nation the King certainly did not neglect his own welfare. He arranged matters carefully so that the royal treasury had ample funds, kept a close watch on government expenses and suggested to wealthy nobles that gifts were always acceptable. Wisely, too, he avoided fighting foreign wars because they were too expensive.

Through many sources of income, Henry VII became independent in a financial way, so that he did not have to call Parliament to raise taxes. The result was Parliament's power was reduced as the King's authority grew. Members of Parliament interfered very little with the firm rule of the first Tudor King because strong government was popular after the lawless days of the Wars of the Roses.

Trade

Interested in strengthening the nation's prosperity, Henry VII promoted trade with other countries by making treaties and by encouraging merchants to sell their goods abroad. An old organization of traders known as the *Merchant Adventurers* was granted a seal, a coat of arms, and a new charter giving special privileges to the association.

Vital changes were taking place in the ancient trade which for centuries had existed between the Orient and Europe. Eastern traders had long carried goods by caravan and ship to the Mediterranean land, and from there these had been taken by Italian merchants to the countries of western Europe. So long as the Mongols controlled the overland trade routes, trade was constant, peaceful and prosperous. But when the Turks captured lands about the eastern Mediterranean, trade slowed to a mere trickle.

With the closing of the eastern trade, Europeans looked for new routes to the Orient, new sea lanes which could not be blocked by the stubborn Turks. During the gigantic search which followed, the Portuguese seaman, Diaz rounded the Cape of Good Hope; Columbus stumbled upon America; Vasco da Gama sailed from Portugal around Africa and on to India.

John Cabot, 1496

Aroused to action by these exciting explorations, King Henry VII gave permission for an English expedition under John Cabot, an Italian adventurer, to sail westward across the Atlantic. The two voyages made by the navigator in 1496 and 1497 were disappointing, for Cabot neither reached the Orient nor returned with rich cargoes of goods. Furs and fish from what is now eastern Canada were not of interest to the sponsors of the expedition. In spite of the first dis-

134

appointment, Englishmen gained a lasting interest in the New World, an interest which led to more long voyages and further discoveries. Important events were to follow.

The age of Henry VII saw new and striking developments in learning which were caused in part by events taking place in Italy. During the fourteenth and fifteenth centuries a movement called the *Renaissance,* meaning "re-birth," was taking place in the old land of the Romans. The Renaissance was more than a study of the ancient civilization; it was an active period in which books were written, pictures painted, statues carved, buildings erected and schools established. So much interest was aroused by the work and study of the Italians that the Renaissance movement spread to other countries of Europe. *The Renaissance*

Young Englishmen who studied in Italy returned home bubbling over with ideas, and anxious to spread the new gospel of learning. Some of them found their way to Oxford University where they remained to teach Latin, Greek, medicine, philosophy, religion and other subjects. Their influence upon English students increased as the years went by, so that the "new learning" had its effects upon the nation.

Many of the great scholars were more than students and teachers: they were reformers who were anxious to have changes made in the English way of life. One such scholar, Thomas More, wrote a book called *Utopia* in which he described many of the unsatisfactory conditions existing then in Europe, and then he went on to tell the story of a make-believe country in which all evils had been removed. More's book caused great interest, making men think seriously of improvements which might be made in governments and in social conditions. Even today we use the word "Utopian" when we wish to describe a situation which is nearly perfect.

One of the great events of the Renaissance was the development of printing which had its European origin in Germany. Printing had been invented centuries before in China, but it was the people of Europe who brought the process to a high level of perfection. An Englishman, William Caxton, who learned to print in Holland, brought the first press to England, in 1476, just nine years before Henry VII came to the throne. Near Westminster Abbey he set up shop in a house with the sign of the "Red Pale." The first book to come off Caxton's press was *Dictes or Sayings of the Philosophers,* which had been translated from the French. During the first three years of *Development of printing*

John Cabot sights the coast of Newfoundland. This picture gives us a good idea of the vessels common in the fifteenth century. They were known as round ships, having generous curves at the stern and mid-ship sections. The square mainsail is very big, probably taking in twice the area of all the other sails put together. Below-deck quarters for the crew are crude, cramped and very uncomfortable.

business, Caxton published no fewer than thirty books, a surprising number for that time. Among the most important of these was Chaucer's *Canterbury Tales*—748 pages in length.

William Caxton believed in advertising, for he printed letters and display bills to promote the sale of his books. One such advertisement read as follows:

If it plese ony man spirituel or temporel to bye ony pyes of two and three commemoracions of Salisburi use enpryntid after the forme of the present lettre, whiche ben wel and truly correct, late hym come to West-monester in to the almonesrye at the reed pale and he shal have them good chepe.

Henry VII and Strong Monarchy

It is difficult for us today to appreciate how wonderful, how important the first printed books were to the people of the time. No longer was it necessary to copy books laboriously by hand, for now they could be turned out quickly in great numbers. Before the arrival of printing it is thought that there were no more than 100,000 written copies of books in all Europe. Fifty years later there were at least 9,000,000 printed books. The growing quantity of books was most helpful to schools and universities, and encouraged the learning of reading among the common people.

After Caxton had established his printing shop, other printing establishments appeared in England, so that soon they were competing with each other for business. Such competition resulted in the improvement of printing quality and led to the introduction of illustrations to make books even more attractive.

Although the English people never learned to love King Henry VII, they appreciated some of the things he accomplished during his Death of Henry VII, 1509

This is the first print shop operated by William Caxton. The man at the right is setting type from a type case, and in the centre another man is turning the handle on a printing press. The process was slow because each sheet of paper had to be printed singly by hand. Presses of this kind were used until the nineteenth century with little improvement.

reign. He established peace and order, brought the barons under control, avoided war, encouraged trade, built up the Royal Navy and placed the government on a sound financial basis. It is true that he was a dictator who often ignored the wishes of Parliament, but he did give England an opportunity to grow, to prosper and to become important in an international sense.

When Henry VII died in 1509, he left to his son Henry VIII a vigorous kingdom and a full treasury.

24

HENRY VIII VERSUS THE CHURCH

Henry VIII came to the throne in 1509, at a time when an English monarch no longer needed to fear the power of the barons, but the Church still remained as a wealthy and vital force in national life. The new reign was to see a long and bitter struggle between the King and officials of the Church.

Henry VIII had not expected to be King of England, because his older brother Arthur, married to a Spanish princess, was heir to the throne. But when Arthur died, Henry's right to the throne was clearly established.

The handsome young King, eighteen years old, was friendly, frank and good natured . . . qualities which made him popular with the English people. Here is the way the Venetian ambassador described Henry VIII in 1519:

Henry VIII, 1509

". . . the handsomest potentate I ever set eyes upon; above the usual height, with an extremely fine calf to his leg, his complexion very fair and light, with auburn hair . . . and a round face so very beautiful that it would become a pretty woman, his throat being rather long and thick."

Henry had been well educated and trained for a life in the Church, so he was well versed in Latin, French, Italian, music and religion. He wrote poetry and composed music. In addition to being a clever scholar he was an athlete of unusual skill, interested in riding, hunting, fencing, jousting and the game of tennis. Such were his vigour and energy that on long hunting trips he could wear out eight or ten horses before the sport was over. It was not surprising that the big, red-headed monarch was given the nickname of "Bluff King Hal."

Henry VIII versus the Church

A few weeks after he became King, Henry VIII married his brother Arthur's widow, Princess Catherine of Aragon. This appeared to be a wise union, for it insured peace with Spain, but Henry was not merely making a convenient marriage; he professed to be in love with the young lady.

Henry VIII, like his father, was determined to rule the country himself with little interference from the nobles, Parliament or anyone else. His advisers were able men most of whom came from among the common people of the nation. One of these, Thomas Wolsey, who had served under Henry's father, became the leading official of government during the new reign. Wolsey, a clergyman and a graduate of Oxford, gradually rose to such high positions as Archbishop of York, Cardinal, representative of the Pope in England and Lord Chancellor of the Kingdom. Because he received a large income from various estates, church properties and offices, he became a wealthy man. His haughty manner and his dictatorial ways, however, made Wolsey an unpopular man with other officials of the government. They were jealous of a man who had a thousand servants and palaces better than those of the King.

Henry was not as careful in avoiding foreign wars as his father had been, a fact which cost him much money and considerable trouble. With Wolsey's approval in 1512 he joined Spain in a minor war against France. This expensive adventure brought neither fame nor conquest to England.

In the meantime the Scots, hoping to lend a helpful hand to France, invaded England with an army of 50,000 men. The invaders and the English clashed in 1513 at the Battle of Flodden Field, a hard-fought engagement in which many lost their lives. This was the last great victory of the English longbow.

During the first fourteen years of Henry's reign, Wolsey was the supreme official under the King. During the course of England's history probably no other Lord Chancellor had held so much power. Like the King, he believed in a strong monarchy comparatively free from control by the people. Parliament was called into session only at rare intervals. The Court

Soldiers equipped with matchlocks took a long time to prepare their weapons for firing, during which time they were virtually unarmed. Pikemen accompanied the gunners into battle to protect them while the guns were being reloaded. The long spear, or pike, probably was developed from the lance used by knights. Some of the pikes were twenty-two feet in length.

Here is a dockside scene in Tudor England. In the background can be seen a small part of the town whose timbered buildings and pointed wooden gables were so much a part of the Tudor scene. At the right is the *Great Harry*, much bigger than any other ship of her day. Her high sides covered with Gothic

of the Star Chamber which had been founded by Henry's father, continued its operations, and no one was strong enough to challenge its verdicts.

Local government Henry VIII and Wolsey did not entirely ignore the will and the welfare of the people, for they realized that a partnership between the government and the citizens was necessary in the growth of a prosperous nation. Local government in the towns and rural areas was carried out largely by the citizens themselves, while local unpaid officials called Justices of the Peace held certain powers and tried minor cases in court.

In order to strengthen the defences of the nation Henry VIII and

140

panels and windows are brilliantly painted and gilded. Long forked pennants fly from mastheads and yard arms. The *Great Harry* is well armed with cannons and other weapons. A ship of 1500 tons, the *Great Harry* carried a company of 907 men. It is not surprising that Henry VIII enjoyed entertaining guests on board the big vessel.

Wolsey expanded the Royal Navy until it was able to control the waters **Defence** about the island. The largest and most powerfully armed warship of the time, the *Great Harry,* was a proud possession of the growing fleet.

It was necessary that Henry VIII be kept informed of events taking place on the continent of Europe, so Wolsey organized a group of agents and messengers who reported to the English government. Their despatches gave information on the size of armies, military actions, revolts, amount of taxes, educational developments, appointment of officials and other matters related to the affairs of European countries.

141

The close friendship which existed between Henry VIII and Wolsey gradually cooled as disagreements arose between them. One of the first serious disputes came about over Henry's desire to renew the war with France. By this time the King was in financial difficulties, for he was not as careful in the handling of royal funds as his father had been. To Henry's annoyance Wolsey was not successful in securing enough money from Parliament to send a large force against France. The King was even more annoyed when he discovered that Wolsey was spending large sums on the building of a religious college at Oxford University. In anger he said to the Chancellor: "It is strange that you have found so much money to spend on your college, and yet you could not find enough to finish my war!"

Henry VIII seeks divorce

In the beginning, Henry's marriage to Catherine of Aragon was a happy one, but as time went by all the children born to the Queen died except for a little girl. Disappointed, Henry longed for a strong son who would succeed him to the throne. Deciding that he should get rid of Catherine and marry again, Henry VIII searched about for some excuse for divorce. He had not far to look, for by religious law, a man could not marry his brother's wife. The fact that Henry had married his brother's widow had never bothered him before, but now he brought forward this fact as a good reason for dissolving his marriage with Catherine. At this time, too, he fell in love with Anne Boleyn, a woman of twenty-four, who while not beautiful was very witty and charming. In a letter written to Anne in 1527 Henry admitted that he had "been now above one whole year stricken with the dart of love." Here was another good reason the King decided for breaking his royal union with the Queen.

Henry's appeal to the Church for a divorce *annulment* caused endless discussions and conferences among churchmen which lasted for a considerable period of time. Although Wolsey and the English churchmen were ready to grant Henry VIII his demands, the Pope would not give a decision in the case. Believing that Wolsey had not done all he could to assist in the matter, Henry removed his old friend from office and heartlessly seized his property. Retiring sadly to religious duties, Cardinal Wolsey died within the following year.

Submission of the Clergy 1532

Still determined to secure the divorce, Henry sent more demands to the Pope, and drew a tighter control over Church affairs in England. In a serious effort to crush opposition, he forced English churchmen to agree that he, instead of the Pope, was head of the Church within the nation, and that no Church laws might be passed without his consent.

142

Henry VIII versus the Church

This course of action in 1532 came to be known as the *submission of the clergy*. Even after this bold action, the Pope remained silent concerning Henry's desire for divorce.

Henry's struggle against the Church was aided to a certain extent by the attitude of Parliament itself. During this period the House of Lords was composed of nobles, bishops and abbots, many of whom owed their positions either to the King or his father. The House of Commons was made up of merchants, lawyers and country squires who also had received benefits from the royal house and on the whole, were loyal to Henry VIII, having little interest in the Church or Church affairs. Parliament, therefore, was quite content to pass any laws regarding religious matters which Henry desired.

The ancient rights of the Church were being challenged not only by the King, but by the English people as well. Englishmen were growing impatient with the astonishing power and authority exerted by wealthy churchmen. People were very much aware that churchmen received salaries from parishes in which they did no work, that large sums of English money were being sent to Rome, that the Church charged high fees for certain services, and that the Church demanded gifts from the estates of people who died. The barons had lost their former influence in English life, so why, the people asked, should the Church continue to be a favoured organization? The growing distrust and opposition to the Church was not confined to England alone, for a similar movement had already begun in other countries of Europe.

Scattered throughout England were hundreds of monasteries, some of which were very old and some comparatively new. Some were wealthy and some poor. Some were very small and some were enormous. The monasteries had played a vital part in the religious and educational life of the nation, but by Henry's time they were falling into a condition of decay.

Learning and scholarship were no longer confined to the monasteries, for numbers of bright, young men were attending universities to train as doctors, lawyers, professors and writers. As a result, the monasteries were neither doing the important work they once had done, nor were they enjoying the high respect of the English people.

In these Church properties, Henry VIII saw a chance to strike at the Church and at the same time refill the royal treasury. He persuaded Parliament to pass, in 1536, a law which did away with 300 small monasteries, and gave the land and buildings to the government.

Dissolution of the monasteries, 1536

143

Henry VIII closed the small monasteries and later the larger ones. He confiscated the silver plate and the jewels of the altars. Bells and lead from the roofs were melted down for the metal. Buildings were taken apart and sold as scrap. Because of this merciless action, thousands of monks lost their homes and were set adrift. A few of the largest monasteries and abbeys such as Westminster Abbey became churches.

During the next few years the remaining monasteries were treated in the same manner.

Henry was delighted with the results, for the Church gold, silver, jewels and other valuables poured into the royal treasury. Many of the monasteries were torn down so that lead, glass, stone, metal, doors, windows could be sold as building materials. The land on which the buildings stood was put up for sale, or given to favourites of the King. Monks and nuns living in the monasteries were sent to stay with friends, were given pensions, or were granted other work within the Church. The unfortunate abbots who had been in charge of the monasteries were no longer permitted to sit in the House of Lords. King Henry VIII could have carried out this sweeping change in a more merciful manner. Needless heartbreak, suffering, despair and hardship were caused by the harsh and hurried dissolution of the English monasteries.

Many people undoubtedly sympathized with Henry when he destroyed the monasteries, but they were shocked when he ordered the execution of two noted clergymen, Sir Thomas More and the Bishop of Rochester. These two determined men, both former friends of Henry, refused to recognize him as the supreme head of the Church in England. Accordingly, they were brought to trial on charges of treason, condemned and beheaded. The Pope promptly excommunicated Henry VIII, declaring that he no longer was monarch of England.

Excommunication of Henry VIII

King Henry ignored the order of excommunication. The ancient links which bound the Catholic Church of England to the Pope in Rome were now broken, so that the Church on the island stood by itself under the control of the King. Henry's quarrel with the Pope made it much simpler for new religious ideas to gain a foothold in England. Such ideas were part of a religious movement in Western Europe which is known as the *Reformation*. The movement began as a desire to make certain changes in the life and organization of the Church, but it ended in the rise of various new *Protestant* or *Reformed* churches. Those who joined the new faiths held very different views from those held by the churchmen of the time. Protestants believed that man's responsibility was to God alone and not to the Church. They opposed the frequent use of sacraments and elaborate ceremonies within the Church. They believed that everyone should have the right to read the Bible, and interpret it as he wished.

Reformation

While it is true that Henry had been eager to control religious affairs and to have himself as head of the Church, he had no desire to see Protestantism in his kingdom. But even the King and Parliament could not keep the new faiths from growing and spreading among the people. The Protestant teachings of Martin Luther and others in

Beginning of the religious struggle

Helmet of the early sixteenth century. In this period protection afforded by the helmet was as complete as possible. On either side two hinged pieces protect the cheeks and over these falls the visor. In making a helmet of this type, known as the *armet*, the problem was to permit the wearer to see and breathe without weakening his defence.

Germany were brought into the country by travellers returning from Europe and by pamphlets and books printed on the continent. Scholars at the universities, merchants, tradesmen, farmers and some priests were eagerly accepting the new religious ideas. Men close to Henry VIII and some who held high offices in the Church were turning toward Protestantism. Severe laws were passed by Parliament and King to stamp out religious rebels; some men were placed in prison; some were driven from the country and some were burned at the stake. Three Carthusian priors were used as frightful example to other churchmen, being "disembowelled alive in their canonical habits." This was the beginning of a period of sad religious struggle which was to last long after the reign of Henry VIII.

Anne Boleyn

After five years' waiting for a divorce, Henry VIII finally took the law into his own hands, and married Anne Boleyn. To the King's satisfaction, a court of English churchmen then declared that the new marriage was legal, since Henry had never been wedded lawfully to Catherine of Aragon. Even with a divorce and a charming new wife, Henry VIII was not happy, soon growing tired of his second Queen. To them was born a baby girl with red hair, who later was to become Queen Elizabeth I of England. The birth brought little but anger and disappointment to Henry, because he still wished for a son to succeed him to the nation's throne.

Anne Boleyn's end was a sad and brutal affair which pointed up Henry's change toward heartless brutality. Charging Anne with treason, the King had her brought before a court where she was condemned to death by burning or beheading as the King wished. With amazing courage the Queen declared that she preferred to die by beheading and with a sword rather than an axe. Henry VIII granted this request, and the execution was delayed until a suitable headsman was brought from the continent.

On the day of the execution Queen Anne Boleyn, in a grey gown, ascended a low platform and looked calmly at the gathered people. "Pray for the King," she said, "for he is a good man, and has treated me as well as could be. I do not accuse anyone of causing my death, neither the judges nor anyone else, for I am condemned by the law of the land and die willingly."

Jane Seymour

Just ten days after the execution, Henry VIII was married to an English lady of nobility, Jane Seymour, a quiet woman who became a gentle and gracious Queen. The marriage unfortunately lasted only a year and a half, ending with Jane Seymour's death. Her gift to King

146

Henry VIII versus the Church

Henry and the kingdom was a son, who later was to reach the throne as Edward VI. In genuine sorrow Henry VIII mourned the Queen's passing.

Henry actually married three more times after Queen Jane's untimely death. His fourth Queen was a German Protestant, Princess Anne of Cleves, a plain woman whom Henry disliked. The marriage was quickly dissolved, and Thomas Cromwell, who had arranged the marriage, was executed. **Anne of Cleves**

Henry's next wife, Catherine Howard, was a beautiful and lively woman thirty years younger than the King. Foolishly, Catherine became involved in a love affair with a cousin, and as a result Henry had her beheaded. **Catherine Howard** *executed.*

Catherine Parr, Henry's last wife, was a brave person, for it had already been shown that being Queen of England was an extremely dangerous calling. She proved, however, to be a remarkable and kindly woman who managed Henry VIII with patience and skill. **Catherine Parr**

As the King grew older, he gained tremendously in weight and suffered continuously from an ulcerated leg, a condition which finally killed him. His temper was terrible. He grew suspicious of those about him, fearing that his power and his throne were in danger. The old hostility between England and Scotland broke again into warfare as battles were fought along the border. In a bloody engagement at Solway Moss, 1542, the Scots were defeated, losing 10,000 men. Heartbroken by this disaster, King James V of Scotland died leaving his throne to his infant daughter, Mary Queen of Scots. This daughter in later years was to have a fateful part in English history. **Defeat of the Scots, 1542**

Trouble with France, too, flared and for a time it appeared that both the Scots and the French might invade England. A peace treaty with France, however, ended the danger, saving England from another dreary war.

King Henry's health failed rapidly, so that eventually he was unable to move about the kingdom. In January, 1547, he passed away quietly in his own huge bed. **Death of Henry VIII, 1547**

The reign of Henry VIII was marred by executions, tortures, persecutions and the destruction of the monasteries, but there were other factors which worked for the good of England. Law and order were preserved, Parliament continued to operate, the Royal Navy was strengthened and the English Bible was being read. In spite of his serious faults, hot-tempered, boisterous Henry VIII remained as a hero to many of his subjects.

25

A CHANGING RESTLESS ENGLAND

Henry VIII left one son, Edward, and two daughters, Mary and Elizabeth. All three were to sit on England's throne, but it was Edward who first succeeded his famous father in 1547. Because King Edward VI was just a boy, royal authority was placed in the hands of a Council led by the King's uncle, the Duke of Somerset.

Edward VI, 1547

The struggle between Protestantism and the old Church was still causing an unhappy division among the English people. The Duke of Somerset, acting as Protector, encouraged a number of religious reforms. A prayer book in the English language was prepared by Archbishop Cranmer and others, and was approved by Parliament in 1549. Two years later the book was revised, and has been used with few changes by the Church of England since that time.

The nation was gradually shifting from Catholicism to the new faiths of the Reformation, as changes were made in religious ceremonies and customs. Crucifixes and images of saints were removed from churches and destroyed; religious pictures on church walls were plastered over; stained glass windows were taken down. Clergymen gave up their coloured robes, and began to marry. By 1552 the Reformation of the Church in England was almost complete, but the government was still dissatisfied with conditions as they were. Unwisely, it was decided to force all the people into the new faith whether they believed **Act of Conformity, 1552** in it or not. By the Act of Conformity the Church of England became the recognized religion, the *only* religion of the realm. This was an unfortunate decision, for a large number of the people still clung to the Catholic faith, hoping for a return to the old ways of their religion. It was not recognized at the time that without free choice of religion there could be no true freedom for the people, no true contentment for the nation.

Enclosures

There were other matters, too, which were troubling the people of the rural districts. For centuries England had been a nation of little farms cultivated by freemen and serfs, but in Tudor times a new type of farmer was making his appearance. He was a man who bought or rented a large tract of land for the purpose of raising sheep. Enclosing his land with hedges, he proceeded to manage his flocks with the help

148

An arquebusier of the Duke of Somerset's army. He is in the act of firing his arquebus, or matchlock, one of the earliest hand-held firearms invented by the Spanish. When the trigger was pulled, a burning wick, or matchcord, was plunged into a pan of priming powder. As this ignited, it set off the gunpowder lying within the barrel of the weapons. It was an awkward firearm and very slow in operation, for the powder had to be measured carefully, and the gun cleaned after each shot. Notice that the gun is held against the chest instead of against the shoulder as was the practice in later periods.

of a few hired men. The rise of these large sheep farms, of course, put many small farmers off the land which they had worked in years gone by. So many of the sheep farms, or enclosures, were formed that large numbers of workers became unemployed. The new sheep men were growing wealthy and wool was produced in quantity, but too many Englishmen were being turned into beggars and paupers.

As Protector, the Duke of Somerset tried to enforce laws against the increase of the sheep farms, but he was powerless to make reforms, for the landowners were solidly against him. In the end, Somerset was driven from authority by all who were dissatisfied with his rule, or jealous of his power. He was confined to the Tower of London and later executed.

With the fall of Somerset, the Duke of Northumberland became the strong man of England, ruling in the name of the royal house. By this time, however, the boy-king, Edward, was dying of tuberculosis. This situation raised the question of who next should sit on the throne. It was well known that Henry VIII had desired to have Princess Mary, daughter of Henry's first wife, Catherine of Aragon, succeed Edward. The Duke of Northumberland had no desire for this. He realized that his own power would disappear and that Mary would restore the old Church to its place. Perhaps he feared that his life would be in danger at the hands of Mary who was half Spaniard.

In a shrewd and ruthless plot against Mary, the Duke of Northumberland chose Lady Jane Grey, a niece of Henry VIII, to be next Queen of England. Unaware of the danger into which she was being drawn, this gentle, attractive girl married the son of Northumberland. Then, under pressure from the Duke the dying King Edward VI was persuaded to sign a paper stating that Lady Jane should be the next Queen.

When Edward VI died, Lady Jane Grey, seventeen years of age, was crowned as Queen while the Duke of Northumberland carried on the government of the nation. It was a brief and pathetic reign of nine days for the innocent girl, trapped and helpless in the selfish scheme of the Duke of Northumberland.

Princess Mary, daughter of Henry VIII and Catherine of Aragon, declared herself to be the true Queen of the realm. In eager support, a strong group of nobles gathered in her defence, and made short work of Northumberland's rule. In a quick upset of power the Duke was executed and Lady Jane Grey remained a prisoner in the Tower of London.

Most people in England were pleased when Queen Mary was crowned in 1553, because they believed she would rule with fairness and justice. In this hope they were to be disappointed. Queen Mary soon roused anger by her actions and by the plans she announced for the kingdom. Among these was her decision to rid England of Protestantism so that the nation might return to its old religious ways. A violent rebellion led by nobles burst out in Kent, but it was crushed by forces of the Queen. Following this revolt Queen Mary became a bitter woman, determined to punish all those who had opposed her rule. The depth of her anger may be judged by the fact that more

150

than one hundred persons were tried, condemned and executed on charges of treason. Even the gentle Lady Jane Grey and her husband went to the block.

Mary's campaign to restore the Roman Catholic faith was vigorous and stern. In a short time the religious service in Latin was being used, crucifixes and statues reappeared, and once-powerful churchmen took up their former positions. Clergymen who had married were forced to leave their wives or the Church. In time, the religious life of England became very much what it had been during the reign of Henry VIII.

Restoration of the Roman Catholic faith

Still dissatisfied Queen Mary decided that the ancient tie which had bound the English Church to the Pope must be restored. She also decided to marry the Catholic King of Spain, Philip II. Neither of these decisions caused any joy in England, for the people had no desire to have closer association with Spain or Rome.

What the people thought mattered little to Mary, for in spite of open protests she proceeded in 1554 to marry King Philip. It was a short unhappy marriage leading to war and heartbreak for the Queen. Philip, who really disliked Queen Mary, had agreed to the marriage only because he hoped to involve England in a war against France. In this hope he was successful, for war with France followed. It was an unhappy conflict, for Calais was besieged and captured in 1558 by a strong French force. All the English people living in that city were forced to move out, leaving behind their homes and other property.

Marriage to Philip of Spain

Loss of Calais, 1558

It is not easy for us to understand the shock, the anger and the humiliation which spread through England at this defeat. For two centuries Calais had been an English trading centre, an outpost of defence, a doorway to France, and a vital point for control of the English Channel. The loss of Calais was a serious blow to

This is Queen Mary's Chair from Winchester Cathedral. The drawing illustrates the solid, practical furniture used at the time. It was not in plentiful supply, for a writer of the sixteenth century states: "The Royal Treasures in furniture and tapestries are kept only in the palace where for the time being the Queen resides, and when she moves to another, everything is taken away, only the bare walls left standing."

LADY Jane Grey, the unfortunate victim of ambitious relatives, was noted for her beauty and intelligence. She was an accomplished musician and had mastered six languages. Here she is seen as a prisoner of Queen Mary, confined in the Tower of London, not in the usual cells but in the House of the Yeoman Gaoler, from which she went to her execution. In the room we see a typical Tudor chest and chair.

England's pride and a great cause of sorrow to the Queen. Her feelings were not improved when Philip crossed to Holland and from there went to Spain.

Persecution of Protestants Then came one of the darkest and saddest periods in latter English history as Queen Mary and Parliament set about the stern work of wiping out all traces of Protestantism. When the former relationship between England and the Pope was restored, the old laws concerned with the burning of heretics were once again put into force. Church courts, moving into action, began the merciless task of persecuting well-known Protestant leaders.

Most of these courageous men stood firm in their beliefs, refusing to surrender the faith they had chosen for their own. Then, when condemned as heretics, they were handed over to sheriffs or other officials for burning at the stake. Even Archbishop Cranmer, ill and delicate though he was, met a calm and fearless end among the flames. The fearful sight of the stake became all too common in several parts of England. A sixteenth century publication *Book of the Martyrs* describes the fiery execution of two other bishops, Ridley and Latimer. A portion of this description reads as follows:

> And so the fire being given unto them, when Dr. Ridley saw the fire flame towards him, he cried with a wonderful loud voice, "In manus tuas, Domine, commendo spiritum meum: Domine recipe spiritum meum." And after, repeated this latter part often in English, "Lord, Lord, receive my spirit;" Master Latimer crying as vehemently on the other side, "O Father of heaven, receive my soul!"

It is probable that between 250 and 300 unfortunates died in this manner, while unknown hundreds were kept in prisons.

The grim work of the courts had not the effect the Queen desired, because considerable sympathy for the victims was aroused among the people. Crowds gathering at the executions cheered the dying men, and muttered threats against the Church, the Queen and Parliament. Neither Mary's hatred nor the flames could destroy the spirit and growth of Protestantism in England.

During her reign Mary was never loved by the people as her father, **Death of** Henry VIII, had been. She was too serious, too stern, too stubborn to **Mary, 1558** arouse any love on the part of Englishmen. Then, too, she was never forgiven for her marriage to Philip and the loss of Calais. In failing health she spent the last period of her reign in sadness and disappointment, surrounded by people who neither loved nor respected her.

When Mary died in 1558, England looked forward with an eager hope to a new reign under Henry VIII's second daughter, Elizabeth.

This wheel lock pistol was one of the earliest hand guns which could "make its own fire." It was invented about 1515. Before this time hand guns were fired by means of a burning cord attached to the weapon. The heavy ball on the handle made it possible to use the pistol as a club during an emergency.

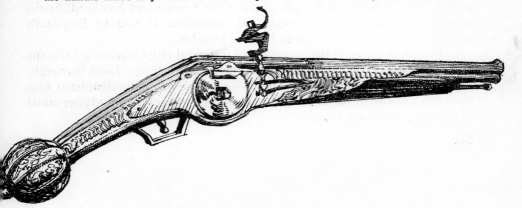

THE EARLY ELIZABETHAN PERIOD

The age which began with the crowning of Elizabeth 1 in 1558 was perhaps the most colourful and interesting in all British history. The Queen's realm was destined to challenge the most powerful countries in Europe, and was to find a new greatness at home and abroad. This was a vital age of warfare, exploration, discovery, piracy, trade and learning which has never been excelled in the island's story. It is astonishing that so many important events could have taken place during the course of a single reign. England's success at this time was in no small measure due to the remarkable personality and talent of the fiery Queen.

Elizabeth I was very much like her father, Henry VIII, in that she was intelligent, energetic, courageous, proud and hot-tempered. At times she struck her treasurer and threw shoes at her secretary, but at other times she was gay, merry and gracious. She loved fine clothes. She enjoyed hunting, hawking, riding, archery, dancing and music. Her education had been thorough, for she could speak six languages, and read well in Latin and Greek.

Elizabeth I, 1558

The Queen was an auburn-haired woman of striking appearance, just twenty-five years of age, when in 1558, she came to the throne. One of her most valuable talents was a genius for gaining the love and loyalty of her people. So great was the nation's lasting devotion, that "Good Queen Bess" enjoyed a united and whole-hearted support never before granted to an English monarch.

The bitterness of Mary's reign had left England in a divided and exhausted condition. There was no strong army to defend the country, the royal treasury was almost empty, the prices of goods were high, there was considerable unemployment, and old religious question was still flaming. If conditions at home were bad, England's relations abroad were worse. There was danger of war with France and Scotland; Spain was not friendly. In her weakened condition, it was to England's advantage to stay out of war as long as possible.

Elizabeth chose as her secretary of state and chief adviser a brilliant and able man, Sir William Cecil, who afterward became Lord Burleigh. The Queen often disregarded his advice and occasionally dismissed him entirely, but the devoted Cecil remained as her friend and adviser until his death forty years later.

The Early Elizabethan Period

Unlike her half-sister, Mary, Queen Elizabeth had been brought up in the Protestant faith. Shortly after her reign began, she managed to repeal the religious laws passed in Mary's time, so that the nation once again became Protestant with the Queen as head of religious affairs. The Church of England which arose from these changes was in reality a new kind of organization which lay half way between Roman Catholicism and the Protestantism of Europe. The Pope no longer had any connection with the Church in England, but the offices of archbishop and bishop were retained. Clergymen still wore the old church robes, but they were permitted to marry. Changes in ceremonies and customs brought in by the Reformation became part of religious life. So it was that the Church of England was a national church, having no connection with religious affairs outside the country, and modelling itself after no other pattern. It was established for all Englishmen, and everyone was expected to worship according to the laws and regulations of the new church. While this settlement had many advantages, it still did not provide for complete religious freedom.

The Church of England was acceptable to most people within the country, but there were some who disliked the new system of worship. There were Roman Catholics who resented the break with the Pope. Such persons were found chiefly among wealthy and noble families in northern England and in some rural areas. There were Protestants who were unhappy because many of the old religious ceremonies and customs had been kept within the Church organization. Among the dissatisfied Protestants was a group known as the Puritans who believed in a simple form of worship. During the reign of Queen Mary numbers of Puritans had been exiles in Europe, and it was there that they gained their extreme religious views.

An Elizabethan silver gilt chalice. Religious and household vessels were frequently made from silver or silver gilt. These pieces used in churches and wealthy homes were examples of superb craftsmanship. Silver vessels were considered more healthy for human use than other types of table ware.

In Tudor times bands of vagabonds and unemployed men roamed the country, often gathering in lawless bands along the fringes of the cities. Robbers and outlaws who infested the forests and roadsides robbed and murdered unwary travellers. Even in the towns the citizens protected themselves with swords and

Some idea of Puritanism may be seen in a series of demands the group made in 1563:

1. That all the Sundays in the year, and principal feasts of Christ, be kept holydays; and all other holydays to be abrogated.

2. That in all parish churches the minister in common prayer turn his face toward the people; and there distinctly read the divine service appointed, where all the people assembled may hear and be edified.

3. That in ministering the sacrament of baptism, the ceremony of making the cross in the child's forehead may be omitted, as tending to superstition.

4. That, forasmuch as divers communicants are not able to kneel during the time of communion for age, sickness, and sundry other infirmities; that the order of kneeling be left to the discretion of the ordinary within his jurisdiction.

5. That it be sufficient for the minister, in time of saying divine service, and ministering the sacraments, to use a surplice; and that no minister say service or minister the sacraments, but in a comely garment or habit.

6. That the use of organs be removed.

The stern, sober attitudes of the Puritans, together with their opposition to music and ceremony in religious affairs was in later years to have a profound influence upon English life.

While it is true that Elizabeth and her Parliament were not as merciless in religious persecution as Mary had been, there were,

lanterns when walking the streets at night. During the reign of Elizabeth I strict laws were passed providing arrest and punishment for idle men moving about the country. The rural roads as seen in this picture were very rough and almost impassable at certain periods of the year.

nevertheless, a number of shocking executions of both Catholics and Puritans. Roman Catholic bishops who refused to accept the Church of England were relieved of their duties and replaced by other churchmen. Of the 9,000 priests and other clergymen in the country, fewer than 1,000 opposed the new Church. These were not permitted to continue in their religious duties.

It would seem that there must have been a goodly number of devout Catholics and Protestants who were willing to sink their religious differences for the sake of religious peace and for the sake of a united nation.

One of the most troublesome problems in England's business life **New coins** had been inherited by Elizabeth from former reigns. It had to do with the peculiar assortment of coins which was used throughout the nation. Issued at various times, some coins were made of almost pure silver or gold while others contained substantial amounts of cheaper metals. Under such a system, a shilling of one kind had a greater value than a shilling of another kind, so that in stores and markets there were different prices depending upon the coins offered in payment. Naturally this caused annoyance, confusion and waste of time. In 1560, two years after Elizabeth became Queen, action was taken to remedy this fault, as old coins were replaced by new ones of fixed and standard value. During the course of nine months, the former coins were collected.

reminted in new form, and issued to the public. This reform of the money system was one of the really important improvements made during the reign of Elizabeth I.

Poor Laws, 1563

There had always been poor people in England, but during the sixteenth century there was an unusually large number of them. The dissolution of the monasteries, the enclosing of fields and the new methods of working all played a part in this situation. Men who were out of work, or did not care to work, wandered about the country, sometimes gathering in lawless bands about the fringes of towns and cities. While Queen Elizabeth sympathized with the poor and the unemployed, she had no intention of permitting them to become a nuisance or a danger throughout the nation.

In 1563, Parliament passed a law providing help for the poor, but forbidding the gathering of large groups of idle people. By this act, men were appointed in each parish to look after needy persons. A list was made of all those who required assistance, and a second list of all those who could afford to help. Once a week money was collected from well-to-do people and then distributed to the poor. Those who refused to make contributions to the poor fund were made to pay property taxes to provide their fair share. Because the poor were now cared for, persons were no longer allowed to beg on the streets, and idle men wandering about the country could be arrested and placed in prison.

27

MARY, QUEEN OF SCOTS

Elizabeth I, like other monarchs before her, had rivals to the throne of England. Among these the most prominent was Mary Stuart, granddaughter of Margaret, the sister of Henry VIII, who had married the King of Scotland. This cousin of Elizabeth, known as Mary Queen of Scots, was next in line to the English throne. Indeed, there were people who believed that Mary had a better claim because the marriage of Henry VIII and Anne Boleyn had been declared illegal.

Mary Stuart

Mary Stuart, eight years younger than Elizabeth, was an attractive, bright, well-educated woman. She was the daughter of a Scottish king, and herself became Queen of Scotland while still a baby, but she was raised and educated in France. There she married the French monarch's

158

son, and, on the King's death, became Queen of France. Still not content with two kingdoms, Mary was bold enough to call herself Queen of Scotland, France and England. It is true that she at first made no strong attempt to gain the English throne, but her use of the title caused a rivalry which sprang up between Mary and Elizabeth.

Mary's connection with the French royal court probably gave her considerable skill in scheming, because the court of the time was filled with intrigue. In her own way, Mary was a ruthless woman who did not hesitate to plot for her own advantage. Her husband the King of France died only a year and a half after he was crowned. Mary felt lonely and discontented in France, so she moved to Scotland where she received a warm welcome from the people. There, in 1561, she took up residence in the old palace of Holyrood in Edinburgh.

Mary Queen of Scots soon discovered that conditions in Scotland were not to her liking. To begin with, the Scots seemed a rough and solemn people in comparison with the polite, gay nobles of the French court. Then too, Mary, as a Roman Catholic, was shocked to find how completely Protestant Scotland had become. Among the devout religious leaders, was John Knox, a fearless, Godly man who spoke his mind to everyone including the Queen herself. Mary, a naturally gay person, resented the stern, cold atmosphere imposed by Scottish religion.

With Elizabeth in England and Mary in Scotland it was inevitable **Rivalry of** that there should be trouble. In an open way Mary tried to persuade **Mary and** **Elizabeth** Elizabeth that she should succeed to the English throne if Elizabeth had no children as heirs. In spite of continued efforts, Mary was unable to secure this agreement, for Elizabeth had good reason to refuse. She feared that if Mary was declared as the heir, some people at home, or abroad, might be tempted to shorten the reign by means of murder. There was danger, too, she believed, that Scotland and France might try a military invasion of England. Elizabeth was clever enough to name no one as the true successor to the English throne.

Disappointed in her attempt to influence Elizabeth, Mary looked **Darnley** about for another means of winning the throne, and it was not long before she had devised another plan. Perhaps, she thought, she could unite the Roman Catholics in England and Scotland, and with their aid she could seize royal power. As part of the scheme she married in 1565 her cousin, Lord Darnley, a Catholic noble of Scotland, who was related to royalty in England as well as in Scotland. Unfortunately for

159

Rizzio was a musician who became secretary to Mary, Queen of Scots, and as such had great influence over her actions. On March 9, 1566, Darnley and others burst into the Queen's chamber at Holyrood Palace, dragged Rizzio into a corridor and murdered him. The assassins in their hatred inflicted fifty-six wounds upon his body. The place where he died may still be seen in the palace.

Mary, Darnley was a weak and vicious person upon whom she could place little trust.

Suspicious of Mary's intentions, a group of Protestant nobles in Scotland rose in armed revolt, but they were defeated and driven to exile in England.

Mary soon lost interest in her husband, Darnley, and in so doing **Rizzio** became friendly with an Italian, Rizzio, who was employed in her service. Darnley, stung by this turn of events, gathered a few nobles together, and killed Rizzio in a brutal manner. Then to make matters even worse for Mary, Darnley recalled the exiled Protestant nobles, and made peace with them.

Still using trickery, Mary pretended to forgive her husband, and waited patiently until she had a strong military force under her command. Again she struck at the Protestant rebels, and once again sent them fleeing into England.

A son was born to Mary Queen of Scots, a son who was named James after Mary's father, James V of Scotland. This Scottish infant, born in a time of turmoil, was later to become King of both Scotland and England.

After the birth of the young prince, Darnley tried to regain the affection of Mary, but by this time the unpredictable Queen was in love with a proud, warlike nobleman, the Earl of Bothwell. The Earl had no intention of allowing Darnley to stand in the way of his marriage to the Queen. One night the castle, Kirk-a-field, inside the walls of Edinburgh blew up with a roar, and the following morning the body of Darnley and that of his page were found on the scene. This cold-blooded murder was either performed or planned by the ambitious Earl of Bothwell. Whether Mary took part in the plan or not is still a mystery.

Following Darnley's murder, the Earl of Bothwell seized Mary Queen of Scots, carried her into captivity, and there he married her. There is reason to believe that Mary was a willing captive.

The Scots, outraged by Mary's behaviour, rose in revolt, defeated the Earl of Bothwell and sent him flying for his life. Mary was not so fortunate, for she was captured and held in prison. Unwilling to keep such a scheming and faithless woman on the throne, the Scots forced Mary to sign papers by which she gave up her royal authority in Scotland and passed it on to her son. Even then, Mary did not give up the fight, for she made good her escape and reached England in safety during the year 1568.

Having arrived in Elizabeth's realm, Mary lost no time in seeking help from her royal cousin. Surprising as it may seem, she dared to ask Queen Elizabeth for an army to march against the Scots.

The presence of Mary in England caused a serious problem for Elizabeth, a problem which held danger for the English Queen. It was therefore decided by Elizabeth and her council that the only safe procedure was to hold Mary as a captive. For nineteen years, 1568 to 1587, Mary remained in confinement, where she spent her days scheming to achieve her desired place.

In the end it was her long-practiced trickery which caused Mary's death. From her place in captivity she kept in touch with five men led by a gentleman named Babington who planned to murder Elizabeth and set Mary free. Eventually the plot was discovered by secret service agents who intercepted messages and kept a close watch on the plotters. It is possible that evidence was invented when it was not available.

Earl of Bothwell

Mary flees to England, 1568

Plots against Elizabeth

161

When the time was right, English justice struck a quick, hard blow. The men were arrested and promptly executed.

Mary was not to escape this time, for her part in the plot had been revealed. Taken before a court of English nobles, she was accused of encouraging the Babington Plot and other plots against the Queen. Evidence brought forward during the trial was so damaging that Mary was declared guilty of attempted murder against Queen Elizabeth.

At the next meeting of Parliament the members asked the Queen to order the death of Mary as a penalty for her treacherous actions. The concern of members of Parliament for the Queen's safety is illustrated in the following passage addressed to Elizabeth:

. . . it may please your Highness to take speedy order, that declaration of the same sentence and judgment be made and published by proclamation, and that thereupon direction be given for further proceedings against the said Scottish Queen, according to the effect and true meaning of the said statute: because, upon advised and great consultation, we cannot find that there is any possible means to provide for your Majesty's safety, but by the just and speedy execution of the said Queen.

It seemed to Elizabeth that Mary did not deserve to live, and yet for a while she could not face the actual task of giving the official command. It was not easy for Elizabeth to send another Queen, even a scheming Queen, to the scaffold. She shuddered, too, at the thought of condemning a woman who was her own cousin. Several times Elizabeth signed papers ordering the execution, and then withdrew them hurriedly. Such delay caused anxiety and impatience among the English authorities, for they were eager to be rid of the dangerous Mary. Elizabeth eventually did give a form of consent to Mary's execution, but it was worded in such a way that its meaning was not clear. Finally the Queen's council took matters into its own hands, and ordered the death of Mary Queen of Scots.

Execution of Mary Stuart, 1587 In February, 1587, with dignity and calmness, Mary Stuart mounted the scaffold and moments later the axe fell on the block. Then, as her severed head was held aloft, there came the harsh cry, "So shall perish all enemies of the Queen!"

Not wishing to bear entire blame for this sad event, Queen Elizabeth declared that she had never ordered the execution, and that her council had misunderstood her meaning. In a rage she scolded her advisers, dismissed an important official, and ordered him off to trial. Such severe treatment was undeserved by her devoted followers, for the Queen knew that Mary's death was necessary for her own safety.

162

However, her protest against the council made it possible for Elizabeth to inform France and Scotland that Mary had died at the hands of her advisers and not through her own desire. Elizabeth had no wish to be on worse terms with either country.

Although Mary Queen of Scots may have been a selfish, ruthless woman, she holds a romantic place in history. To some persons she appears as an unfortunate person whose tragic life was shaped by forces too strong for her restless nature. Perhaps under different circumstances Mary Stuart might have been a great and accomplished Queen.

28

THE NEW WORLD

During the reign of Elizabeth I, English trade with other countries expanded rapidly, bringing a fresh new wealth to the realm. There was a number of large trading companies with royal charters that sent their ships to distant ports in Europe, Africa and Asia. The Muscovy Company traded with Russia; the Levant Company traded with Turkey and other places about the eastern Mediterranean; the Baltic Company traded with Poland and Prussia; the Barbary Company traded with North Africa; and the Guinea Company traded with West Africa. Toward the end of Elizabeth's reign the East India Company, the greatest of them all, began trading with the Orient. With English ships sailing the seven seas, it was inevitable that England should make new discoveries and claim new lands. It was certain, too, that English seamen should clash with those of other lands who were sailing the same waters.

The increasing hostility between England and Spain was partly due to the fact that the former was considered a Protestant country while the latter was considered Catholic. There were other reasons, too, of course, which had to do with trade, commerce, navigation and rivalry in the New World. Spain had been quick to establish colonies in the West Indies following the voyages of Christopher Columbus. Before the reign of Queen Elizabeth, the Spanish adventurer, Balboa, had crossed the Isthmus of Panama, Cortes had captured Mexico and Pizarro had won Peru.

From captured treasures and from mines in Mexico and Peru there **Spanish** poured a steady flow of silver and gold into the royal treasury of Spain. **power**

163

With this newly-won wealth, the Spanish monarch, King Philip, began to build a strong army and a large navy. This growing power of Spain caused concern in England. People asked what was to prevent Philip from crossing the water and invading England.

John Hawkins Elizabeth and her council believed that because Spain's wealth came from the New World, that was the place to challenge the enemy. In spite of Spain's stern laws forbidding her colonies to trade with other countries, daring Englishmen began to engage in this dangerous business. Among the first of these adventurers was Captain John Hawkins of Plymouth. In 1562 he took three ships to Africa, secured several hundred Negroes, crossed the Atlantic, and sold his black prisoners as slaves to the Spanish settlers. On succeeding voyages Hawkins and others forced their unsavoury trade on the colonies. It was a comparatively simple matter for a well-armed English expedition to overawe isolated Spanish settlements. It should be said, too, that in some cases, Spanish plantation owners were only too happy to buy slaves from the English adventurers.

The Spanish monarch protested to Queen Elizabeth concerning the unwanted trade in the colonies, but English seamen still continued to sail the waters of the Caribbean Sea. Such voyages led to sea fights, to shore skirmishes, and to the capture of Spanish treasure ships. English seamen fell into the hands of the Spaniards, and colonial prisoners were seized by English raiders. So it was that from a period of illegal trading the action changed to a violent time of outright piracy. All the quarrelling, battling, raiding and piracy were, of course, strictly unofficial for England and Spain were still at peace.

Aztec goldwork taken from Mexico by the Spanish helped to build the wealth of Spain during the sixteenth century. At the left is a small ornament, and at the right is an ornament with a movable tongue. At the height of her prosperity, Spain had a revenue of millions of dollars from her colonies in America.

Martin Frobisher's ship passes close to icebergs in the north Atlantic. Seamen of the time, and until the nineteenth century, wore no distinctive uniform or clothing. Sailors sometimes wore loose breeches secured below the knee, or very wide, short trousers. A conical cap was frequently part of the outfit. Ships of the time were relatively small, and had none of the carving which was popular a century later. The underwater portions of the ship were covered with a protective substance called "white stuff" which was probably a mixture of tallow and chalk, or lime. Captains of ships were often soldiers, not sailors, and frequently had little experience as mariners.

Captain Hawkins' success against the Spanish was rewarded in 1573 when he became Treasurer and Controller of the Navy. For England, this was a fortunate appointment, because the energetic Hawkins was the right man to rebuild the naval strength of the nation.

A young man from Devon, Francis Drake, who had learned **Francis** seamanship and piracy under Hawkins, became another bitter enemy **Drake** of the Spanish. In a number of voyages he struck swiftly at Spanish settlements, captured treasure ships, and caused alarm throughout the colonies. So clever was he in these movements that he became known to the Spanish as "The Master Thief of the Unknown World." Between

165

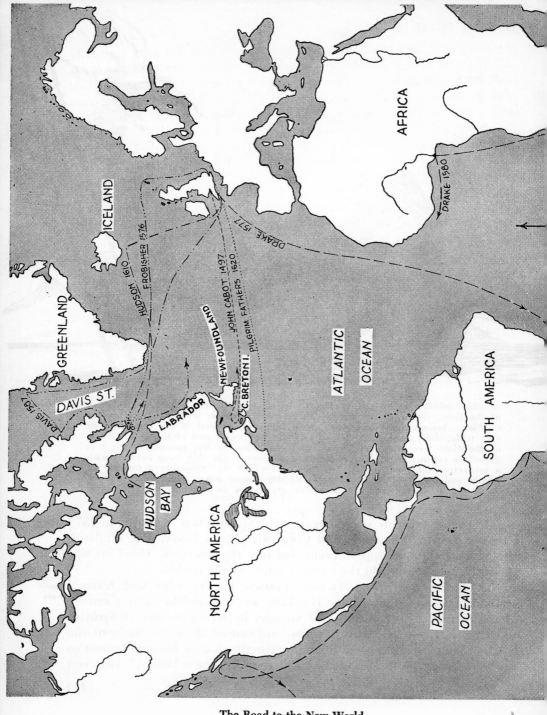

The Road to the New World

the years 1577 and 1580 Drake made a round-the-world voyage during which he attacked Spanish ships and settlements along the western coast of South America. On his return to England he carried with him in the *Golden Hind* a rich cargo of Spanish treasure. For this daring exploit Francis Drake was knighted by Queen Elizabeth.

Spain's efforts to keep other traders and seamen out of the New **Humphrey** World caused men to think of finding other routes to the East which **Gilbert** were not controlled by the Spanish. In 1576 an English gentleman, Humphrey Gilbert, wrote a book entitled, *A Discourse to Prove a Passage by the North-West to Cathaia and the East Indies.* Humphrey Gilbert was referring to a sailing route which he believed to lie in the Arctic Ocean to the north of North America. Of this passage Gilbert said in his book:

It were the onely way for our princess to possess the wealth of all the East parts (as they terme them) of the world which is infinite . . . This discovery hath bene reserved for some noble prince or worthy man, thereby to make himself rich, and the world happie.

Ideas contained in Gilbert's writings inspired a number of English voyages organized to find the Northwest Passage. Martin Frobisher made in 1576, 1577 and 1578 three voyages to the region of Hudson Strait, and found his way into an inlet of Baffin Island. Today we call the inlet Frobisher Bay. Returning excitedly to England with a cargo of black ore, Frobisher was disappointed to learn that it was worthless, and did not contain gold as he had expected.

Humphrey Gilbert was still undiscouraged by the so-called failure of the Frobisher expeditions. His mind turned next to the possibility of founding English colonies in North America to the north of the Spanish possessions. In 1578 he secured from Queen Elizabeth a charter which gave him the right to claim lands in the New World which were not held by other Christian nations.

Along with his half-brother, Walter Raleigh*, and other gentlemen **Walter** Humphrey Gilbert made several voyages to America, but such **Raleigh** adventures brought little result. Still determined to give England a foothold in the New World, Gilbert, in 1583, claimed Newfoundland in the name of Queen Elizabeth. After deciding to establish a permanent settlement on the island, Gilbert set sail for home, but he was not to see England again. During a storm on the night of September

*For a legend concerning Raleigh see page 404.

A recently excavated and restored outdoor oven from early Jamestown. It is made from stone and shaped somewhat like an igloo with a small door. Ovens like this can still be seen in parts of eastern Canada.

9, his little ship, the *Squirrel*, sank beneath mountainous waves as howling winds whipped through the darkness.

Saddened by the death of his half-brother, Walter Raleigh determined to carry on the work of Humphrey Gilbert. In 1585, he founded a colony on Roanoke Island which he called *Virginia* in honour of the virgin Queen. The little colony was short-lived, as was the second one attempted two years later. Raleigh's brave efforts to put England permanently in America were unsuccessful, but they caused an English interest in the New World which was to be renewed in later years. Although Raleigh himself was never in Virginia, his association with the attempted colony enabled him to introduce tobacco and potatoes into England.

John Davis While Raleigh was struggling with settlements in Virginia, an English seaman, John Davis, was making another search for the Northwest Passage. During the course of three voyages he explored 700 miles of Greenland coast, a large portion of southeastern Baffin Island and the whole of the Labrador shoreline. Davis Strait which lies between Greenland and Baffin Island bears his name.

Further attempts at exploration and settlement were brought to a close as England waited anxiously for the beginning of a real war with Spain. It was not for another twenty years that Englishmen could again turn their efforts to gaining a place in the New World.

29

THE INVINCIBLE ARMADA

King Philip of Spain was the former husband of Elizabeth's predecessor, Mary of England. He was an ardent Catholic who ruled not (a) only Spain, but Portugal and what is now Holland. When Queen Elizabeth sent money and men to help the Protestant people of Holland in their struggle against Spain, Philip was annoyed. In preparation for an invasion of England, he gathered together a great fleet which was known as the "Invincible Armada."

Philip's fleet consisted of 130 vessels carrying 2,500 guns and more than 30,000 men, most of whom were soldiers. The ships were of various sizes and shapes, from big high galleons and armed traders to small craft for the transport of an army. While this was an impressive fleet, it did possess several weaknesses. Most of the guns were of a type which could shoot but a short distance. Food supplies were poor. Drinking water leaked from barrels made of unseasoned wood. The soldiers were of poor fighting quality, and their officers had little

This type of swivel gun was mounted on the sides of ships in the time of Queen Elizabeth. It was a simple form of breech loader. The weapon in the picture is being fired, not by a sailor, but by a soldier dressed in breastplate and half armour. Ships of the time also carried pikemen, bowmen and arquebusiers who fired hand guns.

During the latter stages of the English attack on the Invincible Armada fireships were sent among the anchored Spanish vessels. In panic, the Spanish captains cut their cables and put out to sea. Among the ships of the Armada were the

experience with warfare at sea. The Spanish commander, himself a land warrior, was uneasy at the thought of fighting an English fleet.

England prepares for war

In England hasty preparations were made to meet the Spanish threat . . . militia troops were mustered . . . beacon fires were prepared on the hilltops along the south and east coasts . . . groups of vessels under such famous seamen as Hawkins, Drake, Frobisher and Howard waited in harbours from Plymouth to Dover. In addition to the ships of the English navy there were other vessels commanded by traders, pirates and freebooters.

English ships were lower than the high-castled vessels of the Spanish fleet. They were fitted with deep keels and were designed for speed and seaworthiness. Their guns were of the long-range type. Hawkins in re-organizing the Navy had planned a new kind of naval

slender, rakish galleases which resembled Roman galleys. They were rowed by slaves or prisoners of war. Spanish galleons, on the other hand, were large, cumbersome vessels with towering bows and sterns. They were fitted with heavy armaments and had a beak at the bow for ramming other ships.

warfare, a warfare of swift movement and manoeuvre. In the past, naval ships had shot one broadside at the enemy, and then closed in for hand-to-hand fighting on the decks. Hawkins believed enemy ships could be destroyed, or forced to surrender, by the use of guns alone. English captains were anxious to try this new method against the enemy galleons.

In July, 1588, the Armada* moved up the English Channel, **Spanish** heading toward Holland to pick up more invasion troops. Sea fighting **Armada** began. Outweighed by the Spanish, the English stuck to a hit-and-run type of fighting, thus avoiding a head-on collision with the massive enemy. As the Armada sailed on before a brisk wind, small groups of English ships dashed from the harbours to harry the Spanish fleet.

*For a legend concerning this battle see page 403.

Route of the Spanish Armada, 1588

Hanging like wolves about their quarry, the English attacked only under favourable conditions.

For nine days the English harassed the Armada, firing a bothersome hail of balls from the long-range guns. By July 23, however, the wind had died away leaving the ships in a calm. On the still waters, the Spanish launched an attack with galleys rowed by slaves, but this attempt was broken up by Drake and Howard. Two days later near the Isle of Wight there was another clash after which the Spanish withdrew in the direction of France.

Making a fatal error, the Spanish commander ordered his Armada to anchor near Calais. By this time all of the English naval power had been collected together to oppose the advance of the enemy. On July 28, at a conference of English commanders, it was decided to take stronger action against the Armada. In an effort to bring confusion among the enemy ships, it was planned to send fire ships in the direction of the Spanish fleet. The Earl of Monmouth who took part in the engagement describes the action as follows:

. . . in which time our council of war had provided six old hulks, and stuffed them full of all combustible matter fit for burning, and on Monday, at two in the morning, they were let loose, with each of them a man in her to direct them. The tide serving, they brought them very near the Spanish fleet, so that they could not miss coming amongst the midst of them: then they set fire to them, and came off themselves, having each of them a little boat to bring him off. The ships set on fire came so directly to the Spanish fleet, as they had no way to avoid them, but to cut all their halsers, and so escape; and their haste was such that they left one of their four great galeasses on ground before Calais, which our men took and had the spoil of, where many of the Spaniards were slain with the governor thereof, but most of them were saved with wading ashore to Calais. They being in this

172

disorder, we made ready to follow them, where began a cruel fight, and we had such advantage both of wind and tide, as we had a glorious day of them; continuing fight from four o'clock in the morning to almost five or six at night, where they lost a dozen or fourteen of their best ships, some sunk, and the rest run ashore in divers parts to keep themselves from sinking. After God had given us this great victory they made all the haste they could away, and we followed them Tuesday and Wednesday, by which time they were gotten as far as Flamborough-head. It was resolved on Wednesday at night, that, by four o'clock on Thursday, we should have a new fight with them for a farewell; but by two in the morning, there was a flag of council hung out in our vice-admiral, when it was found that in the whole fleet there was not municion sufficient to make half a fight; and therefore, it was **Defeat of** there concluded that we should let them pass, and our fleet to return to the **the Armada,** downs. That night we departed them, we had a mighty storm. **1588**

Had the English not run out of ammunition, very few of the enemy vessels would have survived the conflict. Sailing on after this bitter defeat, the broken Armada made its way northward around Scotland in a desperate effort to reach Spain. It was a tragic voyage, but one which was marked by fine seamanship on the part of Spanish sailors. The Armada had escaped the English, but there were other

dangers and hardships to face. Horses and mules were thrown overboard to lighten the ships and to save water. Two ships were wrecked off the coast of Norway. Drinking water ran so low that the Spanish commanders decided to replenish

The cross-staff was one of the main instruments of navigation in Elizabethan times. It consisted of a straight staff along which could be slid a crossbar set at right angles. The observer applied his eye to one end of the staff and raised it until it was in line with the sun, or star, by which he measured. He then moved the bar until it seemed to touch the horizon and the sun. A marking on the staff indicated the degree of altitude above the horizon. With this information the observer could calculate his position in terms of latitude.

their supply along the Irish coast. It was a costly decision, for high winds drove seventeen vessels ashore with a loss of 5,000 lives. Just one half of the great fleet was able to reach the security of Spanish ports during the autumn months.

Strangely enough, among the English naval captains there was no great amount of pride in the defeat of the Armada. They were disappointed that Spain could muster a greater fleet than England. They were disappointed in the accuracy and striking power of the English long-range cannon. They were disappointed that ammunition had run out at a critical time in battle. They were disappointed that a large portion of the enemy fleet had escaped. The English people, **Results of** however, were overjoyed at a victory which had freed them for the **English** first time in thirty years from the threatening power of Spain. A medal **victory** which was created to honour the occasion bore the words, "God blew and they were scattered."

With the defeat of the Armada, England rose as an important power in Europe, but the conflict with Spain was by no means over. Indeed it lasted for the rest of Queen Elizabeth's reign. It was not a continuous war of great battles, but rather a scattered series of English expeditions sent to harass Spain in Europe and in America. The two old pirate-warriors, Hawkins and Drake, both died while fighting the Spanish in the New World.

England was not yet wealthy enough, or strong enough to strike an overpowering blow at Spain, so the war dragged on in a dismal fashion with no decisive ending. The final result, however, was a stronger England and a weakened Spain.

The importance of the victory over the Invincible Armada was that it gave to the English the power that the Spanish lost . . . a new power and influence which in later years was to lay the foundations of the British Empire.

30
PROGRESS IN ELIZABETHAN TIMES

During the reign of Queen Elizabeth I England found a new wealth and prosperity which brought marked changes into the lives of her people. Such a fortunate condition was due to a number of causes including long periods of peace, the development of industry, expansion of trade and improvements in farming. Population of the country increased rapidly while the number of homes multiplied with surprising speed.

The lower classes of English people in the towns and on the farms built cottages and homes which were much more comfortable than in former times. There were real chimneys on the roofs, and real glass in the windows. Whereas people had once slept on hard straw pallets, many of the Elizabethans became accustomed to feather beds, sheets and pillows. Wooden spoons and bowls were gradually being replaced by those made of pewter.

Progress in farming led to larger quantities of improved foods. **Agriculture** The thin scrawny pigs and sheep of the middle ages had developed into sleeker and fatter animals. Oxen which drew the ploughs were bigger and stronger. Horses, which at one time had been used only in riding, hunting and battle were put to work in the fields and were employed as pack animals. The historian, Trevelyan, states that "the general prosperity of the country demanded more riding horses as in good years we demand more cars." Among the poultry of the farms there were chickens, geese, ducks, pigeons and turkeys, the last of which had been brought into England from Mexico. Gardens contained bright flowers as well as herbs for cooking and medicine. Potatoes brought from America were becoming a new crop on the English farms.

If the lower classes of people benefitted by the new prosperity, **Life of the** the upper classes did even more so. Large, beautiful homes were well **upper** **classes** fitted with furniture, rugs, paintings and tapestries. It was no longer necessary for the wealthy and noble families to build castles for protection, so it was that the homes gained a new and open appearance. High walls, moats, keeps and drawbridges gave way to gracious buildings with large windows, wide doorways and spacious gardens. Many of the stately homes of this period still remain in England, little changed from the time of their construction.

This type of timber frame house was common in the Tudor period. A heavy wooden framework was constructed first, then the spaces between the timbers were filled with wattle which was plastered over. Bricks, which were becoming available, were also used, but they too were given a coating of plaster. The oak timbers were left to grey in the weather rather than being oiled or tarred as is commonly supposed. Roofs were made of thatch, tile, or thin slabs of stone.

The upper classes took great pleasure in the wearing of showy, expensive clothing. Perhaps at no other time in history was English costume so extravagant and so exaggerated. Indeed, at its peak, Elizabethan dress caused smiles and chuckles among the citizens of other countries. Women delighted in dresses made from silk, embroidery, cloth of silver and cloth of gold, while they decked themselves freely with necklaces, rings, bracelets and earrings. Immense skirts were made to stand out in great circles by means of petticoats called farthingales which contained wooden hoops. Men were as vain and colourful in their dress as were the ladies, for they strutted about in graceful jackets, cloaks, short stuffed trousers and long stockings. About their necks both men and women wore wide ruffs which stood out above the shoulders and high behind the head. Queen Elizabeth, like her wealthy subjects, was exceedingly fond of costly clothes, spending large sums of money on finery even though she was rather stingy concerning the purchase of some other things.

In the matter of eating and drinking, too, the upper classes of

176

Englishmen found a new enjoyment. Their long tables were graced by delicate foods and imported wines. Coffee and tea had not reached England in any useful supply, but tobacco smoking had found a place in polite society. Crude eating habits of the middle ages were giving way slowly to more gracious procedures with knives, forks, spoons and plates.

Queen Elizabeth had ample opportunity to display her numerous dresses, for she spent considerable time in the conduct of "progresses." On such occasions she visited a number of country houses, castles and towns, enjoying the hospitality of her hosts. These events pleased her, not only because she enjoyed herself, but because they reduced her own housekeeping expenses. The "progress", sometimes lasting for months, had a sound and practical value in that it kept Elizabeth in close contact with her devoted subjects. During the time that the Queen visited the homes of wealthy or noble families, she was entertained lavishly by means of banquets, balls, musical performances and hunting parties, sometimes sending the host into financial ruin. A proud and vain woman, she found pleasure in the gaiety of the festivities and in the compliments which were showered upon her. In the prosperous towns she was received with a pomp and splendour including speeches, dinners, parades, pageants and mock battles. At the universities the professors read addresses, and the students performed plays in Latin or in Greek. This was followed by a reply from the Queen, who, using the classical languages, praised the efforts of the scholars, or criticized their failures. *Queen's "progresses"*

Trade with foreign countries showed an astonishing growth during the last years of the Elizabethan era. English traders and merchants carried on business with the countries of western Europe, with Russia, with nations near the Baltic Sea, with lands of the Mediterranean, and finally with the Orient. In 1600 Queen Elizabeth gave a charter to the famous *East India Company* which began trade with India and the East Indies. This commercial enterprise was one of the first "joint- *Trade*

This skillet, spelled "skyllet" by the Elizabethans, was used for cooking. Country gentry enjoyed enormous meals which sometimes lasted out over three hours. People of the lower classes lived on bread, bacon, milk, curds, cider and ale. A roast of beef on Sunday was common, but fish were becoming more popular than in former times.

Queen Elizabeth I took extended tours called *progresses* during which she was entertained at castles, towns, schools and universities. Note the costumes represented in the picture. The gentlemen are wearing puffed breeches, long seamless stockings and ruffs about their necks. The Queen, who had 1,000 dresses in her wardrobe, is seen wearing a drum-shaped farthingale and a wired lace collar. In the background may be seen part of a formal garden with yew trees which were often clipped into the ornamental shapes of mushrooms, chessmen, birds and so on.

stock" companies to be established in England, that is the members put all their money in one treasury to meet expenses, and then at suitable times divided the profits which came from the business. From the beginning the East India Company was a prosperous establishment which sent ships to distant ports, and set up trading posts in the Orient. Later we shall see that the company played an important part in securing vital territory in India for the future British Empire.

Literature   Not all the progress of the period was restricted to the practical matters of industry, agriculture, trade, architecture and dress. A fresh current of learning and literature, which had begun in the reign of Henry VIII, poured on with increasing force during the time of Elizabeth. So important was this movement, that the finest poetry and drama yet created in the English language made its appearance. Literature was not only of high quality, but it represented a new and different form of writing. Leaving behind the practices of the past, poets wrote to express their own feelings and thoughts. Among such poets was Edmund Spenser who graduated from Cambridge University, and later became secretary to an important official of the government. Spenser's most noted poem, *The Faerie Queen,* is marked by beauty, delicacy and a remarkable musical quality. The verse form created by the poet is still known as the "Spenserian stanza."

Prose writing, too, displayed rapid growth and surprising variety in the matter of subject material. Hooker wrote on religious matters, Camden produced his annals of the period, Hakluyt edited his famous *Voyages,* Ben Johnson wrote articles and drama, Francis Bacon his witty *Essays,* while Sir Walter Raleigh busied himself with songs, poetry and his *History of the World.* In addition to these important writings, there was a ceaseless outpouring of small pamphlets which performed some of the services now offered by newspapers.

The greatest name in Elizabethan literature, however, was that of the famous poet and playwright, William Shakespeare, who brought a fresh glory and vigour to the English drama. Shakespeare lived at a time when the writing, production and performance of plays held a tremendous fascination for the English people. Plays became the serious work of professional players and the delight of amateur groups made up of all sorts of people from noblemen to schoolboys. Numerous performances were given before Queen Elizabeth at her royal court and during her "progresses." It is estimated that at least 2,000 different plays were produced during the reigns of Elizabeth and her successor, King James. Some of these dramas were written by learned scholars who knew something of the ancient plays of the Greeks and Romans, while others came from the pens of writers who belonged to professional companies. William Shakespeare belonged to the second group of writers.

Sometime before the defeat of the Spanish Armada, Shakespeare arrived in London, and eventually attached himself to a group of active players. It is possible that in the beginning he carried out very humble duties, for legend has it that at one time he looked after the horses belonging to people who attended the plays. Such a situation, of course, did not last for long, because Shakespeare's work led him into acting and into the writing of magnificent plays which appeared from time to time on the stages of the Globe Theatre and Blackfriars Theatre. Fortunately the writer's genius was recognized by the men of the

William Shakespeare

179

The Globe Theatre, built in 1599, was a typical Elizabethan theatre. These were generally round or octagonal in shape, and open to the sky in the centre. The stage was not boxed in like modern stages, but open on all three sides so that the audience could sit around it. No scenery was employed but signs were posted to indicate the location of castles, caves, forests, ships and so on. Wealthy people sat in balconies, while the poorer citizens stood in the central portion of the theatre. Because the streets were not safe at night, plays were performed in the afternoon. Many features of the Elizabethan theatre were utilized in the construction of the Festival Theatre at Stratford, Ontario.

period, so that his plays became popular among theatre-goers. Since that time, 400 years ago, the dramas of William Shakespeare have been performed a countless number of times, and have been translated into many languages. What educated person of today is not acquainted with *Hamlet, Romeo and Juliet, Richard II, The Merchant of Venice, Othello, The Tempest* and other of his plays?

The last years of Elizabeth's reign were not entirely happy, for the elderly Queen was worried by a number of problems and difficulties. Spain still remained a bothersome rival . . . rebellions flared in Ireland against the authority of the English crown . . . Walter Raleigh annoyed the Queen by falling in love with one of her maids of honour . . . young men in the royal court quarrelled with the Queen's older and wiser advisers. The most serious threat, however, arose when the Earl of Essex plotted an uprising in London, and planned to seize Elizabeth so that he might become the strong man of the realm. When this treachery was discovered, Essex lost his handsome head on the block.

Death of Elizabeth, 1603

180

The fiery energy which Elizabeth had held all her life gradually slipped away, so that by the year 1603 she was very ill. After months of silent suffering she died on the twenty-fourth of March.

Queen Elizabeth I was the last of the Tudors, a great line of English monarchs who laid firm foundations for the nation's future greatness. The importance of the Tudors lay in the fact that they were able to remain as strong rulers while at the same time working in harmony with the English parliament. When the Tudors passed from the scene, relationships between royalty and Parliament were not to run so smoothly.

SUMMARY—SECTION IV

Henry VII who came to the throne in 1485 founded the Tudor line of English rulers who lifted monarchy to a new height of strength and power. After the troublesome times of the Wars of the Roses the people were pleased to have a period of justice and order. The already weakened barons were brought under control through the Court of the Star Chamber. Henry VII's reign saw peace with other countries and a growth in trade, commerce and learning. The effects of the Italian Renaissance and the printing of books was being felt in England.

Henry's son, Henry VIII, who was crowned in 1509, was soon in conflict with the Church and the Pope in Rome. Before the end of this struggle Henry VIII had dissolved the English monasteries and had himself become head of the Church in England. During his reign the Protestant faiths gained a foothold within the nation. Henry VIII, having no liking for Protestantism, made unsuccessful efforts to stamp it out. Henry VIII is remembered as the monarch who had six wives during his lifetime. In spite of his many faults, he was popular among his subjects.

King Edward VI, son of Henry VIII, had a short reign of six years—1547 to 1553. During his time the Reformation of the Church was completed as England turned away from Roman Catholicism to the Church of England. In 1549 the English Prayer Book made its appearance.

In 1553 Mary, daughter of Henry VIII and Catherine of Aragon, became Queen and began the work of changing England back to the Catholic faith. Many clergymen were executed for refusing to renounce their Protestant beliefs. Mary made an unpopular marriage when she took King Philip of Spain as her husband. In a war with France England lost her only continental possession, Calais. This was a serious blow to English pride.

181

Elizabeth I, daughter of Henry VIII and Anne Boleyn, came to the throne in 1558. Her reign, known as the "Elizabethan period," was one of tremendous growth for the nation. Having been brought up as a Protestant, she made every effort to wipe out the religious changes made during the reign of her half-sister, Queen Mary. The result was that the Church of England was established as the *only* Church in England. This arrangement was not pleasing to the Catholics, the Presbyterians, the Puritans and other groups. Mary Queen of Scots, Elizabeth's cousin, became a serious threat to the Queen's life and was executed.

Interest in the New World was shown through a number of important voyages made by such noted English seamen as Francis Drake, Humphrey Gilbert, Martin Frobisher, Walter Raleigh and John Davis.

In 1588 a threatened invasion of England by Spain was averted with the defeat of the Invincible Armada. This victory gave England a new power in international affairs which later led to the founding of the British Empire.

The Tudor line of monarchs, beginning with Henry VII and ending with Elizabeth I, maintained a strong monarchy, winning supremacy over barons and Church. In later years there was to be a battle for power between Kings and Parliament.

TIME-CHART

1485-1603

	1485-1509	HENRY VII
Diaz rounds Cape of Good Hope	**1487**	COURT OF THE STAR CHAMBER
Columbus discovers America	**1492**	
Vasco da Gama reaches India	**1496**	
	1497	FIRST VOYAGE OF JOHN CABOT
	1509-1547	HENRY VIII
	1512	WAR WITH FRANCE
	1513	DEFEAT OF THE SCOTS AT FLODDEN FIELD

TIME-CHART—*(continued)*

1519

Magellan begins his voyage around the world	**1519**	
Cortes begins conquest of Mexico	**1531**	HENRY VIII RECOGNIZED AS SUPREME HEAD OF THE CHURCH IN ENGLAND
	1532	SUBMISSION OF THE CLERGY
	1534	
First voyage of Jacques Cartier	**1537**	BEGINNING OF THE DISSOLUTION OF THE MONASTERIES
	1542	DEFEAT OF THE SCOTS AT SOLWAY MOSS
	1547-1553	EDWARD VI
	1549	FIRST PRAYER BOOK
	1553	LADY JANE GREY
	1553-1558	MARY
	1554	REBELLIONS AGAINST MARY MARY MARRIES PHILIP OF SPAIN ENGLAND RECONCILED WITH POPE
	1557	WAR WITH FRANCE
	1558	LOSS OF CALAIS
	1558-1603	ELIZABETH I
	1559	ELIZABETH BECOMES SUPREME HEAD OF THE CHURCH IN ENGLAND
	1576	FROBISHER'S FIRST VOYAGE
	1585	JOHN DAVIS'S FIRST VOYAGE RALEIGH ATTEMPTS TO COLONIZE VIRGINIA
	1587	EXECUTION OF MARY QUEEN OF SCOTS
	1588	DEFEAT OF THE INVINCIBLE ARMADA
	1600	FORMATION OF THE EAST INDIA COMPANY
	1603	DEATH OF ELIZABETH

183

V. THE TRIUMPH OF PARLIAMENT

James I and the "Divine Right of Kings"
• Discontent among the people • A new
version of the Bible • East India
Company establishes itself in India •
Settlements in America • An unwelcome
Prayer Book for Scotland • Parliament
is invaded by Charles I • Civil War
between the Royalists and Roundheads •
Execution of Charles I • The Commonwealth established • Cromwell becomes
Lord Protector • Restoration of monarchy under Charles II • Great Plague
and Great Fire of London • James II
becomes very unpopular • William of
Orange comes to throne on invitation of
the English • Parliament finally holds
greatest power in government

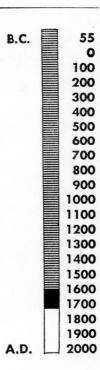

B.C.
55
0
100
200
300
400
500
600
700
800
900
1000
1100
1200
1300
1400
1500
1600
1700
1800
1900
2000
A.D.

31
JAMES I AND AN UNHAPPY PEOPLE

Because Queen Elizabeth had never married, she left no direct heir to the English throne. Ironically enough, the person who held the best claim to the throne was King James I of Scotland, son of Mary Queen of Scots who had been executed for plotting against Elizabeth. With very little opposition to his royal claim, the Scottish monarch was crowned in 1603 as James I of England, first of the Stuart line of kings. The old enemies, England and Scotland, then found themselves living side by side under the rule of a single king.

James I, King of England and Scotland was not a handsome man. In fact Thomas Macaulay, English writer and historian, has described him as having "an awkward figure, a rickety walk and a slobbering mouth." James I, nevertheless, was a well-educated person who took pleasure in the writing of clever essays on many subjects ranging from **James I,** the evils of tobacco to plans of government. From the very beginning **1603** of his reign he expressed the belief that the King ruled by the will of God, and had to answer to God alone for his actions, and that neither the courts nor Parliament had the right to interfere with his rule. This belief, known as the *Divine Right of Kings* was eventually to lead to the downfall of the Stuart line.

Some idea of James' thoughts regarding the high authority of the King may be gained through this passage written by the monarch himself:

And as ye see it manifest that the King is over-lord of the whole land, so is he master over every person that inhabiteth the same, having power of life and death of every one of them: for although a just prince will not take the life of any of his subjects without a clear law, yet the same laws whereby he taketh them are made by himself or his predecessors; and so the power flows always from himself . . .

At the time, European countries were having difficulty with money **Money** problems, because the prices of property and goods were rising rapidly. **problems** One reason for this rise, or inflation, was the plentiful supply of money which resulted from the flow of precious metals from the New World into Europe. During such a period of inflation the value of money

185

becomes less and less as prices continue to rise. During the present century we have experienced just such a condition in our own country.

The decreasing value of English money in the reign of James I meant, of course, that the Royal Treasury needed more funds. King James took for granted that all he need do to secure more money was to demand higher taxes. Queen Elizabeth had managed to get along on her income because she had handled her treasury in a careful manner. But James I had no intention of doing likewise.

Here, then, was one of many disagreements which arose between the King and Parliament. As his court expenses increased, James demanded more and more from Parliament, so that in time he found himself faced with an angry House of Commons. When members of Parliament spoke out against the King's demands, James brushed off their protests, and lectured the men as if they were badly-behaved school boys. Parliament took the attitude that the King should be able to meet his expenses from the income of royal estates and of custom duties collected at English ports. Seeing a chance to increase his income, James I raised the rate of duties, and proceeded to collect large amounts of money. Parliament was greatly displeased, but no serious move was made against the King.

Money problems were not the only troubles which came between King James and his people, for the old religious question made an uncomfortable appearance once again. James had been brought up in Scotland as a Calvinist, one of the Protestant faiths. The English Puritans, believing the King might support their cause, asked for changes in English religious life. As a result, James arranged in 1604 a conference to be held among the bishops of the Church of England and representatives of the Puritan people. The King's hope that the matter might be settled quickly was lost when the bishops refused to make any changes and the Puritans insisted upon their own demands. Angered by the Puritans' stand, James threatened to "harry them out of the land" if they did not obey the Church laws of the nation. The quarrel between the King and the Puritans lasted for years, producing some results which will be noted at a later point in this work.

If the Puritans were unhappy with James I, the Catholics were even more so. Because the King's mother, Mary, Queen of Scots, had been a staunch Catholic, they hoped that James would deal kindly with their problems. In the beginning James did permit priests to move about in their work, and did not fine families who remained away from

186

the parish churches of the Church of England. As time went by, however, he was surprised to find how many people began calling themselves Catholics. In alarm, James I then commenced to take the same
measures against the Catholics as had been taken during the reign
of Elizabeth I.

James' impatience with those who did not belong to the Church
of England stemmed from the fact that he believed no subject could
remain loyal unless he shared the religious beliefs of his monarch.
The Bishops of the Church of England who believed most firmly in
the Divine Right were his strongest supporters and therefore James
was naturally drawn toward them in his beliefs.

Determined to gain rights for the Catholic Church, a small group **Gunpowder Plot, 1605**
of foolish men planned in 1605 to blow up King James I and Parlia-
ment while they were in session. The plotters' hope was that with
Spanish help James' son, Charles or his daughter Elizabeth, might be
placed on the throne of England. The ring-leader of the desperate
plan was Robert Catesby, who was assisted by Guy Fawkes, a former
soldier.

In order to accomplish their object, Catesby and Fawkes dug a
tunnel from a house to a room below the House of Lords in the Parliament buildings. Into this place they carried two tons of gunpowder
all neatly packed in barrels. They felt that here was enough explosive
to kill King James I and many members of Parliament. By a fortunate chance, news of the plot leaked out through an informer, so
that the cellars of Parliament were searched. During the frantic and
hasty search Guy Fawkes was captured, and excitement filled the streets
of London. Since that time November 5 has been celebrated in England as Guy Fawkes' Day with bonfires and fireworks. Even today the
cellars of Parliament are formally searched before the beginning of
each session.

One lasting result which came out of the religious troubles during **The Bible, 1611**
the reign of James I was the development of a new translation of the
English Bible. Before this time various religious groups were using
Bibles which met their own particular needs. Bibles of the time often
contained marginal notes and other interpretations of scripture in
accord with the beliefs of Catholics or Protestant groups. When the
suggestion was made that a new edition of the Bible should be prepared, King James I agreed, believing one standard Bible might improve the religious life of the nation.

About fifty able scholars and churchmen, working in committees,

187

Catesby and Guy Fawkes brought barrels of gunpowder into the basement of the House of Lords and covered them up with coal and pieces of wood. Fortunately this foolish plot to assassinate the King was discovered when one of the plotters wrote an unsigned letter to a relative who was a Lord suggesting he stay away from Parliament "which shall receive a terrible blow yet shall not see who hurt them."

set about the great task of compiling the new version. It was decided that the all important religious groups should be represented among the workers. After three years of careful research, the scholars and churchmen commenced the task of assembling their material. They worked to such good effect that their task was finished by 1609. After careful examination, the Authorized Version of the Bible was published in 1611 by the King's Printer. This famous Bible made its appearance at the time that Champlain was establishing New France on the banks of the St. Lawrence River.

The revised Bible, which came to be known as the *King James' Version* was received with enthusiasm. Many copies were printed, the cheapest edition selling for five shillings. This famous version, still widely used in our own time, has been translated into more languages than any other single book. This is the most important contribution of the period to the religious life of the country.

In his relationships with other countries King James I was a cautious man, at all times trying to avoid war. Indeed, he considered himself the peacemaker of Europe. This was not an easy task, because religious differences and old jealousies made friendship with some nations impossible.

After years of bad feeling between England and Spain, James **Peace with** came to terms by means of a treaty in 1604. To further strengthen **Spain** the understanding he wished to have his son, Charles, marry the daughter of King Philip III of Spain. He discovered, however, that arranging the marriage was a difficult business, because the wily Spaniards wanted too many favours in return. The English people, too, made it clear that they wanted no royal union with a Spanish princess. After years of discussion the plan was given up and young Charles married Henrietta Maria, a French princess, just one year before he succeeded to the throne.

James was anxious to have his two kingdoms of England and Scot- **Union with** land brought more closely together. He held to a dream that the two **Scotland** realms might work together, using the same system of law, religion, **proposed** property and trade. In an effort to gain this end, he requested Parliament in 1607 to pass an act uniting the nations. It is true that men from both countries were appointed to a commission with the purpose of studying the problem of union, but actually very little was accomplished. Neither Parliament nor the English people were ready for union with their ancient enemies, the Scots. England and Scotland continued to live side by side in peace with King James I as the only real link which held them together. The dream of James did not come true for one hundred years.

Sir Walter Raleigh who had been a great favourite in the court of **Execution** Queen Elizabeth, found himself in a much less important position **of Raleigh,** during the time of James. Indeed, some of his high offices and estates **1618** were taken away. Because of this treatment at the hands of the King, Raleigh grumbled openly. He may have said some rather harsh things. Finally he was arrested and placed in the Tower of London on a charge of treason for plotting against the King. It is believed now that he was falsely accused of an act which he had not committed.

After twelve years of imprisonment, Raleigh was finally released in 1617 so that he might lead an expedition to the Orinoco River of South America. There in the New World, he hoped to find a rich gold mine which would perhaps regain the King's favour. Although James I did not forgive Raleigh, he did consent to the expedition because the King could see the possibility of gold for the royal treasury. Unfor-

189

tunately the venture proved to be a disaster: no gold was found, Raleigh's son lost his life, and Englishmen fought Spaniards on the Orinoco River.

This action, rousing considerable anger in Spain, caused the Spanish to lay a protest before James I. Still unwilling to risk war, James decided to punish Raleigh in order to satisfy the Spanish. As a result Sir Walter Raleigh was condemned to execution on the old charge of treason. In 1618 the daring, clever courtier of Elizabethan times climbed to the scaffold, and touching the executioner's axe, he said, "This is sharp medicine, but it is a sound cure for all disease."

Many an Englishman, still hating Spain, groaned in despair as he heard the news of Raleigh's death.

While James I was quarrelling with Parliament over the Divine Right, money problems and foreign affairs, important events were taking place abroad. The East India Company was establishing itself in India, a foothold was gained in the West Indies and settlements were being formed in America.

32

TRADING POSTS AND SETTLEMENTS

If the reign of Elizabeth I had been a time of adventure and exploration, the reign of James I was a time of settlement and trade in distant places . . . America, Africa and India.

While Raleigh was still a prisoner, men were busy making preparations to carry out the plans for colonization which had formed in his fertile mind. In 1606, a group of English business men, the *Virginia Company,* was granted a charter to found settlements in America. **Jamestown, 1607** Members of the company were interested in more than settlement; they hoped to make profits from future trade with the colonies they formed. Before the end of the year 1607 three vessels carried 105 people across the Atlantic, and landed in Virginia, establishing a settlement at Jamestown, named in honour of the King. This was to be the first permanent settlement of Englishmen in the New World. It was just one year later, in 1608, that Samuel de Champlain founded Quebec on the St. Lawrence River.

Until more permanent dwellings could be constructed, settlers lived in crude shelters of many kinds including dugouts and the wigwam-like structure shown here. Based upon English, not Indian, design, these wigwams were generally built over a framework of hickory saplings with a large stone fireplace forming the wall at one end. A heavy door, often of oak, was placed at the other end. The framework was sometimes covered with a mat woven from bulrushes, and this was covered with pine bark lapped to shed the rain.

After a horrible winter in Virginia, half of the colonists were dead **Captain John Smith** as a result of cold, hunger and malaria fever. Captain John Smith, a former soldier, took command of the colony, and enforced such a rugged programme of strict discipline and hard work that Jamestown managed to survive. John Smith's rescue from death at the hands of Indians by Pocahontas has become a romantic legend in the history of the colony, but we are not certain of its truth. We do know, however, that when a colonist, John Rolfe, took Pocahontas as his bride, the marriage caused excitement and some astonishment in London.

More settlers arrived in Virginia, and the serious work of estab- **Tobacco** lishing farms was carried forward with vigour. It was a happy piece of good fortune when it was discovered that the soil and climate of Virginia were ideal for the growing of tobacco. There was an excellent market for tobacco in Europe as smoking became an established practice among gentlemen of the continent. As years passed by, the tobacco crops of Virginia were sold readily; thus bringing important profits to the colony. Small farms were bought up so that large tobacco plantations could be formed for the production of huge crops. Prosperity brought fine homes, graceful living and a spirit of independence to the wealthy planters of Virginia.

In 1612, three years after the founding of Jamestown, a settlement **Other settlements** was made in Bermuda. In the same year the East India Company

191

established a trading post on the western coast of India, and came into conflict with traders of the Dutch East India Company. There was action, too, in 1618 when trading forts were built in the Gold Coast and Gambia on the west coast of Africa.

Puritans at Plymouth, 1620

The work of founding another colony on the mainland of North America was in progress. Some Puritans in England found conditions so unhappy that they had moved to Holland to carry on their own religion in a peaceful manner. Conditions in Holland, however, were rather trying because the Puritans found it very difficult to earn a satisfactory living in the kind of work that was open to them. Moreover, the English were unwilling to lose their own language and customs in the life of Holland.

Unhappy in Dutch surroundings, the Puritans began to think that perhaps America could provide the freedom they desired. Eventually with the help of the Virginia Company, and with the consent of King James, arrangements were made for the establishment of a Puritan colony in the New World. Thirty-five of the Puritans from Holland and sixty-four others from England collected at Plymouth in Devon. Leaving this port in the ship *Mayflower,* in September, 1620, they sailed across the Atlantic for Virginia.

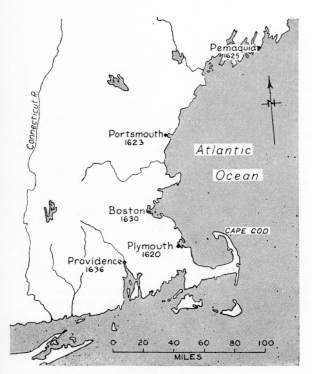

Early New England Settlements

After two and a half months they reached, not Virginia, but the shores of Cape Cod in what is now Massachusetts. In spite of the fact that the Puritans had no permission to settle a colony at this point, they landed at Cape Cod Bay and established the town of *Plymouth*. Like the colony in Virginia, the settlement at Plymouth suffered great hardships during the first years. Unlike the colony in Virginia, however, it made no great profits for the English company. By 1627 the Virginia Company had cut its connections with Plymouth, leaving the Puritans to look after themselves. Prob-

The Puritan settlers at Plymouth wore clothes which were basically Tudor in style, although of simple materials and less elaborate design. Settlers were forced to manufacture at home most of the things they required in daily life. Soap was made by boiling grease and lye outdoors in a huge cauldron over a wood fire. Washing was usually done on the banks of a stream or pond.

ably no one at the time foresaw that this was the beginning of the *New England Colonies* which were to become even more important than Virginia.

As the reign of James I drew to a close many of the English citizens were becoming dissatisfied under the dictatorship of the King and the strict authority of the established Church. Like the Puritans, more people turned their eyes toward America, hoping to find more freedom and a happier way of life. In consequence, *The Company of the Massachusetts Bay in New England* founded in 1629 still another settlement at Salem to the north of Plymouth. Puritan leaders of the Salem venture were thus enabled to found the self-governing colony of Massachusetts. Because conditions were favourable for the settlement of small English farmers and poor workers, Massachusetts grew rapidly

Salem, 1629

in population. Between the years 1629 and 1640 the number of colonists increased from 300 to 14,000.

Connecticut and Rhode Island

Religious troubles had followed the settlers to America however. Not all the people there could agree with the stern, sober views held by leaders of the colony. Indeed some of the Puritans were as unyielding in their attitudes as were the bishops of the Church of England. As time went by, groups of colonists broke away from the main colony in Massachusetts. Some journeyed to the banks of the Connecticut River, there founding Hartford and other places which later became the colony of Connecticut. Another group left Massachusetts, and moved southward, setting up towns and farms which later formed the foundation for the colony of Rhode Island.

Thus by the year 1640, there were five English colonies in America —Virginia, Plymouth, Massachusetts Bay Colony, Connecticut and Rhode Island. In addition to the cold winters and the Indians, French colonies on the St. Lawrence and Dutch colonies on the Hudson posed a constant threat to the safety of the English settlers.

Barbadoes

For years England had been anxious to hold territory in the West Indies, but the Spanish reigned supreme in this area. An important foothold was gained, however, when the Barbados Islands were occupied by the English in 1624 and a colony established a year later.

The foundations of the future British Empire were being laid even though the English people themselves did not realize it.

33

CHARLES I AND AN ANGRY PARLIAMENT

When James I died in 1625 he was succeeded by his son Charles I. The quarrels between King and Parliament were to be much more violent during the new reign than they had been during the previous one. The time was fast approaching when a definite answer had to be found to the question, "Who is supreme in English government — Parliament or King?"

The new monarch was a handsome young man, twenty-five years of age at the time he came to the throne. During his boyhood Charles I had suffered from an attack of paralysis which left him with a stammer in his speech, but the disease seemed to have left no other ill effects. An expert hunter and horseman, Charles could handle a crossbow or gun with remarkable ease. He was neither as intelligent nor as well educated as his father had been, but he did enjoy reading and could write with skill. Holding the pride of the Stuarts, he was fond of ceremony and believed firmly in the Divine Right.

(a)

Charles I, 1625

Unlike his father, Charles I had no desire to avoid war with his enemies in Europe. Before James' death, Charles I had gained a feeling of hatred for the Spanish, and now as King he determined to strike. With the help of his friend and chief minister, the Duke of Buckingham, the King made a number of reckless treaties and plans without consulting the English Parliament. Misfortune followed misfortune as Charles and Buckingham tried to put their plans into action. One English army was riddled by disease; a fleet loaned to France was used against rebellious Protestants instead of against Spain; and an expedition sent in 1625 to Cadiz to capture Spanish treasure ships failed miserably.

War with Spain and France

(b)

By 1627 Charles was at war with France, and in this effort he had no more success than before. The truth was that the English people had no enthusiasm for these battles planned by Charles and his adviser, Buckingham. The military plans had not been approved by Parliament or supported by the interest of the citizens. Men fought because they had no other choice. Military equipment was in short supply. Leadership was poor. It was not surprising then that English expeditions failed to meet success on the continent.

Many English citizens were compelled to provide food and accommodation for the troops of Charles I. Here a housewife is seen serving food to soldiers who have been billeted in her home. The roast of meat she has prepared was cooked on a spit by the fireplace. Notice that the soldiers are wearing half-armour consisting mainly of a breastplate.

Charles I called three Parliaments during the first four years of his reign and quarrelled with each one of them.

Charles and his first Parliament soon were arguing over the matters **First** of taxes and the place taken by the Duke of Buckingham. Members of **Parliament** Parliament disliked the King's minister heartily, considering him a meddler and bungler in the nation's affairs. They wished to remove him from office, but Charles I refused to abandon his friend. The dispute ended when the King, in anger, dissolved Parliament.

The second Parliament of the reign was even less friendly toward **Second** Buckingham than the first, because it charged the minister with a long **Parliament** series of crimes and offences. Considering this to be a dangerous situation, Charles dissolved Parliament once again.

196

Meanwhile discontent was rising among the people, and there was good reason for such unrest. One of the causes for dissatisfaction lay in the fact that many soldiers were sent to live in homes without the consent of the owners. It was an easy way for Charles I to have his soldiers housed and fed at little cost to himself. Families who complained of this injustice were punished or brought before military courts to have their cases settled. Discontentment among the people

Because Parliament had refused to vote money for the King's private wars on the Continent, Charles found it necessary to secure funds in some other way. This was accomplished by means of "forced loans" from the citizens. Sheriffs and other officials throughout the kingdom put pressure upon property owners to lend money to the royal treasury. Very few of these people offered up their money with willingness, because they realized that there was little chance of the loans being repaid. Nevertheless, most of them feared the King's officials and did as they were commanded. Those who refused were punished, some being put into prison without trial.

When the third Parliament met in 1628, the members were determined to protest vigorously against the injustices brought about by Charles I and Buckingham. A few strong leaders within Parliament saw an opportunity to force the King into improving his conduct. To do this they drew up an act, the *Petition of Right,* which declared that in future the compulsory placement of soldiers in homes, trial of citizens by military courts, forced loans and taxes, and imprisonment without trial were to be illegal throughout the nation. Third Parliament

The Petition of Right was passed by the House of Commons, by the House of Lords and then came up for the King's signature. For some time Charles refused to sign the document, but eventually his need for money became so desperate that he gave in. This was an important victory for Parliament. Like *Magna Carta,* signed 400 years before, the new act was to become a vital part of English government and freedom.

Having rid themselves of certain injustices, the members of Parliament began to launch fierce attacks against the hated Buckingham, but Charles put an end to this by postponing the session for six months. Before Parliament could meet again, the problem of Buckingham had been solved, for he was murdered by a personal enemy.

Even then troublesome questions still remained between the King and Parliament. Among these was the old religious question which smouldered like a slow fire among the people. There was less ill feeling Religious question shown against the Catholics; indeed, the Church of England began to adopt a number of Catholic religious practices. Charles was in full agreement with this movement, giving solid support to the established Church of England.

On the other hand Puritanism had displayed such surprising growth in England that many of the citizens and most members of the House of Commons were of this faith. Impatient with the Church of England, members of Parliament desired to punish clergymen who had introduced changes in religious life. King Charles I, however, took a firm stand, refusing to permit action against the churchmen.

Customs duties
Trouble also developed over the customs duties which, according to practice, were granted by Parliament to the royal treasury. When the members seemed slow in voting these funds, Charles commanded his officials to collect the duties without consent of Parliament. The King's income from this source appeared so promising that he considered himself to be almost independent.

When the third Parliament met in 1629, the members were once again prepared to take strong measures against the illegal actions of the King. They summoned before them a number of customs collectors accused of seizing property from citizens who would not pay duties. Also summoned before Parliament was a group of clergymen who had used various Catholic ceremonies in the services of the Church of England. Such clergymen were said to be members of the High Church of England.

Revolt in Parliament
In answer to this bold challenge by Parliament, Charles I ordered his customs collectors not to appear before the House of Commons. He sent word, too, that the session was to be postponed. Then followed one of the strangest and wildest events ever to take place in an English Parliament. As the Speaker of the House of Commons rose to read the King's order, two men dashed forward, seized the Speaker, and pushed him roughly into his chair. Then, as the struggling Speaker was held in place, a member read a number of resolutions dealing with matters of importance. The resolutions stated that anyone making unapproved changes in religious practices, and anyone collecting or paying customs duties without consent of Parliament would be considered an enemy of the state.

There was an immediate uproar in the House of Commons with men shouting, jostling and shoving. Some tried to rescue the Speaker. Some barred the way to the chair. Others locked the doors of the chamber. For an instant it appeared as if the excited members might

198

take to their swords and engage in a pitched battle. But the tense moment passed away. In spite of the confusion, the resolutions were put to the House of Commons and passed in triumph. With a victory won, the members released the Speaker, opened the doors and left the House. None realized that it would be a long time before Parliament assembled again.

King Charles was so annoyed when he learned of this uproarious session that he dissolved Parliament, and took over full control, or personal rule, of the government. It was not to be for another eleven years that representatives of the people were to meet again in the House of Commons.

The ancient struggle for supremacy in England was reaching a **King versus** climax. Power of the barons was gone, the authority of the Church had **Parliament** waned, and now King and Parliament were engaged in a last-ditch fight for supremacy in government. During the time of the Tudors the monarchs had retained royal power but had respected and consulted Parliament. During the reign of James I there was a constant battle for supremacy with neither side gaining much. Under Charles I it seemed as if monarchy stood at the peak of power.

The Puritans and the High Church group within the Church of England were still violently opposed to one another. Each side had among its members strong earnest leaders, all of whom believed in the righteousness of their causes. If they had been sensible enough to give and take a little, England would have been spared a bitter period of religious quarrelling.

Archbishop Laud, the King's chief adviser, persuaded Charles that troublesome Puritans might be tried before the Court of the Star Chamber. This famous court, founded during the reign of Henry VII, had been established to deal with people who were too powerful to be tried by the ordinary courts of the land. Under Charles I, however,

A man being punished publicly in a pillory. This instrument of punishment consisted of a post and wooden frame through which the head and hands were thrust. After 1637 it was used chiefly to penalize persons for such offences as printing books without a license, or libelling the government. The pillory continued in use until it was abolished in 1837.

the Court of the Star Chamber became a means of carrying out the wishes of the King and Archbishop Laud. Another court composed of churchmen called the Court of High Commission held authority in the trial of persons charged with religious crimes. Unfortunate Puritans brought before either court were seldom found innocent because there was no one to defend the accused.

In 1638, by order of the Court of the Star Chamber, a Scotsman was beaten and had his ears cut off for writing a number of articles criticising the English bishops. William Prynne, a noted lawyer and Puritan, wrote books condemning drinking, fashionable dress, long hair worn by men and the sinful life of people in the theatres. Unfortunately for Mr. Prynne, his writings were interpreted as being attacks on the King, the Queen and important officials. As a result the Court of the Star Chamber sentenced Prynne to pay a fine of 5,000 pounds, to stand in the pillory, to have his ears cut off, and to remain in prison until set free by the King. After four years of captivity, he was tried again with others and was condemned to prison for life.

It should be said that there were not many such sad cases, but the impression they made upon the English was great. The King and Laud were determined to secure obedience to their wishes, but in so doing they were arousing a deep and lasting hatred among the English citizens.

Neither the King nor his chief adviser seemed to understand the dangerous situation which was building up within the nation, for they continued to enforce strict measures. Archbishop Laud annoyed the strict Puritans by reviving an old law, the Declaration of Sports, which encouraged football, folk dancing and other pastimes on Sunday afternoons.

Because there was no Parliament to vote money, Charles was forced to secure funds by various means to carry on the government. In doing this he supported the use of practices which, if not actually unlawful, were very close to being so. One of the most successful means of collecting money discovered by Charles I was the imposing of heavy fines upon men who broke the laws. Two lawyers, Noy and Finch, set to work to revive old practices by which the King could collect money without Parliament.

Old laws revived

By one old act men who owned property bringing in a rent of at least forty pounds a year were required to become knights. At one time this amount in rent had been considered real wealth, but by the reign of Charles I even small landowners were securing more than forty

There were many types of English ploughs, most of which resembled the one shown above. Oxen were still used generally in the fields, but as the horse became less important in warfare, it came into greater use on the farm. From such stock there arose such famous breeds as Shires, Suffolks and Clydesdales which we know today.

pounds from their properties. This old law enforcing knighthood had fallen into disuse, so that many men had never bothered to take up this honour and duty. This proved to be a mistake on their part, because the King's officials proceeded to fine them heavily for neglecting their duties.

Another old law which brought Charles I a pleasing sum of money in fines was one dealing with the ancient Royal Forests. Here, too, was a law which over the years lay almost forgotten. This, however, did not prevent Charles from using it to fine subjects who held enclosed land within the boundaries of what had once been the royal hunting lands.

Another scheme used by Charles to raise funds was the securing of *ship money* to build vessels for the English navy. By custom, the seaport towns had either to build the necessary ships, or to provide the money for their construction. Charles now demanded money, not only from the coastal towns, but from all the counties of England. He claimed that this was not a true tax, but merely a sum paid instead of military or naval service. The amount of money raised in this manner was so great that the English people feared it would never be necessary for the King to call Parliament again. A squire, John Hampden, refused to pay, claiming the tax was illegal since Parliament had not voted it. He was tried and the judges decided against him, saying that the tax was legal if the country was in danger and only the King could decide if it was in danger.

It is true that order was being kept at home, peace existed with other countries, and the government was able to conduct its affairs, but the bitterness of the people was so strong that an explosion was bound to follow. It was not long in coming.

201

34

REVOLT IN PARLIAMENT

The first thing to cause a serious crack in the personal rule of Charles I was religious trouble in Scotland. This country, too, was under Charles' rule, for he had inherited the Scottish crown from his father, James I. The Protestant religion as practised in Scotland did not please Charles I chiefly because it was not organized in the same manner as the established Church of England. There had developed in Scotland a system in which the Church was governed, not by bishops, but by committees of churchmen and citizens which were called presbyters. Thus arose the name Presbyterian Church.

King Charles undertook to reorganize the Scottish Church, placing its rule under bishops who were given wide powers. While it is true that this change angered most of the people, a number of noble families gave support to the King's action. When Charles 1, in 1637, forced a new Prayer Book on the Scots, there was real trouble in the north. Some citizens disliked the new Prayer Book because it seemed Catholic in form, and others disliked it because they felt English customs were being forced upon them.

New Prayer Book for Scotland

The first time the Prayer Book was used at a church service in Edinburgh a woman threw a stool at the minister, and the congregation rose in a shouting mass. Excitement spread through the country. So alarmed were the Scots that during the following months thousands of them took a pledge, the *National Covenant*, by which they swore to win back the old form of religion which they loved.

National Covenant, 1638

King Charles, surprised by the determination of the Scots, withdrew the Prayer Book, and promised that the Scottish bishops should not have too much authority. It was too late, however, for these promises; the anger of Scotland had been aroused to a dangerous pitch.

During the autumn of 1638 at a large meeting, the Glasgow Assembly, Scottish clergymen and others declared that they and not the bishops had the right to govern the Church in Scotland. A representative of the King warned the Assembly that it had no such authority, but the determined men paid no attention to him. They set about the task of abolishing the bishops and regaining the presbyteries.

Because these bold actions amounted to rebellion against the King,

Revolt in Parliament

Charles I marched northward with an English army. At the Scottish border he was alarmed to discover that the Scots had already gathered forces which were stronger than his own. It was such an uncomfortable position for Charles I that he made peace, promising that the religious problems of Scotland would be solved in a satisfactory manner. Having made this agreement, the King promptly proceeded to prepare for war against the Scots.

Charles I had enough income to operate his government, but not enough to support a large army. He had no wish to call Parliament to raise the necessary money, but it seemed the only way by which he could meet military expenses. When Parliament, after twelve years **Short** of recess, finally met in 1640, the session lasted only three weeks. **Parliament** Charles I and the members quarrelled continuously. The House of Commons demanded an end to injustice, and advised the King to forget the war with Scotland. Finding that he was gaining nothing through Parliament, Charles I dissolved it. For obvious reasons this particular session has become known in English history as the Short Parliament.

Charles I was now in a desperate situation, for a Scottish army was poised on the border, ready to invade England. By gathering some funds and by forcing men into military service, he managed to organize an army. Then he marched northward to Scotland. It was a poor army with which to fight the Scots, because the English soldiers saw no reason for war. The result was that no fighting took place immediately—just a series of discussions with Scottish leaders. It was a humbling experience for Charles I when he agreed that the Scots might hold two English counties in the north, and that large sums of money would be paid if the invaders would march no further south.

Although Charles I had avoided what might have been a disastrous battle on the Scottish border, he was still in difficulty. He had no funds to pay off the Scottish army. At long last, pride, stubbornness and selfishness had caught the King in a trap of his own making. His position was hopeless unless he could appeal to the English Parliament.

At the royal call Parliament met again in November, 1640, to **Long** face a King who realized his power was no longer as great as it had **Parliament,** been. From the beginning of the session, known as the *Long Parliament,* **1640** members took control, acting in a vigorous manner. A number of the King's chief advisers were placed under arrest, but some managed to escape to the continent. Archbishop Laud and the Earl of Strafford were imprisoned in the Tower and later executed. It was a stern

203

and merciless Parliament which took vengeance upon those who had advised the King.

The danger of a Scottish invasion disappeared after a number of conferences and the payment of agreed sums of money.

Having regained some measure of authority, the members of Parliament began to make their position more secure than it had been at any time during the reign of Charles I. The King was forced to sign a bill stating that Parliament could not be dissolved without its own consent. Another bill required Parliament to meet at least once every three years whether there was a royal summons or not. Then a series of acts were passed to remedy the hardships and injustices which had appeared during the reign. So complete was this work that it seemed impossible for the King to rule the nation without the assistance of the House of Commons and the House of Lords.

The religious issue, however, was not managed so easily, for even in Parliament the members were divided in their opinions. Men of moderate views wished only for certain controls to be placed on the Church of England. Puritans, on the other hand, hoped to get rid of bishops so that religious affairs might be placed under the control of the clergy and the people. In the end Parliament did pass an act changing organization of the Church, but there was such an outcry against it, the bill was withdrawn.

Irish rebellion

An Irish rebellion in 1641 caused alarm and anger because English and Scottish settlers on the island had been tortured and killed by the Irish. A cry for war against the rebels rang from one end of England to the other. Parliament had no wish to see Ireland escape from England's power, but the members hesitated to place an army under Charles. There was an uneasy fear that the King might use the troops to regain his former power within the realm.

This sturdy oak chair of Stuart times shows the effects of earlier styles. About the middle of the seventeenth century furniture design found new life and new beauty. There was an increasing use of upholstery. Interiors of wealthy homes were magnificent with fine furniture and elaborate carvings. The master carver of the period 1670 to 1700 was Grinling Gibbons whose work still adorns some of England's stately buildings.

Charles I arrives at the Guildhall in London to seek the five members who were reported to have taken refuge there after their flight from Parliament. Sessions of Parliament were at this time held at Westminster which was a separate city two miles from London.

By this time Charles was convinced that Parliament was not as united as it had been. He felt safe in making a bold move. In January, 1642, he stationed armed men about the Houses of Parliament, strode into the House of Commons, and declared that he had come to arrest five members who were traitors to their King and country. With flashing eyes Charles looked about the assembly in an effort to find the men he wanted. They were not there and no one offered to help the King find them. Feeling angry and a bit foolish at his failure, Charles I muttered, "The birds have flown," and hurried from the House.

Members of Parliament were annoyed, not only at the King's haughty manner, but because he had dared to invade the House of Commons. By tradition when English kings wished to address the members of the lower House, they did so only in the chamber occupied by the House of Lords. Charles I had committed an act of bad manners which served only to increase the ill will which already existed. Both King and Parliament realized by this time that conditions had become so serious there was no longer a purpose in discussion or noisy quarrelling.

Each side thought only of war.

35

CIVIL WAR

Following Charles I's daring intrusion on the House of Commons in 1642 London was in an uproar as mobs roamed the streets and howled outside the royal palace. In haste the King left the city travelling to Newmarket, to Nottingham and then to York where he set up a temporary court. So it was that the nation found itself with two separate governments—one under Parliament and another under the King.

Roundheads and Royalists

It soon became evident that the break between crown and Parliament could never be closed, and that war was fast approaching. Men rushed to the aid of either cause, some gathering about the King and some moving into London. Supporters of Parliament were given the name *Roundheads* because the Puritans wore short hair, while followers of Charles I were graced with the more elegant name of *Royalists* or sometimes *Cavaliers*.

The question of choosing sides caused anxiety to many Englishmen, for they felt certain loyalties to both King and Parliament. To some rebellion against the crown was a dangerous step to take, and disloyalty to the Parliament equally distasteful. Most of the nobles and High Churchmen became Royalists. Most of the Puritans espoused the Roundhead cause. Other men who were neither nobles, churchmen nor Puritans gave support to whichever party they felt had the more just cause. Families were split by these decisions, so that before the bitter period had passed away fathers were fighting against sons, and brothers were battling brothers.

Battle of Edgehill

At first Charles' army was a small one, but as time went by his military forces grew to the point where he felt safe in challenging the

206

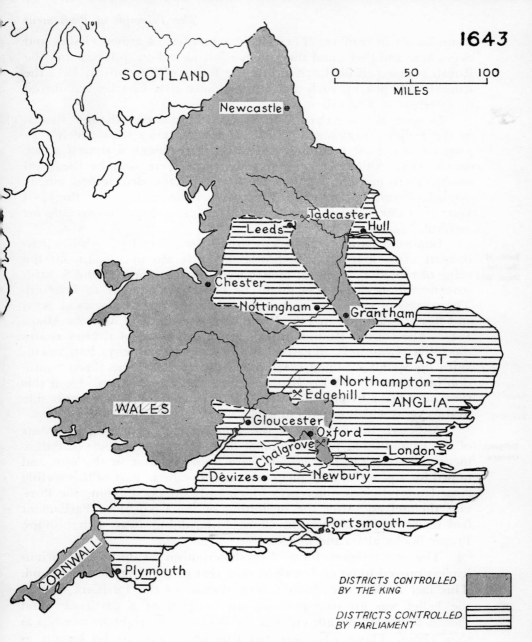

SCOTLAND

0   50   100

MILES

Newcastle

Tadcaster

Leeds   Hull

Chester

Nottingham   Grantham

EAST

Northampton

Edgehill   ANGLIA

WALES

Gloucester

Oxford

Chalgrove   London

Devizes   Newbury

Portsmouth

CORNWALL

Plymouth

DISTRICTS CONTROLLED
BY THE KING

DISTRICTS CONTROLLED
BY PARLIAMENT

The Civil War, 1643

Roundheads in conflict. There were a number of armed clashes and sieges here and there, and then in an effort to make a quick victory the Royalists marched on London. At the Battle of Edgehill in 1642 the Roundheads put up such a fierce resistance that Charles was forced to withdraw to Oxford.

In spite of this setback, the Royalists gained considerable success in the military campaign. They had three armies with which they planned to cut off London's trade, and then launch a frontal attack on the city. Although many small victories were won by the royal troops, their master plan was frustrated by the determined enemy defence of towns in scattered districts. It became clear that the Civil War was to be no short simple campaign, but a desperate struggle for survival.

Battle of Marston Moor, 1644

Important assistance was lent to the Roundhead party when Parliament made a treaty with Scotland which was once again on the verge of rebellion. Sums of money were hurried north to the Scottish government so that forces might be collected and sent to England. The success of this move was shown when the united armies of Scots and Roundheads defeated the Royalists at the Battle of Marston Moor, 1644. The rugged Roundhead officer in command of cavalry troops was Oliver Cromwell, an earnest Puritan and a member of Parliament. With his well-disciplined cavalrymen, the *Ironsides,* he threw confusion into the ranks of Royalist horsemen and foot soldiers. From this time on, Oliver Cromwell was to play an increasingly important role in the events which were to follow.

Religious changes

Although the fortunes of war appeared to be turning in favour of the Roundheads, by the summer of 1644 many members of Parliament and some military leaders were losing interest in the war, and hoped for a peaceful settlement with the Royalists. Part of this feeling arose from religious differences which had developed among the Puritans themselves. After the beginning of the Civil War, Parliament had made drastic changes in Church life, doing away with bishops, Prayer Books, altars and images.

The new religious form of Presbyterianism set up by the Puritan leaders proved to be no less rigid than that of the Church of England. This fact caused uneasiness among certain of the Puritans. Slowly the belief was growing that no one religion of a particular kind should be forced on all; citizens should have the right to worship as they chose. Those who accepted this idea came to be known as *Independents.* It was at this time that new religious groups began to

208

Oliver Cromwell's soldiers prepare for the Battle of Naseby. This engagement turned out to be a decisive victory for the New Model Army. Most of its officers were young men, and the troops were newly trained and untried in battle. Cromwell said, "If you chose honest, godly men as to be captains of horse, honest, godly men will follow them." The men seen here are wearing three-quarter cavalry armour. When the battle was over, artillery, baggage and even royal papers fell into Cromwell's hands.

take form, groups which later were to become such denominations as Baptists, Unitarians, Quakers and others.

Because of these developments, there arose two opposing factions within the Roundhead party—the Presbyterians and the Independents. The Presbyterians wanted peace because they believed they could make a suitable settlement with Charles I. The Independents desired to continue the war because they had no desire to live under Presbyterian domination. In addition to this fact, they did not trust the King as long as he had an army at his command.

Oliver Cromwell, who was an Independent, was more anxious **New Model** than ever to smash the power of the Royalists. He and others who **Army** had the same desire had enough influence in Parliament to secure authority for the complete reorganization of the Roundhead army. In time, then, there appeared a smaller, but stronger and better equipped military force which was named the New Model Army. This

209

army of about 50,000 men was well officered and extremely well disciplined. The second officer in command of the New Model Army was Oliver Cromwell.

It was not long before the New Model Army had the chance to show what it could do. Following a few unimportant clashes with the enemy, the Roundheads met the Royalists in a major engagement, the Battle of Naseby, in June, 1645. In sweeping cavalry charges Cromwell threw such confusion into the enemy infantry and horsemen that the battle was won. It was a costly defeat for Charles because he lost half his cavalry, most of his infantry and artillery, and many of his best officers. An historian of the time said, "The King and the Kingdom were lost at Naseby."

Battle of Naseby, 1645

Charles I was forced to flee from the battle-field with only a small guard of cavalrymen for protection. No less damaging to the King than the defeat itself was the capture of his military correspondence. Letters falling into the hands of the Roundheads are supposed to have revealed that Charles I had planned to bring a foreign army into the Civil War.

Warfare continued for a few months, but it was a one-sided conflict now as the New Model Army captured towns, forts and castles which had been held by the Royalists. Finally conditions became so desperate for Charles that he had no other choice but to give in. In May, 1646, he rode unhappily into the lines of the Scottish forces and surrendered himself to the commander. Shortly after this event the King was handed over to Parliament by whose command he was placed in "honourable imprisonment."

End of Civil War, 1646

Charles surrender

Following Charles' surrender there was a lengthy period of discussion regarding a proper settlement of matters between King and Parliament. Although various plans were put forward by which Charles might be returned to the throne and the liberties of the people insured, none of these seemed to suit both Charles and members of Parliament. Hoping that some miracle would save him, the King kept the discussions going as long as possible. In the meantime he made secret bids for help from the French, the Irish, the Scots and others. His actions proved beyond a doubt that he could not be trusted.

Ill-feeling between Presbyterian and Independents continued within the Puritan party, causing endless quarrels. One difficulty was that Parliament was controlled largely by Presbyterians and the New Model Army by Independents. Members of the House of Commons wished to disband the Army because the Civil War was over, while

1645

Philiphaugh

Newcastle

Carlisle

Scarborough

Marston Moor York
R. Ouse
Preston
Bolton Pontefract

Newark

R. Trent
Lichfield

Naseby

Worcester

Cropredy Br.

R. Severn

Gloucester
R. Thames Oxford

London

Maidstone

Sedgemoor
Taunton
Lyme

Exeter
Braddock Dn.
ostwithiel Plymouth

CONTROLLED BY THE KING
AT THE END OF 1645

CONTROLLED BY PARLIAM-
ENT AT BEGINNING OF 1645

LOST BY THE KING DURING
1645

The Civil War, 1645

A Royalist or Cavalier soldier. The costumes of the Royalists were many and varied, but generally more dashing in appearance than those of the Roundheads. This cavalryman wears a broad-brimmed, felt hat with plume, wide soft collar, high-heeled leather boots, a thick leather coat, and his hair is worn shoulder length. At times he might wear a breastplate. Cavalrymen were considered much more valuable than infantry, and were paid three times as much, although they had to provide their own horses.

the military men were determined to hold the Army together until a final agreement was made with Charles I.

Oliver Cromwell, who was both a member of Parliament and a military leader, tried in vain to reach some sort of suitable settlement. The stalemate was finally brought to an end when the Army took swift action to gain its own goal. King Charles I was seized, troops were sent into London, and charges made against eleven important members of Parliament. The accused members promptly fled to the continent. Even after these strong measures had been taken, the Army found itself in difficulty, for a series of uprisings in favour of the King took place in various parts of England and Scotland. In the Second Civil War which followed the veteran troops of Cromwell soon won victory.

In spite of the Army's powerful position, Parliament still kept up **Pride's Purge** a bold front, continuing to treat with Charles I. Deciding that affairs had gone far enough, Cromwell in December, 1648, sent troops into London. The soldiers under Colonel Pride took up a position outside the House of Commons, refusing entrance to any members known to be favourable to the King. By this action called *Pride's Purge* 143 Presbyterian members of the House were removed from Parliament. The remaining members, mostly Independents, then declared themselves to be the highest authority of government in England.

212

The time for action against Charles I had come. One hundred and thirty-five men were appointed to a High Court of Justice which was to try the King on a charge of high treason. Although a large number of men refused to act, sixty of the appointed members were determined to carry out their duties. Charles, grasping at any means of escape, refused trial on the ground that no court could try an English monarch. His protest was ignored as the High Court of Justice proceeded.

In the formal charge made against Charles during the trial the grievances of the people were summed up. The long charge finished with the following paragraphs:

All which wicked designs, wars and evil practices of him, the said Charles Stuart, have been and are carried on for the advancement and upholding of a personal interest of will, power, and pretended prerogative to himself and his family, against the public interest, common right, liberty, justice, and peace of the people of this nation, by and from whom was entrusted as aforesaid.

By all which it appeareth that the said Charles Stuart hath been, and is the occasioner, author, and continuer of the said unnatural, cruel and bloody wars; and therein guilty of all the treasons, murders, rapines, burnings, spoils, desolations, damages and mischiefs to this nation, acted and committed in the said wars, or occasioned thereby.

Charles I was found guilty and sentenced to death.

Throughout the trial the King conducted himself in a resolute and gentlemanly manner, a fact which aroused considerable admiration among the people. As he was led away from the court chamber there was a persistent sound of "God Save the King!"

Execution of Charles I, 1649

The last day of January, 1649, was set as the date of execution. Snow was falling and the air was cold as the fateful hour approached. Groups of alert soldiers stood guard to prevent disturbances or attempts at rescue. Charles I walked calmly to the scaffold, delivered his last words, helped the executioner adjust a white cap over his long hair, and then knelt before the block. There was an agonizing hush over the observers as Charles himself gave the signal . . . and the axe fell.

A King had paid a terrible penalty for being unable to recognize or understand the will of his people.

213

36

THE COMMONWEALTH

English people soon forgot the faults of King Charles I, remembering only a glorified legend which bore little resemblance to the monarch's true character. The eldest son of the dead King, then in exile, was considered by many to be the rightful ruler, and in private they called him King Charles II.

Prince Charles had very little chance of gaining the English throne while a determined assembly sat in the House of Commons. The members could not forget the injustices and bloodshed which had been suffered during the last reign. Sixty men who still held seats in the Long Parliament considered themselves the only true government, for they had been elected by the people.

The Common-wealth, 1649

Setting their minds to the task of reorganizing the English form of government, the House of Commons abolished Kingship and the House of Lords. By such action England ceased to be a monarchy and became a republic or Commonwealth controlled by Parliament and a Council of State. As might be expected Oliver Cromwell was appointed to the Council, and in the following years proved a useful link between army and government.

The actual declaration, May, 1649, which brought in the Commonwealth read as follows:

Be it declared and enacted by this present Parliament, and by authority of the same, that the people of England, and of all the dominions and territories thereunto belonging, are and shall be, and are hereby constituted, made, established and confirmed, to be a Commonwealth and Free State and shall henceforth be governed as a Commonwealth and Free State by the supreme authority of this nation, the representatives of the people in Parliament, and by such as they shall appoint and constitute as officers and ministers under them for the good of the people, and that without any King or House of Lords.

Rebellion in Ireland

Following the execution of the King, the unpredictable Irish rebelled, as Catholics and Protestants united to drive English power from the country. Not content with mere rebellion, the Irish were bold enough to name Prince Charles as their King. The newly formed Commonwealth was not prepared to accept what it felt was an Irish insult. Accordingly, Cromwell went to Ireland with an army of hardy veterans who had no great difficulty in crushing the revolt. Cromwell remained in Ireland for about a year before returning home for other military duties. His son-in-law took over the Irish command and carried a harsh campaign through all the island. Cities were captured, castles smashed and lands taken away from the rebels. By 1652 Ireland lay wholly under the control of the Commonwealth.

The Scots made the same costly mistake of naming Prince Charles **Rebellion in Scotland** (d). as their rightful ruler. Cromwell, then home from Ireland, led a powerful force to Scotland. In September, 1650 he defeated the Scottish army at the Battle of Dunbar and captured the city of Edinburgh. Even then the Scots were not humbled, for the following year Prince Charles with an army at his back marched southward, hoping that the English would rise in his support. It was a vain hope broken by a smashing defeat at Worcester where Oliver Cromwell once again showed his military skill. The power of the Commonwealth was now supreme. No one dared challenge the government.

Although matters seemed secure at home, Parliament did have **Rivalry with the Dutch** (e) problems abroad, problems in trade and commerce. English seamen sailing the distant parts of the world found themselves faced with the (i) Dutch wherever they went. Holland had become a first-rate commercial nation, building excellent ships and pushing trade to faraway places. In Europe, Africa, the East Indies and America the English and the Dutch were competing for business. Such a situation, of course, resulted in quarrels among merchants and indeed between the two governments. Prince Charles, who was living as an exile in Holland, did not improve relations.

In an effort to curb Dutch prosperity, the English Parliament passed a Navigation Act to control the means by which trade goods (ii) reached the nation. By this act, goods from America, Asia and Africa could only be carried to England in vessels owned and operated by Englishmen; goods from Europe could only be transported to England in vessels owned by the country producing the goods. Holland was very much annoyed by this act which had the effect of reducing Dutch trade in the British Isles. Bitterness reached such a high point in (iii) 1652 that war was declared. A series of naval battles were fought in the English Channel and North Sea. After two years of conflict in which the English won most victories a treaty was signed, Holland agreeing to recognize the Navigation Act.

In spite of the Commonwealth's recent successes the government was not popular throughout the country. Because the Long Parliament had actually been in power for thirteen years without re-election,

English seamen sailing to distant parts of the world found themselves faced with the Dutch wherever they went. Dutch ships, like the one on the right, were a little smaller and drew less water than those of rival nations. Most ships of the time had elaborately carved sterns which were decorated with gold leaf. Upper parts of the hulls were painted in brilliant colours, while the lower sections were heavily oiled or varnished.

there was a desire among the people for a change of members. Oliver Cromwell and the Army were among those who saw advantages in a fresh election. Parliament, however, was opposed to its own dissolution, because the members feared another assembly might give up the Commonwealth and accept Prince Charles as King. Probably there was good reason for such a thought.

Oliver Cromwell Oliver Cromwell had become the most powerful and most respected or hated man in the nation, depending on the viewpoint. Coming from a good family, he was first elected to Parliament at the age of twenty-nine. His military career had begun in 1642 when he was forty-three years of age. His success as a commander had largely arisen from the fact that he could organize and train skilful cavalry

216

troops. During the Civil War he proved that he was a genius in detecting weak spots in the enemy and in taking advantage of these weaknesses.

His rise from an unknown cavalry officer and member of Parliament to military commander and national figure was remarkable. Although Cromwell was not a handsome man, he was tall, dignified and impressive. He was deeply religious but practical in his views. The advice he gave to his soldiers was, "Trust in God, and keep your powder dry."

Cromwell, fully convinced that the Long Parliament had outgrown its usefulness, hoped that conditions would force a new election. His anger burst forth when he learned that the members were on the point of passing an act which would prolong its life. With thirty musketeers he hurried to the House of Commons and, leaving his men outside, took his place in the assembly. After listening impatiently for a short time, he leaped to his feet, shouting, "Come! Come! I will put an end to your prating. You are no Parliament!" Then calling his musketeers he cleared the members from the House and ordered the door to be locked.

Cromwell expells Parliament, 1653

By this high-handed action, Oliver Cromwell swept away centuries of progress in the slow development of English government. By a single sharp command representatives of the people were thrown from office at the point of muskets. For the moment there was just one strong man in command of English government.

During the night some London prankster wrote on a Parliament door, "This House to let—unfurnished."

Cromwell did not want to rule by himself, but at the same time he did not dare risk a free vote in the election of a new Parliament. A free election, he feared, might pave the way to return the monarchy. He solved the problem by having members of Parliament appointed instead of elected. This method was not democratic, but very useful from Cromwell's standpoint. So it was that in a few weeks' time an assembly, sometimes called the Little Parliament, met for its first session. Cromwell tried to stay on the sidelines, hoping that the new assembly would manage affairs in an able manner. Unfortunately most of the members were unacquainted with government business, and some demanded ridiculous changes in national life. The people as a whole neither respected nor trusted the Little Parliament. Before the end of the year the members voted themselves out of office and placed authority in the iron hands of Oliver Cromwell.

217

37

THE PROTECTORATE

Once again England found itself without a government, but with a powerful military commander backed by armed forces. With Oliver Cromwell's approval a group of leading army officers created a new plan of government, a Protectorate, which gave highest power to the Lord Protector who was to be assisted by a Council and by a Parliament meeting every three years.

In December, 1653, during a ceremony Oliver Cromwell sat in a chair of state, and was made *Lord Protector of the Commonwealth of England, Scotland and Ireland*. From that time on he acted as a king, receiving the kind of homage and respect as is accorded to royalty. Although he did not bear the title "King," he held more power than most monarchs of the time. He was a true dictator with a devoted army at his call.

In his dealings with other nations, the Lord Protector was most skilful. He made useful treaties with France and Holland and fought a war against Spain in which a Spanish fleet was destroyed and Jamaica was captured.

The first Parliament of the Protectorate met in 1654. Trouble **Exclusion** flared immediately as one hundred members of the House of Commons **of members** refused to sign an oath of loyalty which read in this way, "I do hereby **from** **Parliament** freely promise and engage, that I will be true and faithful to the Lord Protector and Commonwealth of England, Scotland and Ireland and that according to the terms of the indentures whereby I am returned to serve in this present Parliament, I will not propose, or consent, to alter the government as it is settled in a sole person and the Parliament."

Members who refused to sign the oath were prevented from entering the House by armed guards. A member of Parliament named Goddard has described the scene in these words:

Going by water to Westminster, I was told that Parliament doors were locked up and guarded with soldiers, and the barges were to attend the Protector to the Painted Chamber. As I went I saw two barges at the Privy Stairs. Being come to the Hall, I was confirmed in what I had heard.

218

As a result of voyages of exploration and discovery, the Englishman's table was enriched by a number of foreign foods during the sixteenth and seventeenth centuries. Among these were pears, green peppers, maize, potatoes, pineapples, lemons, oranges, coffee and tea. Tobacco as well came into popular use during the same period.

Nevertheless, I did purpose not to take things merely upon trust, but would receive an actual repulse, to confirm my faith.

Accordingly, I attempted up the Parliament-stairs, but there was a guard of soldiers, who told me there was no passage that way; that the House was locked up, and command given to give no admittance to any. That, if I were a member, I might go into the Painted Chamber, where the Protector would presently be.

The members of Parliament who signed oaths of loyalty began the session, but they accomplished very little. Some of them wanted to reduce Cromwell's army to cut down expenses. Some wanted to make drastic laws against citizens whose religious beliefs were not agreeable to Parliament. Oliver Cromwell hoped that the members would deal with practical and useful matters, but in this he was disappointed. After five months he dissolved his first Parliament.

A soldier of Cromwell's New Model Army. He wears three-quarter armour and a "lobster-tail" helmet. Like the Royalist soldier, he is wearing heavy leather boots. A variety of guns was in use at the time of the Civil War. The matchlock and wheel lock were in wide use, but a newer and simpler flintlock was gaining in favour. This latter weapon "made its own fire" by means of a flint striking a metal flange and igniting the charge of powder. This soldier carries two guns which were hung over his horse near the pommel of the saddle.

Sober Puritan life Cromwell tried a new kind of local government which displeased the English people. England was divided into eleven districts each under a Major-general. These officials were required to command local troops, to prevent Royalist plots and to oversee local officers in the maintenance of law and order. The enforcement of law was no easy matter because the Commonwealth and Protectorate had introduced a series of laws in keeping with the sober views of Puritan life. There were heavy fines for swearing, playing cards and the use of dice. No Christmas puddings were allowed, no theatres, and no dancing. Music, in which England had reached a foremost position in Europe, under

220

Elizabeth with such composers as Purcell and Byrd, became a lost art because no song was permitted. Even the May-poles in the villages were cut down. It is not surprising then that the English people wished for the "good old days" in spite of mistakes made by Charles I.

Cromwell still wished to rule the Commonwealth with the help of a Parliament, so, in 1656, he called his second Parliament of the Protectorate. One hundred members, however, were prevented from taking their places in the House because it was believed they were opposed to the Protectorate. Those who actually were allowed to enter presented Cromwell with a new plan of government. By this plan, Cromwell was to become King, the Council was to be abolished, and the House of Lords was to be brought back into Parliament. Cromwell, after some hesitation, refused to become King, but he agreed to the other changes suggested by members. Cromwell refuses to be king

The second Parliament of the Protectorate accomplished little more than the first one had. Members of the House of Commons spent a great deal of time discussing matters which were unimportant or which did not apply to the business of the lower House. On the other hand they neglected to deal with problems of importance. Finally after two years this Parliament, too, was dissolved. The problem of operating an English government by means of a Lord Protector and an elected assembly had not been solved.

By the summer of 1658 Oliver Cromwell was ill, and as the days passed, his condition grew worse. Lying in bed, he was saddened by the thought that his efforts to bring strong government to England had been a failure. In spite of his many faults Cromwell was a sincere and religious man who firmly believed that God had chosen him to rule the nation. As he lay dying, he prayed, using these words: Death of Cromwell, 1658

Thou hast made me, though very unworthy, a mean instrument to do them some good, and Thee service; and many of them have set too high a value upon me, though others wish and would be glad of my death. Pardon such a desire to trample on the dust of a poor worm, for they are Thy people too; and pardon the folly of this short prayer, even for Jesus Christ's sake, and give us a good night, if it be Thy pleasure. Amen.

The Lord Protector's funeral took place with all the splendour and pomp customarily accorded to kings, and his body was laid to rest in Westminster Abbey.

38

THE RETURN OF MONARCHY UNDER CHARLES II

Because even the great Oliver Cromwell had experienced difficulty ruling England as Lord Protector, it seemed unlikely that anyone else could succeed in the same post. Cromwell's son, Richard, who became the new Protector certainly was not the man to win such success. Nevertheless, the English people welcomed the change, believing they had been delivered from a tyrant.

Richard Cromwell proved to be a feeble but inoffensive ruler, quite incapable of governing the Commonwealth. The historian Kennett describes the new Lord Protector in this way:

. . . neither a military man nor a statesman; rather an honest country gentleman, bred to privacy and sports, and willing to serve his neighbours, and even the cavaliers, by the little interest he had in his father's court. His own father seemed to have the least affection and the lowest opinion of this son among all his other children. He never trusted him in any command, nor employed him in any true business.

Richard Cromwell resigns, 1659

The unfortunate Richard Cromwell, who became known as "Tumbledown Dick," recognized the hopelessness of his position, and so resigned quietly from his office as Lord Protector.

The New Model Army, now without its commander, Oliver Cromwell, broke into a number of rival factions quarrelling among themselves. The cleverest general of the Army, George Monck, was a patriotic, unselfish, strong leader who gained control of the quarrelling groups. Desiring to see a proper government formed, Monck occupied London with troops, and called for a free election. The Parliament thus elected then invited Prince Charles to take the throne which had been vacant since the execution of his father, King Charles I. On May 29, 1660, Charles entered London. A description of the scene in the city states that "the ways were strewed with flowers, the bells ringing and the streets hung with tapestries."

Charles II, 1660

The new king was a handsome witty fellow, thirty years of age, who really was more interested in his own pleasures than he was in his duties as monarch. Like his father he was selfish and proud, but he lacked the determination and stubbornness of Charles I. The new King had no intention of losing his own head by the executioner's axe,

Return of Monarchy Under Charles II

(2)

Charles and Parliament busied themselves with matters still left over from the bitter days of the Civil War. The New Model Army was paid its back wages and then disbanded. Laws were passed doing away with the old feudal duties. Lands seized from the King and Church during the war were handed back, but other properties lost by Royalists were left in the hands of the new owners. The most difficult problem lay in the pardon, or punishment, of those who had rebelled against Charles I. While it is true that Parliament proceeded to pardon most of those who had engaged in the rebellion, still there was a long list of names issued for punishment. Some of the accused persons were forced into exile; some were fined; some imprisoned and some put to death. Among those who suffered execution were thirteen men who had been members of the High Court of Justice which had sent Charles I to the block. A more shocking and barbarous act than this was carried out when the bodies of Oliver Cromwell and others were removed from their graves, hung in chains, and later thrown into a pit.

It was most unfortunate that the perpetual religious troubles **Church of England restored** could not have been settled at a time when England was starting afresh under Charles II. The Parliament of 1661, in no mood for religious freedom, and under the King's first minister, Clarendon, did everything possible to restore the authority of the Church of England. The bishops and the Prayer Book were brought back. Not content with this change, members of Parliament required the clergymen of England to make a statement saying that they agreed with all things contained in the Prayer Book.

During the protest which followed, about 2,000 ministers, mostly Presbyterians, resigned their offices rather than bow before the demands of the Church of England. Presbyterians, Baptists, Quakers and others who were opposed to the established Church came to be called *Dissenters.* Undoubtedly these Dissenters would have been satisfied if they had been allowed to form their own congregations and to worship as they pleased, but this was not permitted by law. King Charles II would have been willing to permit more religious freedom throughout the nation, but Parliament was determined to have one strong Church.

A pewter tankard of the time of Charles II. The use of pewter in England extended back for many centuries, and its manufacture was regulated. Pewter was commonly produced by a mixture of two metals—four-fifths tin and one-fifth lead. In appearance, pewter is a soft, silver-grey colour. By the time of Charles II dishes and cups were made not only of pewter, but of silver, pottery and wood. In the early part of the eighteenth century chinaware was becoming popular.

In a short time the Church of England had regained all its former authority in England. Its members controlled Parliament, offices within the government, education, charity and all Church affairs. No other religious group dared to stand out against its powerful organization.

War with the Dutch England and Holland were still active rivals in trade, as seamen, traders, merchants and adventurers scrambled for trade and land in distant parts of the globe. Both countries were seeking goods and founding colonies in the East Indies, in the West Indies and on the mainland of America. Both countries fished in the North Sea, hunted whales in the Arctic, and held trading settlements on the west coast of Africa. It was not surprising, then, that war once again broke out between England and Holland. Battles were fought in America, Africa and the English Channel.

After a number of enemy victories, a Dutch fleet sailed up the Thames and burned shipping at Chatham. They boasted that the English fleet had been swept from the sea. In fact Charles had neglected the fleet to pay his father's debts. The English and Dutch were so evenly matched that, in 1667, they made peace on a give-and-take arrangement. England gave up the Spice Islands (Moluccas) of the East Indies, agreeing to restrict her eastern trade to the mainland of India. Holland, on the other hand, gave up the American settlement of New Amsterdam (New York) and certain forts on the coast of Africa. English coins called *guineas* were made during the reign of Charles II from gold brought from a stretch of the African shore known as the Guinea Coast.

Hudson's Bay Company, 1670 Two French bush rangers, Radisson and Groseilliers, arrived in London with tales of fabulous fur lands in northern Canada. The King's cousin, Prince Rupert, and others took such interest in these stories that in 1668 they outfitted an expedition to Hudson Bay under the two Frenchmen. The voyage was an astonishing success when a shipload of furs arrived in England the following year. As a result King Charles II granted in 1670 a charter to Prince Rupert and seventeen others who formed a company known as the *Governor and Company of Adventurers of England trading into Hudson's Bay*. By this charter the Hudson's Bay Company was granted all the land drained by rivers flowing into Hudson Bay. No one at the time realized that Charles II was disposing of a vast territory stretching from northern Quebec to the Rocky Mountains.

224

The Dutch people were persuaded by Prince William of Orange, who later became King of England, to open their dikes and flood the land over which the French were advancing. Soldiers in small boats are seen rowing over Dutch farm land past their well known windmills.

After a trade and colonial settlement was made between England The Triple Alliance, 1668 and Holland, the two nations became more or less friendly. Such friendship grew as France under King Louis XIV developed into a dangerous nation with strong armed forces at its command. The English realized that with such a threat lying next door, it would be wise to keep Holland as a friend and ally. In consequence, England, Holland and Sweden joined in a pact, *The Triple Alliance,* with the aim of keeping France in her place.

King Charles II was not altogether pleased with the signing of the Triple Alliance because he did not trust the Dutch, and because he wished to remain on good terms with the French monarch. He could not forget that his own uncle had once been Louis XIII of France. Secretly, he made a treaty with King Louis XIV, offering English troops in a war against Holland, in return for which he would receive sums of money.

225

By 1672, in spite of the terms of the Triple Alliance, the English

More war with the Dutch and the French were fighting the Dutch on land and sea. After two years of rather useless fighting, the war was brought to a close.

The hearts of the English people had not been in this struggle with Holland, for the French were their old enemies. King Charles II and his cousin Louis XIV realized that the English people could not again be brought to fight the Dutch. The only hope of the two scheming monarchs was to keep England out of war on the continent. In order to accomplish this, Louis paid Charles II large sums each year so that the English King would not have to ask his Parliament for money. It was a strange situation—an English monarch being paid to keep his nation at peace by a neighbouring country which threatened at any time to become a dangerous enemy.

During the reign of Charles II political parties made their first

Whigs and Tories appearance in England. Because Parliament met often, its members had the opportunity of forming themselves into groups to support causes or to gain the goals they desired. From these groups there developed two political parties. Members of the first group, the Tories, believed in strong government, monarchy, and the Church of England. Country gentlemen, and clergymen belonged to this party. Members of the second group, the Whigs, believed in democratic government, a controlled monarchy, and religious freedom for Protestants. Noblemen, merchants and city-dwellers made up much of this party. In the beginning the names applied to the parties were terms of scorn: Tories meant "wild Irish outlaws or highwaymen," while Whigs meant "fanatical Scottish Dissenters." As time went by, the original meaning of the names was forgotten so that they were used in a serious and polite manner. Even today the word Whig is sometimes used to mean "Liberal," and the word Tory is sometimes used to mean "Conservative."

During the reign of Charles II there were two great writers work-

John Milton ing in England. The first of these, John Milton, was a Puritan whose writings during the Civil War had spoken in the cause of liberty. By the time monarchy was restored, Milton had lost his sight and was unable to write except by dictating his words to others. His most famous work, *Paradise Lost,* is one of the greatest poems ever written in the English language.

The second writer, John Bunyan, was at one time a soldier in the

John Bunyan Puritan army, and later a Baptist minister. Because he continued to resist the authority of the Church of England during the time of

226

Charles II, Bunyan was kept in prison for a long period of time. While in captivity, he wrote pamphlets and articles on religious subjects. In 1678, his greatest work, *Pilgrim's Progress,* made its appearance. Although this book appears to be a simple story, it had deep religious and political meaning. *Pilgrim's Progress* represented the feelings and hopes of the Dissenters in England at that time.

Of all the acts of Parliament passed during the reign of Charles II none was more vital than the Habeas Corpus Act, 1679, because it brought to English law a fresh feeling of true justice. *Habeas corpus* meaning "You may have the body," was a court order requiring jailers, or others, holding a captive to release him to a court, and to state the reason for confinement. Although something like this had been part of law since the days of *Magna Carta,* there were periods in English history when men were held captive without a stated reason or a proper trial. Kings and powerful ministers had found this a useful method of removing bothersome enemies. **Habeas Corpus Act, 1679**

The Habeas Corpus Act was drawn up by Parliament to prevent further injustices of this kind and to protect the freedom of citizens. By the act any prisoner might claim a writ of Habeas Corpus, so that he could be brought before a court, and have the reason of his captivity stated. During the following years the act became so effective that it protected Englishmen from illegal imprisonment and limited the powers formerly used by the King. Habeas Corpus still remains an important and respected part of law in the British Isles, in United States, in Canada and many other countries of the modern world.

Charles' religious troubles seemed never to be over. He made a Declaration of Indulgence, which did away with penalties against both Dissenters and Catholics. The King hoped that the Dissenters would be so happy with the new freedom that they would not notice that Catholics had received the same treatment. Instead, it united the Protestants and even though the Declaration was withdrawn because Parliament declared it illegal, the way was left open for more harsh treatment of Catholics. For more than a century and a half neither Catholics nor Dissenters could hold public office or hold commissions in the army or navy because of the Test Act which required individuals holding office to take sacrament according to the rites of the English Church. Later, false rumours of a plot by Catholics against the government brought a wave of panic and many innocent men were put to death. **Declaration of Indulgence, 1672**

227

39

JOY AND TRAGEDY UNDER CHARLES II

After the grim struggles of the Civil War and the restless days of the Commonwealth, the English people entered a new period under the restored monarchy of Charles II. Their former ways of life were changed and their habits altered by a number of practices which were fresh to the nation.

Newspapers were being published and read as never before, causing public interest in events at home and abroad. By the latter part of Charles II's reign a number of important papers expressing both **Changes in** Whig and Tory views were sold in London. Besides political informa-**English** tion, news events and social activities, the newspapers began to print **life** advertisements, many of which throw light on English life of that time. The *Public Advertiser* published on Tuesday, June 16, 1657, contained the following:

In Bishopsgate Street, in Queen's Head Alley, at a Frenchman's House, is an excellent West India Drink, called chocolate, to be sold, where you may have it ready at any time, and also unmade, at reasonable rates.

If chocolate was new to the English people, tea must have been equally so, for another advertisement, appearing in 1658, had this to say:

That excellent, and by all physitians approved, China drink, called by the Chineans Tcha, by other nations Tay, *alias* Tee, is sold at the Sultaness Head, a cophee-house at Sweeting's Rents, by the Royal Exchange, London.

Mention of the coffee-house in the above advertisement indicates **Coffee** that these shops had become very popular. The first of the coffee-**houses** houses was opened by a Greek in London during the year 1652. So successful was this business, that dozens of others made their appearance, thus attracting great numbers of citizens. It was here in the coffee-houses that Englishmen, especially wealthy men, gathered to read newspapers and to discuss politics, sports, fashions, books and other subjects of interest. The coffee-houses were much more than restaurants serving beverages; they were social centres where men met to exchange opinions. Certain groups gathering over cups of coffee undoubtedly criticized the government and made harsh statements concerning the

Men gathering in a coffee-house. A custom of the time led men of similiar interests to gather in the same coffee-houses. Thus classical scholars met at the "Grecian", poets met at "Will's", and men of the shipping companies met at "Lloyd's." Clothing worn by gentlemen of the time was ornate with lace and linen. Cleanliness was not fashionable, so that men bathed infrequently and had their linen laundered just once a month. Instead they used perfume. Wigs made from horse hair or goat hair were commonly worn because those made from human hair were very expensive. The gentleman in the foreground is smoking a long clay pipe known as a "churchwarden."

King. Believing this to be the case, Charles II ordered all the coffee-houses to be closed, but after a short time he approved their re-opening when the owners promised to stop all disloyal discussions.

During this period gentlemen appearing in the coffee-houses were **Clothing** wearing costumes far different from the greys and blacks of Puritan gentlemen. The long cloak and the puffed trousers of Elizabethan days had given away to tunics, vests and tight knee breeches. Boots were no longer in style except for riding, so that men walked about in low shoes fitted with high heels and large metal buckles. Men's hats were wide, low in the crown, and decorated with a bow to one side, but there were no feathers. Perhaps the most startling article of dress worn by some gentlemen was a muff hung about the neck by means of a ribbon. Samuel Pepys, the famous English diarist, used his wife's old muff after she had purchased a better one. As a final touch to their costumes, the men wore large wigs which they enjoyed combing while they watched plays and other amusements.

Entertainment

It would seem that London people who could afford to do so were very hospitable, for they entertained at dinners beginning at one o'clock in the afternoon. After the meal was over, guests remained until evening, drinking, smoking, playing cards, and watching tricks of magic. Guests of this period must have been hearty eaters. Samuel Pepys says that on one occasion he served the following small dinner:

. . . a dish of marrow-bones; a leg of mutton; a loin of veal; a dish of fowl, three pullets and a dozen larks all in a dish; a great tart, a neat's tongue, a dish of anchovies; a dish of prawns and cheese.

Great Plague of London, 1665

Although the English may have eaten well, their standard of health was low in comparison with that of today. Medical science had not developed to the stage where it was skilful in surgery or in the prevention of serious diseases. Indeed, a number of old superstitions concerning healing existed among the people. By one of these it was believed that the King could cure certain diseases by a touch of the royal hand. Although Charles II himself considered this to be superstitious nonsense, he continued the practice on the advice of his ministers.

Diseases of many kinds harassed the English from time to time, but none was more dreaded than the bubonic plague. Several epidemics of this illness had occurred since the Black Death in 1348 and 1349, but none of these were disasters. In the summer of 1665, however, the "silent killer" returned to London, spreading death and terror, as it had three hundred years before. The narrow crowded streets of the city and the unsanitary conditions within the homes helped the swift growth of the epidemic.

At the height of the disaster in September, 1665, one thousand people a day were dying in London from the effects of the Great Plague. Shops were closed, streets lay almost deserted, and coffins remained at doorways, awaiting burial. Most of the churchmen, magistrates, many of the doctors and all of the wealthy people fled from the city seeking safety in the country or in Europe. Although the exact number of citizens who died in the Great Plague of London is not known, it may have run as high as 75,000, almost one-sixth of the population.

A fire-engine of about 1675. The round tank of the engine held water, but it had to be re-filled constantly by men with buckets. While a man on top directed a stream of water shooting from a leather hose, four others worked the long double hands of the pump. Fire-engines of this type, even if they had existed at the time of the Great Fire, would have been ineffective for they developed a low pressure stream.

Shortly after the Great Plague had spent its force, another tragedy fell upon the city. A small fire which started in a bakery on Pudding Lane near London Bridge was suddenly whipped into a raging sea of flames spreading across the city. When King Charles II heard the news of this shocking new disaster, he ordered the Lord Mayor to have homes pulled down in the path of the flames so that the fire might be brought under control. Citizens, however, were more interested in saving their own household articles than they were in tearing down buildings. Consequently the Lord Mayor stood by helplessly as much of London felt the fiery touch of the crackling flames.

John Evelyn, a diarist and friend of Samuel Pepys, described the fire in these words:

The stones of Paul's flew like grenadoes (cannon balls), the melting lead running down the streets in a stream, and the very pavements glowing with fiery redness . . . God grant my eye may never behold the like. I now saw about ten thousand houses all in one flame. The noise and cracking and thunder of the flames, the hurry of the people, the fall of the towers, houses and churches was like an awful storm. The air was so hot that at last men were not able to approach the fire, and were forced to stand still and let the flames burn on, which they did for nearly two miles in length and one in breadth. The clouds of smoke were dismal, and reached nearly fifty-six miles in length. London was, but is no more!

Charles II was far more heroic during the crisis than was the Lord Mayor, for the King hurried into the very centre of danger, issuing orders like an army officer. He called seamen and soldiers, ordered houses blown up, passed pails of water, and helped citizens to safety.

After three days the Great Fire had destroyed most of the city, wiping out many ancient and historical buildings. Although the fire appeared at the time to be a major misfortune, it eventually proved to be a blessing. Hundreds of dirty, unhealthy, crowded structures were gone, and so were the disease germs which lingered on after the plague.

King Charles and Parliament took prompt action to rebuild London, but in so doing they were careful to avoid many of the mistakes which had been made in the past. By proclamation there were to be no more wooden houses, no narrow lanes, and no smoke-producing factories or shops in certain areas of the city. Christopher Wren, the greatest architect of his time, worked unceasingly in the enormous task of restoring the city. Although he designed no less than fifty-two new churches, his greatest problem was in the reconstruction of St. Paul's Cathedral. For thirty-five years, 1675 to 1710, this clever little man supervised the slow work of building the enormous Cathedral which is today one of the best known buildings in the world.

In spite of such misfortunes the reign of Charles II was a comparatively gay period in England. Released from the stern restrictions of Puritan rule, the people entertained themselves by a number of amusements. Theatres, horseraces and cock-fights drew constant gatherings. The playing of cards and the dancing of French dances caused considerable interest among society people. Ancient English sports such as bull-baiting and bear-baiting were still enjoyed by the lower classes, but were no longer fashionable among gentlemen who preferred to watch boxing or sword fighting.

Travel During this period people gained a desire to move about the country with the result that travelling conditions improved. Stage coaches which appeared in the time of Oliver Cromwell became common in the reign of Charles II. The famous "Flying Coaches" of 1677 could travel about fifty miles a day, a journey costing passengers the sum of ten shillings. New inns with soft beds and good dining rooms were built along the highways to care for travellers who rode the stage coaches or in private carriages. It must not be imagined, however, that travel was comfortable or completely free of danger, for rough

232

roads and sometimes highwaymen added adventure and risk to the journeys.

Although the reign of Charles II was marked by religious bitter- **Death of** ness, by disease and by fire, the English people as a whole grew to love **Charles II, 1685** their King. As he took his vigorous morning walks through the streets of London, Charles II and his devoted subjects exchanged cheerful greetings. He was a man of many weaknesses, but a man gifted with a certain measure of generosity, sympathy and common sense. He was the only Stuart monarch of England who tried to understand his people, or who realized the limits of royal power. Charles II recognized that King and Parliament must work together in government, and that the Divine Right of Kings was a delusion.

When in January, 1685, he took seriously ill, the churches of London were filled with people praying for the King's swift recovery to health. When he died, the city felt a deep sorrow.

40

JAMES II AND A TROUBLED NATION

Shortly after Charles II died in 1685, his brother was crowned as King (d) **James II. The new monarch had all the stubborn pride and determination of the Stuart family. He did not have, however, the easy manner, the wit or the good humour of Charles II. A staunch Catholic, King James II was eager to gain a place for his own faith in England.**

Not everyone was pleased with the crowning of James II, for many citizens would have preferred a Protestant. The only possibility was (d) the Duke of Monmouth who was not recognized legally as the son of Charles II. He decided to attempt a seizure of royal power. Arriving **James II,** in England, he declared himself to be the rightful ruler of the nation. **1685** Large numbers of Dissenters and others from the lower classes rallied about the Duke of Monmouth with the purpose of placing him on the throne. Excitement spread through the country, causing Parliament to label the Duke as a traitor. In spite of this action, "King Monmouth" marched on London with a motley army of poor farmers, miners and

Here is a small gun, or mortar. This weapon, the idea of which originated in Holland, had a barrel about twice as long as the bore, and fired its charge at a high angle so it would drop on the enemy. At about this time gunners discovered that if a cannon ball was fitted with a fuse and powder, it would explode when at, or near, the target. Cannon balls of this kind, of course, were much more destructive than the ordinary kind.

cloth workers. They carried a queer assortment of weapons ranging from guns to bill hooks and pitchforks. It was a keen disappointment to Monmouth that none of the wealthy or noble gentlemen of England joined his cause. A few powerful men of importance would have given him much greater power in his fight for the crown.

Monmouth Rebellion   James II, rallying his own troops, marched from London with a force of regulars and militia, meeting Monmouth at the Battle of Sedgemoor, July 6, 1685. The untrained and undisciplined men of the rebel force were easily defeated and scattered by the King's soldiers. His dreams of glory lost on the battlefield, the Duke of Monmouth was placed in prison and a few days later was executed.

The Battle of Sedgemoor was followed by a series of harsh trials called the Bloody Assizes in which rebels were tried on charges of treason. Chief Justice Jeffreys, who conducted the trials, was a merciless man issuing harsh sentences to the prisoners appearing before his court. During the course of the Bloody Assizes, 300 men were hanged, another 851 were sent to slavery in the West Indies, and an aged woman, Alice Lisle, was beheaded because she had sheltered two rebels in her home.

As a reward for his merciless work in conducting the Bloody Assizes, Chief Justice Jeffreys was appointed by James II to the high post of Lord Chancellor. Such an appointment as this indicated that the new King held very little regard for the feelings of his people. This foolish action was soon followed by others, so that in a short time James

II found himself to be a very unpopular monarch. He made no effort to gain the support of either Whigs or Tories, a fact which lost him the favour of Parliament. He quarrelled with his ministers, clashed with the Church of England, and increased his own power by enlarging the standing army.

During the reign of Charles II the Church of England had gained **Religious troubles** supremacy because its members alone could hold offices in the army and in the government. James II refused to accept such laws and named Catholic officers to posts in the army. When members of the House of Commons protested, James silenced them by dissolving Parliament. In order to support his right to make appointments as he desired, the King had a high court of judges agree to a plan by which appointments made by James II were to be lawful in England. With this authority in hand, he then proceeded to name Catholic officials within the Church and within the universities. When the King's policy came to be known, there was an uproar among the leaders in the Church and the universities, an uproar which resulted only in more trials, punishments and dismissals. James II was rapidly losing many friends and supporters who had been loyal to the royal house during the reign of Charles II.

King James II, determined to break the power of the Church of England, decided to secure religious freedom within the nation. This plan in itself was a good one, and one which might have been achieved by a strong and popular monarch. James II, however, was not the man to win success in such an effort. At first he tried persuading Parliament to pass a new religious act, but the members of the House of Commons were not in favour of change. Even this rebuff did not stop the King, for he proceeded to issue in 1687 the Declaration of Indulgence which did away with laws against Catholics and Dissenters, and gave citizens the right to worship as they pleased. Although many of the English people longed for religious freedom, they did not want it by a royal decree which broke the laws of the land.

The following year, 1688, James II put forth a second Declaration of Indulgence which contained more instructions regarding religious matters. In order that all citizens might be informed of this Declaration, the King commanded that it be read in all churches during the services of two Sundays. The royal order caused such anger among churchmen, that very few of them obeyed the King's instructions. Strangely enough a bishop in Westminster Abbey commenced to read the Declaration, but as he did so, his congregation stood up and hurried from the Abbey.

In an effort to avoid a direct clash between Church and King, the **Trial of the Seven Bishops, 1688** Archbishop of Canterbury and six other bishops begged James II to withdraw his command concerning the reading in churches. Considering the bishops' appeal to be a form of rebellion, the King had the seven men arrested, and brought to trial. Far from improving the King's position, the holding of the churchmen actually won support for the Church of England. Then, when a jury found the seven bishops not guilty, there were noisy celebrations of joy. Even the soldiers of the standing army rejoiced.

The release of the bishops following the trial in 1688 was the worst defeat an English king had suffered since the days of the Civil War. Perhaps James II began to realize that there are limits even for a king.

So unpopular had James II become that the citizens of the nation **Problem of succession** looked forward wistfully to the next reign when they would be free of a man who flouted English laws. The King's oldest daughter, Mary, who had married a Protestant Dutch prince, William of Orange, because Parliament had exerted pressure for her to do so, appeared to be the one who would next wear the crown. However, the whole situation changed in June, 1688, when a son was born to the King and Queen. The baby boy by tradition took precedence over his sister Mary.

English Protestants, fearing that the baby prince would in time become a Catholic King, decided that quick action should be taken at once. Accordingly a group of important leaders, bishops, nobles, Tories and Whigs invited William of Orange, ruler of Holland, to come to England and take over the government. This invitation interested William very much, because, engaged in a war with France, he saw that England might be a useful ally. While making ready to land in England with an army, William sent a message to the English people saying that he was coming to protect the people from a tyrannical King. He promised, too, that a free election would be held to form a new Parliament.

James II at long last came to the realization that he was in a dangerous position. Frantically, he tried to correct the mistakes he had committed, but time was passing swiftly, too swiftly to regain the good will of his people.

William of Orange disembarked on the southwest coast of the **William of Orange** island close to the spot where the Duke of Monmouth had landed three years before. The Dutch ruler, however, was to have much greater success in his campaign than the luckless Monmouth. William of

236

Prince William of Orange marches triumphantly toward London. Just a few days before his fleet of 600 transports and fifty men-of-war had landed 10,000 of his troops. Now as he proceeds toward the capital, he is joined by English nobles and country gentry. From windows and doors the people watch, hoping that the Dutch prince will win the throne from the unpopular King, James II.

Orange was a highly respected man in Europe, and a military commander of skill and experience. In addition, his position was strengthened by his marriage to the English Princess, Mary. William was no weak adventurer grasping for a hopeless cause; he was a strong determined man in conflict with his own father-in-law, King James II.

As the King prepared to meet the invasion, William of Orange marched slowly and triumphantly in the direction of London. As he moved along, hundreds of the lower class people, country gentlemen and nobles joined his growing forces. Throughout the nation many of the most powerful men declared their intention of supporting William in his bid for power. Thoroughly alarmed by the situation, James II marched with troops to meet the invader, but as he advanced his officers and soldiers slipped quietly away to join the enemy. So many of the royal followers disappeared that the King, losing confidence, turned back to London without meeting the enemy. At one time James was a prisoner but Prince William ordered that he be allowed to escape.

James II flees to France
Completely broken by the desertion of his subjects and the neglect of his friends, James II offered no resistance to the fate he saw ahead. Sending his family to the Continent, he tried to make terms with William of Orange, but saw no hope of saving the throne. After destroying some official papers and dropping the great seal of government in the Thames River, he attempted to escape in disguise to France. Even in this pathetic effort he failed, for he was recognized and taken back to London. William of Orange had no desire to imprison or execute his father-in-law because he believed that such action could only win sympathy for James II. Therefore, he commanded that the King be given every assistance in his flight to France.

Just one week before Christmas, 1688, James left for the Continent, and William of Orange installed himself comfortably in the royal palace of Whitehall.

41

WILLIAM AND MARY

At the time William of Orange arrived in London, 1688, there was actually no real government in England. James II had left for France and the Parliament was helpless. Calling together the House of Lords, all members of the House of Commons who had served under James, and other English leaders, William asked their advice as to what action should be taken. The assembled members suggested that a convention of men representing the English people should be called to discuss the nation's future. This appeared to be good advice, so William of Orange ordered the organization of a convention which would act as a form of Parliament.

When the members of the convention met, they wasted no time in coming to grips with problems which lay waiting for solution. They worked to such good effect that their decisions were not long in coming. James II was deposed as King, the throne was declared vacant, and a declaration of rights was prepared. By this declaration the members of the convention listed the rights which people and Parliament should have completed this work, the convention then offered the crown to William of Orange and Mary jointly. This offer was accepted with the result that King William III and Queen Mary were crowned on February 13, 1689.

The rebellion against James II and the crowning of William and Mary is known as the Revolution of 1688, an event which was extremely important in English history. The new King and Queen ruled not by "Divine Right", but through authority granted them by the representatives of the people. This measure was the turning point in the ancient struggle for supremacy between King and Parliament. The victory was won by Parliament. In future no English monarch was to rule without the help and approval of Parliament.

Following the coronation the King and Queen authorized the convention to become a true Parliament so that it could pass a number of acts. Among these was the *Bill of Rights* which made lawful the declaration of rights that had been accepted by William and Mary.

Among the important points were the following:

The king could not change or set aside the laws of the nation.

Parliament was to be elected through free elections.

Parliament was to meet frequently.

Parliament was to have freedom of speech.

There could be no taxes without consent of Parliament.

The king could not be a Roman Catholic, nor could he marry a Roman Catholic.

Subjects might freely petition the king.

No standing army might be kept in time of peace without consent of Parliament.

A number of other measures were taken to increase the power of Parliament and to reduce the authority of the King. During previous reigns monarchs had received the income from certain duties or taxes during their lifetime. Parliament now changed this practice so that sums of money were voted each year to the royal treasury and the national government. In much the same manner Parliament gained control of the army, making it necessary to vote each year the money

William III defeats James II at the Battle of the Boyne. The Irish with 7,000 French in support were posted on the south side of the Boyne River. A group of William's men crossed a bridge some distance up river and struck at the Irish wing. Then as William's main force crossed the river, the day was won.

needed for military expenses. These matters, of course, made it necessary for Parliament to meet anually.

Toleration Act, 1689 Some progress was made toward a settlement of the religious question, but even then there was no complete freedom for everyone. Through the Toleration Act, 1689, Dissenters were allowed to form congregations and worship as they chose. Roman Catholics were not allowed the same liberty, but they did hold services in private. As time went by, their form of religion was gradually recognized within the nation. The Church of England still held a superior position among the various denominations because its members only could hold positions in government.

Freedom of the press One other step taken at this time in the direction of freedom was that concerned with the liberty of the press. Ever since printing had appeared in England, the government, the courts, and some powerful officials had exercised controls over newspapers, books and pamphlets. For a time the Court of the Star Chamber had used its authority to examine publications. Shortly after William and Mary came to the throne, all of these old restrictions were removed, so that writers no longer needed to fear unjust punishment for statements they made in print. Members of Parliament who brought about this improvement

240

probably did not realize how important their work was to be in future centuries. Today, freedom of the press is one of the most precious rights enjoyed by the people of democratic nations.

While it is true that James II had fled to France, this did not mean that the former King had given up entire hope of regaining the English throne. He realized that William III was secure in England, but that his authority over Ireland and Scotland was very shaky. There were a great many Scots and Irish who felt little loyalty to the Dutch King who sat on the throne. This fact gave James II an opportunity to win supporters for an attack upon William and Mary.

With some help from the French, James II went to Ireland where **Ireland** he was welcomed by the people and where the royal rights were recog- **supports** nized by the Irish Parliament. Except for a few Protestant towns, all **James II** the nation declared its loyalty to James II. In the meantime King William III had collected his own seasoned troops, and moved quickly to Ireland. He captured virtually all of Ireland save only the towns of Londonderry and Enniskillen. Londonderry was besieged for 105 days in 1689. The people were starving when William forced the blockade and relieved the town. William took over the army and in the next year defeated James at the Battle of the Boyne, 1690, a victory still celebrated by some on July 12th. James fled to France.

Although the Irish were keenly disappointed in the leadership shown by James II, they continued to fight against the English, hoping to win new liberty for the nation. Battles were fought here and there during the years 1690 and 1691, with the English finally winning a costly victory. Ireland was once more conquered. By the terms of settlement those Irish fighters who wished to do so were allowed to leave for France. As a result about 12,000 of the Irish, many of them nobles and excellent warriors, left their homeland to join the French forces. This development gave the English more enemies on the Continent, and lost for Ireland many of her powerful citizens and natural leaders. Unhappy days fell upon the island as the Catholic people were oppressed by the English government and by the Irish Protestants.

In Scotland, too, there was unrest under the rule of King William **The** III and Queen Mary. A group of Scottish noblemen, still loyal to James **Jacobites** II, began organizing resistance against the throne. These nobles and their followers, the Highlanders, came to be known as the Jacobites, a name derived from a Latin word "Jacobus" meaning "James." During the conflict which followed the English were defeated in 1689 at the

241

A Scottish clansman of Killiecrankie. He wears the traditional Highland kilt, and is armed with a sword called a claymore—a two-edged weapon with a basket-type handle.

Battle of Killiecrankie, but by 1691 the rebellion was completely crushed.

Scotland and Ireland were now firmly under English control, but a powerful enemy, France, was offering a dangerous threat. There were several reasons why the French bore no love for the English. To begin with, France had become the European champion of Catholicism just as Spain had been in former years. She was opposed to nations like England which held Protestant governments. Then, too, in addition there were certain jealousies between the English and French concerned with trade and settlement in America and in India.

In the face of the French threat, England made an alliance with Holland, Spain, and Germany and soon the rival navies were fighting in the English Channel. In 1690 the French defeated the English and Dutch fleets, but two years later in a battle near La Hogue in France, the French navy suffered a sharp defeat. These were the days when press gangs captured citizens and forced them into naval service. After sea battles in the Channel the bodies of English sailors were washed ashore still dressed in their "Sunday best." The Battle of La Hogue, the greatest sea struggle since the time of the Invincible Armada, was a fortunate victory for England, because her shores remained safe from invasion.

Although the naval fighting was over, land battles continued on the continent with victories and defeats on both sides. In 1697 the war came to a close with the Peace of Ryswick which on the whole left England in a strong position.

William and Mary

King William III had gained control of the British Isles and had thrown some fear into France, but his life at home was not a happy one. He was a silent, gloomy man who had none of the gay, cheerful habits which win popularity for kings. He was hardworking, faithful, and devoted to duty, but gave no effort to winning the love of his people. After the death of Queen Mary he sank even lower in the affections of English citizens.

A Jacobite party which now actually existed within England even hoped for the return of the exiled James II. Some of the Jacobite members, discovered in a plot to kill William III, were captured and later executed. In spite of this, it should not be imagined that the great mass of the people hated the King. The truth is that they respected him, even if they could not bring themselves to love the moody monarch.

Jacobite plot in England

Under William III Parliament continued to grow in power as the party system of government developed. In the beginning the King chose his ministers from both the Tory and Whig parties of Parliament. This plan did not work well, because the members of the cabinet frequently quarrelled among themselves. In 1694, the plan was changed when William III chose a complete cabinet whose members came wholly from the Whig party. The result was that there were fewer disputes, and the government operated more smoothly. So it was that it became the custom for English kings to select their ministers from whatever party had the greater number of members in the House of Commons. In Canada today this practice is followed.

Changes in cabinet system

After the death of Queen Mary there arose the question as to who should be monarch after William III. The answer to this question was not a simple one, for William and Mary were leaving no children. Queen Mary's sister, Princess Anne, was still alive and held the strongest claim to the crown. It was decided, therefore, by the *Act of Settlement* that Anne should be the next Queen, and she on her death would be succeeded by Sophia, granddaughter of King James I. By the *Act of Settlement*, too, it was declared that all future rulers of the nation must be members of the Church of England.

Act of Settlement, 1701

England was not the only nation in Europe having problems regarding royal succession. In Spain the weak-minded King had neither children nor close relatives to accept the crown on his death. This situation caused some alarm in Europe because there was reason to believe that Spain and its colonies might fall into the hands of the French. These fears proved justified when the Spanish ruler died,

A carriage used during the reign of William III and Mary. Although beautifully constructed, it was not comfortable as a travelling vehicle. The passenger compartment is suspended by straps from posts above the axles. This arrangement absorbed very few of the riding shocks. Surprisingly enough city streets had more bumps in them than did the country roads, because they were constructed from granite cobble stones which shook the carriage badly.

leaving his realm and some possessions to the grandson of King Louis XIV of France.

Now completely alarmed by the thought of a united Spain and France, other nations joined in the Grand Alliance to face the dangerous growth of French power. The long War of the Spanish Succession broke out in the year 1701. Although England was not concerned with the first stages of the conflict, she eventually found herself allied with Holland and Austria against France.

In the meantime the exiled James II died in France where he had lived comfortably as a guest of the French government. King Louis XIV unwisely recognized the dead man's son as King James III of England, Ireland and Scotland. The result of this action was that the angry English rallied an army of 40,000 men, strengthened the navy, and voted large sums to carry on a war. William III planned himself to lead the army into France, but fate decided otherwise. In 1702 the King fell from his horse, suffered serious injury, and died a short time later.

Then, in accordance with the *Act of Settlement,* Princess Anne was crowned as Queen.

244

SUMMARY—SECTION V

Elizabeth I was succeeded in 1603 by James I, son of Mary Queen of Scots. The new King was a proud man who believed in the "Divine Right of Kings." His attitude led to continuous squabbles with Parliament over money and other matters. James I supported the Church of England and encouraged the publication in 1611 of a new Bible which came to be known as the King James Version. Neither Puritans nor Catholics were happy with religious conditions during the reign. James I had hoped that his kingdoms of England and Scotland might be joined, but Parliament refused to pass an act of union. During this period the East India Company established itself in India, a foothold was gained in the West Indies and settlements were made on the mainland of North America.

After the death of James I in 1625 his son, Charles I, came to the throne. Like his father, Charles I quarrelled constantly with members in the House of Commons. Charles dissolved the third Parliament of his reign and began his period of personal rule. Strong measures were taken against the Puritans as severe sentences were handed down by the Court of the Star Chamber and the Court of High Commission. Charles I ignored English law as he raised money through a number of illegal measures. When he attempted in 1637 to force a new Prayer Book on the Scots, they rose in rebellion. In 1640 after twelve years of recess a determined Parliament met to face the king. Two years later Charles I invaded the House of Commons to arrest five members. This action so angered the House that a peaceful agreement between king and Parliament was impossible.

In 1642 the Civil War broke out as Royalists and Roundheads fought for the power of government. Oliver Cromwell, a Roundhead military commander, played an important part in the final defeat of the Royalists. King Charles I was beheaded in 1649.

In the same year the Commonwealth form of government was established without King or House of Lords. The Parliament of the new Commonwealth was so ineffective that Oliver Cromwell took over ruling power as the Lord Protector. In this position he became a true dictator. Cromwell and Parliament did not work well together so that the Protectorate proved to be an unsuccessful form of government.

After Oliver Cromwell's death in 1658 his son, Richard, attempted to act as Lord Protector, but he soon resigned from office. By 1660 monarchy was restored when the handsome, witty Charles II was crowned. Charles II had no desire to lose his head, so he worked in cooperation with Parliament. During his reign England gained new settlements in America, placed trading posts in western Africa, and founded the Hudson's Bay Company. The Habeas Corpus Act was passed. Tragedy struck London with the Great Plague in 1665 and the Great Fire in 1666.

King James II, brother of Charles II, was crowned in 1685. The Duke of Monmouth in an unsuccessful attempt to seize the throne was defeated and executed.

Being a Catholic, James II quite naturally attempted to secure a higher place for his faith in England. In so doing he appointed Catholic officials to the army and the universities. This caused anger and alarm because by law only members of the Church of England could hold such positions. Quarrels between James II and Parliament became so bitter that eventually the King's daughter, Mary, and her Dutch husband, William of Orange, were invited to take the throne. After William of Orange arrived with an army and reached London, James II fled to France. The revolt against the King is known as the Revolution of 1688.

During the reign of King William III and Mary, Parliament established itself as the real head of government, working in cooperation with the royal rulers. The Bill of Rights was passed. By the Toleration Act religious freedom was given to the Dissenters but not to Catholics. Freedom of the press was gained. William III repressed rebellions in Ireland and Scotland, thus bringing these nations securely under his control. France, too, was beaten in an important naval battle at La Hogue. William III died in 1702.

With the reign of William III and Mary, Parliament finally had won victory in the long struggle for supremacy in English government.

TIME-CHART

1603-1702

	1603-1625	JAMES I
	1605	GUNPOWDER PLOT
Settlement of Jamestown	**1607**	PARLIAMENT REFUSES TO UNITE ENGLAND AND SCOTLAND
Champlain founds Quebec	**1608**	
Henry Hudson discovers Hudson Bay	**1610**	
	1611	KING JAMES VERSION OF THE BIBLE
Virginia plants a colony in Bermuda	**1612**	
Trading posts set up on west coast of Africa	**1618**	EXECUTION OF WALTER RALEIGH

TIME·CHART—*(continued)*

Puritans found Plymouth	**1620**	
Barbados Islands settled	**1625**	
	1625-1649	CHARLES I
Settlement at Salem in Massachusetts	**1629**	
Virgin Islands acquired	**1635**	
Post established by East India Company at Madras in India	**1639**	
	1640	THE SHORT PARLIAMENT THE SCOTS INVADE ENGLAND MEETING OF THE LONG PARLIAMENT
	1642	BEGINNING OF THE CIVIL WAR
	1644	THE BATTLE OF MARSTON MOOR
	1645	THE BATTLE OF NASEBY
	1646	CHARLES I SURRENDERS TO SCOTS
	1648	THE SECOND CIVIL WAR
	1649	EXECUTION OF CHARLES I
	1649-1653	THE COMMONWEALTH
	1653-1660	THE PROTECTORATE
Capture of Jamaica	**1654**	
	1660-1685	CHARLES II
Bombay is secured by the English	**1661**	
English capture New Amsterdam (New York) from the Dutch	**1664**	
	1665	THE GREAT PLAGUE OF LONDON
	1666	THE GREAT FIRE OF LONDON
Formation of the Hudson's Bay Company	**1670**	

PA—9

TIME-CHART — *(continued)*

Count Frontenac in New France	**1672**	
	1679	Habeas Corpus Act
Pennsylvania founded by William Penn La Salle on the Mississippi	**1682**	
	1685-1688	James II
	1685	Monmouth defeated at Sedgemoor
	1688	Trial of the seven bishops William of Orange arrives in England James II flees to France
	1689-1702	William III and Mary II
	1689	Bill of Rights English defeated at Killiecrankie
	1690	Irish defeated at battle of the Boyne
	1692	French defeated at La Hogue
Calcutta is founded	**1696**	
	1697	Peace of Ryswick
	1702	Death of William III

VI. GROWTH OF BRITISH POWER

England involved in the War of the Spanish Succession • Scotland and England are joined into Great Britain • Beginning of the Hanoverian line of Kings with George I • The Scots rebel under the Pretender • War of the Austrian Succession • Bonnie Prince Charles, the Young Pretender • Britain fights France in the Seven Years' War • India is opened to the British after Clive's victory at Plassey • James Wolfe captures Quebec • Canada becomes British

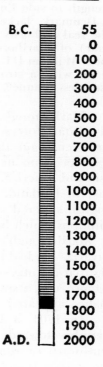

B.C. 55
0
100
200
300
400
500
600
700
800
900
1000
1100
1200
1300
1400
1500
1600
1700
1800
1900
A.D. 2000

42

UNION WITH SCOTLAND

Princess Anne, second daughter of James II, became Queen Anne in 1702 on the death of William III. She was not suited by intelligence or strength to rule England in a firm manner. Her husband, Prince George of Denmark, lacked the will-power to strengthen the crown's position. The real authority fell into the hands of John Churchill, Earl (and later Duke) of Marlborough, an outstanding soldier who had risen to fame under William III. In his search for power, Marlborough was ably assisted by his wife, a strong-minded woman who dominated Queen Anne in a shameless manner.

War of the Spanish Succession, 1701

Marlborough, who had been appointed as commander-in-chief of all military forces, began at once to carry on a serious campaign against the French on the continent. The War of the Spanish Succession developed into an endless series of widely scattered conflicts in Europe, Asia and America. In Europe itself English troops and their allies were busy in Holland, southern Germany, Italy and Spain. Although the English suffered some defeats, Marlborough won a group of brilliant triumphs which became famous in history.

Marlborough's first great battle was fought near Blenheim in Bavaria. He had been holding a large English force in Holland, guarding that country against attack by the French. Realizing that the best defence was a surprise attack, he determined to move whenever the chance appeared.

Battle of Blenheim, 1704

In 1704, a French army was pushing down the valley of the Danube toward Vienna. Marlborough planned a quick march southward to attack the French force from the side, by surprise. It was a long march and had to be carried out in utmost secrecy, but Marlborough overcame all these difficulties. The battle at Blenheim was long and indecisive, with heavy casualties. Finally, a cavalry charge led by Marlborough against the centre of the French army cut their forces into two parts and the right wing, with the river at its back, was forced to surrender. The French army, long believed invincible, had been crushed. It seemed an accident at the time, but Marlborough was to repeat the victory at Ramillies in 1706, Oudenarde in 1708 and Malplaquet in 1709.

Union With Scotland

A grateful country awarded Marlborough with a generous pension and a fine new home, Blenheim Palace, which still ranks as one of the best in England. It was the birthplace of one of the Duke's most famous descendants, Sir Winston Churchill.

The Grand Alliance was in a good position to receive generous terms of peace. On several occasions France offered to end the war, but Marlborough himself persuaded the English Parliament that the war should continue until France was totally defeated. This proved an expensive and unwise decision. The *Treaty of Utrecht* was finally signed in 1713. England gained nothing which could not have been secured at an earlier time. By the terms of the treaty, the French prince was permitted to keep the throne of Spain, but France lost considerable amount of territory. England actually gained more from the treaty than any other single nation.

Treaty of Utrecht, 1713

In Europe England kept Gibraltar and the island of Minorca in the Mediterranean Sea, both places having been captured by the English navy during the war. In the New World England secured control of Nova Scotia, Newfoundland and the region about Hudson Bay. In addition to these gains, England acquired a valuable trade agreement with Spain which was called the *Assiento Treaty*. By this arrangement the English held the right to carry slaves from Africa to the Spanish colonies in America, and the right to send one ship of trade goods each year to Panama. Here were trading privileges for which English seamen had fought since the days of Hawkins and Drake.

At the close of the War of the Spanish Succession in 1713, England possessed the most powerful navy in the world. The mighty fleet of Spain had dwindled away since the time of the Invincible Armada, and the once great fleets of France and Holland were now no match for English naval squadrons. With the new lands won by the *Treaty of Utrecht,* newly gained mastery of the seas, and prospects for better trade, England was in a position to spread her influence abroad in the world. How the little nation took advantage of this opportunity is an amazing story which will be developed in the following chapters.

Mastery of the seas

In the meantime another important event had taken place. It will be remembered that James I, King of England and Scotland, had hoped to join his two realms into one. Neither the English nor the Scots, however, had been willing to accept such a union, because they had been natural enemies for centuries. During Queen Anne's reign, feeling had changed so that people were willing to talk of such a union. There were some difficulties to settle, many of them concerned with

At the Battle of Blenheim the English defeated the French and Bavarians who lost 30,000 men killed, wounded and taken prisoner. The English commander, the Duke of Marlborough, was a brilliant general, very popular with his men who gave him the nickname "Corporal John." Marlborough taught his cavalry to use shock tactics and rely upon the sword rather than the pistol.

the prosperous trade which England had established. The canny Scots were anxious to take part in this trade, but the English were a bit slow in approving the idea.

Act of Union, 1707

Nevertheless, these and other matters were settled agreeably, so that in 1707 England and Scotland were joined together in the Kingdom of Great Britain. The Act of Union began with the following words:

That the two kingdoms of England and Scotland shall upon the first day of May, which shall be in the year one thousand seven hundred and seven, and for ever after, be united into one kingdom by the name of Great Britain; and that the ensigns' armorial of the said united kingdom be such as her Majesty shall appoint, and the crosses of St. George and St. Andrew be conjoined in such manner as her Majesty shall think fit, and used in all flags, banners, standards and ensigns, both at sea and land.

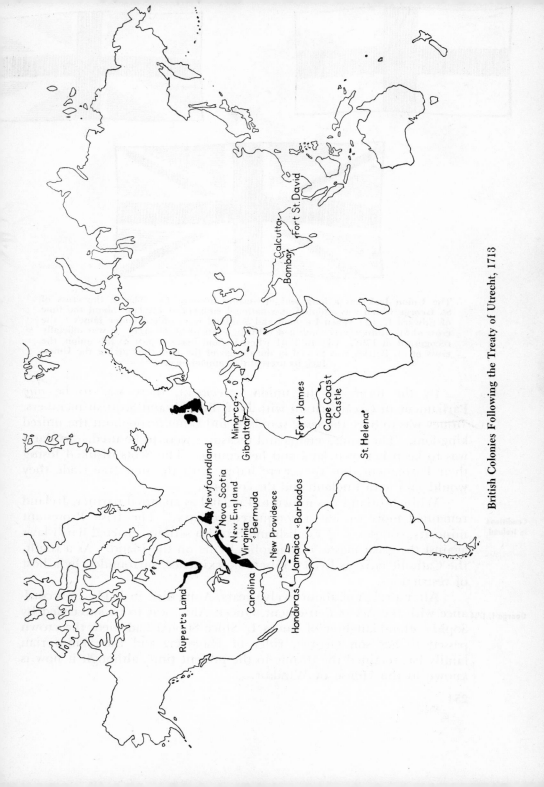

British Colonies Following the Treaty of Utrecht, 1713

Ruperts Land

Newfoundland
Nova Scotia
New England
Virginia · Bermuda
Carolina
New Providence
Honduras · Jamaica · Barbados

Minorca ·
Gibraltar ·

Calcutta ·
Bombay · Fort St. David

Fort James

Cape Coast
Castle

St. Helena ·

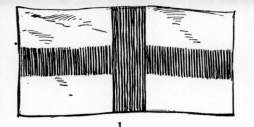

3

The Union Jack has a long and interesting history. (1) This is the cross of St. George which was adopted as a national emblem of England about the time of Edward I. (2) When England and Scotland were united under James I, the cross of St. Andrew was combined with the cross of St. George. It was officially recognized in 1707. (3) In 1801 when Ireland became part of the union, the cross of St. Patrick was placed in the design of the flag, thus giving the Union Jack its present day appearance.

By the terms of the union agreement, there was to be one Parliament in Great Britain with both English and Scottish members. Money was to have the same standard and value throughout the united kingdom. The same weights and measures were to be used. Scotland was to keep her own laws and her courts. The Scots disliked losing their Parliament, but they were happy with the new free trade they would gain with England and the colonies.

Conditions in Ireland

While Scotland was joined to England as an equal partner, Ireland remained more or less a conquered country. The Irish Protestant minority, composed of English and Scottish settlers, enacted harsh laws against the great masses of Catholics living on the island. As a result, the Catholic citizens lived a miserable existence, surrounded by a host of restrictions.

George I, 1714

After a reign of about twelve years, Anne died in 1714. In accordance with the Act of Settlement, Queen Anne was to be succeeded by Sophia, granddaughter of James I. Since Sophia had died, the crown passed to her son George, ruler of Hanover, and the Hanoverian family has retained the throne to the present time, although it now is known as the House of Windsor.

254

43

LAST OF THE STUARTS

George I, crowned in 1714, had no particular liking for England or for his duties as King. Nevertheless, he clung firmly to his royal rights throughout the thirteen years of his reign. Though not distinguished for his brilliance, he did possess a certain shrewdness and common sense. Speaking German as his own tongue, he had neither skill nor interest in the English language.

In the time of George I new trading companies were formed, and startling plans were made to win large fortunes. Shortly before the beginning of the reign, 1711, the South Sea Company was granted a charter from the government, permitting it to trade with the Spanish colonies and with various parts of Asia. This business enterprise was a joint-stock company which sold shares to anyone who wished to become a partner in the company. Thousands of Englishmen, eager for profits, scrambled to get possession of the shares. They sold land, borrowed money, and gave up their savings so that they might have a part in this promising business. Because of the great demand, the price of the shares went up as mining shares occasionally do in our own day. Wild speculation lasted for weeks, and then, as people began to worry about the safety of their money, some sold shares. In the panic which followed everyone wanted to get rid of his holdings, with the result that the price of shares collapsed. On January 1, 1720, the price of the shares was 128½. On July 16, of the same year, the price of shares had risen to 1,000. But by November 16, the price of shares had fallen to 135. **The South Sea Bubble, 1720**

Literally thousands of citizens lost everything they owned. Because the fantastic dream of wealth burst like a bubble, the event is sometimes called the *South Sea Bubble*. Quite naturally, deep anger was directed against the government and the South Sea Company, because the people considered themselves to have been victims of fraud. One disgusted nobleman suggested that the directors of the company be sewn up in bags and thrown into the Thames.

In 1721, Robert Walpole, a Whig member of Parliament, rose to importance. He was appointed First Lord of the Treasury and Chancellor of the Exchequer. At the height of the South Sea Bubble **Robert Walpole**

Here are a Chippendale bed and table. A period of great elegance and beauty in furnishings gave us several brilliant furniture makers and designers—Thomas Chippendale, George Hepplewhite and the Adam brothers. Furniture based on their designs is still widely manufactured today, an indication of the superb quality of these designs.

Walpole had warned the public of danger. Because of this he was called upon to restore public confidence in the time of distress. One of Walpole's first problems, then, was to straighten out the tangled affairs of the South Sea Company. Under his direction, the properties of the Company and those of its directors were sold, and the money handed over to the people who had bought shares. By this means the unfortunate investors regained some of their losses, though not all of them.

In ensuing months Robert Walpole became the most valuable official in the government, and the most honoured of the King's ministers. There had been important ministers before in English history, but none who were held in such high respect by King and Parliament. Because George I spoke no English, he was forced to use Latin when discussing matters with the ministers of his cabinet. None **Walpole** of the gentlemen were fluent in the classical language, so that their **becomes** conversations were slow and a bit ridiculous. Under such awkward **Prime** **Minister** circumstances, the King stopped attending cabinet meetings, permitting

256

Walpole to preside in his place. Thus Walpole became England's first
Prime Minister, a position he held for twenty-one years with remarkable success.

Great Britain was fortunate in its choice of the first Prime
Minister, for Walpole was moderate, cautious and reasonable in his
actions. He tried at all times to keep the nation at peace abroad, while
at home he avoided religious and political quarrels. His purpose was
to give England a chance to develop her agriculture, her industry and
her trade under peaceful conditions.

Just one year after George I came to the throne, the Stuarts made **The**
another attempt to secure royal power. In Scotland, the Duke of Mar, **Pretender**
a Jacobite leader, gathered forces to fight for James Edward, son of *1715*
James II. The rebellion was a short one, for the royal rebel known
as the *Pretender* was a slow-moving man who lacked the qualities of
leadership necessary to win success.

After a reign of thirteen years, King George I died and was **George II,**
succeeded by his son, George II, who was crowned in 1727. The new **1727**
King, who understood the English language and spoke it with a heavy
accent, took a greater part in public affairs than his father had. George
II was not a brilliant man, but he did have a high respect for justice
and possessed some interest in military matters. Because George II
had always disliked Robert Walpole, it was thought that he might
choose another Prime Minister. It is probable there would have been
a change if Queen Caroline had not persuaded the King that there
was not another man who could take Walpole's place. The Queen,
like many another wife, knew how to manage her husband.

By the *Treaty of Utrecht* which closed the War of the Spanish
Succession, the British had been allowed only a limited trade with the
Spanish colonies. As a result, British seamen engaged in the smuggling
of trading goods — a dangerous business which annoyed the Spanish
government. A number of Englishmen were captured, imprisoned,
and even tortured. One of these, Captain Jenkins, appeared before *1739*
the British Parliament, complaining that his ear had been cut off by
Spanish officers. This story caused such a storm of anger, that not even
Walpole could keep the nation out of war in 1739. A few naval battles
and land attacks took place with very little glory for Britain. Soon
the "War of Jenkins' Ear" was brought to a close.

Another and more serious conflict followed as the War of the **War of the**
Austrian Succession broke over Europe in 1740. In a quarrel between **Austrian Succession,**
the German states of Austria and Prussia, the leading European nations **1740**

257

London Bridge of the eighteenth century was an elaborate structure with shops and houses lining both its sides. It appeared more like a street than a bridge.

broke into two armed camps. England and Holland supported Austria, while France and Spain supported Prussia. Walpole, having little interest in the new war, made no effort to bring Britain's full power into the conflict. When a naval attack on a Spanish colony failed, Walpole's enemies in Parliament combined to force him to resign as Prime Minister.

Lord Carteret, who became the next Prime Minister, put more energy into the war effort. King George II led an army to the continent. There he presented a brave but ridiculous figure. He was the last of the British kings to command forces in actual combat. It was a costly **Treaty of** and useless war, for neither side made any substantial gains. The **Aix-la-** French stronghold of Louisburg in what is now Nova Scotia was **Chapelle,** captured by British forces, but was returned when the *Treaty of* **1748** *Aix-la-Chapelle* was signed in 1748.

Before the end of the War of the Austrian Succession, the Stuart **The Young** family made one last attempt to seize royal power in Great Britain. **Pretender,** It was not James Stuart, the Pretender, who led this final gamble, but **1745** his elder son, Charles Stuart, who is known as the Young Pretender. He was a grandson of King James II. This young man travelled to

258

The thick piers supporting the span acted as a kind of dam in the river, creating rapids which were dangerous to navigation. Buildings on the bridge were removed in 1756.

Scotland in 1745 where he laid his claim to the Scottish throne before the Highland chieftains.

Charles Stuart was a handsome, dashing fellow whose charming manner appealed greatly to the Highlanders. It was not long before they were calling him "Bonnie Prince Charlie" and "The Chevalier." His request for help found ready acceptance among the Highlanders who always seemed ready for adventure, especially when it meant war with England. Marching toward Edinburgh with an army of followers, Charles gathered more supporters as he advanced. So great was his power that he was able to have himself crowned as King of Scotland. Shortly afterward, he defeated the national army stationed there, but even in this victory he was in a dangerous position.

Bonnie Prince Charlie knew he must gain control of England if his cause were not to be lost. Although some of his Highland followers left him and returned to their mountain homes, money and arms arrived from France. So, with an army of 6,000 men he crossed the Scottish border in the hope that the English would join his standard. But the feelings of the English had changed with the years toward such

259

Methodist preachers travelled widely, speaking to masses of people outdoors in the streets and town squares. In the picture are seen an assortment of people

romantic adventurers as Charles. The people were no longer keenly interested in royal struggles for the crown. Only 300 recruits were picked up in England.

In the meantime the British government had called out militia troops and commanded two armies to stand in the path of the invaders. Bonnie Prince Charlie wanted to make a bold dash for London, but his officers persuaded him not to take this dangerous step. Then, as time went by, the rebels lost courage, beginning a slow retreat with the enemy pressing at their heels. Prince Charles was able to defend himself in a number of attacks and skirmishes, but finally in 1746 was forced into battle at Culloden Moor on the edge of the Highlands. The Scottish rebels were badly beaten and scattered. The last charge of swordsmen in Scottish history was broken by cannon loaded with grape shot, and by volleys of musket fire from infantry men lined three deep. To this day the grass-covered mounds still mark the spot where the Highlanders fell, and were buried in their clan groups. These were great common graves marked now by small stone tablets: "Here lies the Clan MacDonald," and so on.

Following the Battle of Culloden Moor, harsh measures were

Battle of Culloden Moor, 1746

260

including beggars, business men, merchants, serving maids, peddlers and house-wives. In the background are ruins of a Norman castle. During the Civil War many of the old castles were destroyed by artillery fire.

taken against the Scots; prisoners were shot in cold blood and a number of leaders beheaded. Prince Charles became a hunted man, hiding in the Highlands. Although there was a large reward offered for his capture, the loyal Highlanders refused to betray their beloved Charles. After some months, he was able to escape to France. Sad to relate, the Young Pretender became a lazy, worthless person in later life, with none of the fine qualities he held as a young man. On his death and that of his brother, Cardinal York, the last of the male line of Stuarts was gone.

The religious life of the time was comparatively quiet with none of the fierce conflicts that had taken place during the Tudor and Stuart periods. Much of the deep religious feelings held by the Puritans during the time of the Civil War had disappeared, leaving a rather cold and formal kind of worship. It is true that clergymen did teach proper behaviour and the doctrines of Christianity, but it cannot be said that any deep religious feeling was there. Only among a few scattered groups was there any desire to engage in earnest religious life.

Among these groups was a band of students at Oxford University
The who between the years 1729 and 1735 held meetings for discussion,
Methodists prayer and worship. These men, all members of the Church of England, carried out their religious duties in a devout manner, for they fasted, visited persons in jails, and did many other acts of Christian service. Such unselfish behaviour caused laughter and scorn among the other students at the University. Members of the group were called *Methodists* because they led a methodical and well-regulated way of life.

Among the Methodists were two brothers, John and Charles Wesley, who were destined to play an important part in religious history. John was to become a famous preacher, and Charles a famous writer of hymns. After leaving Oxford University, the Wesleys entered the service of the Church of England, but unlike other clergymen, they did not take special parishes. Once when John Wesley was criticized for not having a church of his own, he replied, "The world is my parish!" In a way this was true, for John Wesley, Charles Wesley, George Whitefield and others travelled about the nation speaking here and there in churches whenever invited to do so.

Unlike most sermons of the time, the Methodist sermons were exciting, enthusiastic, appealing and sometimes filled with dire warnings. Aside from their preaching, the Wesleys and their fellow workers established church groups which carried on activities similar to those of the Oxford group of students.

Many of the clergymen of the Church of England refused to allow the Wesleys and others to preach in their parishes, because they felt the Methodist services were disorderly. Nevertheless, many of the English people enjoyed the services, and flocked to hear the travelling preachers. Methodist chapels began to appear here and there as citizens left the regular churches to join the new religious group. Another change was the growing custom of Methodist preachers to address great masses of people in open air services. John Wesley was especially successful in this kind of service, sometimes speaking to crowds as large as 20,000 people. During his career of fifty years he probably travelled more than 250,000 miles and preached more than 40,000 sermons. John Wesley was not welcomed everywhere he went, for he himself describes one occasion when "The mob pelted us with stones, the greater part of the day. The congregation was larger the next evening, and so was the mob, and likewise in higher spirits, being ready to knock out our brains for joy."

Although John Wesley had no desire to form a new religious denomination separate from the Church of England, conditions seemed to force the Methodists in that direction. By 1760 many of the Methodist clergymen named themselves as "dissenting ministers," and formed the Methodist Church with its own officials, buildings, congregations and conferences. In the English colonies of America, Methodist preachers and missionaries carried their work into the wilderness in the tracks of the explorers, fur traders and settlers.

Another change in England was in the Julian calendar which **Gregorian** had been established in Europe in Roman times. Because the calen- **calendar** dar was imperfect, there had grown over the years an error of several days in the recording of time. This mistake had been discovered and the proper correction developed by Italian astronomers in 1582. Pope Gregory XIII had wisely suggested that European countries should change their calendars to make the proper correction. England had stubbornly refused to do so.

However, in 1751, one hundred and sixty-nine years later, the British Parliament finally adopted the Gregorian calendar. In so doing, Parliament declared that September 3 by the old calendar would be named September 14 on the new one. Unfortunately, many of the citizens thought that they were being robbed of time and of the money they would have earned in that time. It is amusing now to think of people in mobs shouting angrily, "Give us back our eleven days!" By the same reform measure, the next calendar year would begin on January 1 instead of March 25 as formerly.

44

THE BRITISH WIN CANADA

The smouldering rivalry of Great Britain and France in America, burst into fresh flame with the opening of the Seven Years' War in 1756.

The Seven Years' War was no simple contest between two nations, but a complicated struggle with Britain and Prussia on one side, Austria, France and Spain on the other. Britain actually took little part in the European fighting, but she did help Prussia with sums of

263

British troops wade ashore at Louisburg after the fleet had waited off the coast for six days during a period of wind, fog and high waves. Louisburg was one of the great French strongholds in America. Here, too, was a town of 4,000 people who transacted a rich trade in silks, cambrics and laces from France, together with rum, molasses and sugar from the West Indies.

Seven Years' War, 1756
money. The truth of the matter was that Britain was badly prepared for war. Her army was poorly disciplined and her officers lacked experience. To make matters worse, a blow to the nation's pride was suffered when a British fleet fled from French ships after a clash near the island of Minorca. The British were so angered by this event that the British admiral was executed on his own quarterdeck.

William Pitt
Fortunately for Great Britain there rose to importance a minister having the ability to prepare the nation for war. He was William Pitt, Earl of Chatham, a man who in former years had opposed the peaceful policies of Robert Walpole. There was nothing modest about Pitt. He said confidently, "I am sure that I can save this country, and that nobody else can." Pitt was not named Prime Minister, but he was placed in full charge of the war effort. Pitt's plan was to avoid battles in Europe itself, while striking hard at France in America and India. Time proved that he was right.

264

The British Win Canada

In North America the French had settled in the valley of the St. Lawrence and in Acadia, and were pushing southward into the Mississippi basin. The British had established themselves along the Atlantic coast, and were eyeing the land across the Appalachian mountains. It was in the district south of the Great Lakes where the British and French clashed on so many occasions. By the time of King George II this colonial struggle between the two nations appeared to be going in favour of the French. An English force under General Braddock had been cut to pieces at Fort Duquesne (Pittsburgh) on the Ohio River. Soon afterward Fort Oswego on Lake Ontario and Fort William Henry south of Lake Champlain, were captured by the French.

British and French in America

The British position in America changed rapidly when William Pitt put his military plans into action. It is important to realize that Pitt was not primarily interested in gaining more territory, but in expanding trade. Trade meant wealth and power for Great Britain. By defeating France in America a new opportunity for commerce would be opened up. With this aim in mind, Pitt hoped to gain the whole American trade in furs and fish. He hoped to cut off the supply of lumber moving from New France to the French West Indies. He hoped to force up the price of French sugar so that British sugar would find new markets. He hoped to deprive the French navy of wooden masts and timber. He hoped, too, that by defeating France a new security might be obtained for the British colonies along the Atlantic coast.

By the military plan of the year 1758, the British were to attack three important French strongholds—Louisburg in Cape Breton, Fort Duquesne on the Ohio River and Fort Ticonderoga near Lake Champlain.

Louisburg was garrisoned by 3,000 regular troops and protected by a fleet of twelve ships. The rugged shore offered only three possible landing places, and these were strongly fortified. Jeffrey Amherst, the British commander, pretended to attack all three landing places at once, but threw the greatest force at one point. Here the British troops were led by a young officer, James Wolfe. With only a cane in his hand, Wolfe pressed the assault through heavy French fire and succeeded in making a landing. Fearing a rear attack, the French shore guards left their positions, making a hasty retreat into the town of Louisburg.

Capture of Louisburg, 1758

During the siege which followed, cannon were dragged overland

A section of the fortification of the French stronghold at Ticonderoga near Lake Champlain. Most of the French forts were of heavy stone construction. Ticonderoga was eventually captured in 1759 by British troops under Amherst.

and set up behind the town. A battery of French guns located on a point to one side of the harbour was captured, leaving the water open to the British fleet. Now in a desperate position, the French garrison gave in.

The British attack on Fort Ticonderoga near Lake Champlain was a sharp defeat, for in a terrible slaughter the British lost 1,900 men killed and wounded.

Disappointment at this defeat was countered by an unexpected victory at Fort Frontenac on Lake Ontario. There a British expedition of 3,000 men fell upon the fort, captured the garrison and seized an enemy fleet. This action was a severe loss for the French, because it cost them the control of Lake Ontario.

At Fort Duquesne on the Ohio River the British found that the French had destroyed the buildings and retreated north to Lake Erie. The possession of this spot, which was renamed Fort Pitt, was an advantage to the British, for it opened the way to the west, and cut off some of the Indian tribes friendly to France.

Capture of Quebec, 1759 Having thrown fear into the French in America, Pitt decided to attack Quebec in the very heart of New France. For this important and difficult task he chose Wolfe, who was by this time a general, though only thirty-two years of age. Although still a young man, Wolfe had already served in the army for seventeen years. He had fought at Culloden Moor against Bonnie Prince Charlie and had been with Amherst at Louisburg.

In 1759 James Wolfe sailed up the St. Lawrence River with a large fleet and a total force of 27,000 men. There is no need here to recount the familiar story of the siege of Quebec, of Wolfe's Cove, of the climb up the cliffs, and the Battle of the Plains of Abraham.

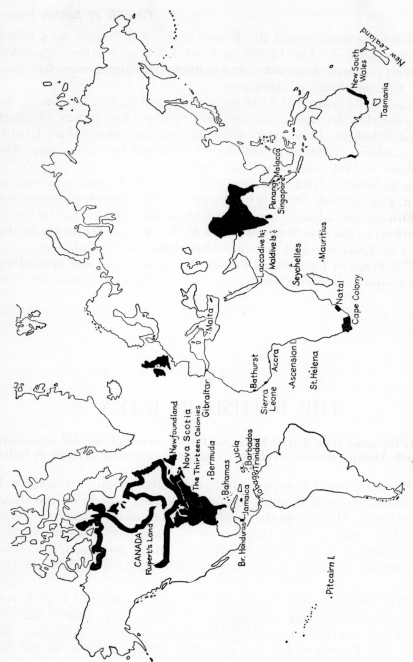

The British Empire Following the Peace of Paris, 1763

New South Wales

Tasmania

New Zealand

Penang
Malacca
Singapore

Laccadive Is.
Maldive Is.
Seychelles
Mauritius

Natal
Cape Colony

Bathurst
Accra
Sierra Leone
Ascension I.
St. Helena

Malta
Gibraltar

Newfoundland
Nova Scotia
The Thirteen Colonies
Bermuda
Bahamas
St. Lucia
Barbados
Trinidad
Br. Honduras Jamaica Tobago

CANADA
Rupert's Land

Pitcairn I.

In this famous engagement the British suffered fifty-eight men killed and 579 wounded. The French suffered 1,200 men killed, wounded and taken prisoner. Each side lost a gallant commander—the victorious Wolfe and the defeated Montcalm.

During the winter of 1760 the French gathered at Montreal. In the spring they attempted to recapture Quebec, but it was an effort doomed to failure. Before the end of the summer months three British forces totalling 17,000 men had circled Montreal in a grim ring. On September 8, 1760, the French surrendered.

Peace of Paris, 1763 In February, 1763, by the *Peace of Paris,* France gave up to Britain, Canada and all her territory east of the Mississippi except for New Orleans and adjacent land. All that remained to France in North America were the two little islands of St. Pierre and Miquelon in the Gulf of St. Lawrence and certain fishing rights on the east coast.

The Peace of Paris closed French rule in Canada, and opened up a new chapter of British history on the continent of North America.

45

THE BRITISH IN INDIA

At the same time that Britain and France were fighting for supremacy in North America the two rivals were engaged in a similar struggle in India.

British trading centres The East India Company, founded in the reign of Elizabeth I, had established itself in three important trading centres on the mainland of India. Madras, on the east coast was acquired in 1639; Bombay on the west coast of 1668; Calcutta on the east coast in 1690. At each of these centres were a fort, warehouses and a settlement protected by a garrison of native troops, sepoys, under the command of British officers.

Over the years the Dutch, the Portuguese and the French had also established trading settlements in India. The Dutch and the Portuguese centres, however, declined in importance, leaving the British and French as the two powerful trading nations on the big

268

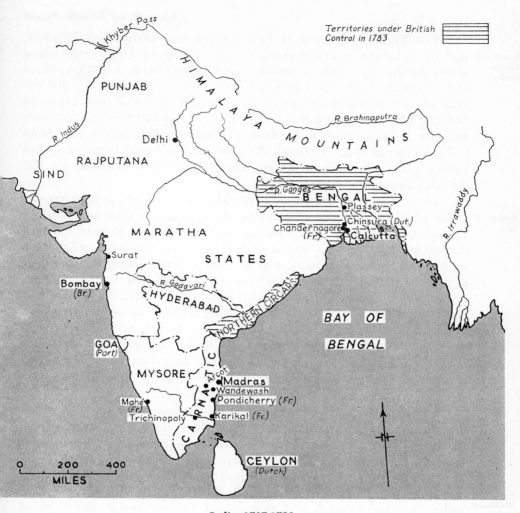

India, 1707-1783

peninsula. In 1674 the French Compagnie Des Indes Orientales had gained trading rights at Pondicherry and at Chandernagore.

Such distances separated the various trading centres that for years there was little trouble between the East India Company and the French traders. But during the reign of King George II the British at Madras came into conflict with the French at Pondicherry, eighty miles to the south.

French and British rivalry

The French governor at Pondicherry, the Marquis of Dupleix, was an ambitious man dreaming of a great French empire spreading across India. He made a number of alliances with Indian princes, and gradually built up a strong force of native troops. During the War of the Austrian Succession the French attacked and captured Madras, but when peace was signed in 1748 Madras was handed back and the French received Louisburg, Cape Breton, which had been taken by the British. Through the years that followed Dupleix spread French power to such an extent that it seemed impossible for the British to hold their rights in India.

Robert Clive

Many times during history, British causes which seemed on the point of failing have been saved by the appearance of strong leaders. In India this miracle was repeated with the rise of Robert Clive, a daring military genius. Robert Clive had come to India as a clerk in the East India Company, but he had so little liking for this sort of work that he left it to seek adventure in army life.

It was a happy move both for Clive and for Britain, because the young man soon displayed an amazing ability in military affairs. Following the example of the French, the British now strengthened their forces and made alliances with native leaders who were unfriendly toward the French. This was the same pattern of conflict as was set in America, for there, too, tribes of North American Indians were allied with either the French or the British.

Robert Clive was so successful in his campaign against the French that in a few years, the tide of fortune had turned in favour of the British. In 1753, Clive returned to England in poor health, and Dupleix was recalled to France to explain his lack of success.

Black Hole of Calcutta, 1756

In 1756 an event occurred in northern India which caused shock and anger in Britain. Ill feeling had developed between the East India Company officials at Calcutta and Siraj-ud-daulah the ruler of Bengal. This Indian prince, marching on Calcutta, captured the English trading centre and took a number of prisoners. Unknown to Siraj-ud-daulah the remnant of the British garrison was placed on June 20 in a prison cell, the Black Hole of Calcutta. According to British reports of this affair thirsty men went mad as they fought and trampled one another in crazed efforts to gain places near the windows. Men screamed, clawed at their own throats, and died panting for air. In the morning, it is said, 123 of the prisoners lay in still heaps on the floor. Some modern historians are inclined to believe that

270

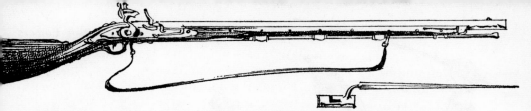

This famous British flintlock was known as *Brown Bess*, probably in honour of Elizabeth I, while the adjective "brown" referred to the colour of the weapon. The flintlock, weighing eleven pounds and four ounces, held a bayonet seventeen inches in length. Bullets, weighing a little more than one ounce, were powerful enough to break a horse's leg. Soldiers using the *Brown Bess* were allowed three new flints for every 600 rounds fired.

the horrors of the Black Hole have been exaggerated in written accounts of the past.

Determined to wipe out British influence in Bengal, Siraj-ud-daulah expelled all the remaining British in the province, and seized the property of the trading centre. The startling news of the Calcutta defeat reached Madras shortly after Robert Clive had arrived back in India. Within a few months this bold commander had recaptured Calcutta and had forced Bengal into an alliance with Britain.

When the Seven Years' War broke out in Europe, fighting between Britain and France continued its course in India. Clive, in a rapid move, attacked and destroyed the French post at Chandernagore which stood west of Calcutta. This event, however, brought Clive once again into conflict with the British-hating ruler of Bengal, Siraj-ud-daulah. In 1757, just two years before Wolfe took Quebec, Clive clashed with the Indian prince at the famous Battle of Plassey. With a small army of 900 British troops and 2,100 sepoys, Clive faced Indian and French forces of 50,000 warriors.

Clive took up a protected position in a grove of mango trees **Battle of** situated near the Bengal village of Plassey. On a cloudy June morn- **Plassey,** ing, he watched as the glittering columns of turbaned fighters advanced **1757** in a great sweeping semi-circle. On they came . . . 35,000 footsoldiers armed with matchlocks, swords and spears . . . 15,000 cavalrymen armed with lances and shields . . . fifty-three cannon mounted on massive platforms drawn by white oxen and pushed by elephants.

Beginning at eight o'clock in the morning, the Battle of Plassey lasted for most of the day, as the Indian troops sought to overwhelm the little British force which lay behind earthen embankments among the mango trees. Siraj-ud-daulah's artillery did little damage, but the British guns maintained a steady fire on the Indian lines.

By noon the clouds let loose a sudden shower of rain which stopped the Indian guns, for the gunners had no canvas covers to keep their

271

A fierce charge by the British at Plassey breaks the enemy ranks. Although very striking, uniforms of the period were tight and uncomfortable . . . red coats, white knee breeches, stiff belts and gaiters. The soldier with the tall hat is a grenadier who, in addition to his regular infantry weapons, carried a pouch containing grenades. These grenades were small hand bombs with fuses attached. Having lit the fuse, the grenadier threw the bomb at the enemy.

powder dry. British guns, however, continued against the enemy. Discouraged by this, the Indians began to move back toward their own entrenchments. Clive had decided to remain in his own position until nightfall, and then launch a sharp attack. However, when the dispirited Indians continued to retire, he ordered heavy artillery fire and began an assault. As Indian soldiers, horses and oxen fell, the enemy ranks fell into confusion and the frightened elephants stampeded. Siraj-ud-daulah, mounting a swift camel, fled from the scene accompanied by 2,000 horsemen. Across the battlefield of Plassey lay abandoned guns, wagons and tents, while elephants, oxen and horses milled in bewildered groups.

This was an amazing victory, for Clive lost but eighteen men killed, forty-five wounded and two missing. The enemy suffered 500 killed and wounded according to British figures.

Even the British were astonished with the wealth of the conquered Bengal. Macaulay, the English historian, wrote:

The treasury of Bengal was thrown open to him (Clive). There were piled up after the usage of Indian princes immense masses of coin, among which might not seldom be detected the florins and the byzants with which, before any European ship had turned the Cape of Good Hope, the Venetians purchased the stuffs and spices of the East.

The Battle of Plassey was one of the greatest triumphs in all British history. The winning of Bengal threw India open to the British, and spelled the end of French power on the peninsula. Plassey was more than a military success; it introduced a rich new world of trade and commerce. The wealth of India brought huge fortunes to British subjects, and this money flowing back into Britain financed the industrial growth of the nation. Much of British power and influence during the following century was based on Clive's success at Plassey.

Results of Plassey

SUMMARY—SECTION VI

On the death of William III (William of Orange) in 1702, Anne became Queen of England. Because she was weak, much of the power in government fell into the hands of the Duke of Marlborough. As England became involved in the War of the Spanish Succession, Marlborough won a number of brilliant victories against the French. Among these was the famous Battle of Blenheim fought in 1704. The war closed with the Treaty of Utrecht by which England gained Gibraltar, the island of Minorca and Newfoundland.

In 1707 England and Scotland were united into the kingdom of Great Britain. By the terms of the agreement of union there was to be one Parliament and one flag, the Union Jack.

George I, a German prince from Hanover came to the throne in 1714. He was the first monarch in the Hanoverian line which has ruled Great Britain to the present time. Financial ruin came to many Englishmen with the bursting of the South Sea Bubble in 1720. Robert Walpole, who became Chancellor of the Exchequer in 1721, helped to straighten out the tangled affairs of the South Sea Company. Walpole rose to even greater fame when he became Britain's first Prime Minister.

In 1715 the Scots rebelled in support of James Stuart, the Pretender, but this uprising was soon crushed.

King George I died in 1727 and was succeeded by his son, George II. In a half-hearted way Britain took part in the War of the Austrian Succession. By the Treaty of Aix-la-Chapelle Britain gave up captured Louisburg, but received Madras which had been captured by the French in India.

In 1745, the Stuarts made their last attempt to regain royal power. The Scottish Highlanders supporting Bonnie Prince Charlie, the Young Pretender, invaded England but withdrew before the advance of a British army. At the Battle of Culloden Moor, 1746, the Scots were defeated, and Bonnie Prince Charlie fled to France.

During the Seven Years' War, 1756 to 1763, the French and British fought for control in America and India as well as in Europe. William Pitt, who was placed in charge of the war effort, brought new vigour into the British fighting spirit. After a series of victories in America during 1758, the British under James Wolfe captured Quebec in 1759, thus winning Canada.

In the seventeenth century the British had established trading centres in India at Madras, Bombay and Calcutta. By the time of George II they were in conflict with the French who also had trading interests in the peninsula. Robert Clive, a military commander of genius, led the British in the struggle against the French. After a number of successes, Clive won, in 1757, the decisive Battle of Plassey against Indian and French forces. Through this victory Bengal was conquered, French power was broken, and the riches of India were opened to the British.

The trade, the lands and the wealth acquired by Great Britain in the period from 1700 to 1760 laid the foundations for her amazing expansion in the nineteenth century.

TIME-CHART

1702-1763

	1702-1714	ANNE
British capture Gibraltar	1704	BATTLE OF BLENHEIM—MARLBOROUGH DEFEATS THE FRENCH
	1707	UNION OF ENGLAND AND SCOTLAND
	1713	TREATY OF UTRECHT ENDS WAR OF THE SPANISH SUCCESSION—BRITAIN GAINS GIBRALTAR, MINORCA AND NEWFOUNDLAND

TIME·CHART — *(continued)*

	1714-1727	George I
	1715	Scottish rebellion in favour of the Pretender
	1720	Bursting of the South Sea Bubble
	1721	Robert Walpole becomes Chancellor of the Exchequer and First Lord of the Treasury
	1727-1760	George II
Western journeys of La Verendrye	**1731-1743**	
	1740-1748	War of the Austrian Succession
Russian expedition under Vitus Bering reaches Alaska	**1741**	
	1746	Bonnie Prince Charlie, the Young Pretender, is defeated at Culloden Moor
	1748	Treaty of Aix-le-Chapelle ends war of the Austrian Succession—Britain gives up captured Louisburg but received back Madras
Madras occupied by the British	**1749**	
	1756-1763	The Seven Years' War
Black Hole of Calcutta	**1756**	
	1757	Battle of Plassey—Clive wins Bengal
Capture of Louisburg	**1758**	
	1759	Wolfe captures Quebec in battle of the Plains of Abraham
Capture of Montreal by the British	**1760**	
	1763	Peace of Paris ends Seven Years' War—Britain gains Canada

VII. REVOLUTIONS AND WARS

The industrial revolution brings changes to life and industry • New spinning machines • Importance of steam power • Iron and coal • The colonists seek freedom during the American Revolution • The United States of America • Fury of the French Revolution • Ireland joins Great Britain to form the United Kingdom • War with France and Napoleon • Battle of Waterloo • New power and influence for Britain

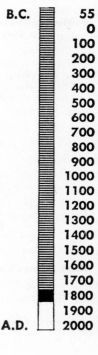

B.C. 55
0
100
200
300
400
500
600
700
800
900
1000
1100
1200
1300
1400
1500
1600
1700
1800
1900
A.D. 2000

46

THE INDUSTRIAL REVOLUTION

During the latter part of the seventeenth century, English industry had gained through the immigration of foreign workers from Europe. Among these were skilled experts in cloth-making who brought ideas and processes for the manufacture of beautiful fabrics. Other artisans from the continent established new industries for the making of glass, paper, toys, clocks and watches. Even this remarkable growth was dwarfed by developments in the eighteenth century which came through the invention of machinery and the use of coal.

In 1760, one year after James Wolfe captured Quebec, George II died, and was succeeded by his grandson who was crowned George III of Great Britain and Ireland. The newly-crowned King had been born in England, and was first of the Hanoverian line to act and speak like a true Englishman. George III possessed qualities both good **George III,** and bad, for he was faithful but narrow minded, religious but preju- **1760** diced, kindly but obstinate. This strange mixture of good and bad was to lead him into difficulties that were to have an unfortunate effect upon the growing British Empire.

Following the death of his father, the Prince of Wales, George had been raised by his mother who had very definite ideas as to what a king should be. Very often when speaking to her son the Queen had said, "George, be a king!" The Queen Mother's idea of monarchy unfortunately was based on her knowledge of other European countries and not upon conditions in England. Her advice, nevertheless, made such an impression upon the Prince that when he became George III, he was determined to choose his own ministers and to have a strong say in government.

As a result, George III's cabinet was changed from Whig to Tory ministers for the first time in forty years. Even the great William Pitt was forced to resign in 1761 when his plans were not supported. By 1770 George III's place in government was a strong one, for his friend, Lord North, was Prime Minister, the cabinet was Tory, and even the House of Commons supported the King. It was rather odd to find the monarch in such a strong position, particularly at a time when the nation was undergoing marked changes in ways of living and working.

About the year 1775 women's hair arrangements had become enormous in size
and elaborate in style. They were built up over thick pads of horse hair concealed
beneath the tresses. Some head pieces became so large that ladies had to kneel
when travelling in carriages. Endless hours were spent in the creation and care
of the intricate structures. They were greased, powdered white, and frequently
decorated with fruit, flowers and even ship models. Because the hair was washed
infrequently, the high towers were frequently not too clean.

New methods in industry   The changes which came about at this time are known as the *Industrial Revolution*. The word revolution here is not used to indicate struggle, conflict, fighting and bloodshed, but simply refers to the changes brought about by new methods used in industry, particularly manufacturing. The period might be compared with the time in which we live — the beginning of a new era of electronics and atomic power. The people of those days were beginning to use new machines and new sources of power just as we are today. It is probable, too, that their new developments appeared as wonderful to them as electronic devices and earth satellites do to us.

The flying shuttle   Among the first inventions which became important were those which brought improvements in the manufacture of thread, yarn, cotton goods, and woollen goods. Up to this time the weaving and spinning of yarn and of thread had been a cottage industry practised by people in their own homes. Weaving had been a slow process, for the yarn of the weft had to be threaded by hand through the yarns of the warp on the loom. In 1738, a man named John Kay had invented the *flying shuttle* which passed mechanically across the entire warp in one rapid motion. The flying shuttle meant a man could work twice as quickly and he could weave cloth twice as wide as before. As the demand for yarn, thread and cloth materials grew, inventors searched for still more rapid methods of production.

New spinning machines   In 1764, four years after George III came to the throne, James Hargreaves invented the *spinning jenny* which he named in honour of his wife. This new spinning machine had a wheel which turned

278

sixteen spindles all at once instead of a single spindle as in former machines. By its use one operator could spin sixteen cotton threads at the same time. Shortly after the spinning jenny came another invention when Richard Arkwright created a spinning machine, the *water frame,* using rollers turned by water power. Still later Samuel Crompton invented the *spinning mule* which combined ideas used in both the spinning jenny and the water frame. Perhaps most remarkable of all the inventions was the development in 1785 of a large loom powered by steam. The odd fact concerning this invention was that it was created by a clergyman, Edmund Cartwright who had no experience with weaving or with looms. The British were not slow to put these machines to work, so that spinning and weaving became a growing and prosperous industry. The high cost of machinery and the necessity of producing large quantities of materials, however, took the industry out of the homes and placed it in large factories.

For a long time it had been realized that in steam there lay a **Steam power** great source of power, but no one had found a way to harness such power and put it to work in an effective manner. In 1769, James Watt, a maker of mathematical instruments, improved a crude machine

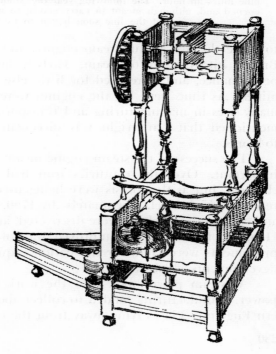

Arkwright's spinning machine made in 1769. Arkwright had been a barber and a maker of wigs. While moving about the mills fitting his customers with wigs, he learned of the attempts being made to improve methods of spinning and weaving. Becoming interested in these problems, he began experimenting and eventually developed the spinning machine shown here. It was so successful that Arkwright became a wealthy man, and was knighted in 1786 for his contribution to industry.

George Stephenson's locomotive, the Rocket, was a colourful engine painted yellow and black with a white chimney. In a famous competition with three other locomotives, 1829, the Rocket won easily after reaching a speed of twenty-nine miles an hour. The following year the Manchester-Liverpool Railway was opened and, although meant to carry goods, so many people desired to travel that the line soon began to take passengers.

to make the first useful steam engine, and in so doing pushed Great Britain into the age of steam. Early steam engines were limited in performance, and were used for little else than to pump water from mines. As time went by, the engines were improved and adapted to many uses in manufacturing and transportation. It has already been mentioned that Cartwright was successful in applying steam power to looms.

The success of the steam engine meant that iron now became very important. Over the centuries iron had been smelted by burning charcoal, but as the forests were being used up, the price of charcoal reached a high level. Fortunately, by 1760, new methods of using coal and coke in the smelting were discovered, and, in 1770, an Englishman Henry Cort, created an improved way of refining iron. These improvements were vital, for the nation required iron for use in many developments which lay ahead.

As steam power took over the work of hand power and water power, manufacturing tended to collect about the coal fields in northern England. Places lying away from the coal fields declined in pros-

280

perity, and agriculture suffered from loss of workers. Large numbers of men, women and children were employed in the factories, and the old practice of spinning and weaving in the homes gradually disappeared. No longer was it possible for the cottage weavers to compete with the fast machines of the factories. Such conditions caused unemployment and misery for some who had depended upon their own looms and spinning machines to earn a living. There were thousands, of course, who were young enough and willing enough to adapt themselves to the new ways, and these found work in the factories.

Developments, too, were taking place in the field of transportation. In 1761 the first English canal was opened, and this was soon followed by others. A network of canals provided simple and cheap transportation for goods, foods and raw materials. The canals were of particular benefit to makers of china dishes who had suffered great losses as carts bounced over rough roads.

Transportation

Through the centuries, English roads had become very poor because no effective road building programme had been put into force since the days of the Romans. The care of roads was the responsibility of local authorities who neglected their duties through lack of money or interest. Carts and stagecoaches jolted over rough roads in fine weather and stuck in the mud during rain periods. Many people actually found it more comfortable to

Dresses of this style were worn in England during the period 1780 to 1790. Materials utilized in their making were products of the new and faster looms being used in the mills. So skilful were the clothing designers that England became the acknowledged leader in fashion and clothing. Even the fashionable people of Paris were dressing *à l'Anglaise*. Costumes of casual appearance were designed for outdoor life. Large broadbrimmed hats of Italian straw were popular, and English women wore their hair in long soft curls liberally dusted with grey powder.

Wig styles for men are shown here. In Stuart times gentlemen wore shoulder-length wigs but in the Georgian period wigs became shorter and more formal in style. Boys of noble families wore wigs and, like their fathers, carried their hats in hand. Formal wigs are still worn in British law courts.

travel by horseback. By 1800, as the necessity for travel increased, greater interest was shown in the repair of old roads and the building of new ones. A Scottish engineer, John Macadam, developed in 1811 a method of road building by the use of layers of crushed stone rolled into a hard surface with a mixture of tar. In 1816 Bristol roads were "Macadamized" so successfully that other places showed a willingness to make improvements. About this time, too, a number of turnpike companies were formed to build roads for profit. Such companies secured rights of way, constructed good roads, and gained profits by charging tolls to travellers.

After the steam engine had established itself in manufacturing, it began to appear in transportation. In 1801 Richard Trevithick produced the first steam carriage ever to carry passengers. This astonishing affair, looking like a wagon with a steam engine behind and a steering rod in front, was the ancestor of the automobile as well as of the train. By 1812, the *Comet,* one of the first steamboats, sailed the River Thames. In 1814 George Stephenson startled England with his steam locomotive, the *Rocket,* which could travel twenty-nine miles an hour. A few years later he superintended in England the building of the world's first steam railway. Through such inventions as these, sailing ship and stagecoach were to be pushed from the scene.

Land holding While manufacturing and transportation were making such strides, agriculture was not standing idle. Improvements were made in the breeding of farm animals, in crops, and in methods of cultivation. The old problem of enclosures arose again as certain "open lands" were purchased and turned into private farms, but this action was carried out in a different manner than it had been 200 years before.

There was not the same conflict and the same disregard for rights which had existed in former years. By an act of Parliament, the enclosing of "open lands" was to be done only after the proper consideration of all rights belonging to tenants and small landowners. In spite of this, considerable suffering followed, because the small farmers found it difficult to compete with the big farms which were appearing. Numbers of labourers who had used "open lands" to graze animals and geese, now lost their old privileges as the common pastures disappeared. Many of the small farmers found it necessary to give up their little holdings, and work for others or find employment in factories. Many of those affected by the enclosures emigrated to British colonies, including a great many of the settlers who came to Canada in the early nineteenth century.

During the course of the industrial revolution of the eighteenth century, population grew rapidly and British exports increased to five times the former figures. One of the most striking effects was the change in the classes of British people. Among the upper classes there appeared a new group of wealthy manufacturers to join the ranks of the nobles, the big landowners, the merchants and traders. Among the lower classes there appeared a new group of factory workers quite distinct from the tradesmen, the labourers and the small farmers.

Trade and industry

47

THE AMERICAN REVOLUTION

King George III in his efforts to be a strong king, gradually aroused the opposition of the people even though he was supported by his ministers and by Parliament. Some of this feeling was shown in letters and articles appearing in newspapers, attacking the king and his friends. These writings were read by the people, causing further restlessness throughout the nation. Citizens of the time were inclined to feel that George III and his supporters were operating the government for their own good rather than for the benefit of the whole nation.

This dissatisfaction spread to the British colonies in America where the colonists had an even better opportunity to express their resentment. It is true that there had been differences of opinion between the colonies and the mother country, but none of these had caused any serious amount of bitterness. At this time, as in previous times, the nations of Europe operated their colonies in such a way that the greatest profits could be gained from them. There was little thought given to building up the colonies for their own sake. When the British colonies in America began to manufacture goods, laws were enacted controlling the sale and export of goods. Manufacturing did not expand as it might have, so that the colonies remained largely as agricultural settlements.

Even agricultural products such as sugar and tobacco were controlled with the purpose of sending all such exports to England. This was a handicap to the colonists, because they might easily have secured higher prices if their products were sold to other nations. Goods imported into the colonies were either produced in England or brought to England by means of British vessels. In spite of trade laws the colonists managed to smuggle goods into America from other countries, and carried on an illegal trade with French, Spanish and Dutch settlements in the West Indies.

Colonists desire self-government George III and his government would not have recognized it, but there was growing in the American colonies a desire for freedom and liberty. While Parliament was thinking only of trade, the colonists were thinking of their own lands and their rights as citizens. Even though the British at home did not realize it, the colonies could no longer be treated as mere trading centres. They had become political units of importance. Colonists were seeking, not complete independence from Britain, but a self-governing condition which today we would call a "Dominion."

After the close of the Seven Years' War in 1763, Britain began to tighten her trade laws in relation to the colonies. In addition to the thirteen colonies along the Atlantic coast, she held, by the peace treaty, the additional territories of Canada and Florida. Having now to protect this vast land area from the French, the Spanish and Indians, Britain made preparation for defence. It was decided to establish in America a standing army of 10,000 British troops to meet any emergencies. The **Stamp Tax, 1765** mother country would pay two-thirds of the cost of these troops, leaving the colonists to pay one-third. To raise this money, import duties were increased and the *Stamp Tax Act* of 1765 was passed. This made it necessary for the colonists to place official stamps on newspapers and legal documents. In effect, then, the sale of stamps was a special tax levied on most colonists.

In spite of the fact that the stamp tax was created to supply protection, the colonists fought strongly against it. Each of the Atlantic

284

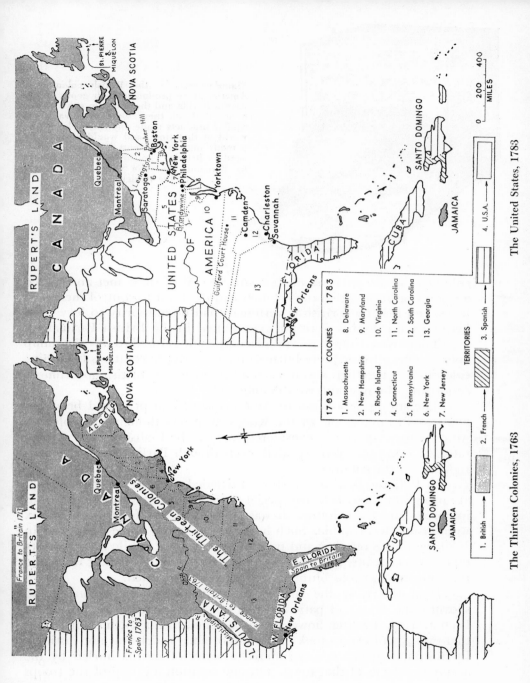

The United States, 1783

COLONIES 1783

1763 COLONIES
1. Massachusetts
2. New Hampshire
3. Rhode Island
4. Connecticut
5. Pennsylvania
6. New York
7. New Jersey

8. Delaware
9. Maryland
10. Virginia
11. North Carolina
12. South Carolina
13. Georgia

TERRITORIES

1. British ──▶   2. French ──▶   3. Spanish ──▶   4. U.S.A. ──▶

The Thirteen Colonies, 1763

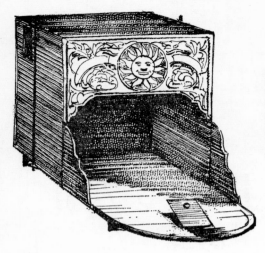

Manufacturers in the British colonies of America were producing such goods as the Kentucky rifle and the Franklin stove shown here. Both of these were in advance of similar products made anywhere else in the world at that time, and would have found a ready market if export had been encouraged by Britain. The stove invented in 1742 by Benjamin Franklin was the forerunner of the modern stove.

colonies had a legislature of its own. Several of these met and passed a resolution stating that the colonies had the right to control their own taxes, and that the British government had no authority to levy taxes because the colonists were not represented in the British Parliament.

There were riots in several places; people refused to pay the stamp tax and tax collectors were burned in effigy. Representatives from nine colonies met together, and drafted a protest to the British government concerning the new and troublesome tax.

The strong opposition in America caused surprise and bewilderment in Britain. Some of the King's ministers thought the colonists **Stamp Tax** were right, while others considered them to be foolish rebels. At any **repealed,** rate, the stamp tax was repealed, even though Parliament asserted its **1766** right to tax the colonies.

In 1767 the British government decided to make another attempt at raising funds and so levied special duties on tea, glass and other goods imported into the colonies. It was hoped that a different kind of tax would cause less trouble. Such hope was in vain. Three years later in 1770 the duties on glass and paper were removed, while a single duty on tea was kept just to show that the government could tax if it wanted to. This was a serious blunder, as events soon revealed.

If at this time the British government and the colonists had shown some degree of patience with one another, trouble could have been averted. Feeling, however, had reached such a pitch of bitterness that even small events took on an importance which was not justified. In Boston, British soldiers suffered a series of insults hurled by the annoyed citizens of that town. On one occasion a group of the troops

286

was surrounded and taunted with such terms as "rascals," "lobsters" and "bloody backs." Not content with mere words, the Bostonians made snowballs and threw them at the soldiers. In the confusion which followed, guns were fired, and four colonists fell in the snow. As the story of this unfortunate event spread among the colonies, it grew and grew in the horror of the telling until the people were talking of the *Boston Massacre*. Another affair which caused anger in England was the destruction of a British ship by colonists who went aboard and set fire to the vessel.

During this period the ships of the East India Company were allowed by the government to sail directly from India to America with cargoes of tea. After the vessels put into port, an import duty of three pence was levied on each pound of tea. In a gesture of defiance, a small group of adventurous colonists, in 1773, dressed as Mohawk Indians, boarded several vessels and dumped 340 chests of tea into Boston harbour. This escapade, known as the *Boston Tea Party*, was a joke in America. Its real importance, however, was that it committed the colonists to violence and caused deep anger in Britain.

Taking measures to prevent other such incidents, the British government closed Boston harbour, named a new governor for Massachusetts, and forbade the citizens to gather in public meetings. Far from frightening the colonists, these measures strengthened a growing desire on the part of the people to control their own affairs. Representatives from all the colonies, except Georgia, met at Philadelphia and there they drew up a *Declaration of Rights*, demanded the repeal of certain laws, and organized a boycott of British goods. Realizing by now that the American situation was serious, the government tried to reach a settlement with the colonists. It was too late for such measures, for the fighting had already commenced with the Battle of Lexington in 1775.

During the following year, on July 4, 1776, the *Declaration of* *Independence* was signed. By it the colonies broke their ties with Britain, and declared their own independence, thus creating the United States of America.

The *Declaration of Independence*, drafted mainly by Thomas Jefferson, revealed clearly the wishes of the American colonists. Their new democratic government was to be controlled by the people for the good of all the people. In part, the Declaration reads as follows:

We hold these truths to be self-evident, that all men are created equal, that they are endowed by their Creator with certain inalienable

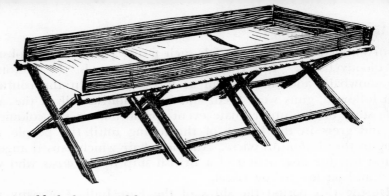

This portable bed was used by George Washington at Valley Forge where he and 10,000 of his men spent an uncomfortable winter suffering from cold, lack of warm clothing and scanty supplies. This bed is not unlike some modern portable beds, but has sides attached.

rights, that among these are life, liberty and the pursuit of happiness. That to secure these rights governments are instituted among men, deriving their just powers from the consent of the governed. That whenever any form of government becomes destructive to these ends, it is the right of the people to alter or abolish it, and to institute new government, laying its foundations on such principles and organizing its powers in such form, as to them shall seem most likely to affect their safety and happiness.

The *Declaration of Independence* was signed, but the fight for independence was not yet won. Britain had no intention of letting the American colonies slip away without an effort to hold them within the Empire. The war which followed is known in history as the American Revolution or the War of American Independence. Military difficulties which faced the British government during eight years of fighting were very great. The colonists were fighting on their own territory and so were close to their sources of supply. British troops, on the other hand, were 3,000 miles from home, far from their bases of supply, trying to cope with an enemy spread over a wide territory. To the British advantage, however, was the fact that the colonists were not trained soldiers. They lacked discipline. They did not care to stay away from their homes for long periods of time. In addition, more than half of the upper class people in America were opposed to the revolution.

In spite of the serious situation known to exist in America, the British government underestimated the determination and the fighting strength of the colonists. Insufficient reinforcements were sent to bolster the troops already stationed in America, and no capable general was placed in command of the forces. The Americans, meanwhile, had secured an energetic leader in the person of George Washington, a

George
Washington

288

wealthy Virginia plantation owner, who was able to rally forces and sustain the fighting spirit of his men.

It will be necessary here to give but a short description of the military campaign which took place in the bitter years between 1775 and 1783. In the beginning, the conflict centred about Boston, as the British clashed with the Americans at Lexington, Concord and Bunker Hill. The Americans sent a half-hearted expedition against Canada in the hope of capturing Quebec. It was a failure. For a time the British seemed in control as they defeated General George Washington at Brooklyn in 1776. One year later, however, the Americans won a solid triumph at Saratoga, and from that time on the fortunes of war remained largely with the Americans.

To complicate matters, a number of Britain's enemies lent their support to the American cause, as Holland, Spain and France entered the war. A French general, Marquis de Lafayette, offered his services to Washington and was made a major-general in the American army. Spain attacked Gibraltar and stood as a threat over the British trade routes to India. The French fleet entered American waters to aid Washington's troops. A British force in Virginia, caught between the

American troops with bayonets charge the British at Saratoga, 1777. The British lines of supply were over-extended, and the men exhausted by an arduous march. Uniforms worn by the Americans are similar to those of the British, although white and blue in colour. The American rifle is a flintlock weapon modelled after the British *Brown Bess*, but having simpler lines in its design.

French fleet at sea and the Americans on land, was forced to surrender. In the meantime French soldiers were landed in the north. Britain eventually was left holding no other territory but New York.

The British position was improved somewhat in 1782 when the French fleet was defeated in the West Indies, and the siege of Gibraltar broken up. These successes, nevertheless, were not enough to turn the tide of war. By 1783 all nations in the conflict were quite content to lay down their arms and talk of peace. The war closed with the *Treaty of Versailles,* which recognized the independence of the United States of America.

Treaty of Versailles, 1783

The loss of the American colonies was a humiliating defeat for Great Britain. It marked the end of the first British Empire, but it left a valuable lesson which aided in building the second Empire.

The rise of a new democratic nation in America was to have its effects upon thinking in the Old World and the New, bringing fresh ideas of liberty and justice.

48

GREAT BRITAIN AND THE FRENCH REVOLUTION

The American Revolution showed that the policies of George III and his government had been very costly to the nation. Not only had Great Britain lost her American colonies, but during the course of the war Ireland had won partial independence. As a result of the American crisis, George III was forced into a less important position through the action of the House of Commons. No longer was he able to choose ministers to suit himself, and no longer was he able to control Parliament. In one way, then, the American Revolution brought benefit, for it saved Britain from a return to strong monarchy.

In 1783, William Pitt, second son of the famous William Pitt, became Prime Minister. This young man, then twenty-four years of age, is known in history as William Pitt the Younger. Although the new Prime Minister did not have all the talents of his father, he was an extremely clever statesman. In the beginning Pitt was a Whig, but as time went by, he formed a new Tory party which remained in power for years.

Skating is one of the oldest sports known in England. In earliest times the shin bones of animals were tied to the feet, and skaters propelled themselves over the ice with the aid of spiked poles. In the period illustrated here, iron and steel blades were in use, and skating had become a very popular pastime. The long coat and dress worn by the woman skater bears little resemblance to the skating costumes of today.

Pitt the Younger was concerned with the way in which members of Parliament were elected to the House of Commons. According to law, two members were elected in each county and two from each town of reasonable size. This system had been satisfactory at one time, but with the passing of years it brought unfairness and inequality. It meant that unimportant little towns had as many members in the House of Commons as did some of the larger cities. The situation was plainly unfair to many districts. In certain places, where population was small, powerful landowners controlled the election of members. Actually at one time more than 300 members were elected through the influence of a small group of nobles and country gentry. On the other hand, prosperous towns had grown up having no members in Parliament except those representing the counties.

A great many British citizens were unable to vote because they did not own enough property. In 1768, only 160,000 people out of the 8,000,000 living in England, Wales and Scotland were qualified to vote at elections.

These conditions left the great mass of British people without representation in the House of Commons. It was quite possible for Parliament to operate the government without meeting the wishes of the people. The only effective method the people had of expressing their desires was through a show of force. At various times mobs collected to demand rights or to shout insults at officials of the government.

After William Pitt the Younger became Prime Minister, he made several attempts to change the system of electing members to Parliament, but he was unable to secure the approval of the House of Commons, even though the British people were demanding a change. The chance of reform was handicapped by a startling event taking place in France. This event persuaded the upper classes in Britain that it would not be wise to place more authority in the hands of the lower classes.

Conditions in France This event was the French Revolution, 1789, a savage class struggle which brought about the end of monarchy in France. The people of France had grown restless under heavy taxation and under a government in which they had no representatives. The French *States-General*, which was like the British Parliament, had not met for 175 years. In 1789, however, King Louis XVI was forced to call the States-General because his government needed money. The nation was hopelessly in debt.

Because France had taken part in the American Revolution, the French people knew of the freedom that had been won by the colonies. They desired some degree of liberty under their own government. When the States-General finally met, the members made very firm demands for changes in national life. Peaceful measures soon gave way to violence as mobs stormed and captured, on July 14, 1789, the Bastille, a strong fortress in Paris where many political prisoners were kept.

Among the participants in the French Revolution were women, some of whom were even more violent and more bloodthirsty than the men. Shown here is a typical female revolutionary dressed in what is basically a peasant costume. Because red, white and blue were the symbolic colours of the revolution, they appeared somewhere in the clothing of both men and women.

A French nobleman is led to the guillotine during the Reign of Terror which formed part of the French Revolution. In those violent days, hundreds of men and women were executed after hasty trials for being unsympathetic toward the Revolution. The guillotine shown here was invented in 1789 as a humane means of execution by Dr. Joseph Guillotine. After the heavy blade dropped from above, the victim's head fell into a basket.

The fall of the Bastille was a blow to King Louis XVI and a shock to the citizens of other European countries. With the growing power of the French lower classes, many reforms were made in the system of government. Had King Louis XVI been willing to co-operate with the French reformers he might have saved his throne. Foolishly, he acted in an uncertain manner so that his people did not know whether to trust him or not. In 1791, he fled from Paris, hurrying in the direction of eastern France with the hope of escaping from the country. His freedom was short-lived. He was captured and held as a traitor.

The September massacres which occurred the next year brought death to hundreds of French prisoners who were beheaded by the guillotine. Among these unfortunates were many men and women of nobility who were accused of being enemies of the Revolution. In

September, 1792, a new assembly of representatives, the Convention, met and declared France to be a Republic. In January of 1793, King Louis was executed, and a few months later Queen Marie Antoinette followed him to the guillotine.

Execution of King Louis, 1793

Events of the French Revolution had a marked effect upon every country in Europe. The new French motto, "Liberty, Equality and Fraternity," won sympathy and admiration in the hearts of people across the continent. In the beginning, British poets and authors wrote glowing passages concerning the French freedom, while clergymen preached sermons on the glories of the newly-won liberty. The leader of the Whig party became so enthusiastic that he said the capture of the Bastille was the greatest event that ever happened in the world.

Effect of the Revolution in Britain

Much of the interest shown in the French rebels was caused by the feeling that the Revolution would improve matters in France. Successes of the French in gaining reforms caused the British to think more seriously of their own situation. The Whig party urged changes in Parliament, the abolition of slavery, and the removal of injustices. Some of the British even talked of doing away with monarchy and forming a republic. When the French Revolution turned into its violent and merciless stage, British feelings changed so that there was less demand for reform in government. By 1795 the outcry for change had almost disappeared so that even pressing needs were put off for another twenty years.

Union of Britain and Ireland, 1801

In unhappy Ireland, the French Revolution made a greater impression than it did in England and Scotland. One result was the organization of a revolutionary party, the United Irishmen, which aimed at winning independence for Ireland. After a period of plotting and the training of troops, a revolt broke out in 1798. During the fighting shocking cruelties were committed by both the Irish and British troops. In a short time, however, the rebellion was crushed, and a number of Irish leaders were executed.

At the close of this affair the British government came to the conclusion that it would be wise to unite the Irish Parliament with the Parliament of Great Britain. Although the Irish were opposed to the plan, in the year 1801 the union was accomplished. The first portion of the Act of Union read as follows:

> That it be the first article of the Union of the kingdoms of Great Britain and Ireland, that the said kingdoms of Great Britain and Ireland shall, upon the first day of January which shall be in the year of our Lord, one thousand eight hundred and one, and for ever after, be united into

one kingdom, by the name of the *United Kingdom of Great Britain and Ireland*; and that the royal style and titles appertaining to the imperial crown of the said united kingdom and its dependencies; and also the ensigns, armorial flags, and banners thereof, shall be as his Majesty, by his royal proclamation under the great seal of the united kingdom, shall be pleased to appoint.

From that time, Irish members sat in the House of Commons and the House of Lords of the united Parliament in London. A new national flag, the Union Jack as we know it today, was formed when the cross of St. Patrick was added to the crosses of St. George and St. Andrew.

Even with the union of flags and parliaments, discontent remained in Ireland. This was due in part to the law which prohibited Catholics from holding seats in the House of Commons, and to the fact that they had been forced into this unwelcome union.

49

WAR WITH FRANCE AND NAPOLEON

One year before France became a Republic, the nation unwisely declared that it would give support to any people who would overthrow their kings and seek liberty. This bold statement was equivalent to a declaration of war against the monarchies of Europe. The conflict began in 1793 as Britain, Austria, Prussia, Holland, Spain and Sardinia ranged themselves against France.

Pitt the Younger was still Prime Minister in Great Britain, but he was not the wartime leader his famous father had been. His plans for war actually misused the nation's sea power, and caused the organization of some fruitless expeditions. Pitt was so sure France could be easily overcome by the allies that he failed to make sufficient preparation for a long and serious struggle. France, on the other hand, showed astonishing resistance to her enemies, so that invading armies were driven from the country.

France had gained a great military leader, Napoleon Bonaparte, **Battle of** who won startling victories in Italy against the King of Sardinia, and in **the Nile,** Austria where the French advanced almost to the city of Vienna. **1798** Encouraged by these victories and feeling safe in the Mediterranean,

Napoleon decided on an invasion of Egypt. This was a costly blunder, for he reckoned without the daring English admiral, Horatio Nelson.

Finding the French fleet anchored close to the mouth of the Nile River, Nelson launched an overwhelming attack which ended with the destruction of the enemy vessels. The Battle of the Nile, 1798, was a brilliant victory for Nelson, a victory the British very much needed, for the war had been going badly. Nelson became a hero in Britain, and with very good reason.

Following the Battle of the Nile, Napoleon deserted his troops in Egypt and made his way in a small boat to France. By this time his power at home had become so great that he was able to take over the government of France as First Consul of the nation. In this high post, he acted as a dictator with almost complete control of national affairs.

Treaty of Amiens, 1802 As the war continued, the British won some naval successes in the West Indies and defeated Napoleon's army in Egypt, but during nine years of fighting Britain had lost her allies. By 1802 both sides engaged in the struggle were so exhausted that they were relieved to sign the *Treaty of Amiens.*

The peace which came with the Treaty of Amiens was no more than a recess period in the long struggle, for Napoleon still held ambitious thoughts for a great French empire. He meddled in the affairs of other European countries, and he looked at South Africa, India and Australia. It was inevitable that the conflict should break out once more.

Napoleonic War, 1803 The struggle which started in 1803 is known as the Napoleonic War because it was no longer a fight against France but against the dictator who became Emperor Napoleon I. The French leader's plan of action included an invasion of England by means of a powerful army and fleet. In preparation for this venture, Napoleon collected a force of 100,000 men and readied a flotilla of flat-bottomed boats. There was just one weakness in this invasion plan, but it was fatal. The British controlled the waters lying between England and France.

So effective was the work of the British navy that for a time the French fighting ships were kept bottled up in harbours along the coast of France and Spain. However, in 1805 a group of French ships escaped from Toulon harbour, joined an allied Spanish fleet, and sailed to the French West Indies. Then began a gigantic game of hide-and-seek, as Nelson hunted for the enemy ships. Not knowing where they had gone, Nelson searched the Mediterranean, and then crossed the Atlantic to the West Indies. Here, too, he missed them, for the French and

296

A naval gun of 1805. The aiming of guns was still a crude and inaccurate operation although this was not considered a serious matter because naval action was conducted at close range. Many types of ammunition were employed, including bar shot, grape shot and chain shot. Chain shot was created through the joining of two half-balls by a long length of chain. As they emerged from the gun the two halves remained attached by the chain and in their whirling motion did great damage to sails and rigging of enemy vessels.

Spanish had slipped back to Europe. The hunt came to an end off Cape Trafalgar in Spain just to the north of Gibraltar. It was October 21, 1805. Here took place the great Battle of Trafalgar.

In a slightly curved line, almost five miles in length, lay the French and Spanish fleets. Most naval commanders of the day would have fought the enemy in a parallel line of attack. Nelson, however, advanced on the French and Spanish in two columns at right angles to the enemy line, an action which surprised and bewildered the enemy commanders.

The battle began about noon. As both columns of the British fleet engaged the enemy, guns roared, muskets rattled and clouds of smoke rolled across the waters. When Nelson's flagship the *Victory*, fired her first broadside, the enemy lost twenty guns and 400 men killed and wounded. The work of the British gunners was vital. They were not only more accurate than the French, but they could shoot twice as fast. Their swift actions took a frightful toll.

As the fleets came to close quarters, the battle broke up into duels among small groups of vessels. When the *Victory* turned sharply into the side of an enemy vessel the two ships became locked together by tangled rigging. A musket shot from the mizzen-top of the French ship

Admiral Nelson's flagship, the *Victory*, engages the French at the Battle of Trafalgar. Action shown here took place just after the British had broken through the French line. The *Victory*, which is still preserved at Portsmouth, was already forty years old at the time of Trafalgar. She is 226 feet long, weighs 2,162 tons and carried 104 guns. Because the fighting vessels were wooden sailing ships, wind played an important part in naval battles. British tactics were to keep windward of the enemy, for the windward fleet could choose when to start the battle.

struck Nelson's epaulet, passed through his chest and lodged in his spine. As he was raised from the deck, he cried, "They have done for me at last, Hardy . . . my backbone is shot through."

As the battle raged on, French and Spanish ships began to surrender. A British captain describing the scene on a captured vessel, said that "The dead, thrown back as they fell, lay along the middle of the decks in heaps, and the shot passing through these, had mangled the bodies . . . More than four hundred had been killed and wounded."

Before Nelson died, he knew that the French and Spanish had

been beaten. By 4.30 p.m. thirteen enemy ships were in flight, seventeen were totally disabled, and one was afire. Not a single British ship was lost.

Trafalgar was an important battle. It defeated Napoleon's plan for an invasion of England and brought to a close a century of naval rivalry between France and Britain.

Even though Napoleon had lost control of the sea, he was still **Austerlitz,** **1805** strong on the land. Two months after the Battle of Trafalgar he defeated Britain's ally, Austria, at the Battle of Austerlitz, and so forced this nation out of the conflict. The news of this defeat alarmed Britain, and so shocked William Pitt the Younger that he died shortly afterward.

The war situation became worse as Napoleon beat the Prussians and then the Russians. Only Great Britain stood between the French dictator and his dream of controlling Europe. Napoleon realized he could neither defeat the British navy nor invade England with an army. He planned to use another method to force a British surrender. By this plan he hoped to starve out the enemy by cutting off trade with other nations.

In order to cripple the British, Napoleon issued decrees ordering Prussia, Austria, Russia and other countries to have no further trade with the British Isles. In reply, the British navy blockaded continental ports, preventing ships from landing cargoes on enemy shores. The general result of these actions was to disrupt all trade, so that both sides suffered. Actually Great Britain was in the stronger position because her ships could go and come as they wished.

On the continent, Napoleon controlled Holland, Belgium, Italy, **Fighting in** part of Germany, Portugal and Spain. Austria and Prussia stood as **Spain and** **Portugal** neutrals, but Russia was an ally of France. Napoleon made an error when he occupied Portugal in 1807, because the British considered Portugal to be a friend and ally. British forces were sent, in 1808, to check Napoleon's power in Spain and Portugal. The struggle which followed is called the Peninsular War.

British forces were led by Arthur Wellesley, a skilful commander who later became the Duke of Wellington. For several years he fought the French in the rough, mountainous land of Portugal and Spain. Although he won no decisive victories, he succeeeded in holding the **Napoleon** enemy in check. His opportunity came in 1812, when Napoleon **invades** **Russia** turned against his ally, and led an army of 600,000 men into Russia.

299

This was a disastrous campaign for the French, for only 20,000 of the troops straggled back to Warsaw.

While Napoleon was pushing into Russia, the Duke of Wellington invaded Spain, taking advantage of a good opportunity. He defeated a French army, sending it in retreat to the north, but for a time he was unable to occupy the whole country.

In the meantime the British government was putting fresh vigour into the long struggle against Napoleon. A new alliance with Prussia, Sweden and Austria made a strong combination which threw its energies into a powerful blow at the French. In 1813, these allies clashed with Napoleon's forces at Leipzig in Germany and there the four-day Battle of the Nations was fought. It ended with the defeat of the French, and the retreat of Napoleon into France.

Napoleon defeated and exiled While these events were taking place, the Duke of Wellington smashed a French army in Spain, crossed the Pyrenees Mountains, and marched into France. The hard-pressed Napoleon was now caught between enemy forces advancing from two directions. Wellington's veterans pushed on relentlessly, winning a victory at Orthez, and finally forcing the complete surrender of the French. Napoleon, the little dictator who had dreamed of a mighty empire, was banished to the island of Elba in the Mediterranean Sea.

War of 1812 in America While the Duke of Wellington was fighting the Peninsular War in Spain and Portugal, Britain was engaged in another conflict on the other side of the Atlantic. The trade struggle between Britain and Napoleon had caused some unpleasant incidents between British and American ships. As a result, war broke out in 1812. On the high seas and on the Great Lakes the Americans won some victories, but on land their military movements were failures. The Canadians fought bravely to turn back invading forces. Among the land engagements was the Battle of Queenston Heights in which the Americans were defeated and the British commander, Isaac Brock was killed. Following the downfall of Napoleon, the British government sent a fleet and an army to America. The city of Washington was captured, but an attempt to take New Orleans failed. Both nations were content to end the dispute with a peace treaty in 1815. As a result of the war there was increased bitterness between United States and Britain, but in Canada there arose a feeling of nationalism.

300

50

WATERLOO

After the defeat of Napoleon in 1814, the allies met at the Congress of Vienna to settle the complicated terms of peace. They were still quarrelling over the settlement, when shocking news was received by the assembly. Napoleon Bonaparte had escaped from Elba!

During the short absence of the British frigate which guarded Elba, the little prisoner had slipped away from the island and landed in France. There he was welcomed with joy by his old soldiers, and he **Napoleon** arrived at Paris without firing a shot. Then began the short, stirring **escapes** period in European history which is known as "the Hundred Days." **from Elba**

King Louis XVIII of France fled for his life, Napoleon reorganized the government, and proclaimed that he was willing to live at peace with the other nations of Europe. His old enemies, however, knew Napoleon so well that they put no trust in his word. Quickly Great Britain, Austria, Russia and Prussia made plans to place a large army in the field against France.

The allies hoped to advance directly on the city of Paris, but by June, 1815, only the British and the Prussians were ready for military action. In Belgium the Duke of Wellington stood ready with an army of British, German, Dutch and Belgian troops. To the right of the British position the Prussian general, Blücher, commanded a large force of Germans. Extending in a line almost one hundred miles in length the forces of Wellington and Blücher remained a few miles outside the French border. Napoleon planned to strike hard at the centre of the allied line so as to separate the enemy armies. Then having split Wellington from Blücher, Napoleon hoped to defeat them one at a time.

On June 12, 1815, Napoleon left Paris and three days later was facing the allied armies. So swift and unexpected was this action that it caught Wellington and Blücher by surprise. The British commander himself admitted that the French move was "the finest thing ever done, so rapid and so well combined."

On June 16, there were two short battles in which the Prussians **Battle of** were beaten, but the British stood firm. At dawn the next morning **Waterloo,** Blücher retreated northward, and a few hours later Wellington, **1815** too, began a retirement. The French were so slow in pursuit that by evening Wellington had settled himself in a strong position near Waterloo. The Prussians unfortunately were sixteen miles away. During the night, however, Blücher sent a message promising reinforcements, so that Wellington decided to face Napoleon at Waterloo.

As Napoleon's troops came up to the British position, the two armies faced each other across a shallow valley. Because the ground was soft and wet from a night rain, Napoleon delayed his attack. It was not until 11.30 on the morning of June 18, that the French cannon opened fire. As a large portion of Wellington's troops were lying in the protection of a small ridge, they suffered very little during this first bombardment.

Anxious to break through the centre of Wellington's line, Napoleon launched attack after attack of foot soldiers supported by cavalry and terrific artillery fire. In spite of this merciless pressure, the British infantry stood as steady as a fortress wall. As large cumbersome masses of French soldiers advanced, Wellington's men sprang up from behind the ridge, pouring a withering fire into the enemy ranks.

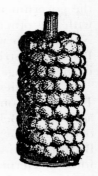

Hour after hour the battle raged on. Dense clouds of smoke from the firing of black powder floated in clouds across the valley. As the action continued, there were moments of high danger for the British cause. In one gallant, sweeping charge French cavalrymen overwhelmed and captured a battery of guns, but were forced to retire before the rush of British horsemen. Could the French have disabled the guns or dragged them away, the Battle of Waterloo might have ended in a different manner.

Later in the afternoon, another crisis loomed as an advance point in the British position was taken, placing the whole centre of the line in danger. Fortunately for Wellington, Napoleon did not realize the serious damage which had been done, and so failed to press his

Grape shot shown here was very effective in "softening up" a line of enemy troops. A charge of grape consisted of a large number of one-inch iron balls bunched around a wooden rod which had its lower end set into a wooden disk. The whole was held together by a cloth bag laced with twine. The bag caught fire when the gun was discharged, releasing the balls which flew in a shower from the muzzle.

advantage. In haste, Wellington filled the gap with troops and himself remained on the spot.

By 4.30 p.m. the advance guard of Blücher's Prussians were on the scene and were engaging the French. Prussian guns were in action, providing one more worry for Napoleon.

The battle dragged on until seven in the evening when Napoleon decided on one last powerful attack. As the French guns renewed their fire, the attackers moved forward up the slope shouting, "Vive l'Empereur!" Then, in a vicious encounter on the hillside, Napoleon's famous soldiers broke in confusion and began a ragged retreat. Seeing the break in the enemy ranks, the Duke of Wellington waved his hat to signal a general advance of the British forces. In a great awesome surge 40,000 troops poured into the valley and hurled themselves on the French. A British officer describing the scene wrote, "I have seen nothing like that moment, the sky literally darkened with smoke, the sun going down, and which till then had not for some hours broken through the gloom of the day, the indescribable shouts of thousands, where it was impossible to distinguish between friend and foe. Every man's arm seemed raised against that of every other. Suddenly, after the mingled mass had ebbed and flowed, the enemy began to yield; and cheerings and English huzzas announced that the day must be ours."

The French in full retreat, Wellington and Blücher met at nine o'clock, shook hands, and congratulated each other on the successful events of the day. It was decided that the Prussians should take over the task of pursuing the French.

The losses suffered during the Battle of Waterloo were shocking even in comparison with those of the World Wars of our own century. Wellington lost 15,100 killed and wounded, Blücher 7,000, and Napoleon 25,000. The French, too, gave up 8,000 prisoners and 220 guns. These are staggering losses for an engagement lasting but nine hours.

A week after the battle, Napoleon Bonaparte abdicated as head of the French government, and on July 7 Wellington and Blücher marched triumphantly into Paris. Failing to make an escape to the United States of America, Napoleon surrendered himself to the commander of a British naval ship, and was exiled to St. Helena. There on this island lying 1,200 miles west of Africa the little Emperor died in 1821.

Napoleon exiled to St. Helena

303

The last charge at Waterloo. Napoleon threw his crack Imperial Guard into the attack, but the British wore them down with cannon fire, using case and grape shot. Then, as the French faltered, the British launched an overwhelming assault which threw the enemy ranks into disorder. Casualties were so high that, it is said, Wellington wept as he rode across the area after the close of battle.

After the defeat of Napoleon, the Congress of Vienna, which had been in session before "the Hundred Days," finished its work and signed the *Treaty of Paris,* 1815. Of the conquests made by Britain during the war she kept the island of Malta in the Mediterranean Sea, the island of Mauritius in the Indian Ocean, and Cape Colony.

The conclusion of the conflict left Britain in an enviable position, for she had gained mastery of the seas and had won a great new opportunity for trade and commerce. In the years to follow she was to be "the world's workshop and banker."

304

SUMMARY—SECTION VII

In 1760 George II died and was succeeded by his grandson, George III. The new king tried to be a strong monarch, but his efforts only brought trouble and humiliation for the nation. His reign, however, was marked by changes known as the Industrial Revolution, brought about through the use of new machines, the steam engine and coal. Manufacturing cities grew up in northern England about the coal-mining districts.

The American Revolution, or the American War of Independence, 1775 to 1783, developed as a tax quarrel between Britain and her colonies in America. Although the colonists did not wish to break away completely from the mother country, they did want self-government. Feeling became so bitter that war broke out, and the colonists threw off British rule. After the signing of the *Declaration of Independence,* the colonies became a new nation, the United States of America. This action was a severe blow to Britain.

The French Revolution, 1789, was a revolt for freedom launched by the French lower classes against the tyranny of Louis XVI and his government. France was declared a Republic and King Louis was executed. In the beginning, people of other nations applauded the French fight for liberty, but as the revolutionists turned to unnecessary violence and mass executions, there was less admiration for the French cause.

In 1801 Great Britain and Ireland were joined together in the United Kingdom of Great Britain and Ireland. From then on, Irish members sat in the Parliament which met in London. A new Union Jack, as we know it today, was formed, when the cross of St. Patrick was added to those of St. George and St. Andrew.

Between the years 1793 and 1802 Britain and other countries were at war with the new Republic of France. Napoleon Bonaparte rose to importance as a great French military commander and First Consul of the nation. After nine years of conflict the war came to a close with the *Treaty of Amiens.*

In 1803, Britain was engaged in the Napoleonic War against the little dictator who dreamed of a French empire. By 1804 he was crowned as Emperor Napoleon I of France. His hope of invading England was shattered when the French fleet was defeated at the Battle of Trafalgar. Failing in the invasion plan, Napoleon next tried to cut off Britain's trade but this attempt, too, was a failure. After victories and defeats, Napoleon was decisively beaten in 1814 and banished to the island of Elba in the Mediterranean Sea.

In 1815 the captive Emperor escaped from Elba and returned to France where he again took over the government and the army. Then began the stirring period known as "the Hundred Days." British troops under Wellington and Prussian troops

305

under Blücher eventually faced and defeated Napoleon in Belgium at the Battle of Waterloo. Following this defeat the Emperor was confined to the island of St. Helena where he later died.

The end of the wars with the Republic of France and Napoleon Bonaparte placed Britain in a powerful position. She had gained control of the oceans and won for herself a new position in trade, commerce and industry. Her greatest days lay just ahead.

TIME-CHART

1760-1815

	1760-1820 GEORGE III
	1763 PEACE OF PARIS / END OF THE SEVEN YEARS' WAR
	1765 PARLIAMENT PASSES THE STAMP TAX
	1766 REPEAL OF THE STAMP TAX
First voyage of Captain Cook	**1768-1771**
	1769 JAMES WATT'S STEAM ENGINE
	1770 ALL DUTIES EXCEPT ON TEA REPEALED BY PARLIAMENT
Second voyage of Captain Cook	**1772-1775**
Boston Tea Party	**1773**
	1775-1783 THE AMERICAN REVOLUTION
Battles of Lexington and Bunker Hill / George Washington becomes American commander	**1775**
Declaration of Independence	**1776**
Captain Cook's third voyage	**1776-1779**

TIME-CHART — *(continued)*

	1783	TREATY OF VERSAILLES END OF THE AMERICAN REVOLUTION
	1785	CARTWRIGHT'S POWER LOOM
Colony of Sierra Leone founded in Africa	**1787**	
	1789	FRENCH REVOLUTION BEGINS CARTWRIGHT'S LOOM POWERED BY STEAM
Captain Vancouver charts the west coast of Canada	**1792-1794**	
Alexander Mackenzie reaches Pacific overland from Canada	**1793**	WAR WITH THE REPUBLIC OF FRANCE EXECUTION OF LOUIS XVI
	1798	BATTLE OF THE NILE—NELSON DEFEATS FRENCH FLEET IN EGYPT
	1801	FORMATION OF THE KINGDOM OF GREAT BRITAIN AND IRELAND
	1802	TREATY OF AMIENS CLOSES WAR WITH REPUBLIC OF FRANCE
	1803	BEGINNING OF THE NAPOLEONIC WARS
	1805	BATTLE OF TRAFALGAR—NELSON DEFEATS FRENCH FLEET
Simon Fraser explores the Fraser River	**1808**	
David Thompson explores Columbia River	**1808-1811**	
	1809	WELLINGTON BEGINS PENINSULAR WAR AGAINST THE FRENCH IN SPAIN AND PORTUGAL
	1812-1814	WAR OF 1812—BRITAIN AND UNITED STATES
	1814	NAPOLEON DEFEATED AND BANISHED TO ELBA GEORGE STEPHENSON'S ROCKET
	1815	NAPOLEON ESCAPES FROM ELBA BATTLE OF WATERLOO TREATY OF PARIS—BRITAIN GAINS MALTA, MAURITIUS AND CAPE COLONY

307

VIII. THE REFORM PERIOD

Hard times after the Napoleonic War •
Demand for reforms • Death penalty
removed from many offences • Reform
Bill of 1832 brings vote to middle classes
• Improvements in child labour and
education • Queen Victoria comes to
the throne • The People's Charter •
Potato famine in Ireland • Repeal of
the Corn Laws • Penny postage •
Expansion of railways • Growth of
manufacturing trade and commerce •
International Exhibition in London

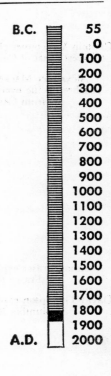

B.C.   55
        0
        100
        200
        300
        400
        500
        600
        700
        800
        900
        1000
        1100
        1200
        1300
        1400
        1500
        1600
        1700
        1800
        1900
A.D.   2000

51

DEMAND FOR REFORM

After the long struggle with France and Napoleon, Britain suffered conditions which follow most wars. There was heavy taxation, alarming prices and widespread unemployment. Hundreds of British soldiers and seamen found it difficult to secure work. The cost of food was higher than in former years. Manufacturing and trade had been dislocated by the years of warfare.

These unfavourable conditions caused the British people to turn their minds once again to reform in government. They were encouraged in this by a newspaper, the *Weekly Political Register,* which stated that conditions would only improve when changes were made in the operations of Parliament. When, in 1816, the *Weekly Political Register* was reduced in price from one shilling to twopence, great numbers of the people bought and read it regularly. For this reason, then, the newspaper had an important influence upon the British public.

The movement for reform soon passed the stage of quiet grumbling, as men demanded swift changes in national life and engaged in noisy demonstrations. Groups of people from among the lower classes took part in riots, collected at mass meetings, started reform groups, and even gathered military weapons.

Parliament was controlled by Tory members, very few of whom **Six Acts,** were interested in any changes being made in government. They **1819** much preferred to have things remain as they were. In order to fight the strong demand for reform, members of Parliament, in 1819, passed the *Six Acts* which forbade noisy mass meetings, and provided punishment for those who disturbed the peace. Under the new acts some writers were prosecuted for statements they had made in newspapers and pamphlets. In general the government was following a plan of crushing all the popular demands for change.

It was certain that sooner or later the people would clash with **Manchester** officials of government. One such clash came at the city of Manchester, **or "Peterloo"** in 1819, where reformers planned a large mass meeting to hear several **1819** speakers. When the city authorities heard of the planned gathering, they sent out orders that the meeting was unlawful and could not be held. In spite of this command the reform leaders called the meeting, and on the set date gathered in St. Peter's Fields. A group of police officers trying to shove their way through the crowd was pushed about and jeered by the people. Seeing that the police were helpless, the city authorities commanded cavalry troops to break up the meeting. In the swift rush of horsemen several men were killed and a large number wounded.

This event which came to be called the *"Peterloo" Massacre* caused hot anger among the people, but the government sent messages to the city authorities praising them for the strong action they had taken. Parliament, annoyed by the rebellious event in Manchester, passed even more severe laws against reformers. It seemed for a time that the nation might split into two hostile camps—one working for reform and the other fighting against it.

Beginning about 1816 large numbers of people from the working classes who were unhappy with conditions in Britain began leaving the country to seek new homes in Canada, Australia and the United States of America.

An important new change in government thinking came with the appearance of some Tory ministers who were not seriously opposed to reform. Among these was George Canning who became Prime Minister in 1827. Canning and other ministers made the government more popular among the people and paved the way for some much needed changes in law and in national life.

One of the first matters to receive attention was the heavy penalties **Changes in death penalties** which by law were imposed upon persons convicted of crimes. In 1800 there had been no less than 200 offences which were punishable by the death penalty. These offences included such crimes as sheep stealing, forgery, shoplifting and pocket picking. Literally hundreds of citizens had been hanged for criminal acts which today would receive light fines or short prison sentences. Boys and girls as young as eleven or twelve

A chair of the early nineteenth century. Such furniture was solid in construction and graceful in appearance. One of the last great English furniture styles, it was not so elaborate or so ornamental as the designs of the eighteenth century.

The Carron range, an early nineteenth century stove. On its left side is an oven and on the right side a boiler. The oven was equipped with a revolving shelf so that foods being cooked could be turned at intervals to prevent burning on one side. Open stoves of this type together with new larger factories were a factor in the serious air pollution which existed in London. One celebrated doctor of the time estimated that a cubic mile of London air contained six tons of soot, a condition leading to hundreds of deaths.

were sentenced to death. The odd thing concerning the criminal laws of those days was that they made little or no distinction between such crimes as petty theft and the monstrous crimes of murder or kidnappings. It is a sad commentary that large crowds of people gathered to enjoy the horrible spectacle of public hangings.

So heavy were penalties that they sometimes led to the miscarriage of justice. Juries, feeling sorry for accused persons, sometimes brought in verdicts of not guilty, even when it was clear that the culprits had committed crimes. Punishment was uncertain, for death sentences were sometimes reduced to complete pardon, to life imprisonment or to transportation to prison colonies.

British writers, speakers, a few statesmen and others had begged Parliament to change the laws so as to lighten the sentences for small crimes. In 1824 the death penalty was removed from a long list of crimes. In 1828 another step was taken when execution was reserved for major crimes such as kidnapping, murder and treason. In the

Daniel O'Connell addresses a gathering of Irish citizens during his campaign for Parliament in 1828. This was a period of wide variety in clothing as can be seen by the illustration. Men's trousers were held straight and neat by small leather straps which passed beneath the insteps of shoes. Coats were long, and were fitted with sleeves called "leg-of-mutton" because of their shape.

meantime imprisonment for debt and the public whippings of female criminals were abolished. It was not until 1836, however, that accused persons were allowed to have lawyers defend them in all cases.

While important changes were taking place in criminal law, equally important changes were developing in religious matters. According to the *Toleration Act* passed by Parliament in 1689, Dissenters had been given the right to worship as they chose, but only members of the Church of England were allowed to hold office in local and national government. Roman Catholic citizens had been granted neither religious nor political freedom.

As time went by, feeling softened so that some Dissenters had actually found their way into official positions. Catholics, too, had gained through the winning of religious freedom in 1778. Because reform was in the air, there was a constant demand for greater liberty for Dissenters and Catholics. As a result, by 1829 these groups were given most of the advantages enjoyed by members of the Church of

England. However, an oath affirming the monarch to be the head of the Church had to be taken by all members of the House of Commons, thus excluding all sincere Roman Catholics and some Dissenters. Although many members of the House of Commons wished to waive this oath, a group of Tories and the King were opposed to the change.

The matter was finally settled by an event which took place in Ireland. There, a brilliant and popular Catholic, Daniel O'Connell, ran for Parliament against two candidates favoured by the government. Although O'Connell knew that because of the oath, he could not sit in the House of Commons, nevertheless he was elected by a large majority.

The government of the United Kingdom realized then that it had the choice either of granting Catholics the right to sit in Parliament without the oath or of facing the unwelcome prospect of putting down a rebellion in Ireland. By 1829 Parliament passed the *Catholic Emancipation Bill* which permitted Catholics to hold any but a few of the highest positions in the nation. Catholic Emancipation Bill, 1829

The long, bitter, religious struggle which stretched back over the centuries of British history was almost at an end.

52

THE REFORM BILL OF 1832

When King George III died in 1820, he was succeeded by George IV, a man who had ruled for years as Prince Regent during periods when George III suffered from mental illness. Unfortunately his behaviour did not become his position. He spent money foolishly, he was often in debt, and he had gathered about him a crowd of notorious friends. Actually he took little part in government, except at times when he spoke out against reform. Despite a pleasant personality, he was neither an able nor a useful monarch. After a reign of ten years he died, and was followed to the throne by his brother, William IV. Important events were to take place in the new reign.

With the coming of the new King, a general election was called in 1830. Winning the election was important to both parties, Whig and Tory, because the future of reform hung in the balance. The Tories had been in control, with one short exception, for a period

The steam coach shown here, built by Walter Hancock, made an average speed of about fifteen miles an hour on a trip. The boiler and fire-box were beneath the body of the coach, the smoke passing out between the wheels. Royal commissioners decided that steam carriages were too dangerous, and for this reason the Red Flag Act was passed. By this Act a person carrying a red flag was required to walk in front of self-propelled vehicles moving along the British roads.

of forty-six years. The Duke of Wellington, a Tory, was Prime Minister, and he had no intention of allowing any further reforms. Seeing that there was very little chance of gaining reforms while the Tories were in power, a large number of the British people cast their votes for the Whigs. Defeat was a bitter blow to the Tories.

Proposed changes Shortly after the Whig party took control of the government, a Reform Bill proposing changes in the election of members for Parliament was introduced. By this Bill, the electoral districts throughout the nation were to be redivided more fairly than they had been for centuries. Some old towns which had not grown would lose members entirely. The Bill caused alarm among the Tory members, and, indeed, some of the Whigs themselves were not happy with the suggested changes.

Opposition was so strong that when the Reform Bill finally came to a vote it was passed by a majority of one. Parliament was dissolved and an election called. This time all the members who had supported the Bill were re-elected, while many of those who had fought against it lost their seats in the House of Commons. Following the election, the Bill was passed easily. This, however, was not enough to place the

314

Bill in British law, for it had yet to be approved by the House of Lords. Such approval was not granted; the Lords voted firmly against it. The following year, 1831, the same thing happened as the House of Commons voted for the Bill and the House of Lords against it.

With a deadlock in Parliament, excitement rose throughout the country. Riots flared here and there as citizens expressed their anger against the House of Lords. Groups of reformers made all sorts of wild suggestions such as marching against the Lords and even doing away with British nobility. Conditions became so dangerous that for a time it appeared as if another civil war might burst into flames. **Deadlock in Parliament**

As a remedy for deadlock in Parliament, Whig ministers suggested to the King that he might appoint to the House of Lords new peers who were in favour of the Reform Bill. The suggestion placed William IV in a difficult position, for a strong group of Tories, churchmen and nobles pleaded with him not to take such action. Eventually William did agree to the Whig plan, and the Lords withdrew their opposition. When the Reform Bill came up again in Parliament it was approved by both Houses and became law in 1832. **First Reform Bill 1832**

To the British people who had waited so long for change, the passing of the Bill was a cause for celebration. Lord Macaulay who had supported the Reform Bill describes his own feelings in this way,

> We shook hands and clapped each other on the back, and went out laughing, crying and huzzaing into the lobby. And no sooner were the outer doors opened than another shout answered that within the House. All the passages and the stairs into the waiting rooms were thronged by people who had waited until four in the morning to know the issue. We had passed through a narrow lane between two thick masses of them; and all the way down we were shouting and waving our hats, till we got into the open air. I called a cabriolet, and the first thing the driver asked was, "Is the Bill carried?" "Yes, by one." "Thank God for it, sir!" And away I rode to Gray's Inn — and so ended a scene which will probably never be equalled till the reformed Parliament wants reforming.

The Reform Bill of 1832 took away 143 parliamentary seats from thinly populated districts and gave them to counties, new industrial towns and cities having large populations. Another change lay in the fact that whole new groups of citizens were given the right to vote in elections. Previously in rural districts only well-to-do landowners had the right to vote, but by the Reform Bill the value of land (owned or rented) necessary for voting privilege was reduced. In towns people

315

An English policeman of the early nineteenth century. In 1829 Sir Robert Peel, Home Secretary, established in London the first efficient system of law enforcement. His force consisted of 2,000 men who were commonly called "Peelers." In the beginning citizens feared that such a body of policemen would be a threat to personal liberty. Public hostility was so great that a number of riots followed. In time, however, people learned to accept and respect the police constables.

who lived in homes worth a rent of ten pounds a year were also permitted to vote.

Importance of Reform Bill These changes really meant that the middle classes were given a new power in government, but working men still remained without a voice. The old tight control which had been held for centuries by the nobles and wealthy landowners was now broken, thus opening a new period in British government.

The reform had come not through ministers, or Parliament or King, but through the steady demand of the people. Here was an exciting movement which might well be compared to the barons' struggle with King John for the rights included in *Magna Carta,* 1215. The Reform Bill of 1832 was one of the first steps in the gaining of self-government for all the people. In future years this Bill was to be followed by other reform bills which brought true democracy to the nation.

316

53

SOCIAL REFORMS

Other reforms followed swiftly after the passing of parliamentary reform in 1832. The Whig House of Commons set itself to the work of making improvements in social matters, for many problems had arisen to cause misery and suffering.

One of the most pressing problems was the question of the thousands of children who were working in factories. Instead of attending school and enjoying sports, thousands of boys and girls were working ten to fourteen hours a day in factories. Other children were forced to labour in dark, damp mine pits far below the surface of the ground. Today we cannot fully appreciate the cruel hardships these **Child** children suffered through frightful working conditions and harsh **labour** masters. Many of them, ill-fed, poorly dressed and overworked, died at an early age.

A boy drags a cart of coal through the narrow passage in a mine. Some of these tunnels were no more than twenty inches in height. Children often became crippled or deformed as a result of these working conditions. A commission under Lord Shaftesbury reported in 1842 that thousands of children, some as young as three years, were employed at underground work, never seeing the light of day except on Sundays.

The historian, J. E. Symes, has described the situation in this way:

Employers soon found that children could do much of the factory work; and children were plentiful at a penny a day. They were often swept into factories when they could hardly walk. The Poor Law authorities of London began carting off wagon loads of pauper children to Lancashire. The workingmen were driven by poverty or greed to send their own children to work in the factories and thus, in the long run, to beat down their own wages by the competition of their own children. Many of them hated the necessity and some saw that they were really injuring their own class. But what could a man do but imitate his neighbours? His own wages, perhaps, a shilling a day. His half-dozen children could add fifty per cent to this; and it was almost impossible to feed them otherwise. Children of eight, seven or even six were frequently employed in the factories. The poor little mites often had to work twelve or thirteen hours a day. Children of both sexes were growing up in a sort of slavery, broken in health and brutalised in mind.

Factory Act, 1833 Fortunately there appeared in England at this time a strong champion of working children who fought in their cause. He was Lord Shaftesbury, a gentleman who had never known misery, but who still held a deep sympathy for the poor people of the nation. Shaftesbury's first attempt to secure improvement was to demand shorter working hours in factories. This idea, of course, caused loud protests from factory owners who said that if working hours were reduced, the factories could make no profits and so would close down. Factory owners were not alone in this belief. Even officials in government were fearful that industry might suffer. Nevertheless, Parliament was so moved by descriptions of child labour in the factories that it passed the *Factory Act* of 1833 which had to do with the cotton and woollen industry.

By the Factory Act no child under nine years of age might work in a factory; no child under thirteen might work more than nine hours a day; and children between the ages of thirteen and eighteen might not work more than twelve hours a day. These new regulations contained in the Factory Act improved conditions, but by today's standards conditions were still causing much hardship.

Those people who had foretold the ruination of British industry by the shorter working hours were proven wrong when the production of labourers increased, industry expanded and trade flourished in Britain.

Education Act, 1833 With so many children set free from working duties, there arose the problem of education. There was no national system of schools to provide education for all. Indeed, schooling for all children was con-

Many homeless children of the nineteenth century wandered the streets begging by day and at night sleeping wherever they could find meagre shelter. Some slept on roofs, some under arches and steps, and some in barrels.

sidered a dangerously progressive idea. There were, however, two large charitable societies which had set up schools in many districts for poor children, and early in the Industrial Revolution Robert Raikes had started Sunday schools for working children. The societies had raised their own funds and operated the schools as best they could in spite of difficulties. Recognizing the good work that was being done, the government in 1833 began to give a grant of £20,000 per year to the societies to assist in education. The government also passed a law requiring all children who worked part of the time in cotton mills to attend school for at least two hours each day. These actions on the part of Parliament were really the first steps taken in the development of a state educational system which is now one of the most advanced in the world.

Another social reform came with the changing of the old Poor Laws which dated back to the reign of Queen Elizabeth I. Poverty was so widespread that many districts found it necessary to help needy families through the payment of relief money. In some cases this was not a good thing, for lazy men grew to expect a steady income from relief payments. Employers, too, took advantage of the situation by paying very low wages to those who received relief. The cost of assistance was running so high that it placed a heavy burden on taxpayers. So burdensome were the taxes that some farmers were forced to give up their lands because they could not meet the payments. It became clear that this system of helping the poor was not a good one.

In 1834, Parliament passed the *Poor Law Amendment Act* which **Poor Law Amendment, 1834** made important changes in the former laws. One of the regulations contained in the new Act required able-bodied persons receiving relief to live in workhouses. Because there were different workhouses for men

319

and women, it meant that members of the family were separated from one another. The result was that many poor families having no desire to live in workhouses struggled along as best they could. Employers were forced to pay higher wages, and many lazy people went back to work. While it is true that the Act caused some suffering through the breakup of families, it did improve other conditions and reduced the amount of taxes needed for charity.

Abolition of Slavery, 1833

Still another social reform came with the complete abolition of slavery in the United Kingdom and in the colonies. For a long time European countries had taken part in this inhuman trade. Negroes were snatched from their homes in Africa, carried to distant places, and sold into slavery. Although this business was considered respectable by those who profited from slavery, there were others who considered it a crime little better than murder. Steady protest against slavery in Great Britain had brought about in 1807 its abolition within the nation, but the trade was still carried on in Jamaica and in South Africa. Plantation owners argued that their lands could not be cultivated without the use of slaves. Even this argument, however, did not save colonial slavery, when in 1833 the government ordered its end in the British colonies. The close of slavery came through the *Emancipation Act* which caused considerable debate in Parliament. The Bishop of Llandaff said that the abolition of slavery was "an act of national humanity and justice." The Earl of Westmoreland, on the other hand, said, "that no good would come from it, while it might be attended with much mischief."

In order to repay the plantation owners for their losses in slaves, Parliament granted a large sum of 20 million pounds. In South Africa this action caused considerable trouble, because a large group of Dutch farmers, the Boers, considered the black slaves an inferior race. The Boers saw no reason why such people should not be treated as slaves. As a result, many of the angry Boers left their lands and moved some distance northward into new African lands. The bitterness which arose between the British and the Boers of South Africa was to remain for a long time, and eventually to lead to war.

54

CHANGES UNDER QUEEN VICTORIA

King William IV died in 1837 and his niece, the eighteen-year-old Princess Victoria, was crowned as Queen. British people were frankly pleased that a young princess was to succeed to the throne so long occupied by rather clumsy and incapable men. The people, however, did not suspect that she was to become a really great ruler, and one who was to enjoy the longest reign in British history.

Queen Victoria was practically unknown to her subjects at the time of her coronation because she had been brought up quietly at home. Her careful training and sound education soon revealed itself, showing that she was a woman of judgment, moderation and good sense. Three years after she came to the throne, she married a German prince, Albert of Saxe-Cobourg-Gotha. Although the British were not altogether happy about the German marriage, Albert proved to be a wise and kindly man who made an excellent husband for the young Queen.

The two parties in Parliament continually quarrelled with one another over matters of reform, but certain changes were being felt in their acting and thinking. Gradually the Whigs began to call themselves *Liberals,* and the Tories began to call themselves *Conservatives,* so that in time the old names almost disappeared from use. Some Conservatives had accepted the ideas contained in the Reform Bill of 1832, but they insisted that any more changes should be made in a slow and careful manner. After the middle of the century even the Liberals themselves began to lose interest in parliamentary reform, for they believed that much had already been gained. Some actually voted against suggestions for change. _{Liberals and Conservatives}

England had become a wealthy, industrial nation whose manufactured goods were used widely at home and across the world. Even though wages for working people were a little higher than formerly, and factory conditions somewhat improved, there was still much dissatisfaction among the workers. The lower classes were engaged in a constant struggle to gain a better standard of living.

Working men of the time, who were interested in more than wages and hours, urged that the lower classes be represented in the House of Commons. During the year that Queen Victoria was crowned, 1838, a _{People's Charter}

321

conference of working leaders and some members of Parliament drew up a People's Charter which asked for more changes in government. Among these demands were: (1) the vote for all adult male citizens, (2) a new Parliament each year, (3) vote by secret ballot rather than public voting, (4) no property qualifications for members in the House of Commons, (5) the division of the nation into electoral districts having equal population. These demands seemed extreme at the time but virtually all have since been granted.

The People's Charter became the symbol of freedom for the lower classes, causing the formation of a new party named the Chartists. Although the members of the group had very few votes, they were large in numbers and very active in several ways. They held meetings, formed parades and sent petitions to the government. In 1839 when the Chartists presented a monster petition containing millions of names, the government became so alarmed that it made preparations for trouble.

In spite of the tense situation in London, the event passed without serious disturbance. In the following years the Chartists continued to petition the government to accept the People's Charter, but members of Parliament refused. Members of both Houses considered the Chartists to be rude, disorderly and violent. Discouraged by their lack of success the Chartists eventually gave up further efforts and disbanded the party.

Suddenly in 1845 a disastrous famine broke out in Ireland. The potato crop, which was the chief food of the Irish peasantry, failed. In order to feed the starving people, foreign wheat had to be imported, for in that same wet summer there was insufficient English wheat.

The potato famine had one good result in that it caused the

The Corn Laws government to face the problem caused by the Corn Laws. These laws had for many years forced importers to pay heavy duties on shipments of grain brought into the United Kingdom. The purpose of the Corn Laws had been to protect the farmers and to encourage them to produce more grain on their lands. In the beginning such a plan had been sensible and useful, but as the population of the nation grew, there was not enough grain grown to meet the demand. Under such conditions the Corn Laws only served to increase the price of grain and foodstuffs made from it.

In Parliament there was no desire to change matters because among the members were wealthy farmers and landowners who gained through the high price of grain. However, in 1839, there appeared in the

In England a post box is still called a pillar box because it was made to resemble a pillar. Some early boxes are in use today. In the illustration is shown a well-dressed gentleman of about 1885 who is posting a letter. He wears a high hat, checkered trousers and a brightly coloured vest.

manufacturing city of Manchester an organization called the *Anti-Corn-Law League* which began a fight against duties on foreign grains. Two eloquent merchants, Richard Cobden and John Bright, became brilliant leaders in this movement, because they believed that the Corn Laws caused real hardship among the working people.

Cobden, Bright and their followers carried their message through England by means of pamphlets, newspapers and public addresses. Money poured in to help them in their efforts. Their campaign had remarkable success among the people, but still no great impression was made upon Parliament.

Matters improved when Cobden and Bright became members of Parliament and pushed their fight to the very heart of government. So persuasive were the two gentlemen that many Liberals and even some of the Conservatives were convinced that some action should be taken. It is possible even then that very little would have been done if the tragic Irish potato famine had not brought some harsh realism to the

Repeal of the Corn Laws, 1846

This Victorian chair is representative of one of the ugliest periods in the whole history of furniture. Designers were obsessed with the capacity of new woodworking machinery, and in consequence used the machine to add unnecessary ornament as a substitute for good design. Plush, velvet and woven horsehair were employed in conjunction with such woods as mahogany and rosewood.

question. In 1846, Sir Robert Peel, the Prime Minister, was able to pass a bill doing away with duties on wheat and other grains. This had the effect of lowering prices on foreign and home-grown grains, so that bread could be bought at a reasonable price by working people.

The removal of duties on grains was just the beginning of a *free-trade* programme in the United Kingdom. During the same year that the Corn Laws were

Repeal of the Navigation Act, 1849 abolished, duties on sugar were dropped. Then, the old *Navigation Acts* established during the sixteenth century were abandoned, so that foreign ships were permitted to move freely in and out of British ports. In the years that followed, duties on hundreds of different articles were removed, leaving only a handful of import duties which provided some income for the treasury.

International Exhibition, 1851 Britain felt confident in her free trade programme with other countries because she led them all in manufacturing, commerce and agriculture. Realizing this, Prince Albert suggested that an International Exhibition be held in London during 1851. Albert could see a number of important advantages in a great exhibition where many nations displayed their products side by side. It is true that he was interested in advertising British goods, but he desired also that all countries should benefit. Although the Prince in the beginning had some difficulty arousing interest in the Exhibition, he persevered to the point where the nation became enthusiastic, thus lending full support to the idea. Held in the Crystal Palace* which was specially built for the occasion, it was a complete success.

*The Crystal Palace was completely destroyed by fire during World War II. Its site is now occupied by a television station.

Changes Under Queen Victoria

At the beginning of Victoria's reign the Post Office had not **Penny postage** developed a cheap and rapid system of handling mail. The cost of postage for letters varied with the distance carried, so that it cost five pence to send a letter from London to Windsor, and eight pence from London to Cambridge. A letter posted on a Friday night at Uxbridge would not reach Gravesend, forty miles away, until Tuesday morning. In Britain people of the time received an average of four letters per person per year. Today the average would be about 150.

An English gentleman, Rowland Hill, pressed the government for improvements in postal service. He proved that the expense of handling letters did not vary much with the distance carried. His plan was to use postage stamps, and to make a uniform charge for letters being carried within the nation. The postmaster-general of the day was opposed to Hill's plan because he believed cheap postage would result in a flood of letters which would burst the walls of the Post Offices.

By 1840 penny postage was introduced by Parliament, and this action was of great benefit to business and to private individuals. In the following years a similar plan was established in a number of the British colonies. By 1851 the first Canadian postage stamps were printed, and two years later the Canadian ocean mail service was in operation.

The growth of railways during the reign of Victoria was amazing. **Growth of railways** Britain's first railway was opened in 1825 and the second in 1829. When it was proved that railways were both useful and profitable, wealthy men formed companies for more construction. Queen Victoria took her first train journey in 1842. By 1850, just twenty-five years after the building of the first line, there were 6,000 miles of railway carrying 70,000,000 passengers a year. Industry gained greatly by the new method of transportation because coal and other raw materials could be carried easily to the places where needed.

The period of reform from 1815 to 1852 was a peaceful time insofar as war with other nations was concerned. It was a useful period because it permitted the people and the government to consider some of their problems, and to remove old injustices. Marked improvements were achieved in the operation of Parliament, in working conditions, in child labour, in education, in health, in transportation and in communication. No longer was it possible for the upper classes to control government, because Parliament had reached the stage where it was passing laws for the good of all the people.

SUMMARY—SECTION VIII

Following the long struggle with France and Napoleon, Britain was troubled by heavy taxation, high prices and widespread unemployment. From among the lower classes there arose a strong demand for reform. Such demands were accompanied by mass meetings, noisy demonstrations and riots.

During the reign of George IV, 1820 to 1830, the death penalty was removed from all but a few major offences. By the Catholic Emancipation Bill, Catholics were granted the right to hold positions in government.

The reign of William IV, 1830 to 1837, saw a series of important changes. By the famous Reform Bill of 1832 many people among the middle classes gained the right to vote, and seats in Parliament were distributed more fairly throughout the nation. By the Factory Act of 1833 the serious problem of child labour was partly solved. In the same year the government began to take an interest in the education of children from poor families.

When Victoria came to the throne in 1837 the demand for reform was still strong. The Chartists who supported the People's Charter wanted the vote for all adult male citizens and other changes. In spite of parades, demonstrations and petitions the Chartists could not get Parliament to accept their demands. In 1846 and 1847 the potato famine brought tremendous suffering in Ireland. Meanwhile in England the dispute over the Corn Laws was raging. In 1846 Parliament abolished duties on foreign grain so that the price of flour and bread was reduced. This was the beginning of a free trade period for Britain.

Through the urging of Rowland Hill, Parliament improved mail service by the establishment in 1840 of penny postage. Railways had been expanding so rapidly that by 1850 there were 6,000 miles of railroad lines.

By the middle of the nineteenth century Britain led the world in manufacturing, trade and agriculture. She had the opportunity to display her goods along with those of other nations at the great International Exhibition held at London in 1851.

The period of reform from 1815 to 1852 brought important improvements in government, working conditions, child labour, education, transportation and communication. Parliament had reached the stage where it was giving greater attention to the welfare of all citizens within the nation.

TIME·CHART
1819-1851

	1819	SIX ACTS PASSED TO CONTROL VIOLENCE AND DEMAND FOR REFORM
		"PETERLOO" MASSACRE REFORM MEETING BROKEN UP BY CAVALRY
	1820-1830	GEORGE IV
Union of Hudson's Bay Company and North West Company	**1821**	
Monroe Doctrine in America	**1823**	
	1828	DEATH PENALTIES REMOVED FROM ALL BUT A FEW MAJOR OFFENCES
	1829	CATHOLIC EMANCIPATION BILL
	1830-1837	WILLIAM IV
	1832	REFORM BILL
	1833	FACTORY ACT
		EDUCATION ACT
		EMANCIPATION ACT—SLAVES FREED IN BRITISH EMPIRE
	1834	POOR LAW AMENDMENT ACT
	1837-1901	VICTORIA
	1838	PEOPLE'S CHARTER
Lord Durham's Report	**1839**	MONSTER PETITION OF THE CHARTISTS
		FORMATION OF ANTI-CORN LAWS LEAGUE
Union of Upper and Lower Canada	**1840**	PENNY POSTAGE
	1846-1847	IRISH POTATO FAMINE
	1846	CORN LAWS REPEALED
	1849	REPEAL OF THE NAVIGATION ACTS
	1850	6,000 MILES OF RAILWAY
	1851	GREAT INTERNATIONAL EXHIBITION IN LONDON

327

IX. GROWTH OF DEMOCRACY

Britain and France against Russia in the
Crimean War • Florence Nightingale •
The Indian Mutiny • Gladstone and
Disraeli as great leaders • Reform Bill
of 1867 brings votes to lower classes •
Britain buys shares in the Suez Canal •
Egypt and the Sudan come under British
Control • British growth in Africa •
Canada • Australia • New Zealand
• South Africa • Second Boer War •
British Empire at its height • Life in
Victorian England • Queen Victoria's
Diamond Jubilee

B.C.

A.D.

55
0
100
200
300
400
500
600
700
800
900
1000
1100
1200
1300
1400
1500
1600
1700
1800
1900
2000

THE CRIMEAN WAR

The long period of peace for Great Britain came to an end in 1854 when the nation was drawn into a conflict known as the Crimean War. This struggle among European nations arose from rivalries existing at the eastern end of the Mediterranean Sea. Russia and Turkey were traditional enemies who had fought many times for various reasons. By the middle of the nineteenth century Russia had emerged as the stronger power. She stood as a serious menace over Turkish territories.

The Turkish Empire at this time was extensive, including the Balkan countries of Serbia, Bulgaria, Rumania, Greece, together with Egypt, Syria and Palestine. But, because Turkey's power was waning, **Reasons** it was a shaky empire whose members were seeking freedom. Russia **for war**

The charge of the Light Brigade was a famous event in the Crimean War. The Light Brigade was composed of dragoons, hussars and lancers all of whom were lightly armed cavalry. They carried lances and wore metal helmets not unlike those worn by the men of Cromwell's New Model Army. Canada's first Victoria Cross was won by Alexander Dunn of Toronto in this famous charge.

South-east Europe, Scene of the Crimean War, 1854-1856

was anxious to gain control of some of the Turkish territories, so she invented an excuse for war. As a Christian nation, Russia claimed the right to protect Christians in the Turkish states, and the right of guardianship over the "Holy Places" in Jerusalem and Bethlehem.

Czar Nicholas of Russia, feeling that Turkey had no friends in Europe, made the mistake of invading Turkish lands, and sinking a Turkish fleet. Britain and France were alarmed by these actions, for they believed the Russians were interested more in power than in Christianity. As in our day, Britain feared an unfriendly power standing astride the trade routes to India.

330

The Crimean War

Britain and France became allies of Turkey, and declared war on Russia in 1854. In the beginning, the allies planned only to drive Russian influence from some of the Turkish states, but eventually it was decided to strike a blow directly at Russia itself.

The war which followed was a "history of blunders," largely because there had been no major wars for some time, and the nations had forgotten how to fight effectively. Armies were bady dressed, armed, equipped and fed. It was the last of the old-fashioned wars fought according to the traditions of centuries.

Actual fighting was confined to Russian territory in the Crimean Peninsula, located on the north shore of the Black Sea. There were several sharp engagements shortly after the British and French landed, one of these being the battle of Balaclava, October, 1854. In this battle, the famous charge of the Light Brigade took place. Through a misunderstanding of the British general's commands, an officer ordered a cavalry group, the Light Brigade, to capture a battery of enemy guns located at the end of a long narrow valley.

It was a hopeless task, for the line of charge lay open to Russian guns on the surrounding hills. Through a deadly crossfire, 673 British horsemen galloped along the valley, losing men and horses as they pressed forward. With amazing dash and daring they reached the enemy guns, held them for a time, and then retired to the British lines . . . but out on the valley lay the bodies of 247 men. A French officer who witnessed the charge shook his head sadly and remarked, "It is magnificent, but it is not war."

The main target of the British and French was the capture of Sebastopol, the fortress which formed the centre of Russian defence. Because this stronghold held firmly against allied attacks, the British and French were faced with a winter campaign in the Crimea. They were ill-prepared for such hardship, because clothing and supplies were low, the animals used for transport had died, hospitals were in terrible condition, and the winter was cold. To make matters even more alarming, diseases such as dysentery, fever, cholera and scurvy broke out among the troops, causing illness and death. These patients, added to the thousands of wounded, created an impossible situation for the medical authorities. If there had been hospital supplies and equipment ready for use, something might have been done by the doctors and orderlies, but there were few beds and bandages and little in the way of soap, drugs and disinfectants.

When the news of the disgraceful conditions in the army camps

331

Florence Nightingale arrived at the military hospital in Turkey just as thousands of wounded were received from the battle of Inkerman. Beds were filled and wounded crowded together on the floors. "I think," she wrote, "we have not an average of three limbs per man." The devoted nurse on days of emergency worked twenty hours with scarcely a pause for rest. She was able to improve the hospital's unenviable record of fifty per cent. loss of its patients.

reached Britain, there was deep anger among the people and an uproar in Parliament. It had become evident that incapable officials and dishonest authorities were responsible for the tragedy which was taking place in the Crimea.

Florence Nightingale   One of the really important results, which came from the anger aroused at home, was the sending of Florence Nightingale to the scene to organize a nursing service for the military hospitals. Miss Nightingale had entered nursing at a time when it was not considered a respectable profession for a lady. In spite of ridicule and opposition, she had trained as a nurse in Germany, and later returned to England where she took charge of nursing in a sanatorium.

In 1854, with thirty-four nurses, she sailed to Scutari intending to bring some sort of order to the frightful hospital conditions there. It was not long before Florence Nightingale with the help of her assistants had created a miracle. Soldiers were well cared for in clean hospitals equipped with beds and other necessary equipment. This was not accomplished without a struggle, because the medical and military authorities were slow to make changes, and many resented the presence of nurses on the scene of war. Particularly they resented this woman who exposed the bungling and did something about it.

Neither the army officers nor the medical doctors were a match for Florence Nightingale. She bullied officials, wrote letters to British newspapers, and demanded what she wanted from the government. It was the wounded and sick men in the hospitals who learned to love and respect her as she moved about quietly with a light in her hand. To them she became the honoured "Lady of the Lamp."

With the coming of another year, 1855, the military prospects of the allies improved. With renewed vigour the British and French fought the Russians with increasing success until even the powerful Sebastopol fell before the attackers after a siege of 308 days. The fall of the Russian stronghold brought the war to a close, and peace was settled by the *Treaty of Paris,* 1856.

Following the war, Florence Nightingale returned home and continued her nursing duties there. The British government, however, paid her no special honour, although Queen Victoria did send her

Cantinières were women employed by the French army during the Crimean War to work in canteens and cookhouses. Although they were not soldiers, the women on occasions attacked their own troops with sticks when the men broke ranks under enemy fire.

a brooch. It was not until 1910, when the great nurse was a very old lady, that the Order of Merit was bestowed upon her.

In spite of this early neglect, Florence Nightingale has taken her place among the greatest heroines in British history. It was through her devoted service that nursing became a respected profession for women, that hospitals became cleaner and healthier places, and that the training of nurses was transformed. Her work was one of the few compensations for the waste and horror of the Crimean War.

56

THE INDIAN MUTINY

After the successes of Robert Clive and others in India, most of the great peninsula was controlled by the British under several types of authority. Madras and Bengal were governed by the East India Company which had been a force in the East since the days of Elizabeth I. Other districts in India were native states under princes who recognized British power within certain limits.

To the east of India lay Burma, and to the northwest lay the wild mountainous country of Afghanistan. The British fought some battles with the Burmese, and had no great difficulty in securing land conquests there. It was against the fierce, proud warriors of Afghanistan that the British forces had their greatest trouble. British authorities in India had hoped to remain on friendly terms with the Afghans, but this became impossible when Russian agents began stirring discontent among the warlike tribesmen.

The Afghans Believing that the only solution to the problem was a conquest of Afghanistan, the British sent troops into the mountains and occupied the restless land for two years. For a time the conquered people appeared to have accepted defeat, but in a sudden uprising in 1841, they seized the British stores of military equipment. Without ammunition, the British occupation army was so helpless that it had to make terms and leave the district. In a winter retreat through the Khyber Pass, thousands died of cold and starvation, and others fell before the attacks of mountain raiders. A futile attempt was made the following year to avenge the British defeat.

Thereafter, it was considered useless to consider a permanent conquest of Afghanistan.

Following the Afghan campaign, Britain found herself fighting **The Sikhs** against the fierce Sikhs of the Punjab region in northwestern India. These Sikhs, the best warriors in all India, poured out of their own lands and attacked British forces. It was only after a series of desperate battles that the Sikhs were defeated and forced to make peace. Quiet in this area did not last long, for the second Sikh War broke out in 1848, bringing another group of sharp engagements. Some idea of the fighting quality of the Sikhs may be judged by the fact that they killed over 2,000 British troops in a single action, even though they did not win the battle. Eventually the war came to a close when the British improved their artillery. By 1849 the Punjab became part of British India. Perhaps the conquest of the Sikhs may appear a harsh and stern measure, but British rule of the Punjab brought peace and a measure of prosperity to the region. The loyalty of the Sikhs to the British in future years proved that the relationship between the two people was not altogether an unpleasant one.

Still more Indian lands fell to the British, as the State of Oudh in the Ganges Valley was taken over, and placed, in 1856, under the control of the East India Company. Lower Burma, too, became another conquest after some fighting.

On the whole, British authorities were well-meaning in their rule **British** of India, but a number of things were done which caused discontent. **rule in** It had become the custom of Indian princes who had no children to **India** adopt sons who eventually became rulers on the death of the princes. To the Indians this seemed to be a sensible practice, but the British refused to recognize it, maintaining that in cases where there were no natural sons to accept power, the lands should come directly under the control of Britain. Quite naturally, this decision caused resentment among princes who were affected by its terms.

Roads were built, railways expanded, telegraph put into use, a mail system established, and irrigation projects created, though these improvements caused suspicion among some of the Indians. Instead of considering these changes to be for the good of the country, the people believed that they were new forces for military control. Public transportation in railway trains was believed to be anti-religious because people of different castes had to ride in the same coaches. Even the sound of wind moaning about the telegraph lines was said by the superstitious to be the voice of evil demons.

Thus, for a variety of reasons, distrust and discontent rankled in the minds of natives scattered here and there through the vast territory of British India. Also, the defeat of the British by the Afghans and the desperate struggle with the Sikhs led some Indians to believe that British troops were not, after all, invincible in the face of a determined enemy. All of these things eventually paved the way to the *Indian Mutiny* of 1857.

Indian Mutiny, 1857

This was a mutiny of native troops, the *Sepoys,* against British authority and not a general rebellion on the part of the Indian people. The event which touched off the mutiny was the issuance of the Enfield rifle to native soldiers. In order to use the greased ammunition for the new weapons, the men were required to bite the cartridges before placing them in the rifles. Anger swept through the Sepoys when a rumour was spread that the ammunition grease was made from the fat of cows and pigs. Because cattle were sacred to the Hindus and pigs were considered untouchable by the Mohammedans, the use of grease made from these animals was considered sacrilegious by the native troops. Historical records seem to disagree as to whether the grease was actually made from animal fats or mineral oils.

In May, 1857, Sepoys at Meerut mutinied, killing their officers and spreading revolt to the northern and central parts of the peninsula. The victorious mutineers of Meerut marched off to Delhi where they were strengthened by the addition of other rebels. There they set up

The Sikh warriors of India dressed colourfully in loose, cool clothing. Shown in the illustration is a Sikh with a massive curved sword which he has been carefully trained to use. At times the Sikhs carried in their turbans a number of sharp quoits which were used as missiles in battle.

British troops come to the relief of Lucknow which is besieged by Indian forces. Highlanders are shown fighting alongside the English. On the way to Lucknow the relief force passed the well at Cawnpore where British women and children were massacred.

a government of their own with Delhi as the capital. In the restless state of Oudh other garrisons mutinied, laying siege to the British in Lucknow and in Cawnpore across the Ganges River.

At Cawnpore one of the most treacherous events of the mutiny took place. There a group of 200 British troops and a body of civilians surrendered to a powerful Indian force with the understanding that the defenders would be permitted to leave in safety. After the surrender was completed, the men were placed in boats and ordered to move across the river, but as they did so the natives opened fire, killing most of the occupants. Shortly afterward the women and children were killed and their bodies thrown down a well. The day after this massacre a strong relief force reached Cawnpore, sending the Indian rebels flying from the scene.

At Lucknow the defenders had better fortune, but they were forced

Sieges of Cawnpore and Lucknow

337

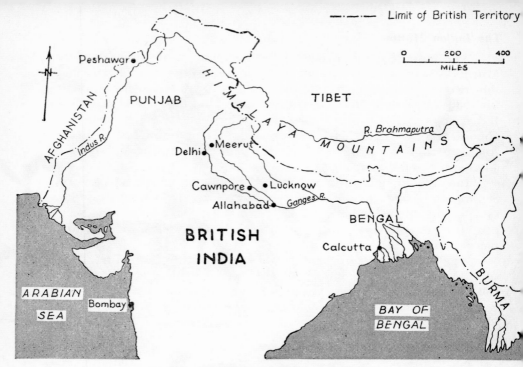

The Indian Mutiny, 1857

to endure a siege of eighty-seven days. A force of 1,000 British troops and 700 loyal Sepoys fought day after day against an immense body of mutineers armed with cannon. Reinforcements arrived to help the defenders, but even with this aid the British were besieged for two more months.

Not all the Sepoys across India joined in the Mutiny, for there were districts where the Indians took no part in the revolt, or where they fought side by side with the British. In addition to the loyal natives at Lucknow, there were others near Delhi. At Bombay and Madras the Sepoys refused to revolt, while the Sikhs of the Punjab region fought like tigers for the British.

Results of the Mutiny In a few months' time, the Mutiny had spent its first energy, and British authorities began to regain control. Fresh troops from Britain joined loyal Indian forces in mopping up the remaining pockets of resistance. In crushing the Mutiny, the British authorities used measures which today would seem excessively stern and cruel. Many of the known rebels were executed on the order of military courts, some by very cruel means.

338

The most striking change in the government of India after the Mutiny was the end of rule by the East India Company. Events had shown that a business corporation was not a suitable organization to wield authority over such a territory. Therefore, the control of British India passed directly into the hands of the home government which appointed a cabinet minister known as the Secretary for India. In the colony itself a Viceroy represented the British crown, and he was advised by several councils.

In order to reduce dissatisfaction among the native soldiers, the Sepoys were made part of the official British forces, which maintained a ratio of one British soldier to every four Sepoys. This arrangement proved very satisfactory, for no other incidents of a serious nature took place.

The Indian Mutiny had shown the need for improving social conditions within the country, because it was evident that the lower classes were suffering from disease, famine and a very low standard of living. British authorities commenced the almost impossible task of solving problems in health, education, industry and agriculture. Solution of these problems was extremely difficult because the government was dealing with a teeming population which was unskilled, uneducated, superstitious and divided into different castes and religions. Not all of these Indian problems have been solved even today, but the British went a long way toward improvement.

It is very easy to criticize the British actions in India on the basis of conquest, or greed, or selfishness, or cruelty or fancied racial superiority, but this does not do justice to the whole situation. It is difficult to assess all the rights and wrongs of the events which took place a hundred years ago. The fact remains that the British moulded an important country from a group of quarrelling states which had done very little for their own people. The fact remains that the British united, maintained and developed this country at a high cost in money, energy and lives. No one can dispute the fact that devoted British civil servants created one of the most efficient colonial governments of all time. India of today would not be the respected, independent nation that she is, if Britain had not taken steps to establish transportation, communication, education, industry and agriculture.

57

REFORMS UNDER GLADSTONE AND DISRAELI

Twenty years passed after the Reform Bill of 1832 before there was any strong demand from within the House of Commons for further reforms in Parliament. By 1852, however, a need was felt for extending the vote to more people among the working classes. In Parliament itself William Ewart Gladstone championed this cause, speaking firmly in its defence.

Gladstone, a graduate of Oxford University, began his political Gladstone career as a Conservative, but with the passing of time he became interested in reform, and so shifted over to the Liberal party. From then on he was a vigorous supporter of reform measures. Gladstone was more than a man crying out for change ... he was a skilful and intelligent minister of government who became Chancellor of the Exchequer in 1853. So eloquent were his addresses in the House of Commons that he could hold the members spellbound while he explained details of financial affairs in the British government.

Disraeli Meanwhile there had arisen in the Conservative party a brilliant young man named Benjamin Disraeli, who became a leading figure in the House of Commons. Disraeli, who came from an Italian-Jewish family, left school at fifteen, began work in a lawyer's office at seventeen, and entered Parliament at thirty-three. Because of his eccentric dress and ways, he was not popular among his fellow members. One of his costumes is described as having purple trousers, a black velvet cloak lined with satin, a red waistcoat and white gloves with a number of rings worn outside. In spite of this, Disraeli was highly respected by both parties in Parliament because of his outstanding ability and his skill in debate.

It is not surprising that Gladstone and Disraeli disliked each other, or that they became bitter rivals in the House of Commons. Seldom in British history have two more able men served in Parliament at one time.

Public opinion through the nation was running so strongly in favour of parliamentary reform that even the Conservatives began to think that some sort of action should be taken. It should be remembered that numerous changes had taken place since the passing of the

A political meeting in 1865. Well attended by the citizens, political rallies were lively, interesting affairs marked by fiery speeches and hot debates. Before 1872 voting was done publicly and election days were frequently marred by squabbles, fist fights and serious riots.

Reform Bill in 1832. Rapid communication, better newspapers, cheap postage and more schools had served to enlighten the people as to events at home and abroad. The working classes had grown in number and importance, so that their power was becoming evident. The greatest single influence for reform among the workers, however, came from the young people who had never known conditions before the *Reform Bill* of 1832. It was the younger generation who believed that further improvements were natural and desirable.

In 1867 Disraeli introduced into Parliament a new Reform Bill which included moderate reforms, but this was not acceptable to the Liberal members. In the hot debates which followed, the Liberals

Second Reform Bill, 1867

341

fought for more reforms, and the Conservatives yielded step by step. So many changes were made in the original bill that in the end Parliament went further than either party had originally intended. There is no doubt, too, that the decisions of members were affected by the amount of agitation which was going on among the people as a whole.

By the second Reform Bill of 1867 eleven small towns lost both members in Parliament, while thirty-five others lost one member each. These vacant seats were distributed among cities and counties having greater populations. But even more important than these changes was the extension of voting rights to people who had never enjoyed them before. In the rural districts any man who owned or rented land worth five pounds a year, or more, could vote for county members of Parliament. In the towns men who owned or rented houses worth ten pounds a year and paid the usual taxes, or who occupied lodgings worth ten pounds a year, had the right to vote. Accordingly, in the towns nearly every man had the privilege of voting. The only group of men who still lacked the vote were labourers who neither owned nor rented land and whose houses had very little value.

It would seem that the second Reform Bill created even greater changes in government than did the first one, for now nearly two-thirds of all men in England were entitled to elect members to the House of Commons. Such newly-won power placed Parliament within the control of the people, and thus constituted a long step in the winning of real democratic government. The first Reform Bill had given power to the middle classes, but the second extended a new influence down into the working classes.

The Education Act, 1870
Other reforms followed quickly. In 1870 was passed the Elementary Schools Act, which laid the foundations for a national system of schools. By this Act districts in England and Wales which had no school were to be provided with one, while districts having schools were to be helped with grants of money. Although Parliament lent generous financial support, schools were not entirely free, for parents were required to pay fees to assist in the cost of education. Compulsory attendance was not included in this Elementary Schools Act, but ten years later children were required to attend school up to the age of thirteen. In 1872 a similar Act was passed to improve Scottish education.

Ballot Act, 1872
Still another vital reform appeared in 1872 through the Ballot Act which introduced voting by the secret ballot to take the place of open voting by word of mouth. This change was important because it did

342

An early kind of English tram car known as the "knifeboard," about 1875. This vehicle appears very small when compared with the buses and the street-cars of today. It has a double deck and advertising posters as do the modern English trams.

away with many abuses which had taken place in elections. It was no longer profitable to bribe persons to vote in a certain way. Then, too, citizens lost their fear of being attacked or abused by others who disagreed with their ways of voting. Today it is difficult to understand why the secret ballot was not adopted at an earlier period in British history. **Civil**

Reform under Gladstone was carried even into the Civil Service and **service** the armed forces. For years many incapable people had been employed in the Civil Service because they had been appointed by friends who were members of Parliament or officials in authority. This was changed when it became necessary for all people desiring positions to pass a government examination in order to prove their ability.

In the army, too, there was a great need for reform. One of the **Army** old abuses in military life was the custom by which young men of wealth and nobility could become officers simply by buying commissions. Indeed, much of the military muddle which had taken place during the Crimean War had been due to mismanagement on the part of untrained and stupid officers. Among the military reforms gained by the Gladstone government were: (a) the elimination of commissions by purchase, (b) the beginning of short term service for young men, (c) the building of reserve army forces, (d) the uniting of many military departments which had operated as separate units.

Suez Canal In 1874, when the Liberals lost an election, Gladstone resigned and Disraeli became Prime Minister. During his term of office Disraeli turned his attention to securing Britain's place among the nations of Europe, and to strengthening the power of the Empire. He was particularly interested in India, a fact which led him to take a number of important actions. By a shrewd move in 1875 he purchased for the nation shares worth £4,000,000 in the Suez Canal. This enabled Britain to hold a controlling interest in the waterway which led to India. Then in 1876 Parliament passed an act granting the Queen the title Empress of India, a title which it was felt would improve British standing with the ruling princes of that country.

Disraeli and the Empire Following an election in 1880, Gladstone at seventy years of age formed a new government. He was pledged to reverse many of the policies followed by Disraeli and he had immediate problems to be solved in South Africa, Egypt and Ireland.

Disraeli's death, in 1881, brought to a close a career which had affected the nation in many ways. Even though he was a staunch Conservative, Disraeli had sympathized with the working classes, and had been interested in reform. Throughout his time as a leader in Parliament he encouraged the development of the British Empire, because he believed that colonial policy brought benefits to the backward countries included within the wide union. His Empire programme was so generally accepted that for years afterward it was supported by the British people. Disraeli himself gave kindly assistance to Queen Victoria, particularly in the days after the death of Prince Albert. While it is true that Gladstone also admired and respected his Queen, he never was able to gain the trust of the Queen which Disraeli enjoyed.

58

THE BRITISH IN EGYPT

At one time it appeared that France might have taken control of Egypt, for she held large territories in northern Africa lying close to the Egyptian borders. Then, too, France had initiated the construction of the Suez Canal joining the Mediterranean Sea with the Red Sea, and passing through Egyptian lands.

The spendthrift ruler of Egypt, the Khedive Ismail Pasha, had owned a large block of shares in the Suez Canal, but at a time when he needed money he sold these to Britain. This purchase of shares in 1875 made Britain a partner of France in the Canal and in certain Egyptian affairs. Egypt, in some respects, was still considered to be part of the old Turkish Empire. Turkey's power, however, had waned to the point

The British fleet bombard the harbour of Alexandria in Egypt. By this time wooden sailing vessels had been largely replaced by iron ships powered with steam. However, even in 1882 some sails were being used on steamships. Seen below is the famous warship *Inflexible*, which had revolving gun turrets housing eighty-ton guns capable of firing shot weighing 1,700 pounds. Heavy armour placed amidships on the vessel was two feet in thickness.

where she could no longer control or administer her outlying possessions. After a peaceful discussion, therefore, Turkey agreed that France and Britain might take over joint control of the Egyptian lands.

These arrangements had been made under the Disraeli government, but it was Gladstone who faced the difficulties which next arose. Dual control of Egypt by France and Britain was so disliked by the Egyptians that they arose in armed revolt. Riots broke out in several places, and a number of Europeans were killed. British and French fleets were rushed to Egyptian waters to support military forces. At this point the French decided that they did not wish to engage in an African war, and so withdrew, leaving the British to fight on alone. France had not retreated from Egypt in fear, but did so because she suspected Germany was preparing an attack upon her in Europe.

The French leave Egypt

The British fleet bombarded the city of Alexandria, and a few months later in 1882 forces under Sir Garnet Wolseley smashed an Egyptian army at Tel-el-Kebir.

South of Egypt lay the sprawling lands of the Sudan where the people had been restless for years under Egyptian rulers. In a sudden revolt, the Sudanese set up their own government and declared themselves independent of Egypt. Gladstone decided that there was no need to wage a war of conquest in the Sudan, but he was obliged to consider the plight of some British officers stationed there. These officers, who had been in the employ of Egypt, commanded garrisons scattered here and there in the Sudan. In order to rescue these, a British force was hurried southward.

The Sudan

The region was familiar country to General Gordon, the commander of the British expedition, for he had served under the Khedive as the Governor of the Sudan. Gordon, who already had a long and distinguished military service, held a reputation for courage and skill in action. He was a deeply religious man, disliking the thought of the Sudanese people being led by a fanatical Mohammedan leader, the Mahdi. Somehow or other, Gordon gained the idea that the Sudanese people should be converted to Christianity and that Britain should gain firm control of the region.

Although Gordon's orders simply required him to withdraw garrisons, Egyptian officials, and British officers from the Sudan, he advanced far up the Nile River to Khartoum. When established in this city, he began to send messages to London, requesting more troops so that he might defeat Sudanese forces under the Mahdi. This news created an uproar in Parliament, as some members argued against war

General Gordon at Khartoum, 1884

346

The gatling gun was the first machine gun employed by the British army. Issued in 1871, it was put into wide use, even in Canada. It had ten separate barrels which revolved as a crank was turned. The gatling gun was capable of firing 800 rounds per minute.

and others demanded that an army be rushed to Khartoum. Gladstone himself was so annoyed with General Gordon's actions, that he refused to support strong action against the Sudan.

In the meantime the small British force at Khartoum was surrounded by enemy troops and placed in a state of siege. With determination and courage Gordon fought off attackers month after month. In Britain the plight of the besieged British forces caught the imagination of the people, causing a loud demand that a relief force be sent to Khartoum. In the end such a force was organized and placed under the command of General Garnet Wolseley, an officer who had fought in the Crimean War, the Indian Mutiny and in Africa.

During preparations for the journey, General Wolseley made a request which seemed strange to some of his fellow officers. He asked for Canadian boatmen to assist him with transportation on the River

Nile. It was not a thoughtless request, for Wolseley had seen the wiry Canadians in action on the rivers and lakes of this country. It was Wolseley who had led the expedition sent from eastern Canada in 1870 against Louis Riel, the half-breed leader. Although Wolseley's request may have seemed odd to the British, a group of Canadian rivermen were sent across the Atlantic and on to Egypt.

Wolsley captures Khartoum, 1885 Unfortunately there were delays in preparing the expedition and more delays on the route, so that the British troops arrived in Khartoum just two days too late . . . Khartoum had been captured and Gordon killed, January 26, 1885. The siege had lasted for 317 days.

News of this disaster raised a fierce storm of anger in England, an anger which was directed chiefly at the Prime Minister. To British citizens, General Gordon, the dashing military commander, had been a martyr sacrificed by the blundering actions of Gladstone. Very few stopped to consider the fact that Gordon himself had been chiefly responsible for his own fate.

Third Reform Bill 1884 Although Gladstone lost popularity because of the Sudan affair, he gained one more success which won him support among the working classes. This was the passing by Parliament of the Country Franchise Act, 1884, which gave the right of vote to the agricultural workers and the town labourers who had been excluded before. By this Act another two million men were added to the voting lists, thus giving much greater power to the working classes of Britain. This legislation is sometimes called the Third Reform Bill.

59

MORE TROUBLE IN IRELAND

The Irish continued to resent the union with Great Britain which had been forced upon them in 1801. Quite naturally, too, they were unhappy at having the Church of England as the established Church in a land which was predominantly Roman Catholic.

Daniel O'Connell Fresh hope for the Irish cause appeared at the beginning of the nineteenth century with the rise of a great national leader, Daniel O'Connell, who is sometimes known as "the Liberator." It was he who formed the Catholic Association to fight for Catholic Emancipa-

During the Irish potato famine thousands of Irish citizens suffered hunger, and large numbers died of starvation. Help was sent from other countries, but even this was not enough to prevent a serious disaster. The illustration above shows people being served at an emergency soup kitchen set up on a city street.

tion—that is the right for Catholics to sit in Parliament and to enjoy other privileges of citizenship. O'Connell's election to Parliament finally led to the passage of the Catholic Emancipation Act of 1829.

By the middle of the nineteenth century, the Irish were still suffering from pitiful conditions which Disraeli attributed to "a starving people, an alien Church and an absentee aristocracy."

Over the years the Irish had grown accustomed to raising immense crops of potatoes, a food on which they depended heavily. So important were potatoes that a crop failure could mean nothing less than a

Potato famine, 1845

349

national disaster. Such a shocking event took place in 1845 when a wet spring promoted the rapid spread of a plant disease which killed the potatoes. That winter there was hunger in Ireland, but it was much worse the following year after the disease struck again. Food was rushed to Ireland from other countries and soup kitchens were set up for the hungry, but in spite of these measures, thousands died of starvation.

Fenian Society Feeling that there was little chance of living a comfortable or happy existence in Ireland, great masses of citizens moved out, seeking new homes in the British colonies and in the United States. Whole townships in Ontario and cities in the eastern part of United States were populated by these unfortunate emigrants.

A Fenian Society formed in the United States tried to attract attention to Irish miseries by committing acts of violence which were directed against the British. Fenian raids were launched against Ontario, Quebec, Manitoba and New Brunswick. Such small raids caused little damage or injury, but they did persuade the people of New Brunswick that union with other provinces in Canada was essential.

Gladstone believed that only by making important reforms in Ireland could the situation be brought back to relative peace and quiet. In 1869 he was successful in having the Church of England removed as the established Church in Ireland.

Land League The next problem which came to his attention was the unjust system by which land was held in Ireland. Landowners, many of whom lived outside the country, controlled large areas of agricultural land which they rented in small lots to peasants. By custom, tenants were required to bear the costs of repairs to buildings, fences and gates, but were never repaid for these expenses. Moreover, industrious tenants who improved their farms found their rents raised, and, if unable or unwilling to pay, they were ruthlessly evicted.

In 1871 a Land League was organized in Ireland with the purpose of uniting the tenants against the landowners. Members of this League planned to act together in opposition to those who took unfair advantages. In such cases the tenants were to ignore the landowner . . . no one was to labour for him; no one was to supply him with food; no one was to act as a servant in his home. The first person to be treated in this fashion was a certain Captain Boycott who found himself suddenly without workers in his fields and without servants in his home. Placed in a helpless position, Captain Boycott was forced to adopt a kindlier attitude toward those around him. Such united action on the part of members of the Land League came to be known as a "boycott." Today we still use the term with reference to situations where goods and services are withheld from individuals, organizations or nations.

In 1879 another potato famine spread hunger and fear across the country, causing misery, want and desolation. Unable to pay their rents, hundreds of tenants were put off their lands by selfish, grasping landowners. Without food, homes or proper clothing, the desperate outcasts turned to acts of hate and violence. Raiding, looting, robbery and even murder became all too frequent as mobs vented their anger upon wealthy landowners.

Such appalling conditions in Ireland gave Gladstone the backing **Land Act, 1881** he needed to pass the Land Act of 1881. This measure was nicknamed the "Act of the Three F's" because it brought "fair rent, fixed tenure and free sale." Tenants dissatisfied with their rents had the right to take complaints before a land court for settlement. Tenants who paid their rents regularly could not be put off their holdings. Tenants who wished to move had the privilege of selling their improvements. The Irish peasants, however, could be satisfied with nothing less than outright ownership of their lands.

Although these were worthwhile improvements in the Irish land **Home Rule Proposed 1886** system, their value was partly hidden by a rising demand for Home Rule. This cry for independent government came most strongly from Charles Stewart Parnell, a gentleman gifted with fluent speech and a talent for organization. Parnell believed that Irish conditions could not be improved through begging reforms from Great Britain, but through a return to the old system by which Ireland had her own Parliament. Gladstone sympathized with Parnell's views, but he could not gain the approval of Parliament, because the Conservatives and some Liberals wanted nothing to do with Home Rule. Ireland had been joined to Great Britain, and that was the way it was going to be.

Angered by violence in Ireland and by the behaviour of Irish members in the House of Commons, Parliament passed severe acts which fixed heavier punishments for tenants taking illegal action against landlords. Gladstone realized that punishing the Irish could never remedy the faults which lay at the roots of dissatisfaction. He knew the best cure was to give Ireland her own Parliament, and accord-

An angry Irish mob vents its wrath on a fleeing landlord. Thousands of Irish tenants lost their homes through the greed of landowners who evicted people from their holdings. Later in the century Parliament passed acts to protect the rights of such unfortunate citizens.

ingly he introduced in 1886 the Home Rule Bill. Unfortunately this bill was defeated in the House of Commons.

In 1892 Gladstone once again made a gallant effort to gain Home Rule for the Irish, and in this attempt he almost succeeded. His bill passed the House of Commons, but was defeated by a stubborn House of Lords.

For twenty years Ireland was kept under strict control through repressive laws. Violence was stamped out, and an uneasy peace settled over the island. The solution of thorny Irish problems was left to the twentieth century.

60

EXPANSION OF THE BRITISH EMPIRE

The imperial policy which had been framed by Benjamin Disraeli continued to hold the attention of government, so that in the latter part of the nineteenth century there was a renewed interest in British colonies, particularly those located in Africa.

In theory, the Khedive was the monarch of Egypt and the Sultan of Turkey was his overlord, but it was the British who did the actual ruling. Marked improvements were made in Egyptian affairs as British officials strengthened the country's finances, checked dishonesty, abolished forced labour and built up a system of irrigation to increase the area of farming lands. With the passing of years, Egypt became peaceful, stable and prosperous.

With Egyptian affairs in such a promising state, the British felt ready to turn their attention to the lawless and turbulent region of the Sudan. Already there existed a well-trained Egyptian army led by British officers. It was this fighting force led by Lord Kitchener which moved southward into the Sudan. During a short and successful campaign, the British defeated the Sudanese army at the Battle of Omdurman in 1898. Kitchener in the Sudan, 1898

Although France had withdrawn from Egypt years before, she gradually became jealous of Britain's triumphs in Egypt and in the Sudan. So strong was this feeling that French troops were moved into the southern part of the Sudan with the purpose of seizing lands along the Nile River. Such action, of course, alarmed the British, because they wanted no other European power stationed along the big river. Acting swiftly, Lord Kitchener sent British soldiers to the scene of invasion where they forced a quick retreat of the French.

These manoeuvres were just part of an immense European scramble for colonies in Africa, a movement which has been called the great "grab for Africa." With imagination fired by such men as Livingstone and Stanley, thousands of Europeans poured into Africa. Some went for the sake of adventure; some went to gain fortunes; some went to Christianize the Africans; and some went in the hope of building settlements. This situation led to clashes of interest among groups The "grab for Africa"

353

David Livingstone and his party travel in Africa. The famous explorer is seen wearing a hat with small trailing cape. As a child of ten Livingstone had worked in a cotton factory as did so many other children of the time. As a man

representing various nations as the race for land and power went on and on.

For years Africa had been the mysterious "Dark Continent" which was an unknown land to Europe except for the coast. The explorations of such men as Speke, Burton, Livingstone and Stanley, however, revealed that the heart of Africa was not a barren desert but a beautiful land of hills, rivers, streams, lakes, grasslands and forests. Accounts of these explorations excited the Europeans, setting them off on dreams of fortune, romance and high adventure.

So much African territory was being claimed and occupied by European nations that it was decided some agreement should be made to prevent useless clashes and disputes on the continent. Before the end of the century there were no less than six different agreements made and recognized by the European powers. By these, France gained a vast region in northwestern Africa, stretching from the Mediterranean southward to the Congo River. Belgium gained the Congo region lying southwest of the Sudan. Spain gained Spanish Morocco near the Strait of Gibraltar. Italy gained Somaliland on the east coast. Portugal gained

he firmly believed that missionaries should do exploration as part of their Christian duties. It is thought that he opened up more African territory than any other one person.

a district in East Africa. Great Britain's control of Egypt and the Sudan was recognized and also her possession of British Somaliland, Uganda, British East Africa, Rhodesia, Bechuanaland and Cape Colony at the tip of the continent.

Many of Britain's colonies scattered around the world had come **More** to her as the result of foreign wars. In the beginning there had been **colonies for the Empire** no thought of a world-wide Empire, but by the latter part of the nineteenth century this feeling had changed. The British were striving for land and power around the globe. The Federation of the Malay States was established in 1896. A protectorate was secured over Borneo and Sarawak. The Fijis and other islands in the south Pacific became colonies. Hong Kong in China was already a thriving centre of British trade.

So it was that between the years 1880 and 1900 the British Empire expanded its territory by thousands of square miles, and added 90,000,000 people to its population. It is little wonder that the British began to talk of an "Empire upon which the sun never sets."

61

CANADA

By the treaty of Paris, Canada ceased to be a French colony and became British territory. French colonists living in Canada were allowed to sell their property and return to France if they wished to do so, but most of them preferred to remain in the land they loved. Peace terms offered to the French were most favourable to the colonists, for they were permitted to retain their own religion, their own language, their own customs and their own system of holding land.

It was fortunate that such a moderate settlement was made for it gained the loyalty of the French in future years. During the American Revolution the French Canadians could have joined the rebels and turned upon the British in Canada. No such action took place.

Conditions in early Canada In the beginning Canada was not a single nation, but simply a collection of colonies, or provinces, scattered along the Great Lakes, the St. Lawrence River and the Atlantic shores. Following the American Revolution the population of most districts was increased by the stream of United Empire Loyalists which moved northward from the United States into Canada.

The most thickly settled regions became Upper Canada (Ontario) and Lower Canada (Quebec). Discontent with colonial rule grew in these two provinces because it was felt that control was kept in the hands of a few powerful persons while the people had very little voice in government. In 1837 this discontent burst into open revolt with a rebellion in Upper Canada under William Lyon Mackenzie and another in Lower Canada under Louis Joseph Papineau.

Because the British government was shocked by the revolts in Canada, Lord Durham was sent out as Governor to investigate conditions. After a careful examination of affairs Durham recommended in his famous Report that Upper and Lower Canada be united into the Province of Canada, and that the province be given greater voice in the control of its affairs through its own Parliament. The Parliament was to have almost the same control over the King's representative in the Province as the British Parliament had over the King.

The union was accomplished immediately but responsible government, not fully understood by successive governors, came more

356

Following the American Revolution thousands of United Empire Loyalists poured into Canada. Their arrival assisted materially in the establishment of Upper Canada and New Brunswick. For most Loyalist families the first years in this country were filled with hardships and continuous labour. Shown above is a log cabin of the type constructed by some of the Loyalists. Notice that it has been created from logs which have been squared by hand through the use of adzes.

slowly. This new treatment of a colony went a long way toward forming the basis of the future British Commonwealth of Nations.

Following the union of Upper and Lower Canada into the Province of Canada, affairs in government ran none too smoothly. Frequent quarrels broke out between the English and French or between the Liberals and Conservatives. For a time it appeared that perhaps union was not such a sound idea after all.

As years went by, there arose among citizens a feeling that the time had come to talk of a wider union among all the British provinces in Canada. A union of the Province of Canada with the provinces by the sea would have many advantages. A railway running from the Atlantic to the Great Lakes could improve trade and speed communication among the scattered districts. Union, too, could mean greater strength and more effective defence in a time of war.

Not everyone agreed that a wider union was a desirable or useful move, but the leading men in government realized that by this means alone could an important nation be developed.

On the Atlantic coast the people were thinking in somewhat the same terms. A conference was called in 1864 to discuss a union of Nova Scotia, New Brunswick and Prince Edward Island. At the conference held in Charlottetown representatives from these provinces, and guests from the Province of Canada, made the first hesitant steps toward confederation. As all Canadians know, the Charlottetown gathering led to the famous Quebec Conference of the following year at which important steps were taken toward the creation of the Dominion of Canada. This historical meeting was followed by still another conference in London, England, where the *British North America Act* was drafted, thus making a new nation which came into being on July 1, 1867.

British North America Act, 1867

Three years afterward, the youthful country gained an important addition to its territory when the Hudson's Bay Company sold to the government its vast Canadian holdings which had been obtained by a royal Charter granted in 1670 by King Charles II.

The four provinces of Ontario, Quebec, Nova Scotia and New Brunswick, which were the original members of Confederation, were not to remain alone for long. Others gradually came into the family, so that by 1905 nine provinces had become part of the Dominion.

There is no necessity here to expand any further the history of our own country. The important thing to keep in mind is that it was in Canada that Britain began her policy of granting self-government to the colonies. Historical events which took place here were to have an effect upon government in Australia, New Zealand, South Africa, India and other territories within the Empire.

62

AUSTRALIA

In 1770 Captain James Cook had explored New Zealand and some 2,000 miles of Australian coastline. On his return to England, Cook reported seeing fertile districts in Australia which he believed were suitable for white settlement, but the British government was in no mood for the establishment of more colonies. The loss of the American colonies was still casting a gloom over Britain.

By 1788 a small settlement was made at Botany Bay on the southeastern coast of Australia in what is now the State of New South Wales. To this spot was sent a group of 700 convicts along with the necessary guards. Some of the prisoners were dangerous criminals and some were unfortunates accused of plotting against the British government. During the following years more settlements sprang up, as prisoners and colonists arrived in the eastern regions of Australia. **Early settlements**

British people who chose to seek new homes on the southern continent were encouraged to do so by the government. Liberal grants of land were given to settlers, to soldiers, and to prisoners who had served their full sentences in the prison camps. Population gradually increased, the city of Sydney developed near Botany Bay, and the surrounding district came to be known as New South Wales. After this colony was established, British settlers began moving into other areas of the continent. Tasmania was settled, and then Queensland, Victoria, Western Australia and South Australia. The development was somewhat similar to that of Canada because the various settlements were spread out over great distances.

Agriculture, the first industry in Australia, gained increasing strength when it was found that sheep could be raised profitably. As early as 1797 a British military officer had imported a few

The natives of Australia used a unique weapon known as the boomerang. Looking like a bent stick, it is slightly concave on one side, and slightly convex on the other. A skilled thrower can hurl the boomerang in such a manner that it flies in a great circle and falls to the ground at the thrower's feet.

merino sheep from South Africa, and these did well on Australian pastures. Discovery of vast grasslands in the interior of the continent provided the wide ranges necessary for sheep ranching. As a result, the raising of sheep became a leading industry just at a time when wool was in strong demand. The great stocks of wool produced on the Australian ranches found a ready market in England where the woollen mills were providing work for thousands of workers.

In 1851 excitement raced across the land when a gold strike was made in New South Wales and shortly afterward in Victoria and

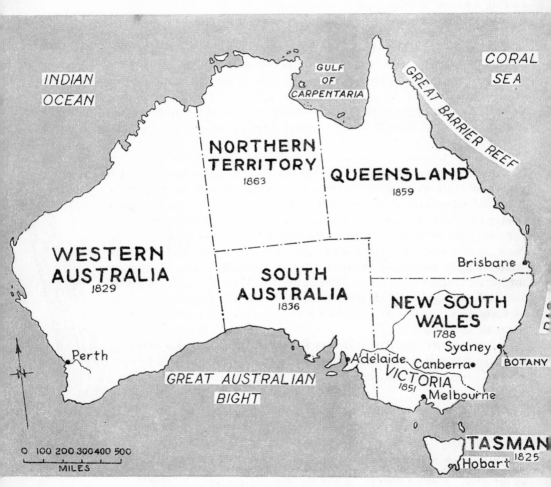

Early Australian Settlements

Merino sheep were imported into Australia and did remarkably well on the grasslands there. The Merino, which was originally a Spanish sheep, has a fine, dense wool growing down to its hoofs. One pioneer sheep breeder in Australia described the wool as being "fine enough to weave into angels' folds."

Queensland. As news of the discovery spread abroad, thousands of miners hurried from other countries to take part in the gold rush. **Gold** Like the gold rushes which took place in Canada, it was a short-lived affair in which some gained fortunes and most found nothing. As in Canada, too, the really important result came after the gold fever had died away and the gold seekers settled down to other occupations. By 1850 the population of New South Wales alone had grown to 250,000.

In the beginning, the various Australian colonies were ruled by **Government** governors sent out from Britain. Subsequently, councils appointed by the governors were given some voice in government, but the people as a whole had no power in the conduct of affairs. Important changes began in 1842 during the early years of Victoria's reign when the Australian colonies were gradually permitted to elect their own councils.

Thirteen years later each of the colonies drew up constitutions which they considered satisfactory, and submitted these to the British government. Eventually these were approved with the result that the colonies became self-governing with some general supervision by the British government. It should be noted that the colonies were still

361

separate units, as the Canadian provinces had been before Confederation. For some time there was no attempt made to draw a closer connection among the Australian districts, but with the passing of years people began to think of this possibility. The first step was taken in 1883 when the Federal Council for Australia was created. This, however, was a very loose organization which brought no close unity to the scattered colonies.

Commonwealth of Australia, 1900

The remarkable success achieved by the form of government established in the Dominion of Canada, in 1867, caused the British Parliament and the Australian people to consider the organization of a more solid type of union than the one which existed. This came to pass in 1900 with the creation of the Commonwealth of Australia which was to have a government very much like our own. There were to be parliaments in each of the seven states and a federal parliament to manage national affairs. Then too, as in Canada, the reigning British monarch was to be represented by a Governor-General.

The federal Parliament of Australia met for years at Melbourne in the state of Victoria, but later, in 1927, the site of the national government was changed to the city of Canberra which was created to be the capital of the nation.

63

NEW ZEALAND

The Australian settlers had found a climate quite different from that of Britain and a native people so shy and primitive that they put up little resistance to white occupation. In New Zealand settlers found a temperate climate similar to that of Britain and a native people, the Maoris, who were skilled and courageous warriors. In time, therefore, it became necessary either to conquer the Maoris or come to some peaceful agreement with them.

Missionaries who arrived in New Zealand during the early part of the nineteenth century were anxious to protect and educate the Maoris, but these noble aims were not always followed by the British settlers who followed. Missionaries and some settlers were established on the islands before the year 1840 when Britain officially declared

New Zealand to be a colony. This action on the part of the government was taken because it appeared that a conflict was developing between the white settlers and the Maoris. There was some reason to believe, too, that the French were ready to occupy the islands. In 1840 the Treaty of Waitangi was arranged between the government and the Maori chiefs. By this agreement the Maoris accepted Victoria as their Queen and thereby became her subjects within the Empire. The British, on the other hand, agreed to respect the land rights of the native people. This was a promise which was to cause trouble in later years.

Early New Zealand Settlements

As more and more settlers came to New Zealand, the rights of British and Maoris to certain lands came into dispute. It was very much like the situation which existed in America when the whites were in conflict with the Indian tribes over the possession of territory. During the years 1860 to 1871 the struggles reached a peak as the British and Maoris waged a costly war which brought suffering and hardship to both races.

In a determined effort to defeat the colonists, the Maoris formed a strong alliance among their own groups and fought the British with remarkable courage. This was no savage, treacherous, merciless struggle, but a hard-fought war in which both sides conducted themselves with gallantry. Records show that at times the Maori warriors risked their own lives to get water for their white prisoners. The long conflict finally drew to a close with a settlement which was agreeable to both peoples. During the struggle British and Maoris had gained a mutual respect and admiration, a feeling which enabled them to settle down at peace with one another.

In the meantime important developments had been taking place **Government** in the government of New Zealand. By 1856 the six provinces had

363

A Maori chief of New Zealand. The Maoris, of Polynesian stock, were tall and muscular with brown or olive skins. They possessed a highly developed feeling for art and design which enabled them to create beautiful canoes, house-posts, sculpture and other objects. Unlike the natives of Australia, the Maoris were courageous and capable warriors.

been granted self-government and a loose kind of federal organization. When communication and transportation were well established, it was found that separate governments in each of the provinces were not necessary, so that in 1876 all affairs were placed under the control of a single parliament. The fact that New Zealand occupied a much smaller area than either Canada or Australia made it possible for the nation to create a different kind of government.

It is rather surprising to find that after the sharp conflicts which had taken place Maori representatives were elected to the New Zealand House of Commons, and a few years later Maoris were sitting in the Upper House, or Senate, which corresponded to the House of Lords in the British Parliament. This swift recognition of the native people illustrates how well the two races had grown to accept each other in the life of the nation.

It is important to realize that British policy had changed remarkably since the loss of the colonies during the American Revolution. Britain had learned that colonial government could never be managed properly by officials who knew little of conditions abroad, and who understood nothing of the colonists themselves. Britain had wisely come to the realization that the sensible plan was to grant self-government to the colonies . . . self-government in a form which was best suited to the local situation.

64

SOUTH AFRICA

Probably the first European to land at Cape of Good Hope was the Portuguese navigator, Bartholomew Diaz, who, in 1486, was searching for a sea route to India. It was the Dutch, however, and not the Portuguese, who made the first important settlements in South Africa. Here was a convenient stopping place for Dutch vessels making the long voyage from Holland to possessions in the East Indies.

During the Napoleonic War, Holland passed under the control of France, and for this reason was considered an enemy nation by Britain. Because British warships held control of the high seas, it was a simple matter to capture the Dutch settlements in South Africa. By the Treaty of Paris, 1815, which closed the Napoleonic War, Britain was required to return conquered colonies to the original owners, but Britain managed to retain South Africa by buying the territory from Holland for a sum of six million pounds.

Colonization of Cape Colony by the British was not accomplished **The Boers** without a struggle, for the land was already settled by people who were not friendly toward British interests. There were the rugged, independent Dutch farmers, the Boers, whose families had held African land for generations. Also, there were the restless native tribes of black people who in later years were to give much trouble to the British.

The Boers had changed very little over the years since their first coming to the Cape. They were an industrious, determined, serious people, religious in their ways, and fully confident of their rights in Africa. Being rather old-fashioned in their views, they had very little in common with the eager, bustling, progressive British who appeared on the scene during the nineteenth century.

Among the natives living in South Africa were the Hottentots, **Native tribes** the Kaffirs, the Zulus and the Basutos. Although many of these peoples lived in a wild and primitive state, numbers of them had served for years as servants and slaves of the Boer farmers. When Britain abolished colonial slavery in 1833, the Boers had been greatly angered, even though they were paid for their losses. The amount of money granted by the British government appeared to the farmers to be very small in comparison with the value of free labour.

The picture above shows native Bantu women of South Africa. One is grinding meal in a stone bowl. The other is carrying water in an earthenware jug balanced on top of her head.

Even greater alarm spread among the Boers when the British began granting to natives the same political privileges as were permitted to white settlers. This was a shocking policy to the Boers who thought of the blacks as being little more than animals. Then, too, there was the fear that the natives, when given the vote, might gain control of the colony. The uneasy situation became serious when the Boers refused to allow political rights for the natives, and the Kaffirs threatened to launch an invasion from the north.

Completely dissatisfied with life under British rule, the Boers **The Great** decided to withdraw from Cape Colony with the purpose of finding **Trek, 1836** unsettled land for themselves. Then began the Great Trek as the **to 1842** Boers, transporting their possessions in wagons, moved northward across the African veldt to unpopulated country. The first district, Natal, which they settled was annexed by the British who disliked a Boer state lying next to Cape Colony. Moving on again, the Boers formed a second colony, Orange Free State, across the Orange River and a third one, Transvaal, on the other side of the Vaal River. These Boer settlements were made up chiefly of scattered farms which possessed little protection against the Kaffirs and Zulus.

Still suspicious of the Boers, the British took over, in 1847, both the Orange Free State and the Transvaal, but shortly afterward handed them back, thus recognizing the states as independent Boer republics. The Boers next found themselves busy in the defence of their holdings against native attacks from nearby districts. In consequence, British forces moved in, defeated the Basutos, and took possession of their territory. In the meantime other conflicts were taking place as the British fought to subdue the Kaffirs who proved so determined that only after a series of campaigns were they brought under control.

In 1871, diamonds were discovered near Kimberley in the Orange **Discovery** Free State, causing a rush of fortune-seekers to the new diamond fields. **of Diamonds** Following this discovery, the district surrounding Kimberley was annexed by the British. Cape Colony, prospering with the growth of industry and population, was given self-government, in 1877, in accordance with British policy toward her larger colonies.

While Cape Colony prospered, the Boer republics of the Orange Free State and Transvaal, enjoyed no such degree of wealth, and stood in perpetual fear of the dreaded Zulus. These tall warriors, the most dreaded in all Africa, presented a fearsome sight in battle as they bounded forward with painted shields and light spears. Time proved that the alarm of the Boers was well founded, for a Zulu chief collected 40,000 fighting men, and announced his intention of invading the Transvaal. The British, anticipating native attacks on all white settlers in Africa, annexed the Transvaal in the hope of discouraging the Zulu invasion.

Up until this time, the Zulus and the British had been on fairly good terms with one another, but the British action in Transvaal aroused an anger among the warriors which led to the Zulu wars. The conflict which followed was a long, bitter affair marked by bloody battles and massacres. In the beginning the Zulus won impressive victories, largely because the British commanders were incapable or did not know how to fight the natives on their home ground. Eventually, through a supreme effort, the British gained the upper

Zulu warriors encounter a small British force. These tall, fierce natives used feathers in their costumes and carried ox-hide shields like those shown above. In addition to their own native weapons, they possessed a limited number of firearms.

hand by 1879, although eight more years elapsed before the Zulu menace was completely removed.

First Boer War, 1881 While the Boers were thankful for the strong action Britain took against the Zulus, they still resented the British annexation of Transvaal. When it became clear that they were not to receive self-government such as had been granted to the settlers in Cape Colony, the Boers arose in armed revolt. In a short conflict, which is sometimes called the First Boer War, the Boers won two military engagements at Laing's Nek and Majuba Hill, both taking place in 1881.

Gladstone, who was Prime Minister at the time, held some sympathy for the Boers, feeling that they should be granted self-government. As a result, he came to terms with the rebels . . . a decision which was by no means popular in Britain. By the agreement which followed, Transvaal was recognized as an independent state to be known as the South African Republic, and it was further agreed that there should be free trade throughout South Africa and that Europeans might live in either the British or Dutch territories.

It was this last item of agreement which during the following years was to cause further hostilities between the British and the Boers.

65

SECOND BOER WAR

During the critical years when the Boers and the British were trying to work out their separate problems in South Africa, there arose two remarkable leaders who were to have a great influence upon the ultimate destiny of the land.

Paul Kruger, the son of a Boer farmer, had as a young boy travelled with his family on the Great Trek of the Boers out of Cape Colony. Even in his youth Kruger was a noted athlete who performed numerous feats of strength and endurance. The story is told that **Paul Kruger** he ran a full day's race against the best Kaffir runners, finally passing them all just before nightfall. A religious man, Paul Kruger in adult life became obsessed with the idea that he was chosen by God to lead his people to liberty, prosperity and power. By 1883 he had gained such respect and popularity among the Boers that he was elected President of the South African Republic. Still not content with his own position or the condition of his republic, Kruger dreamed of a Boer empire extending across all of South Africa.

The second leader to appear at this time was an Englishman, **Cecil** Cecil Rhodes, who was the son of a British clergyman. Because Rhodes **Rhodes** as a boy suffered from poor health, he was sent to South Africa in the hope that the climate there would benefit him, so that even during his college years at Oxford he spent his vacations in Cape Colony. As a man he entered business in South Africa, and acquired a great love for the country of his adoption. Like others of the time, he believed strongly in the expansion of the British Empire throughout the world and particularly in Africa. Like Paul Kruger, he dreamed of an African empire . . . a British one which spread all the way from the Cape of Good Hope to Cairo near the Mediterranean Sea.

Cecil Rhodes, being more than a dreamer of dreams, eventually became an extremely wealthy man through his activities in the diamond industry. Even by today's standards he was a rich person, for his income is believed to have been approximately one million dollars a year. Through his power as a wealthy and successful business man, Rhodes

A typical wagon of the kind used by the Boers in their Great Trek into Natal and the Transvaal. These were sturdy conveyances resembling in some respects the wagons used by settlers on the western prairies of America. During warfare Boer wagons like the one shown above were used to transport military supplies.

had considerable influence with the government of Cape Colony and with the home government in Great Britain. Using this influence to good advantage, he persuaded Britain to declare a protectorate over Bechuanaland, and then proceeded to develop the large territory now known as Rhodesia. Through an organization he created, the Company of South Africa, he built railways and roads, encouraged settlement, and devised schemes for the expansion of mining and agriculture in Rhodesia.

Rhodes continually strove to confine Boer power in South Africa in order to enhance British interests. It is not surprising, therefore, that he was alarmed by the discovery of rich new gold fields in the Boer lands of the Transvaal. So valuable was this discovery that the small income of the Boer government grew by leaps and bounds. Here was a new wealth and a new power which the Boers determined to hold at all costs.

As in the case of all gold strikes, there was a frantic rush of thousands into the fabulous new mining fields. Most of the men, being outsiders, were treated by the Boer government as foreigners, or "Uitlanders", who had no political rights, even though these miners were paying the heaviest share of national taxes.

By this time Cecil Rhodes was Prime Minister of Cape Colony as well as Chairman of the Company of South Africa. Stung by the growing prosperity of the Boer republic, he looked for some means of reducing or destroying the power of the rival government. In Rhodes' opinion, the refusal of the Boers to grant political privileges to the Uitlanders was sufficient reason to take strong action.

Gold Rush, 1886

370

Second Boer War

Learning that the Uitlanders planned a revolt in the Transvaal, Rhodes secretly promised military help by means of troops which were to be sent from Rhodesia under the command of Dr. Jameson. This unworthy plan achieved the failure it deserved, for a series of blunders turned the proposed action into a ridiculous farce. Rhodes, thinking better of his hasty decision, sent a message to Jameson, ordering him not to proceed with plans, but the Rhodesian commander had already set off on his mission without waiting for the Uitlanders to rebel. In 1896, with a meager force of 600 men, Jameson crossed into Boer territory, only to be captured and disarmed.

The failure of this venture and the underhanded nature of the British plot placed Cecil Rhodes in such an embarrassing position that he resigned as Prime Minister of Cape Colony. Already in declining health, Rhodes survived this event by only a few years, dying in 1902. While it is true that the Jameson Raid clouded the end of his political career, Rhodes will always be remembered as one of the great builders of the British Empire. He is remembered with respect and admiration, too, for his connection with the Rhodes Scholarships which he established with his own money for study at Oxford University. Since that time scholarships have been granted to many promising students

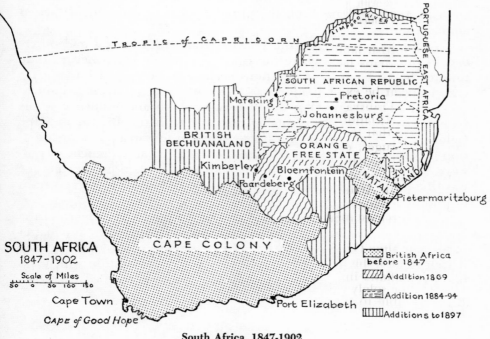

South Africa, 1847-1902

British troops with a gun carriage are attacked by Boers when attempting to ford a stream. Soldiers of the period were provided with a great variety of equipment. Notice the ammunition belts, water canteens, blanket rolls and

living in British lands and in the United States. A number of well-known Canadians have been the proud holders of these highly-prized annual awards.

As might be expected, the Jameson Raid caused anger and bitterness in the Transvaal, where the Boers took an even harsher attitude toward the Uitlanders. Conditions eventually developed into such a serious state that the Uitlanders asked assistance from Great Britain.

Paul Kruger, enjoying the increased wealth and influence of his republic, refused to co-operate in any way with the British in Cape Colony. He would not permit his government to join a postal organization for South Africa, or to take part in the joint development of railways. More dangerous than these actions was his open preparation for war, the purchase of arms, and the use of German instructors to train his troops.

At the time Great Britain had recognized the independence of the Boer republics, she had retained certain authority including the matter of foreign affairs in South Africa. In consequence, she now declared herself to be solely responsible in that region, a declaration which was not acceptable to the Boers. Conditions had now reached the point

Outbreak of war, 1899

sabres. Cavalrymen still carried long lances. The man on the right has a lance made of bamboo. Khaki colour by this time was used in uniforms because it was less conspicuous under battle conditions.

where only war could settle the question as to who should rule in South Africa—the Boers or the British. In October, 1899, the contest began.

This struggle with two small republics was not a situation which appealed to other European nations, so that France, Holland and Germany joined in a chorus of disapproval over British action in South Africa. In addition to this unpopularity on the continent, Britain was embarrassed by the fact that the first portion of the war went very badly.

Remembering the successes of the first conflict with their rivals, the Boers advanced confidently into British territory, and with such success that they hemmed in British troops at Kimberley, Mafeking, and Ladysmith. The besieged forces stationed at these points put up a magnificent defence, while every attempt was made to bring help from outside.

Paul Kruger had hoped for military help from some of the European nations, and perhaps an uprising of the Dutch settlers living in Cape Colony. In both of these hopes he was disappointed, so he had to be satisfied with the sole assistance of the Orange Free State. On the other hand, Britain was gradually gaining military strength as Canada, **Empire troops**

373

India, Australia and New Zealand gathered troops to support the mother country. Shortly after the war broke out, Canadians expressed a clear desire to send soldiers to South Africa, so that in a remarkably short time the first contingent was on its way. Altogether 7,000 Canadians were members of the expeditionary force—the first ever sent abroad by the youthful nation, the Dominion of Canada.

With the arrival of strong reinforcements from Britain and the colonies, the tide of war turned against the Boers, for under the leadership of Lord Roberts and Lord Kitchener British forces occupied Bloemfontein, capital of the Orange Free State, and Pretoria, capital of the Transvaal. As a result of these successful actions, the besieged cities of Ladysmith, Kimberley and Mafeking were relieved to the great pleasure of British citizens everywhere. With these gains in hand, Great Britain promptly annexed the two Boer republics in 1900, and made them part of British territory in South Africa.

In spite of this, an extremely difficult portion of the war was still to be fought as the Boers turned to guerilla fighting. Dividing into small groups equipped with swift horses, the Boers had adopted a hit-and-run style of conflict which proved troublesome to the British for a period of almost two years.

End of the second Boer War, 1902
By the peace agreement made in 1902, Britain extended remarkably generous terms to the defeated Boers. It was felt at the time that every attempt should be made to create conditions by which both peoples might live happily in South Africa. It was agreed that the Boers might use the Dutch language in their schools and courts; that the Boer states might settle as they wished the matter of granting political rights to natives; that the Boer farmers be given help to re-establish themselves; and that the Boer states be given self-government. All of these promises were kept, so that by 1906 the goal of self-government had been reached.

Union of South Africa, 1910
In 1910, the final step in political development took place when the provinces of Transvaal, Orange Free State, Natal and Cape Colony united to establish the *Union of South Africa* which, of course, remained as part of the British Empire. One of the Boer generals, Jan Christian Smuts, was a member of the first cabinet and served later as Prime Minister after World War I and during World War II.

66

THE BRITISH EMPIRE

We have been examining separate developments in the various parts of the British Empire, but we have not taken an over-all view of the scattered territories which came under British rule before the end of the nineteenth century.

In the early days of Queen Elizabeth's reign, no one dreamed that **Early days** the English were capable of gaining an Empire spreading around the **of Empire** world. Spain and Portugal claimed the New World, and conducted a profitable trade with their colonies in America and in the East Indies. England, not yet joined to Scotland, had no settlements of her own beyond the seas.

Nevertheless, before the Elizabethan era was over, English seamen were probing Arctic waters in search of the Northwest Passage, English privateers were challenging galleons on the Spanish Main, and Francis Drake had sailed around the world. Then came the great clash of sea power in which English seamen defeated the Invincible Armada of Spain.

With Spanish power reduced in Europe, the way was cleared for English trade and settlement in various parts of the globe. In 1600 the famous East India Company was founded. It later was to establish British authority in India. Then began a period of English colonization in America as Jamestown was founded in 1607 and Plymouth in 1620. At this time, too, England gained several islands in the West Indies, established posts in West Africa, and set up trading settlements on both shores of India.

For some years the Dutch were aggressive rivals of the English in America, India and in the East, but Holland was unable to maintain the struggle. It was the French who remained a dangerous enemy, particularly in America, until the end of the Seven Years' War when Britain captured Canada. Another vital victory came with Robert Clive's defeat of the French in India.

England and Scotland ceased to be separate kingdoms in 1707 when they were united as a single nation known as Great Britain, and thereafter the English possessions were known as the British Empire.

During the American Revolution, 1775-1783, the Empire received

375

a rude shock with the loss of the thirteen British colonies spread along the Atlantic coast of America. The loss of these important possessions was a shattering experience for Britain, but one which taught her a lesson in the proper treatment of colonies.

Even while the Americans were struggling for independence, the Industrial Revolution was underway in the British Isles. A new and prosperous age was ushered in as men put steam power to work in factories, mines and railways. Benefits won by the Industrial Revolution gave Britain more wealth and more tools for the winning of a greater Empire.

After the defeat of Napoleon Bonaparte at Waterloo, Britain stood as a powerful nation whose warships controlled the seas, and whose merchant ships enjoyed a thriving trade. British goods found a ready market in a hundred ports around the globe.

During the nineteenth century Britain gained control of New Zealand, Australia and South Africa.

To gain some appreciation of the distances which lie between the various parts of the Empire it is necessary to realize that it is 2,744 miles from Eastern Canada to Britain; 5,840 miles from Britain to South Africa; 4,610 miles from South Africa to Bombay; 5,630 miles from Bombay to Melbourne in Australia; and 6,210 miles from New Zealand to the west coast of Canada.

The scattered nature of the Empire made it essential to maintain an effective system of sea communication between the mother country and the colonies. Because Britannia ruled the waves the navy was able to guard the sea routes and lend assistance to any colony in need of help. British blue-jackets were soon on the scene when revolts, earthquakes, floods and fires brought sudden disaster. It was the navy that smashed the slave trade along the coast of Africa. It was the navy which laid the foundations for many new colonies.

Communication and trade

Under the shelter of naval protection, ships of the mercantile marine continued to enlarge Britain's trade through the nineteenth century. Fast new vessels known as clipper ships were used to carry cargoes from the east to Britain. Races between clipper ships often occurred because the first cargoes of wool, tea and other goods sometimes brought better prices than those which followed.

The day of the clipper ship was a comparatively short one, for steamships soon took over the shipping lanes. Steamships brought more rapid and more regular voyages, but they also brought the problem of coal supply. It became necessary to establish coaling stations at

376

Rangoon, in Burma, was twice captured by the British, first in 1824 and again in 1852, after which it became a part of the Empire. As early as 1852 the British had a factory there. In less than fifty years it rose from a minor place to become the third ranking seaport in British Asia. Note in the drawing above the beautiful lofty building in the background and the eastern dress of the Burmese troops.

suitable points along the routes which linked the widespread colonies. Some of these stations were Gibraltar, Malta, Aden, Colombo, Singapore, Hong Kong, West Africa, Ascension, St. Helena, Mauritius, Seychelles and the Falkland Islands.

For years the most rapid method of sending messages within the Empire was by means of letters carried in ships. Weeks and sometimes months passed before such messages could be delivered. Indeed, many important events which occurred in the colonies were not known in London until long after they had taken place.

In 1866 communications were greatly improved when a telegraph cable was laid across the North Atlantic. During the next twenty years more than 100,000 miles of cable were connecting many

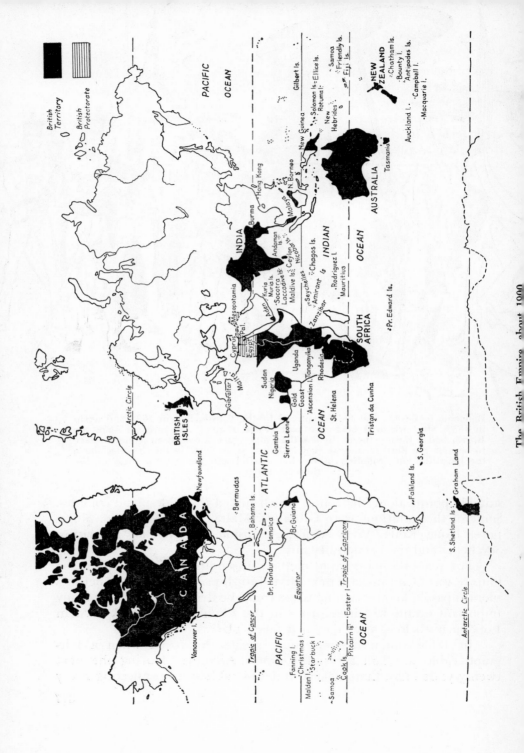

The British Empire about 1900

parts of the world. The new network of communication was so successful that before the end of the century telegraph messages could be
speeded to the most distant regions of the Empire.

The territories existing within the Empire were not all controlled **Kinds of**
or governed in the same way, because conditions differed so widely **colonies**
from place to place. Some of the forms of government used were:

1. *Crown colonies*—In these, government was controlled by officials appointed through the British Colonial Office. Example
—Gibraltar.

2. *Colonies with representative government*—In this type of
colony the chief posts were held by British officials, but an
assembly elected within the territory had a voice in government. Examples—Jamaica and British Guiana.

3. *Self-governing dominions*—These were lands settled by large
numbers of British people where complete self-government had
been granted. Examples—Dominion of Canada and Commonwealth of Australia.

4. *Condominiums*—In a very few cases territories were ruled
jointly by Britain and one other nation. Examples—the Anglo-
Egyptian Sudan and the New Hebrides (Britain and France).

5. *Protectorates*—Britain held limited control over a number of
lands, and extended protection to them. The amount of control exercised often was restricted to the field of foreign
affairs. Examples—Bechuanaland and Uganda.

See Appendix page 406 for complete list.

67

LIFE IN VICTORIAN ENGLAND

The fact that England was comparatively free from long costly wars during the reign of Queen Victoria gave the nation an opportunity to accomplish many things. Industry, trade, transportation and communication all expanded as the decades passed. It was during this period that Britain and the Empire reached their greatest power and influence.

From 1850 to 1870 the English people of all classes seemed to place great importance on the virtues of hard work and respectability. Perhaps they realized that progress and prosperity grew from the practice of these ideals. Their energy and enthusiasm showed results, as coal-mining, iron and steel making, and textile manufacturing showed astonishing growth.

Lower Classes
Many citizens, especially among the working classes, enjoyed a higher standard of living than they had ever known before. Because railways expanded rapidly and new industries were developed, the level of employment remained high. Big trade unions were well organized; they had well-filled treasuries; and they exercised considerable influence throughout the nation. Although the industrial boom lasted for years, it had begun to lose its force by the end of the century, when some unemployment and misery became apparent.

Middle Classes
People of the middle classes lived in large, ornate houses fitted with solid furniture and staffed by able servants. They dressed elegantly, ate heartily, moved about in carriages, and took an interest in art and music. Dignified middle-class parents were deeply concerned with the education and upbringing of their sons and daughters. Boys, after leaving school, were frequently trained to take their father's place in business, while girls were carefully instructed in needlework, housekeeping, music and graceful manners.

Clothing worn by the middle and upper classes was perhaps more sober than in previous periods. Women wore large hats and long sweeping dresses with full skirts, tight waists, bustles, all over a multitude of petticoats. Men, on the other hand, dressed in high hats, long coats, fancy vests, straight narrow trousers, tall collars and cravats.

Inventions
The effects of various inventions made in Britain and other countries were felt during the reign of Queen Victoria. Improved

380

A Victorian crinoline dress of 1857 to 1860. Such costumes had fine flounces in the skirts and pagoda style sleeves. The crinoline itself was a light framework of b a m b o o, whalebone or metal designed to make the skirt stand out in a full, rounded fashion. This was a period of rich materials, including silk, satin, silk damask and brocade.

soaps, matches, oil for lamps, cameras, telephones and sewing machines all became part of middle and upper class life. As bicycles appeared, young people took up the sport of cycling. Among the early bicycles was the "penny-farthing" machine which was fitted with a high wheel in front and a small wheel in the rear. The daring rider sat in a precarious position high above the level of the road. Although the "penny-farthing" bicycle was an improvement over the "hobby-horse" and "boneshaker" models, it was still an awkward machine to handle. When the modern-type "safety" bicycle appeared about 1885, cycling became more popular than ever before.

The development of refrigeration actually brought important changes in trade and altered the eating habits of the people. It had always been possible to transport dried meats and fruits, but fresh meat and fresh fruits had presented serious problems. Between the years 1880 and 1900, however, better ways of freezing and chilling foods were discovered. Such developments made it possible for fresh beef, mutton, pork, fish, eggs, butter, fruits and vegetables to be carried long distances without danger of spoiling. It meant, too, that the English people could enjoy fresh fruits and vegetables in the winter months as well as in spring and summer.

The telegraph during the early years of Victoria's reign, and the telephone in later years not only improved communication for individuals, business and government, but increased the news gathering ability of newspapers. In 1866 the first telegraph cable crossed the Atlantic. Others followed and newspapers were able to receive world-wide news in a matter of hours or even minutes. A new machine called the *linotype* increased the speed of typesetting, and did away with the old, slow method of setting type by hand. Because more attention was being given to education, people were increasingly interested in the reading of daily newspapers.

Before the end of the century electricity was playing a vital part in the life of the nation. Electric street cars were taking the place of the old cars drawn along rails by means of horses. Electric street lamps were replacing gas lamps, and electric fixtures were being installed in stores, offices, theatres and houses. By 1896 electricity for power and light was being produced in many scattered points throughout Great Britain.

Trans-portation Although automobiles followed rapidly upon the development of the internal combustion engine in Germany and were being made in

During Victoria's reign, new and important inventions were introduced, each of which had significance for Englishmen, even though some of these originated in other countries. (1) W. H. Fox Talbot stands beside an early box camera. It was he who discovered the negative-positive principle which permitted photographs to be duplicated. (2) Although delayed by the Red Flag Law, the automobile was well established in England by 1900. By 1910 there were 200,000 motor vehicles of all kinds operating in Britain. (3) The National Telephone Company was established and a telephone exchange in operation in London by 1879. The illustration depicts an early "lamp-shade" switchboard of 1882. (4) A British table telephone of about 1895. (5) Bicycles of many types and designs were common in Victorian England. The first of these, known as the "hobby-horse" appeared about 1818. The large bicycle shown here is a "penny-farthing" of 1885, so called because of its small rear wheel. (6) The telegraph was in wide use by the middle of the nineteenth century. Samuel Morse in America and Sir Charles Wheatstone in England were the men who developed this new means of rapid communication. Wheatstone's A.B.C. transmitter is shown. The hands on the transmitter can be moved to any letter on the dial. On the receiver (7) many miles away, a similar hand points out the letters as received.

1

2

3

7

5

4

6

The Great Eastern, 692 feet in length, launched in 1859, was the largest ship constructed up to that time. Constructed almost entirely of iron, she was fitted with sails, paddle wheels and a propeller. She was supposed to accommodate 4,000 passengers but from the beginning was an engineering failure. In 1860 she reached New York in eleven days but encountered so much trouble that she was never put on a regular run. Later *The Great Eastern* was used to lay cable across the Atlantic.

other countries, their development in Britain was hindered by a curious law, made in 1865, to control the use of steam carriages This law required a man with a red flag to walk ahead of any "mechanically propelled vehicle" moving along British roads. However, when "the red flag law" was repealed in 1896, automobiles soon came into use.

The change from sails to steam took place during the long reign of Queen Victoria. Among many steamships built by the British was the giant vessel, the *Great Eastern,* which was the largest ship of the time. Although a monster ship for the period, the *Great Eastern* was a failure, probably because she was not well planned. In 1860 she crossed the Atlantic to New York in eleven days, and ten years later was employed in laying telegraph cable across the Atlantic Ocean.

While England was gaining great success in material matters, the standard of her literature did not suffer. Despite the emphasis upon trade and industry, and despite the fact that people were inclined to admire those things which were ornate and superficial, the standard of achievement in literature was remarkably high.

Literature Such writers as William Thackeray, Charles Dickens, George Eliot, Robert Louis Stevenson, Thomas Carlyle, Charles Ruskin, Thomas Hardy, Lewis Carroll, Rudyard Kipling and Conan Doyle were producing works which were read enthusiastically at home and abroad.

Life in Victorian England

Poets of the period, too, achieved a fame in Britain and throughout the English-speaking world. Among these were William Wordsworth, Robert Southey, Elizabeth Barrett Browning, Alfred Tennyson, Robert Browning, Matthew Arnold, Dante Rossetti and Christina Rossetti.

The vigour of the Victorian age was expressed also in the field of **Science** science where many discoveries were made. Perhaps the outstanding scientist was Charles Darwin who developed the theory of evolution. During an around-the-world voyage on the ship *Beagle,* Darwin collected and observed thousands of natural specimens which formed the material for a long study lasting over years. In 1859 he published his famous work, *The Origin of Species.* This writing offered the theory that fish, birds and animals have, over the ages, gradually evolved from simpler forms of life. This slow change from one form to another, Darwin believed, was caused by the eternal struggle for existence.

Darwin's theory of evolution, as might be expected, caused both alarm and interest among Victorians. Some welcomed it as a great and important discovery, while others considered it a ridiculous suggestion. Those who scoffed at Darwin's beliefs, however, found it very difficult to reason against the evidence which the scientist had prepared so carefully.

Many games popular today were well known in Victorian times and long before. Football was known in the twelfth century, and cricket seems to have its origin in the thirteenth century. Although tennis courts built in 1530 still exist in England, the game was not widely played until about 1875 when it superseded the popular game of croquet. During the nineteenth century tennis was a lawn game played by both men and women. While playing tennis, women wore clothing which was little different from street attire.

Other scientific advancements were helping in the fight against illness and disease. The necessity of cleanliness during surgical operations and other medical treatments was being accepted seriously. Louis Pasteur the French scientist proved that diseases could be spread by germs in the air or on the bodies of people. A German named Koch showed that germs can cause dangerous conditions in open cuts and wounds. Joseph Lister, an English surgeon, introduced the practice of sterilizing medical instruments by means of carbolic acid or heat treatment. British surgeons gained, too, by the discovery that certain gases and liquids such as ether and chloroform may be used with value as anaesthetics during medical operations. Before this time surgery was performed with little or no anaesthetic.

Considerable interest was shown in the improvement of public health, particularly in the densely populated districts. Many British cities were crowded, smoky, dismal, unhealthy places. A large area of north central England had earned the unenviable name of "The Black Country." Conditions in some communities were so terrible that hundreds died of diseases caused by improper sewage disposal, unclean air, polluted water and damp cold homes. Alarmed by the death rate, authorities began to make major improvements in water supply, sewage systems and other matters concerned with public health.

Education During the early part of Queen Victoria's reign there were numerous private schools charging small fees for instruction, so that working class people could place their children in these if they wished to do so. Some of these schools were operated by churches, some by charitable organizations and some by persons who gained a living through this means. Unfortunately, many of the small schools consisted of only one untidy room where pupils were taught by one untrained and impatient teacher. In Liverpool forty children were crowded into an attic room which was also occupied by three dogs, two hens and a noisy rooster. Under such conditions very little real education could be obtained by the children attending school.

To provide schooling for many children formerly uneducated, monitorial schools were developed, where as many as a thousand pupils sat crowded together on benches in a single huge room with only three or four teachers supervising. The children were divided into small groups of eight or ten, each of which was placed under a pupil called a monitor, who was required to teach the lessons he, himself, had learned. It was a cheap form of education but could not be called effective.

386

Life in Victorian England

As mentioned in an earlier chapter, conditions improved in 1870 with the passing of the Elementary Education Act, by which the country was divided into districts, each one being required to have at least one school not operated for profit. Before the end of Victoria's reign all children were able to obtain an elementary school education, but high school and university education remained only for those who could afford to attend the better private schools and universities.

In the life of England, Queen Victoria played a part which reflected the thoughts and customs of the period. Her marriage to the German prince, Albert, had not been well received by the English people in the beginning, but the Queen outlived this brief unpopularity to regain the love and devotion of her subjects. **End of Victoria's Reign**

Her success as a British sovereign was due to certain personal qualities including a strong will, a religious nature, tactful behaviour, a sense of dedication and a keen mind with a remarkable memory. During her long period on the throne she managed to retain all the recognized rights of a British monarch in the face of strong republican sentiment. More than that, she earned the love of the people for herself and her family as persons, in a way that has carried on past the day when many other monarchs have disappeared. From her reign dates the present popularity of the Royal Family.

The devotion of British subjects to their Queen was expressed in its most colourful form at the time of Queen Victoria's Diamond Jubilee, marking the end of sixty years on the throne. In London, 4,000,000 visitors from all parts of the world were added to the city's usual population of 5,000,000 citizens. On June 22, 1897, the Jubilee was climaxed by a great parade which moved along flag-draped streets swarming with masses of excited spectators. This remarkable scene has been described in the following words:

At the head of the parade came the colonial troops and the Prime Minister. Representatives of the Indian army came next. There were giant Sikhs wearing white turbans. There were cheers for the marchers, from the Canadian mounted forces to the New South Wales cavalry, from the Dyaks of Borneo to the strapping cavalrymen from Jamaica. The procession took forty-five minutes to pass a given point at a quick walk.

Riding ahead of the Queen's carriage was a cavalcade of Princes including relatives or representatives of every notable sovereign in the world. Prince Ferdinand of Bulgaria was there; the Crown Prince of Austria, in a brilliant Hussar uniform; German Princes and Grand Dukes, three of them in the white uniforms of the Emperor, were there; Japanese,

387

These pupils are at work in a *monitorial* school. The master shown here is in charge of the whole school, although most of the teaching was done by pupils called monitors who taught the lessons they themselves had learned. Monitors often wore medals describing their duties, for example, "General Monitor of Reading," or "General Monitor of Arithmetic." Sometimes as many as 1,000 pupils were given instruction in a single large classroom.

Burmese, and Siamese Princes, swarthy little fellows, going on their way with Oriental impassiveness, were in the line.

Then came the Queen's carriage, drawn by eight cream-coloured horses, with their red morocco harness studded all over with burnished gold medallions bearing the Royal Arms, each led by a running groom dressed in a postillion's peaked cap and long coat, covered with gold braid. The Queen sat alone in a rear seat.[*]

Queen Victoria lived three and a half years following her Diamond Jubilee celebration, and then died at the age of eighty-three years, on January 22, 1901. Her reign, the longest in British history, lasted for sixty-three years, seven months and two days.

Victoria's reign brought to a close one of the greatest periods in the island story, a period marked by progress at home and expansion

[*]Coulter and Cooper (ed.) *Queen Victoria, Her Gracious Life and Glorious Reign,* World Publishing Company, 1910.

abroad. The Queen lived to see democratic government established in the mother country; to see self-government created in large colonies; to see the British flag planted on all the continents except Antarctica, and to see millions of additional people become new citizens within the Empire.

At the time of Queen Victoria's death, Britain remained as the most influential nation on earth—a strong power controlling history's greatest empire. As the twentieth century dawned, Britain's future appeared so bright that few people would have dared to prophesy anything but further progress and growing influence. It was not realized that before half a century had elapsed Britain would exhaust herself in two World Wars ... that the Royal navy would be challenged by aggressive enemy fleets ... that the Empire would shrink quickly with the rise of self-governing nations within the British Commonwealth ... that United States and Russia would emerge as leaders in modern world affairs.

But in spite of these startling events, Britain still remains as a significant power, representing a force for good in the world today. She stands with other Western nations as a democratic bulwark against the threatening spread of communism.

It is important to remember that British traditions still exert a tremendous influence upon all English-speaking nations of the present time. Even if the little Isles were to sink into the sea, and the British Commonwealth were to disintegrate, the spirit of Britain would live on for a thousand years. Many of the factors which are basic, permanent and fine in our way of life are of British origin. Unconsciously we think, feel and act in accordance with old patterns born long ago. All unheard by us, all unseen by us, a host of significant events in British history still shape our daily lives and frame the course of the future. The courage of Magna Carta, the privileges of the Bill of Rights, the justice of Habeas Corpus and the integrity of the parliamentary system of government remain as vital parts of our democratic heritage. And over the barriers of time which separate us from the *Proud Ages* we feel the sense of duty, the respect for law, the spirit of adventure and the love of freedom which motivated so many generations of British people.

SUMMARY—SECTION IX

During the latter part of the nineteenth century Britain suffered from a number of wars, mutinies and rebellions most of which were caused by her efforts to extend and protect her colonies. From 1854 to 1856 Britain and France were engaged in the Crimean War against Russia. In 1857 the Indian Mutiny broke out as Sepoys rose against British authority. In New Zealand the British came into sharp conflict with the Maoris. Egypt came under British control after the Battle of Tel-el-Kebir in 1882. In South Africa the British and the Boers carried on a long, bitter struggle which ended in the Second Boer War, 1899 to 1902. Australia was settled, Canada became a nation, and a host of small colonies were drawn into the British family. By the time of Queen Victoria's Diamond Jubilee in 1897 Britain controlled the greatest empire the world had ever seen.

During the period 1850 to 1900 Britain made rapid strides in the achievement of democracy in government. The secret ballot was established and voting rights were granted to people of the lower classes. Parliament elected by a majority of the people stood as the real power in government. Democratic ideas were extended to various parts of the Empire, as such important regions as Canada, Australia, New Zealand and South Africa were given self-government.

Two great political leaders, Disraeli of the Conservative party and Gladstone of the Liberal party, played important roles in Britain's advancement during this age.

Amazing improvements were made in transportation and communication with the expansion of railroads, penny postage and the telegraph. Schools for all children were made possible by the Education Act of 1870. Health conditions were improved through greater attention to sanitation and through new medical discoveries.

Well-to-do citizens dressed well, ate well, and lived in large, finely-furnished homes. They began to enjoy such new inventions as bicycles, cameras, sewing machines, telephones and a few automobiles. Lower class people did not have the same high standards of living, but their wages were higher and working conditions better than in previous periods. They appreciated the fact that their children had some opportunities for education.

Queen Victoria's long and successful reign reached its peak of glory in 1897 when the British Empire celebrated her Diamond Jubilee. On this happy occasion millions of devoted citizens from around the world gathered in London to witness the colourful parades and ceremonies.

In 1901 the Queen died after the longest reign in British history.

TIME-CHART

1851-1902

Gold is discovered in Australia	**1851**	
	1854	OUTBREAK OF THE CRIMEAN WAR BATTLE OF BALACLAVA FLORENCE NIGHTINGALE
Australian Colonies get responsible government	**1855**	FALL OF SEBASTOPOL
Britain acquires State of Oudh in India	**1856**	TREATY OF PARIS ENDS CRIMEAN WAR
Discovery of gold in New Zealand	**1857**	THE INDIAN MUTINY SIEGES OF LUCKNOW AND CAWNPORE
Lands and governing power of the East India Company in India are transferred to British Government	**1858**	
Ottawa is made capital of Province of Canada	**1859**	
Rising of the Maoris in New Zealand	**1860**	
	1861	DEATH OF PRINCE ALBERT
The Maori War in New Zealand	**1863**	
Fenian Raids in Canada Close of the Maori Wars in New Zealand	**1866**	
British North America Act—Canada becomes a nation	**1867**	DISRAELI INTRODUCES REFORM BILL OF 1867
Riel Rebellion in western Canada Hudson's Bay Company gives up its territory to Canada Diamonds discovered at Kimberley	**1870**	IRISH LAND BILL ELEMENTARY SCHOOLS ACT
	1871	ORGANIZATION OF THE IRISH LAND LEAGUE

391

TIME-CHART — *(continued)*

Responsible government is established in Cape Colony	**1872**	THE BALLOT ACT INTRODUCES SECRET VOTING IN ELECTIONS
Britain gains Fiji Islands	**1874**	
	1875	PURCHASE OF SUEZ CANAL SHARES
Large measure of local government granted to New Zealand	**1876**	
Annexation of Transvaal Cape Colony gets self-government	**1877**	QUEEN VICTORIA IS PROCLAIMED EMPRESS OF INDIA
Invasion of Afghanistan	**1878**	
Transvaal Republic proclaimed	**1879**	
	1880	IRELAND IN A DISTURBED CONDITION
First Boer War Defeat of the British at Majuba Hill Boers regain independence	**1881**	SECOND LAND ACT FOR IRELAND
Battle of Tel-el-Kebir resulting in the British occupation of Egypt and the Sudan	**1882**	
Transvaal State becomes South African Republic	**1884**	GLADSTONE AND THE COUNTRY FRANCHISE ACT WHICH GRANTED VOTE TO RURAL LABORERS AND TOWN WORKMEN
Fall of Khartoum—Death of General Gordon Canadian Pacific Railway is completed	**1885**	
Gold rush in Transvaal	**1886**	
	1893	IRISH HOME RULE BILL DEFEATED BY HOUSE OF LORDS
Cecil Rhodes becomes Premier of Cape Colony	**1895**	
The Jameson Raid Rhodes resigns as Premier	**1896**	

TIME·CHART — *(continued)*

	1897	QUEEN VICTORIA'S DIAMOND JUBILEE
Sudanese army defeated by British at Battle of Omdurman	**1898**	
	1899-1902	SECOND BOER WAR
Sieges of Mafeking and Kimberley	**1900**	
Empire troops sent to South Africa		
Australian Commonwealth is established		
	1901	EDWARD VII COMES TO THE THRONE
	1902	END OF THE BOER WAR

APPENDIX

STORIES FROM THE PAST

Many of the stories from Britain's past have been told and re-told so often that it is difficult to say where fact leaves off and imagination begins. For that reason, stories of this nature seldom find their way into a serious history book. Did King Alfred really burn the cakes? Was Robert Bruce really inspired by the persistence of a spider? No one can say with certainty—yet these stories, in their own way, can tell us a great deal about the times and places where they were supposed to have happened.

While the text of *Proud Ages* has been based on the results of extensive research by generations of historians, the stories which follow may or may not be true. Whether they are or not is relatively unimportant, but what does matter is that at some time people must have told these stories believing them to be true, and they should be read in that light.

* * * * *

ST. GEORGE AND THE DRAGON

St. George, the patron-saint of England, is a legendary hero who typifies the highest ideals of heroism and Christianity. The best known story concerning St. George is of his encounter with a fierce dragon which was terrorizing the countryside. So frightened were the people of the dragon's power that they sacrificed their sheep one by one to the monster. When all the sheep were gone, the citizens went through the horrible experience of drawing lots to see which of them would next be eaten by the dragon.

One day as St. George was riding across a marsh, he met a procession of weeping people led by a beautiful princess who was dressed as a bride. St. George was shocked to learn that the king's daughter had been chosen as a sacrifice, and was then on her way to meet the monster.

In anger, St. George advanced ahead of the party, and on seeing the dragon, charged boldly forward. With his magic sword, Ascalon, he struck a mighty blow which wounded the great beast. Then St. George asked the princess to tie her scarf about the dragon and lead him into the city. As tame as a lamb, the clumsy dragon followed the princess into the market place where a great crowd gathered.

And there before the eyes of the citizens St. George with his magic sword killed the evil monster which had caused so much death and sorrow. When the beast lay still on the earth, St. George spoke to the people saying that they had been saved through the power of God. The citizens who were heathens immediately became Christians and destroyed the old idols they had been worshipping.

Edward III of England made St. George the patron of the Knights of the Garter, and a jewelled figure of St. George and the dragon is one of the Order's emblems.

KING ARTHUR

The legends and myths surrounding Arthur are among the best known in the English language. It has not been proven conclusively that there ever was a real King Arthur, but the stories related to this legendary hero may have some factual basis. Some historians are inclined to believe that Arthur was a chieftain of mixed Roman and British parentage who fought against the Saxon invaders during the sixth century. It has been suggested, too, that he was not a king, but a mighty warrior-general who led royal armies.

However this may be, it is certain that any real Arthur bore little resemblance to the hero of the legends. With the passing of centuries, the various tales, poems and ballads concerning King Arthur became ever more romantic and fanciful. According to these, he was an incomparable warrior-king who conquered not only the British Isles but most of western Europe. In time King Arthur appeared in literature as the ideal knight, the model of chivalry, the perfect king, the invincible fighter who held the devotion of Queen Guinevere and the Knights of the Round table. He was a person possessing superhuman power and strength. To prove his right to the throne he drew the sword Excalibur from its place in solid rock.

The adventures of the King Arthur and such knights as Sir Galahad, Sir Lancelot and Sir Gawain have made fascinating reading for generations of boys and girls. Even the death of King Arthur provides a romantic and moving story, for after being wounded in battle, he is carried off in a mysterious boat to Avalon, the earthly paradise beyond the western horizon.

Among the most beautifully told legends of King Arthur are those contained in *Idylls of the King* by the English poet, Tennyson.

ALFRED AND THE CAKES

At one time during King Alfred's fight against the Danes, he was forced to hide in the marshes of southwestern England. It was a desperate period in the struggle, a period in which Alfred almost gave up hope of saving his kingdom of Wessex.

In the course of his wanderings, he took shelter in the humble hut of a cow-herd. As Alfred sat beside the open fire, resting and enjoying the warmth of the flames, the housewife approached. Not realizing that she was addressing her King, she asked the visitor to watch the cakes which were baking on the hearth.

King Alfred readily agreed to do so, but being tired and thoughtful in mood, he forgot the woman's instructions. As Alfred sat making plans for future action against the Danes, the cakes burned to a crisp. When the housewife returned and discovered the blackened cakes, she was furious. She lectured Alfred on his carelessness. An old English song declares that she used these words:

> There, didn't you see the cakes on fire?
> And didn't you see them burn?
> I'm sure you'll eat them fast enough
> As soon as 'tis your turn.

When the cow-herd came into the hut, his wife learned for the first time that she had been scolding the King of Wessex. Embarrassed and frightened by her rash action, the woman begged forgiveness.

King Alfred with his usual gentle manner laughed and admitted that he deserved a scolding for letting the cakes burn.

KING ALFRED'S CANDLES

King Alfred the Great was so hardworking and so methodical that he divided each day into equal portions, and in each portion devoted himself to a set task. To carry out this programme, he employed an unusual system of time measurement. Passage of time was indicated by means of burning candles, marked with a series of notches in the wax. When first used for this purpose, the candles burned irregularly because of the draughts which swept through Alfred's palace. However, this problem was overcome by enclosing the candles in cases made from wood and white horn. Charles Dickens states that these were the first lanterns ever made in England.

KING CANUTE AND THE SEA

Although Canute had been an adventurous and ruthless sea-rover, he tried to be a just monarch when he became King of England. So successful was he in winning over the English, that they grew to respect and admire him.

Surrounded as he was by courtiers, he sometimes grew tired of their eternal flattery. One day they grew so enthusiastic in their praise, that they stated the King was so powerful he could command the waves of the sea.

With some impatience, Canute ordered his golden chair to be carried to the seashore and placed in the path of the rising tide. There he sat in his robes and crown, shouthing at the sea, "Go back, I am master of land and sea. I command you to advance no nearer, nor dare to wet my feet."

As the low waves came higher and higher they washed about his shoes and the legs of his chair.

Turning to his courtiers, Canute cried, "Now you see that I am not master of the waves. Know, foolish men, that such power belongs only to God. He alone rules over earth and sea and sky."

Canute is supposed never to have worn his crown after this event.

SIX FEET OF GROUND

Shortly after Harold Godwin became King in 1066, he was threatened by invasion forces under his own brother, Tostig, and the King of Norway. Marching northward to Stamford Bridge, Harold found his enemies drawn up in a great hollow circle, ready for battle. As Harold inspected the enemy troops from a distance, he noticed an officer thrown from his horse.

"Who is that man?" asked Harold.

"The King of Norway," replied one of his own captains.

"He is a tall and stately king," remarked Harold, "but his end is near."

Then turning to his captain, Harold commanded, "Go over to my brother and tell him if he comes to my side, he shall be made an earl and shall be a rich and powerful man in England."

The messenger rode to the enemy position, and delivered the message. "And what will he grant my friend, the King of Norway?" inquired Harold's brother.

"Six feet of ground for a grave," said the messenger firmly.

"No more?"

"The King of Norway is a tall man—perhaps a little more."

"Go back to your lines," said Harold's brother, "and tell your King to prepare for battle."

In the engagement which followed at Stamford Bridge, Harold Godwin won a victory, while his brother and the King of Norway were slain on the battlefield.

DUKE WILLIAM AT HASTINGS

Following the Battle of Stamford Bridge, Harold Godwin moved swiftly southward to meet a new threat posed by a Norman army under William, Duke of Normandy.

On October 14, 1066, the English and Norman forces clashed at the famous Battle of Hastings. It was a hard-fought engagement between close-standing English footsoldiers and Norman cavalry troops supported by archers. Several groups of eager English rashly left their secure positions to pursue Norman riders, only to be wiped out by the enemy. These facts we know to be true, but we are not certain that Duke William spoke the often-quoted words which have been attributed to him.

After surveying the battle scene, he is said to have shouted, "Still there are thousands of the English firm as rocks around their King. Shoot upward, Norman archers, that your arrows may fall down upon their faces."

HEREWARD THE WAKE

After William the Conqueror became King of England following the Battle of Hastings there was a tragic period of uprisings, battles, sieges and massacres in which the Anglo-Saxons were battered into complete submission. Bands of men taking refuge from the Normans, became outlaws hiding in forests and swamps. Among these was one large group commanded by a powerful leader known as Hereward the Wake. So skilful was he in guerrilla warfare that the Normans believed him to have supernatural powers.

In an attempt to defeat the outlaws, William built a road across the Cambridgeshire marshes lying to the north of London. As the Normans advanced against Hereward the Wake, they are said to have taken with them an old woman who claimed to be a sorceress. It was thought that her powers of magic might work against those of the outlaw leader. According to legend the men of the marshes put an end to sorcery by burning the old woman along with her wooden tower.

Eventually Hereward the Wake was defeated in battle, but his fate is not known with any degree of certainty. Some old tales suggest that he was killed in a skirmish after he had slain sixteen men by his own hand.

THE SARACEN MAIDEN

Once upon a time a London merchant made a long pilgrimage to the Holy Land where, unfortunately, he was captured by a Saracen nobleman. Although treated kindly by his captor, Gilbert Becket was held prisoner for many months. During the course of this captivity, the beautiful daughter of the Saracen lord met Gilbert and promptly fell in love with him. So deep was her love that she expressed a wish to leave her father's house so that she and Gilbert might run off together to a Christian country.

However, when Gilbert Becket one day discovered a way of escape, he and his servant, Richard, left quickly and quietly without the Saracen maiden. Arriving safely in England, Gilbert proceeded to forget all about the young lady in the distant land.

One afternoon as he was busy at work in his office, Richard, the servant, ran in shouting, "Master, master, the Saracen maiden is here. As I live, the Saracen maiden is walking the streets of London crying, 'Gilbert! Gilbert!'"

The merchant strode to the window, and looking out saw a young lady in foreign dress walking slowly and crying, "Gilbert! Gilbert!" She appeared sad and lonely as she moved along, surrounded by a crowd of curious citizens.

Feeling pity, shame and excitement all at the same time, Gilbert rushed into the street. When she saw him coming, the Saracen maiden ran toward Gilbert and fainted in his arms.

Gilbert Becket and the young Saracen woman, after a marriage in London, lived a happy life together. They had one son, Thomas Becket, who was to become an important man in the kingdom.

HENRY II AND BECKET'S CLOAK

When Thomas Becket was Chancellor in England, he lived as one of England's wealthiest and most powerful noblemen. On occasions King Henry II enjoyed teasing Becket over the magnificence and the stylishness of his clothing. At one time, it is said, the two men were riding together on a cold, winter morning, when they encountered a shivering man dressed in rags.

"Would it not be a kindly thing," remarked Henry, "to give that poor old man a warm cloak?"

"Truly it would," answered Becket, "and you do well to consider such Christian duty."

"Come," ordered Henry, "give him your own cloak."

Because it was a splendid cloak of crimson material trimmed with white ermine, Becket showed no instant desire to surrender the garment. In consequence, the King grasped the border of the cloak and began to jerk it from Becket's shoulders. As the two struggled for possession, they almost tumbled from their saddles. Amidst a roar of laughter from other courtiers present, Becket finally gave up his beloved cloak, which was handed over immediately to the astonished man in the street.

ROBIN HOOD

Robin Hood is an English legendary hero whose history appears to have changed considerably with the passing years. It is not known when the earliest tales of Robin Hood were told among the people. The first mention of this hero made in English literature was in *Piers the Plowman* which was written in 1377. It is probable that there were a number of songs and stories concerning Robin Hood before that time. In later years he was mentioned in the writings of William Shakespeare, Ben Jonson and others.

From the host of songs, poems, plays and tales of Robin Hood which have come down to us, we have gained our own particular picture of him. To us he is a daring, handsome leader of a happy band of outlaws hiding in Sherwood forest. He is the skilled master of the sword and the bow. He wages a constant struggle for right and justice against the forces of tyranny and selfishness. With Will Scarlet, Friar Tuck, Little John and the others he robs the rich to help the poor. Always loyal to King Richard I, the outlaw despises the temporary rule of his brother, Prince John.

Just as King Arthur represents the highest form of gallantry and honour among the English nobles, so does Robin Hood represent these qualities among the men of the lower classes.

In the English counties of Yorkshire, Nottingham and Lincolnshire there are a number of places which have been named in the hero's honour: Robin Hood's Bay, Robin Hood's Cave, Robin Hood's Chair, and others.

The legend of Robin Hood is as popular today as it ever was. Indeed, it continues to grow through the magic of television.

DEATH OF RICHARD I

The words of an old French song suggested that King Richard I (Lion Heart) would die by an arrow made at Limoges.

When a French nobleman, the Viscount of Limoges, found on his property a treasure in ancient coins, he sent half of it to his lord, Richard I. Not satisfied with this amount, Richard angrily demanded the whole of the treasure, and, when refused, he lay siege to the noble's castle. Furious at being rebuffed, King Richard swore he would capture the castle and hang its defenders.

One day a young French archer standing on the wall of the castle saw the King riding by. Quickly he fitted an arrow to his bow and whispered, "Now I pray God speed thee well, arrow." The aim was good, for Richard was struck high on the left shoulder. Although the wound was not considered fatal, it was painful enough to make the King retire to his tent. As time went by, blood poisoning developed, and Richard realized he was about to die.

After the castle finally fell, all the defenders were hanged except the young archer who had fired the fatal arrow. When he was brought before the dying King, he stood calm and unafraid. Richard demanded of him, "What have I done to you that you should take my life?"

"You have killed my father and my two brothers, and you will hang me. Let me die now by any torture you wish. What ever you do will not save your own life. I am content that through me the world is rid of you."

For a moment the two looked steadily at each other. Then with a weak smile King Richard said, "Boy, I forgive you. You may go unhurt."

RAVENS OF THE TOWER

One of the interesting sights to be seen in the Tower of London is a flock of ravens. These birds, inclined to be a nuisance at times, are noisy. They pick putty from windows and occasionally peck at the legs of visitors. In spite of the trouble they cause, the ravens are well cared for. Six of them receive special attention, as they are kept in a special cage and are fed meat by the Raven Master. Some of these famous ravens live to a ripe old age. One elderly bird actually lived at the Tower for more than forty-four years.

The attention and interest given the birds originally rose from an old legend which states that when the ravens leave the Tower of London the building will fall and the British Empire will be no more.

ROBERT BRUCE AND THE SPIDER

Robert Bruce (1274-1329), one of Scotland's most beloved kings, was noted in songs and legends as well as in history. Much of his adventurous lifetime was spent in an effort to free Scotland from the rule of the English. After a series of defeats, Robert Bruce was forced to go into hiding. Discouraged by his lack of success, he began to wonder if his long struggle was worth while.

One morning he lay in a hard bed in a humble Scottish cottage. As he looked upward, he saw a spider hanging from a long silken thread which it had spun. It was swinging back and forth, trying to get from one beam to another. With remarkable patience and determination, the spider tried again and again. Fascinated by its actions, Bruce watched with the keenest interest.

After the spider had tried six times and failed, the thought came to Bruce that this was the same number of times he had lost battles. Impulsively, Bruce decided that if the spider tried again and succeeded, he, too, would take up the struggle. He held his breath and waited. Miraculously, the spider's next attempt was a success. Bruce leaped from bed with a smile on his face and hope in his heart.

In 1314 Robert Bruce defeated the English in the famous battle of Bannockburn.

PRINCE HENRY AND THE JUDGE

Before Henry IV came to the throne he was a lively dashing young man who was sometimes called the "Madcap Prince."

On one occasion, according to legend, he learned that a friend of his had been arrested for a crime and was being tried by one of the King's judges. Rushing to the court, Prince Henry demanded that his friend be set free at once.

Unruffled by the young Prince's demand, the judge calmly replied, "Your friend has committed a crime and must be punished. Only your father, the King, can grant him a pardon."

Astonished that a subject would dare to speak so boldly, Henry drew his sword and struck the judge. Still in a firm voice the judge continued, "Your Majesty, now you also must go to jail for attacking one of the King's judges."

Prince Henry's anger disappeared quickly and he hung his head in shame. Willingly he allowed himself to be led away to a cell.

When the Prince's father heard the story of this event, he said, "I thank God that He has given me a judge who fears not to do right, and a son who can obey the law."

DICK WHITTINGTON AND HIS CAT

Richard Whittington, the son of Sir William Whittington, was Lord Mayor of London three times (1397, 1406 and 1419). A legend concerning Whittington as a boy has grown up, but how the story started remains as a mystery. Here it is—

Dick Whittington, a homeless country boy, went to London to make his fortune. In time he arrived at the big city with his pet cat which was his only friend. Finally after some difficult days, Dick found work as a kitchen boy in the large home of a wealthy merchant. Here, after long days of hard work, he slept in a tiny attic room which was overrun with rats and mice. Fortunately, Dick's cat attacked the invaders, and soon had them all killed. Conditions might have been fairly comfortable if the cook had not taken to beating Dick whenever she felt like it.

The wealthy merchant who owned the house sent his ships on long trading voyages to distant lands. Sometimes he permitted the servants to send some possessions on the ships so that the articles could be sold at a high price in foreign countries. Poor Dick wanted to make a profit, too, but he had nothing to sell but his cat. After considerable thought and some tears, he finally allowed his cat to be sent off on one of the ships.

When Dick's pet had gone, the boy was lonesome, the rats and mice came back, the cook beat him more than ever. When he could stand it no longer, he ran away from the merchant's house. But as he walked along, he heard the bells of the Bow church ringing. The Bow bells seemed to say,

> Turn a-gain, Whitt-ing-ton,
> Three times Lord Mayor of London.

Dick listened for a long time and then slowly he turned back toward the merchant's house. No sooner had he arrived, than he was greeted by the most wonderful news . . . his cat had been sold to a foreign king for six bags of gold. The ruler of the distant country had been willing to pay such an enormous price because his kingdom was plagued by an army of rats and mice.

Dick was overjoyed, but this was only the beginning of his good fortune. The merchant took the boy into his family and raised him as if he were his own son. When Dick Whittington grew up, he became a famous man and eventually assumed the important position of Lord Mayor of London.

DRAKE AND THE BOWLING GAME

In July, 1588, the Invincible Armada of King Philip made its way into the English Channel. A small fishing vessel, catching sight of the great fleet, turned tail and sped for the English coast. Spanish vessels gave chase, but could not catch the little craft which escaped to Plymouth where much of the English fleet lay waiting. Immediately the invasion alarm was spread through the port.

According to an old story, on July 19 a group of naval officers were bowling at the Pelican Inn at Plymouth when a sailor burst into their midst. Approaching the Lord Admiral, he cried, "My lord! my lord! They are coming! I saw them off the Lizard last night."

The Lord Admiral was anxious to put to sea at once, but he asked the advice of a senior officer, Francis Drake. While still taking aim with a bowling ball, Drake remarked, "They'll come soon enough for us to show them sport, and yet slow enough for us to be ready; so let no man hurry himself."

After calmly finishing the game, Drake went down to the harbour where his quiet self-confidence raised the spirits of his men.

SIR PHILIP SIDNEY

During the reign of Elizabeth I a small English army under the command of the Earl of Leicester was sent to help the Dutch against the French. The campaign conducted by this force was so ineffective that it deserves no important place in history. One event in this campaign, however, which is said to have taken place, has been told and re-told a thousand times.

Among the English officers was a distinguished writer and soldier, Sir Philip Sidney, who lost his horse during battle. As he mounted a fresh animal he was struck in the thigh by a musket ball. Riding away towards the rear of battle, he suffered greatly from pain and thirst. When finally given a cup of water, Sir Philip noticed a common soldier lying wounded on the ground. Struck by the appeal in the man's eyes, Sir Philip said, "Thy necessity is greater than mine," and passed the cup down.

Of the story Charles Dickens has said, "This touching action of a noble heart is perhaps as well known as any in history—is as famous far and wide as the blood-stained Tower of London, with its axe, and block, and murders out of number. So delightful is an act of true humanity, and so glad is mankind to remember it."

RALEIGH SPREADS HIS CLOAK

Handsome, bearded Walter Raleigh was born in 1552, and later educated at Oxford University. He developed into a clever and versatile man who became a soldier, a seaman, a poet and an author of books. It is not at all surprising that such a personable young man should become a favourite in the court of Elizabeth I.

The Queen showered him with gifts, appointed him captain of her guard, granted him estates and eventually knighted him in 1584. Indeed, Sir Walter and Elizabeth became such close friends that it was rumoured from time to time that they were to be married. While royal favour had certain evident advantages, it also had handicaps for an adventurous gentleman. Elizabeth several times denied Raleigh permission to go on long voyages of exploration, because she wanted him near her at court.

A story which may or may not be true relates the circumstances under which Raleigh first attracted the attention of the Queen. It is said that one day Elizabeth was walking outdoors when she came to a muddy spot lying directly in her pathway. Momentarily she hesitated, not knowing what to do, for she disliked soiling her shoes. Young Walter Raleigh, seeing his Queen's predicament, whipped off his own fine cloak, knelt on the ground, and spread the garment across the muddy area.

"Your Majesty," he said, with a sweeping bow, "do me the honour of walking on my cloak."

Delighted with such gallantry, Elizabeth turned smiling eyes on the young man, and then stepped lightly over the folds of Raleigh's cloak.

KINGS AND QUEENS OF ENGLAND

**EARLY ANGLO-SAXON AND
DANISH RULERS**

758-796	Offa, King of Mercia
802-839	Egbert, King of Wessex
871-901	Alfred the Great
901-925	Edward the Elder
925-940	Athelstan
959-975	Edgar the Peaceful
978-1016	Ethelred the Unready
1016-1035	Canute
1042-1066	Edward the Confessor
1066	Harold (Godwin)

THE NORMAN KINGS

1066-1087	William I (The Conqueror)
1087-1100	William II (Rufus)
1100-1135	Henry I (Beauclerc)
1135-1154	Stephen

THE HOUSE OF ANJOU (PLANTAGENET)

1154-1189	Henry II
1189-1199	Richard I (Lion Heart)
1199-1216	John
1216-1272	Henry III
1272-1307	Edward I (Hammer of the Scots)
1307-1327	Edward II
1327-1377	Edward III
1377-1399	Richard II

THE HOUSE OF LANCASTER

1399-1413	Henry IV
1413-1422	Henry V
1422-1461	Henry VI

THE HOUSE OF YORK

1461-1483	Edward IV
1483	Edward V
1483-1485	Richard III

THE HOUSE OF TUDOR

1485-1509	Henry VII
1509-1547	Henry VIII
1547-1553	Edward VI
1553-1558	Mary I
1558-1603	Elizabeth I

THE HOUSE OF STUART

1603-1625	James I
1625-1649	Charles I
	(1649-1660 Commonwealth and Protectorate)
1660-1685	Charles II
1685-1688	James II
	(1689-1702 William III and Mary II—House of Orange)
1702-1714	Anne

HOUSE OF HANOVER

1714-1727	George I
1727-1760	George II
1760-1820	George III
1820-1830	George IV
1830-1837	William IV
1837-1901	Victoria
1901-1910	Edward VII

HOUSE OF WINDSOR

1910-1936	George V
1936	Edward VIII
1936-1952	George VI
1952	Elizabeth II

THE BRITISH EMPIRE IN 1900

In the Americas	Date of Possession	Status
Canada	1763	Dominion
Newfoundland	1623	Colony
Bermuda	1609	Colony
Bahamas	1647	Colony
Barbados	1627	Colony
Jamaica	1655	Colony
Leeward Islands	1815	Colony
Trinidad	1797	Colony
Tobago	1763	Colony
Windward Islands	1815	Colony
British Honduras	1638	Colony
British Guiana	1732	Colony
Falkland Islands	1833	Colony

In Africa		
Gambia	1618	Colony and Protectorate
Gold Coast	1821	Colony (now Ghana)
Sierra Leone	1788	Colony and Protectorate
Nigeria	1879	Colony and Protectorate
Cape Colony	1795	Colony (part of Union of South Africa in 1910)
Basutoland	1868	Colony within South Africa
Egypt	1882	Protectorate
Bechuanaland	1885	Protectorate within South Africa
Swaziland	1888	Protectorate within South Africa
Southern Rhodesia	1888	Colony
Northern Rhodesia	1889	Protectorate
Nyasaland	1889	Protectorate
Kenya	1890	Colony and Protectorate
Uganda	1894	Protectorate
Zanzibar	1890	Protectorate
British Somaliland	1884	Protectorate
Anglo-Egyptian Sudan	1898	Condominium (with Egypt)
Mauritius	1810	Colony
Seychelles Islands	1794	Colony
St. Helena	1673	Colony
Ascension Island	1815	Dependency of St. Helena
Tristan da Cunha	1816	Dependency of St. Helena

406

THE BRITISH EMPIRE IN 1900— (Continued)

In Australasia	Date of Possession	Status
Australian Commonwealth	1788	Dominion
Norfolk Island		Territory of Australia
Papua	1884	Territory of Australia
New Zealand	1840	Colony (Dominion in 1907)
Cook Islands	1888	Dependency of New Zealand
Niue (or Savage Islands)		Dependency of New Zealand
Tokelau Islands		Administrated by New Zealand
Kermadec Islands	1887	Within the Dominion of New Zealand
Fiji	1874	Colony
Tonga (or Friendly Islands)	1899	Protected State
New Hebrides	1902	Condominium (with France)
Pitcairn Island	1790	Colony

In Asia		
Cyprus	1878	Colony
Aden	1839	Colony and Protectorate
Ceylon	1796	Colony
Maldive Islands		Within Colony of Ceylon
Indian Empire	1766	British India and Indian States
Burma		Colony
Straits Settlements	1786	Colony of four settlements—Singapore, Penang, Malacca and Labuan
Federated Malay States	1895	Four protected states—Perak, Selangor, Negri-Sembilan, and Pahang
British North Borneo	1881	Protected state
Brunei	1888	Protected state
Sarawak	1842	Protected state
Hongkong	1841	Colony

In Europe		
United Kingdom		
Gibraltar	1704	Colony
Malta	1800	Colony

NOTE: Many small possessions have been omitted from the above list.

407

INDEX

408

Index

409

412

Index

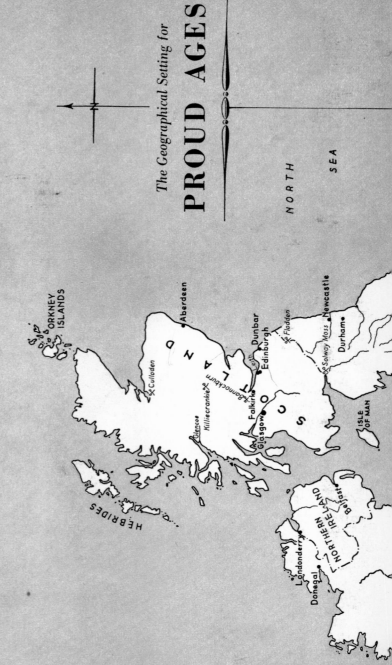

The Geographical Setting for

PROUD AGES

NORTH

SEA

SHETLAND
ISLANDS

ORKNEY
ISLANDS

Aberdeen

S C O T L A N D

Culloden

Glencoe

Killiecrankie

Bannockburn

Falkirk

Leith

Dunbar

Edinburgh

Flodden

Glasgow

Newcastle

Solway Moss

Durham

ISLE
OF MAN

HEBRIDES

NORTHERN IRELAND

Belfast

Londonderry

Donegal